5/14

A Bigger Prize

A Bigger Prize

How We Can Do Better than the Competition

MARGARET HEFFERNAN

PublicAffairs | New York

Published in the United States by PublicAffairs™, a Member of the Perseus Books Group

Book design by Janet Tingey

Library of Congress Cataloging-in-Publication Data
Heffernan, Margaret, 1955–
A bigger prize: how we can do better than the competition / Margaret Heffernan.—First edition.
pages cm
ISBN 978-1-61039-291-4 (hardback)
ISBN 978-1-61039-292-1 (ebook)
1. Business networks. 2. Competition. 3. Strategic alliances (Business) 4. Organizational effectiveness. 5. Creative ability in business. I. Title.

HD69.S8H445 2014
658ʼ.046—dc23
2013044641

First Edition
10 9 8 7 6 5 4 3 2 1

For Lindsay

CONTENTS

INTRODUCTION

On a beautiful August day, the New Hampshire sunshine streams through the tall pine trees surrounding the Cheshire County Fair. On the outer perimeter, cart horses and pigs are scrutinized and judged, some garnering rosettes, others being returned to their owners, for whom they are both livelihood and pets. Kids try their hand at milking cows and goats or driving their first tractor. After lunch, Slackwire Sam unicycles up and down his loose clothesline; in the far corner of the fairground, tug-of-war is scheduled for the end of the day.

An inner circle of food stalls offers fried dough, blossoming onions, corn dogs, and cotton candy. Families four abreast carry paper cartons of calamari and fries or cones overflowing with fluorescent ice cream. Clutching goldfish swimming in plastic bags, three young girls compare prizes while twin brothers walk side by side, sporting matching T-shirts: THE 2ND AMENDMENT: AMERICA'S ORIGINAL HOMELAND SECURITY. In the dusty heat, we are all sauntering slowly, eating, talking, and seeking out small patches of shade, when the announcement comes over the loudspeaker: the demolition derby is about to begin!

Gently—it is too hot to rush—the direction of the crowd turns toward the central stadium and up the bleachers, where seats in the shade are soon occupied. Conceding defeat, the rest of the spectators shift reluctantly toward the sunny side, spread out, and don hats. Aficionados place towels carefully on their laps.

In the center of the arena, eight rusty wrecked cars rev their engines. Car 49 sports flags decorated with skulls; car 38 proudly promotes its sponsor—WB Paint Worx—in hand-painted electric red, white, and blue logos. Car 72 displays steer horns on its roof, while car 3 advertises McCue's billiard hall in nearby Keene.

"Are you ready?" the loudspeaker blares. The crowd starts to join in the countdown—"five ... four ... three ... two ... one"—and the cars reverse out of their alignment, struggling to gain traction in the dust. Now they're off, whirling and spinning as they drag themselves into collisions. The goal is demolition, and the last car left running wins the prize.

"Get serious, guys—we need some contact!"

As the cars drag themselves around the arena, radiators steaming, the spinning tires throw up dirt made damp from oil spills and water. The crowd screams and ducks as the dirt goes flying, landing on laps and smearing my sunglasses. Now I understand why the woman next to me brought her towel: this is part of the fun.

"Eileen, you gotta hit somebody!"

Driving car 23, Eileen can't possibly hear the crowd through her crash helmet, but she knows what to do. Whizzing around, she heads off to smash into car 49, an easy target as its undercarriage drags along the ground. Then she backs up and charges into the corner where Kyle in car 25 is stuck—trapped by three dilapidated vehicles that back up, accelerate, and smash into him. The radiator explodes against the arena wall, the car accordions, and Kyle is out of the game. Once a car can't move, all of the rest move in to pulverize it.

With doors, hoods, and fenders now dispersed across the dirt, just four vehicles remain. Car 72 can only drive in reverse now and limps with a flat tire; everyone is starting to lose power, but the derby can't finish until one more goes down. As if sensing blood, cars 35, 66, and 72 head for Eileen, but she outmaneuvers them, gets behind 35, and, catching it on her front fender, rams it against the wall.

"We've got our three!" and the crowd erupts into applause as the local fire brigade walks onto the field to clear the wreckage and prepare for the final.

As I sat in the stands on that beautiful August day, I couldn't help but think that I was watching some kind of parable. All around the world, rusty, dilapidated institutions and ideas seemed to be crashing into each other, driven by a competitive spirit that offered the brutal simplicity of winners and losers. After five years of corporate breakdowns, ethical corrosion, financial crashes, stalled politics, and overheated rhetoric, all that remained was the grim drama of the contest.

Wherever I looked, competition had become the default motivator, as though, exhausted and demoralized, no culture or politics could proffer a superior driver or decisive alternative. As complex social, financial, legal, and environmental challenges piled up on one another, a kind of despair seemed to descend: we don't know what to do, let the market decide. Put it out to competition, make people compete, the best will rise to the top—won't it?

Fans of competition regularly looked to Charles Darwin for intellectual support. Most cited "survival of the fittest" without recognizing that the term came not from Darwin but from Herbert Spencer, who had handily translated "natural selection," giving it his own favored political spin. Since a world of winners and losers is natural, the social Darwinians argued, we would do better to tone our competitive muscles than question the ways of nature. We are, after all, the product of an evolutionary contest in which the best of our genetic inheritance has survived while the rest has perished. Although even Darwin scholars couldn't agree whether Darwin himself would have been a social Darwinian, nature itself seemed to provide the ultimate alibi.

Social Darwinians were hugely aided by the many people who were familiar with Richard Dawkins's *The Selfish Gene* but who had never read it. No wonder publisher Tom Maschler suggested that the book might better be called *The Immortal Gene*. As Dawkins himself conceded in the thirtieth anniversary edition, many people took the title at face value, didn't bother to read the text, and concluded that the book must be a vindication of raw, unbridled selfishness. The selfish gene is only out for itself, it is who we are, and there's nothing we can do about it. That the book said nothing of the kind—in fact it mounted an eloquent and powerful counterargument—didn't matter. The title had become the work.

Nor were the avid competitors devoid of data. At the end of the nineteenth century, one of the world's first social psychologists, Norman Triplett, had demonstrated that cyclists ride faster against a competitor than when cycling alone. And even though much of Triplett's subsequent work added layers of refinement and contingency to his result, the headline stuck: everyone works harder, faster, better, when they're up against each other. Sport became the ubiquitous metaphor, profusely obscuring what it sought to illuminate.

As a consequence, organizations—public and private—had come to rely on competition to choose and motivate people, to inspire investors and consumers, to justify everything from doomed mergers to sweatshops and price hikes. What had been tested by competition must be better. Never mind the cost, and never mind that competition is designed to benefit the few, not the many—we lived in a dog-eat-dog world and what mattered now was to be top dog. Schools might no longer be about learning, work might now have little to do with self-fulfillment, and society might not be about relationships anymore; what mattered was to read the manuals, bone up on techniques, buy the equipment, pay the trainer, swallow the supplements, and always keep score.

Winners have always, of course, been more susceptible to this argument. Since competitions work for them, they understandably find it hard to see what might be wrong with their strategy. Losers rarely write history. And anyway, competition is fun: it's dramatic and exciting, there's a winner, and you always know just where you stand. At a moment in time when no one seemed to know where to go or what to do, wasn't that clarity good enough?

And yet, just as we'd learned that individuals aren't rational and markets aren't efficient and we went ahead operating as though they are, so we also recognized that competition quite regularly doesn't work, the best do not always rise to the top, and the so-called efficiency of competition seems to throw off a very great deal of waste. It was comforting to designate these ideas "perverse outcomes," as though each one was an anomaly, but as aberrations mounted, they started to look more like a norm.

As this grim contest has played out over the last few years, the "Prisoner's Dilemma" has come into its own.* The Prisoner's Dilemma has been applied to so many problems and settings—from the Cold War to drugs in sports—that it has been called the "E. coli of social science." Game theory is largely absent from this book—I'm far more interested in practice—but in all the many permutations of the Prisoner's Dilemma, one finding remains critical: when each prisoner competes for himself, instead of collaborating with his fellow, they both lose. The individual pursuit of self-interest proves collectively defeating.

Over the last fifty years, we have seen this played out on an epic scale.

---

*Dreamed up and given its name by a Canadian mathematician, Albert Tucker, the game has been used to model competition and the variety of ways in which it can play out. The Prisoner's Dilemma poses what looks like a simple scenario. Two members of a gang are arrested and placed in solitary confinement, where they have no means of communicating with each other. The police don't have enough evidence to convict the two on the main charge, so they plan to sentence each to a year's imprisonment on a lesser charge. But they also offer the prisoners a bargain: if one testifies against his partner, he will go free and the partner will get three years in prison on the more serious charge. As in all good social-science scenarios, there is a catch: if both prisoners testify against each other, they each get two years in jail.

In our quasi-religious fervor to compete, we have expected fabulous efficiencies, miraculous economies, infinite creativity, and dazzling innovation. Instead, we have found ourselves gasping for air in a sea of corruption, dysfunction, environmental degradation, waste, disenchantment, and inequality—and the harder we compete the more unequal we become. This is no coincidence, but the inevitable outcome of our faith in competition as a simple panacea for the many and complex challenges that we face.

Winning always incurs costs. When siblings grow up in rivalry, they struggle to relate with trust and generosity. When schools celebrate the top of the class, they demotivate the rest. When the rich win tax cuts, inequality grows. As sports become fiercer and richer, careers shorten and injuries abound. When executives are encouraged to compete for bonuses and promotions, they pay in lost friendships and stunted creativity. An obsession with score-keeping constrains thinking and undermines the very innovation it hopes to spark. When pharmaceutical companies win patents on lookalike drugs, it costs us the critical new medicines that never get developed. When food producers aim to dominate their markets with low prices, we all pay the costs in environmental and social degradation. And when the pressure to win exacerbates cheating and corruption, it costs us the legitimacy of our institutions and the credibility of our beliefs.

Over the last fifty years, we have leaned heavily on competition, hoping that it will solve our problems, motivate our children, and reinvigorate companies and institutions. But we have shied away from the uncomfortable truth that our outsize veneration of competition has left us ill equipped to solve the problems it has created. If we are to invent new ways to live and work together, we need high levels of trust and give-and-take: attributes that competition specifically and subtly corrodes.

As if in recognition of this, a rising generation is avidly seeking the tools and environments in which sharing, co-creation, and trust are endemic and reinforced. And increasingly, they are not disappointed. Evolutionary science has shown us why we have survived to defy gravity and build monuments of lasting beauty and meaning—because we know how to work together. New models for sharing information, pooling resources, organizing complex projects, and inventing new products abound, amply demonstrating that great work, inexhaustible innovation, and passionate commitment amply and easily supplant exhausting rivalries. The wildly collaborative and creative individuals and organizations described in this book testify to the human capacity to cooperate, to share, to look across broad horizons, and to dig deep together. Our talent for coalitions, our ability to cooperate, even the creation of language itself—the ultimate tool for collaboration—testifies to an immense human capacity for solidarity.

Perhaps the long legacy of the Soviet Union explains the queasiness with which many approach the subjects of collaboration, cooperation, and altruism to this day. Rather as Darwin feared killing God, we fear that any renunciation of competition must kill capitalism and return us to the corruption and cruelty of the Soviet experiment. Such a conception is, of course, historically inaccurate—the Soviet Union incited competition regularly and viciously in all walks of life. But the polarization implicit in it reflects the poverty of our win-lose mind-set, which blinds us to the greater opportunities and energies that lie elsewhere. We can find better ways to live, to work, and to rebuild our failed institutions for the many, not just the few. All around us are examples we can and must learn from.

We are all competitive, but we are not only competitive. No book, sermon, movement, or political party will ever change the insatiable human appetite for status and distinction. But working together is human nature, and if we look carefully, we can see individuals and organizations all around us to show us how. These trailblazers know that growth, learning, and creativity always depend on a vast array of people and ideas, freely shared and generously celebrated. They appreciate that fairness, safety, and trust are essential to the unfettered exploration that generates new ideas. They don't accept that the only measure of success is the number of losers left in the dust. And they entirely reject the idea that true achievement can be measured at any single moment in time. These are people who aren't driven to keep score but rather are motivated by the belief that great work is done together, that efficiency is gained by trust, and that safety opens the floodgates of the mind. They have everything to teach us—and sharing is what they do best.

When I first started to explore these themes, the first response that greeted me was astonishment: You dare to question competition? What else is there? In the years that have passed, that reaction has shifted. Now when I discuss my work, I see in people's faces and hear in their voices a sense of relief and hope. Yes, there *is* a better way to live and work. Yes, the alternatives are real, significant, practical, and sustainable. There are forms of success that are better than winning. For all of us, there is a bigger prize.

PART I

Personal Best

CHAPTER 1

Oh, Brother!

"I want the first one!"

As Alice brings in a plate of cake slices, Harry stretches over to grab his piece. He's wound up, tense, and excited. He's hungry, of course, but it's more than that. He doesn't just want cake. He wants to be the first to get his cake and eat it.

We aren't in a poor home—there's no shortage of food. In this comfortable country house with sunny windows and a big open kitchen, there is more than enough warmth and light and cake to go around. Harry's parents, Alice and Paul Hobbs, are kind, loving, and calm. They're both lawyers; of the two, Alice had the more dazzling career until she stepped down to spend more time with her three boys.

And that's the clue. The tension, the excitement, the slightly wired feeling in the room—it isn't about cake. It's about those three boys, each one of whom wants to come first, get the most, be the best.

Harry is eleven. He competes with Tom, who is eight, and four-year-old Oliver. All three boys are handsome, boisterous, even charismatic in their as-yet undeveloped enthusiasms. You can tell as you watch them that they're neither spoiled rotten nor lacking for anything. Growing up with plenty—of love, attention, stimulation, support, and, yes, cake—has had its effect. The boys are bursting with potential that requires only time to unfurl. So they aren't competing because there's a shortage of anything. They're competing because they're human. And they compete all the time.

The next morning, as the sun starts to burn off the mist on the broad lawns that surround the house, Tom is up early making porridge and getting ready to go for a swimming lesson.

"Where's the chocolate spread?" Harry asks.

His father Paul isn't sure, but Harry knows for a fact that his mother bought some on Friday and that it hasn't been opened yet. He conveys this information with the ferocity of a government minister at the dispatch box arguing his point. His father duly finds the chocolate spread.

"You can't let him have that!" Tom protests.

"Yes, he can!" Harry counters.

"You can't, Dad." Tom is distraught. "You can't let him have the chocolate spread. I'm going swimming. It will all be gone before I get back."

Food isn't the only point of contention in the Hobbs household. Footballs, TV time, Monopoly pieces, outings with Grandma, the place in front of the fire, bedtime—anything and everything can be fought over. It's exhausting for Alice because it never stops.

"If I give them each a candy, there will be endless squabbling—a Smartie is worth more than a Gummy Bear. If I hand them each a cookie, I just have two hands and the third one will always ask: where's mine? As if I'm not going to turn around and get the other cookie. If for some reason I don't give them a candy, they'll argue about whose fault it is that there aren't any candies today."

Alice has invited me to observe her three boys because she recognizes how competitive they are. Their desire to win against each other is so naked and unmediated. Like the rest of us, Alice understands the need for identity and territory to call one's own, but her sons' open fight for it disrupts her family and unsettles her home.

The constant competition is also very draining. Every bedtime the boys fight over something. When they aren't in school, contests, spats, and conflagrations erupt with monotonous regularity, and their mother recognizes that they are competing for her attention and approval, of which there can never be enough. The heat in the household invariably centers on Harry, who is handsome, tall with curly light brown hair, has presence, and exudes a sense of being top dog.

"Harry plays rugby at school," his mother tells me. "After a match, if he hasn't scored a try, he'll have a reason: he wasn't placed right, he wasn't given the chance. He won't ever say the other boy played better. Deep down inside, he cannot bear to say to himself: 'He scored the try because he's better than I am.'"

Tom is smaller, quieter, and a deeper character altogether, as though he has knowledge that he's not sharing.

"Tom will watch Harry play rugby and say, 'He played well,' or, 'That was a great kick,' and he does it without any sense that it has cost him anything to say that. Generosity comes easily to him, but he won't put himself forward. He doesn't do his own PR. He's much quieter, and he won't challenge."

The youngest, Oliver, clearly loves being the baby of the family, the safest spot because no one wants his position.

"Oliver just loves getting stuck in. He's only four, he knows he can't touch his brothers. But he's keen to show that he can play the game, that he counts, and that there's no reason he should be left out. But in the family pecking order, well, he's just above Rocket the dog."

At school Harry has to be—and invariably is—top of his class. He's good, his mother says, at marketing himself. His father Paul thinks he has the makings of a CEO, or perhaps an MP.

"Harry has to be top dog; he has to be. He's very careful to ensure that everyone likes him," Alice says. "The teachers and the kids all like him because, of course, at school they have no idea what a bully he is at home. Because he is a bully. He wants to make Tom feel bad. He can't be generous. He has to be the best. Whenever I praise Tom, you'll see him rise up and have to put him down."

We are sitting in Alice's sitting room, which is lined with deep cream sofas. For the moment the house is quiet, but Alice is on tenterhooks; she knows that moments like this don't last long. And indeed, just a few minutes later, something upstairs crashes to the floor, we hear howls of protest, and somebody starts crying. With a weary sigh, Alice rises out of the sofa and leaves to adjudicate.

Harry has to win. He needs his siblings to lose. You can see it in the way he carries himself, the way he watches every move they make. Later in the day, when Alice tries to tell me what a strong swimmer Tom is, Harry stands in front of me, as though trying physically to block the words from reaching my ears.

Over the next two weeks Alice keeps a diary of her sons' interactions. It is relentless.

> *Wednesday the 12th:* Tom has insisted on a trip to visit his grandparents alone because Harry has had several visits himself; there's an element of evening out the score.
> *Thursday the 13th:* Oliver in a song and dance show at school. We told him how well he'd done. "Tell the others," he said, "because they said it was going to be rubbish."
> *Saturday the 15th:* Major argument over rugby balls.

Sunday the 16ᵗʰ: Much arguing over small things; bickering and unsettled. Particular issue when Harry wanted to go fishing with Granddad and it's only safe for Granddad to look after one boy at a time.
Tom very upset.

Monday the 17ᵗʰ: Huge fight over bathtime. Tom decidedly smug that he
was "getting away with it."

Tuesday the 18ᵗʰ: Argument over a cake Oliver had been given at a
birthday party. He had almost finished it (with brothers pleading for
a piece at every mouthful) when a piece broke off, landed on the
floor, whereupon the dog licked it. Harry then grabbed it—and ate
it. Yuck! He was scolded by me, but the look on his face was telling
me he thought it was worth it for the prize of a piece of unexpected
cake, even if dog-licked. Tom, excluded from it all, with no doggy
cake, went into meltdown.

Wednesday the 19ᵗʰ: Tom invited out to see the new *Johnny English* film.
Harry was clearly envious and disappeared into the study for hours.
He emerged triumphant, declaring he had worked out how to download films and was downloading, yes, *Johnny English 1*. Given our
rubbish broadband speed, it took ages and then even longer to watch
it back on the computer. This did not diminish his pleasure one bit.
Not sure if the film was any good, but he had succeeded in clawing
back a piece of Tom's treat by undermining the novelty. Predictably,
on Tom's return he announced, "Well, I've seen *Johnny English 1*, and
everyone thinks that it's better."

The diary goes on like this, day after day. It's exhausting to read and must
have been enervating to live through. Earlier in the year, Harry had gone
on a weeklong school trip. The difference, Alice tells me, was absolute. The
mood, temperature, conversations—everything in the family changed. It is
sad, she reflects, to be so happy when one of your children is gone.

What Alice and her husband have on their hands is a bad case of "sibling
rivalry." The phrase was first coined by psychologist David M. Levy in 1941.
That it took so long to name such a common phenomenon seems remarkable. Sibling rivalry kicks off the Bible, with the murder by Cain of Abel, the
first act of violence in a very violent book. In the ancient world, Acrisius and
Proteus start their quarrel in the womb. Polynices and Eteocles, the sons of
Oedipus, kill each other over Thebes, and Romulus and Remus do likewise
over the location of Rome. Shakespeare is replete with rivalrous siblings:

King Lear pits sister against sister and brother against half-brother, *The Tempest* encapsulates a lifelong rivalry between Antonio and his brother Prospero, while *The Taming of the Shrew* draws comic steam from the pitched battle between amiable Bianca and the shrewish Katherine. Novelists from the Brontës and Jane Austen through to Saul Bellow and Jonathan Franzen have appreciated the energy and tension that the presence of brothers and sisters is bound to supply.

In contemporary life, the public and bitter feuds between Clement and Lucian Freud, Liam and Noel Gallagher, Peter and Christopher Hitchens, and Rufus and Martha Wainwright testify to the fact that neither fame nor success mollifies the urgent, primal need to come first. Even a delicately presented rivalry, the one between David and Ed Miliband when both competed for the leadership of the Labour Party, ended with David abandoning politics and leaving the country.

Sibling rivalry is a fundamental building block of stories and gossip because we recognize that its raw emotion is real and universal. From the moment we are born, we compete for the resources of survival: attention, food, love, warmth, and protection. For the newborn, securing the mother's (or other caregiver's) undivided attention is an absolute biological imperative. Worldwide today, it's estimated that one out of every four children live in poverty, 24 million have no parents, and every day 16,000 die from hunger.[1] For all children, getting enough—attention, shelter, education, clothing, or even cake—is a real and daily struggle. At the beginning of life, we have no choice but to compete.

Even in comfortable, secure families, infants are alert to the danger of anything that might distract or remove the love, attention, and food that they need. As early as six months, we recognize that some threats are more serious than others: in one experiment, infants were found to be relatively unperturbed if their mother paid attention to a book, but became very unhappy when she interacted with a doll.[2]

But it is the birth of a sibling that provokes the most visceral reaction, for the newborn represents a far bigger challenge than any book or doll, a challenge no mother can deny. Judy Dunn is the doyenne of sibling relationships, having devoted nearly half a century to the observation and study of brothers and sisters in their families over long periods of time. She documented a 93 percent increase in naughtiness after a sibling's birth, almost all of it designed to get attention.

"The upheaval of another baby coming into the family is *enormous*," says

Dunn. "What is so interesting about watching siblings is that theirs is absolutely a no-holds-barred relationship. Most parents are in denial, but however desirable it may be to show your family as all cooperative, brothers and sisters let out their competitiveness very clearly. It just hangs out whenever you observe a family."

In the West, 80 percent of us are siblings. That makes most of us either perpetrators, victims, or, more likely, both. Violence—both emotional and physical—is common. More than half of all children experience violence from a sibling in the course of just one year, and in the United States a national study of family violence showed that 74 percent of children had pushed or shoved a sibling, while 42 percent had kicked, bitten, or punched them.[3] It is thought that sibling abuse (physical and emotional) exceeds parental abuse and is the most abusive relationship to be found in families.[4] So seriously does the National Crime Prevention Council take sibling rivalry that it provides advice to parents on how to manage conflict between their children.[5] We may love our brothers and sisters, but we also hate them with a passion, and accounts of sibling rivalry are ubiquitous.

> "I put my baby brother in the microwave, and it might have worked except I couldn't get the door to shut."
> "I tried to get my baby sister to drink nail polish remover. I put it in her bottle and mixed in milk—but it obviously tasted horrible, so she wouldn't drink it."
> "When we were having a bath, I pushed my brother under, but he just fought like a tiger and kept coming up for air."
> "I threw my sister out of the window."

Many siblings have reminded me that the writer Alice Walker was blinded in one eye when her brother shot her with his BB gun; that they savored this detail attested to their identification with her experience—or with her brother's. But had any of these incidents of sibling violence been perpetrated by adults, we would take them very seriously. That they occur in childhood permits us to hope that they are transitory, that the kids will grow out of these murderous feelings, that love and generosity, self-control, and fairness will overwhelm them eventually, or at least mitigate them. We recognize childhood as the beginning of the social understanding—how to relate to others, how to become social beings—on which our survival keenly depends, and we hope that the violence will recede as this understanding develops.

Such strong emotions, however, rarely do what we might like them to do:

simply evaporate. When they linger and fester, as they did throughout Diane Wilson's childhood, their legacy is enormous.

"I was born one day before my sister Beth's birthday. From her perspective, I stole her thunder!"

Diane Wilson got off to a bad start with her older sister, and looking back, she realizes that no one in the family knew what to do about it. Diane was the last of five children, born into a family of three boys and Beth. The older children had scarcely known their father, who had been away, serving in the army, during the Second World War. Even after his return, emotional and financial resources were thin on the ground, and the rivalry and resentment between the two girls was fierce.

"My mother definitely played us off against each other. I was the good one, Beth was the difficult one. But this was never really talked about, it was just there, an undercurrent the whole time. My father just didn't get involved."

Although the girls weren't physically violent to one another, the emotional violence between them was unmistakable and unforgettable. Beth's resentment of her younger, prettier sister was the background rumble of Diane's childhood: constant, unpleasant, dangerous, and suppressed. Beth was very academic, while Diane was not, which made life at school for the two sisters tense and often humiliating. Beth would regularly chastise her sister for being such a failure and letting her down so badly.

"Even while we were at school, she used to wind me up. She knew just how to do it. When she was head girl, she would go out of her way to belittle me, yelling across the courtyard, 'Where's your beret?' There was just no way I was going to be academic the way that she was. Who would want to be?"

Knowing she could never match Beth's accomplishments, Diane turned instead to dance, for which she developed a real passion.

"I was keen on dance, and on one occasion I remember Beth saying, 'Dancing is a third-rate art—all you're doing is what someone else tells you to do.' Mother's defense of me was, 'Don't pick on her about that, it is the one thing she is any good at!' Between the two of them…. My father by this time had had a stroke, when I was ten. It was all very difficult."

In a household of five children, open conflict wasn't encouraged, and it's clear now that neither parent had the energy or the skills to mediate the intense rivalry between the two girls. An undercurrent of competitive tension was omnipresent, Diane says, but it was never allowed out into the open. Instead, confronted with her sister's unstoppable rivalry, Diane learned to do everything she could to stay out of the way.

"I used to read a lot of European literature—*The Idiot, Crime and Punish-ment*—but I would never read English writers. That was because Beth read English at Cambridge; that was her domain, so I stayed away from English fiction. Later on, people kept telling me I should do a degree; I thought I wasn't clever enough. I couldn't see my own intelligence. I didn't do a degree in order to avoid competing with her—I just wanted to stay out of her way."

Neither girl found in their parents any kind of model of collaboration, and their mother actively stoked the rivalry between them. Dance was a way for Diane to escape into a world where her sister could not and would not follow her. But when physical problems brought her dancing to an end, she was left without any strong sense of her own identity. Instead, she developed a habit of self-subversion by which the mere idea of her sister defeated all her aspirations.

"I kept thinking, 'I don't need to be in competition with Beth, so I don't need a degree.' Everyone could see what was going on but me! As long as I didn't earn much money, didn't have any qualifications, didn't have a house, wasn't like her, I imagined she wouldn't envy me or attack me. She was so competitive that the only way not to be destroyed by her was to keep my head down. Delicate, vulnerable, and a failure—that was how I distinguished myself from my sister."

As we sat in Diane's warm house discussing events long past, the sense of anger, rage, confusion, and fear was present and palpable. She was circum-spect about where we could talk, not wanting the subject to infect other parts of her home. Like many people with painful sibling relationships, Diane is wary of reentering territory that still has the power to frighten and depress her. A slim, attractive woman in her mid-sixties, she leads a lively cultural and intellectual life now. But that life has been hard-won, pulled from the flames of a relationship with a sibling who always, it seemed, tried to make her fail.

Years of standoffs and silence would be interrupted by rapprochements and fresh starts that invariably ended badly. On one occasion, Beth invited Diane to stay with her—but then told her to go out for dinner because guests were invited for whom she was not good enough company. It was as though the sisters were frozen at the moment of Diane's birth, which had spoiled Beth's party and forever stolen attention from her. As their mother aged and needed support, the battle between them revived with all the heat of child-hood, and Diane felt increasingly sidelined and abandoned.

Even the death of their mother, which might have brought about a truce, did nothing of the sort. By this time the sisters were not speaking, and when Diane attended the funeral, she brought a friend for moral support. What she feared was not her grief, but her sister. At the reception afterward, the sisters were never in the same room at the same time. They didn't see each other again for nearly twenty years, and then they did not speak.

Competition stoked by her mother made rivalry the defining characteristic of Diane's childhood and much of her adult life. And it wasn't just her relationship with her sister that was damaged; relating to women generally is problematic for her, and she is still on her guard. If she gets close to anyone, she feels anxious and will start to defend herself—whether or not she's been attacked.

"I don't know how to assert my own point of view," she told me, "while making room for others. It's taken me years to discover how to compromise without *being* compromised. The whole family dynamic has made it impossible for me to think of doing work that is really collaborative; fitting in feels too much like death."

Only the support of friends and allies finally allowed Diane to complete her education and to start to feel that she has a life of her own. Nevertheless, her struggle with—or against—her sister still feels very alive. During our conversations, I couldn't tell whether she was confiding in me because I'd asked her to, or because talking to me was another way to strike back at her sister.

But I was grateful to Diane because, while many people have quickly and eagerly told me stories of their rivalrous siblings, very few have wished to be interviewed on the subject. These feelings are too dangerous—too awkward, uncomfortable, and sometimes even shameful. For many people, the rivalry is as intense in adulthood as it was in childhood, and if some resolution has been achieved, it is only because the siblings moved away from each other socially, professionally, or geographically. Passions may seem to die down, but they can be reignited at the time of a parent's death, when the task of dividing property often proves incendiary.

Diane's sister Beth clearly has to win, in matters both small and large. Similarly, in the Hobbs family, Harry has a fierce need to be top dog, and it's telling that, when he's away, the whole family is so placid. Both Harry and Beth, in their different ways, might be described as hypercompetitive, a characteristic described as an "indiscriminant need by individuals to compete and win (and to avoid losing) at any cost as a means of maintaining or enhancing feelings of self-worth."[6] Hypercompetitive people compete in inappropriate situations because every social encounter represents an opportunity for power, control, or domination that can be either won or lost. Some researchers also regard this trait as an extreme form of individualism because personal advantage and narcissistic self-interest overwhelm all other concerns. Hypercompetitive people feel successful only when others lose.

I recognize now that my father was hypercompetitive. The youngest and smallest of three boys, he was born into a poor Texas family where there was never enough of anything. He hated his brothers, left home as early as he could, rarely contacted them, and didn't attend their funerals. He had grown up with a burning desire to get as far from home as possible. This served him well professionally, but it also left him determined always to prove his superiority. If he met people whom he liked but who were less successful than he, his contempt shone through. Attracted to people who were more successful than he was, his sense of relative failure impeded any friendship. He was an adroit negotiator, but a poor judge of when to stop—good at achieving his goals, but graceless in victory. He negotiated complex agreements between oil companies and national governments with an ambition, he once told me, not to secure a workable deal but to break his opponent's spine. Perhaps he was the only one to be surprised when his employer retired him at the earliest opportunity.

My father's competitiveness made him a bully. That has stood me in very good stead in my own career, in which I have encountered many people rather like him: gifted, intelligent thugs. This experience isn't industry-specific: such thugs are as prevalent in broadcasting as they are in software development, venture capital, and consulting. Many have a great deal of power, which is the chief reason people end up working for them; no one would choose such a boss, and most leave at the earliest opportunity. Growing up around this kind of personality left me with a shrewd idea of how to deal with it—I'm good at avoiding confrontation but canny when accepting it—but mostly with a profound sense of waste: talent undermined by aggression, the desire for human connection perpetually subverted by the need to triumph. I loved my father, but I see that he was trapped, isolated, and ostracized by a drive he could not control.

Like many hypercompetitive people, he was also attractive, even charismatic. The energy and drive of the hypercompetitive is dynamic and alluring, a siren song that lures others unaware onto the rocks of relationships that must fail. As a result, the achievements of hypercompetitive people are often short-lived and always costly—in terms of damaged relationships, missed opportunities, and lost connections. Because we can all readily think of high-achievers who fit this profile, it's easy to imagine that hypercompetitive people are always successful, that their drive is some kind of guarantee worth its high price. But we should beware ascertainment bias: what the world doesn't celebrate are the vast numbers of hypercompetitive people whose drive subverts them. I've met plenty of those too.

One in particular, a brilliant BBC trainee with a double first from Oxford, I'll call Tim. Tim's older brother had also gained a double first from Oxford but had gone into finance. I was asked to oversee the production of Tim's first film, which I did with some difficulty, as he made it very clear to me that no help was needed. He bridled at being a trainee, and although he was rapidly accepted as a peer, his need to prove himself made him spiky company. Assigned a gift of a subject and, as was usual in television at the time, a fantastic crew of prize-winning technicians, Tim had no reason not to succeed. Yet, when I viewed a rough-cut of his program, it was a complete mess. Afterward, the film editor explained the mystery. Listening to soundtrack of the crew recorded during the making of the show, it became clear that Tim would take suggestions and advice from no one but instead would insist on getting exactly what he had asked for. In the end, the seasoned crew stopped helping and submitted to his every direction. They stopped collaborating and started following orders.

After we reshot and recut the film, I tried to explain to Tim what had gone wrong. He listened politely and then demurred. He had not, he said, gone into television to learn how to be nice. Many years later, I encountered him again. Still working in television, he had moved from company to company—each one was originally enticed by his intelligence, but then each one eventually decided the costs of working with him were too high.

The problem with competitiveness like this is that, in requiring others to fail, it is fundamentally antisocial. Yet many social Darwinians, inspired by the visible successes they observe in highly competitive people, connect the drive of such people with high levels of productivity and achievement. If only everyone, they argue, were so driven and determined to win, economic growth would skyrocket and vast human potential would be unleashed. Some parents—like my grandparents—studiously fuel their children's rivalry, hoping it will toughen them up for the real world. David and Ida Eisenhower brought their children up this way, as did Joseph Kennedy Sr., who was famous for proclaiming that he wanted no losers in his family. "Life is a fight," one parent explained to me, "and the sooner my kids get good at winning the fight the better."

Why does the desire to make others fail feel natural, while the ability to play well with others does not? Perhaps the sheer drama and excitement provoked by hypercompetitors feels more real, raw, and authentic than pro-social behavior. But the problem with this crude misinterpretation of natural selection is not just that hypercompetitiveness is associated with all kinds of high costs and antisocial tendencies—bullying, narcissism, and Machiavellianism—but that it is *not* associated with higher levels of success.[7] Becoming vicious in order to win is no guarantee of victory.

Why are some people hypercompetitive while others are not? For biologists, the prime suspect is testosterone. Everyone—both male and female—is exposed to testosterone in the womb, at adolescence, and in adulthood, and most scientists believe that testosterone levels play a role in brain development. By adulthood, we each have a basal level of testosterone that stays fairly stable throughout our lives. Men with higher basal testosterone have been found to be less likely to marry, more likely to divorce, and less likely to achieve higher education or income. Because testosterone is sometimes associated with aggression, it has been thought that higher basal levels might be correlated with a greater demand for dominance. But the voluminous studies on this topic have failed to prove a clear correlation.

What has emerged, however, are some intriguing details. When challenged, a man's testosterone levels will rise, and they will rise again if he wins; they fall if he loses. It may be that this creates a hormonal feedback loop in which those who need power get it—and are therefore more likely and better able to continue to demand power. This is not true for women, whose testosterone does not rise at a challenge.[8]

What is most striking about testosterone, however, is that it is implicated in poor judgment and weaker emotional intelligence. In one experiment, supervised by the renowned autism expert Simon Baron-Cohen, testosterone was administered to women, who were then asked to take a test that measured their ability to read people's faces. As the research team had anticipated, the testosterone impaired the women's ability to infer intention, emotions, and other mental states, confirming the hypothesis that high testosterone levels negatively influence social intelligence.[9] Other experiments that monitored naturally circulating testosterone have similarly found that it appears to counteract empathy.[10]

Most intriguing of all is research looking at the relationship between testosterone and collaboration. In a study conducted by British researcher Nicholas Wright and his colleagues, several pairs of volunteers were given testosterone orally while another group of volunteers were given a placebo. Everyone was asked to work in pairs, watching a screen and anticipating the moment at which a target would appear. At first, each participant had to reach a decision independently; then they had to make their choices collaboratively. The researchers were pretty sure that the collaborative decision-making would be more accurate, which it was. But the question they really wanted to answer was this: would testosterone improve or inhibit the quality of the collaboration?

What they found was that testosterone caused a marked decrease in the capability of the collaborative pairs. This effect was primarily ascribed to an "egocentricity bias": each participant was more likely to overvalue his or her own opinion and to undervalue the opinions of partners. Raised testosterone levels, in effect, made participants more self-centered and much less capable of working with other people, with the result that they failed to capture the value of collaborating.[11]

We can see that there is a relationship between testosterone and high degrees of competitiveness, but we don't know why some people have higher levels of testosterone than others. This difference sheds light but doesn't fully explain the complexity of behavior and real life outside of experiments. We will not—and should not hope to—see the day when hormone testing is used in interviews or job recruiting. As complex as it is, the science is clear on one thing: biology alone can never account fully for the complex interaction of the social and psychological processes that drive behavior. Hormone levels on their own—before or after birth—can't explain personality, and even the most neurochemically minded of researchers end up talking about the importance of parental attachment and environment. There are simply too many other factors to consider—hundreds of other hormones for a start.[12] Temperament, preexisting behaviors, social support, and culture all play their role in a rich brew in which we still can identify only a few ingredients at a time. The fact that identical twins, raised in the same family, will develop different immune systems testifies to the complexity of the interplay between all of these factors. Most influential of all is experience—what happens to us and what we do.

Our brain's wiring is critically determined by the experiences that we have throughout life, but much of the basic platform, we now can see, is laid down in early life. This was most vividly illustrated in a series of experiments in which young kittens had one eye sutured shut for the first three months of life. This was not deliberate cruelty; the goal was to ascertain how the parts of the brain responsible for visual cognition would develop. The results were striking: the part of the brain responsible for vision for the closed eye could not develop. Brain scans could identify clear, defined differences—big black blobs—marking the areas where neural pathways had not grown. What is more important is that, after a certain age, the cats' brains could not change. What had happened early in life was fixed. These were some of the first dramatic experiments that demonstrated both the plasticity of the brain and the degree to which it is minutely sculpted by experience.[13]

Since that work, neuroscientists have been uncovering the stages at which those critical pathways of the human brain are laid down. What is clear is that connections that aren't used die off (as with the kittens), but also that connections that are richly stimulated wire together. This has been described by neuropsychiatrist Allan Schore as a "use it or lose it situation. Cells that fire together wire together. Cells that do not, die together." One of the conclusions Schore has drawn from his work is that, while too much stress may stop cells from developing, experiencing conflict *that can be and is resolved* may be how we develop the neural networks we need for collaboration.[14]

The family is a learning environment where we are introduced to and learn to imagine the minds of others.[15] It can and should provide the safe environment where children's rivalrous feelings can emerge and be expressed as a way of learning about conflict. The important work of a family is not to eliminate arguments and negative emotions, but to create a safe place where they can be challenged, understood, and resolved with love by people who won't give up. That's what family dinners are for: not just the food fights but the lessons learned from the give-and-take, the cut-and-thrust, of passionate debate.

Ezekiel Emanuel, today a medical ethicist at the University of Pennsylvania, wrote tellingly about growing up with his brothers Rahm (who grew up to become chief of staff in President Barack Obama's administration) and Ari (a Hollywood agent and reputedly the model for Ari Gold in the television show *Entourage*). At the brothers' family meals, passion, solid information, honesty, and argument were expected and respected. There were rules—no cruelty, no prejudice, and no stupidity—but swearing was allowed. What Emanuel describes is common to the experience of many siblings who, looking back, say that their childhood rivalry made a profound contribution to their social competence, their emotional development, and, ultimately, their parenting skills. Families were where they first experienced hatred—but also where they learned to deal with it.

Conflict is critical not only to brain development but to emotional and social learning. Children need to experience conflict, but they also need to have the positive experience of finding solutions to it: losing sometimes, winning other times, but always surviving it. And many siblings believe that expressing their rivalry in their youth made them closer in adulthood. Hypercompetitive people may never have these experiences, however, because they dominate too quickly, and their submissive siblings (like Diane Wilson) never have these experiences because they get so good at avoiding the fight.

Experiments with families in which some parents were trained in mediation skills demonstrate that even very young children have an immense capacity to learn how to resolve conflicts constructively and creatively. Parents without mediation training tended to intervene and adjudicate more; their children were more contentious, demanding, and self-justifying. In families where parents did have mediation training, the disputes were more severe, but the children became better problem-solvers and crafted more creative resolutions for themselves. In these families, parents helped but did not design the final outcomes because the children learned to do so for themselves—and they did it better.[16] What the experiments illustrated was children's profound capacity to learn from each other and from their parents the prosocial skills they needed to collaborate and to integrate different interests, needs, and perspectives.

The most creative response to sibling competition is "deidentification," a term coined by psychologist Frances Schachter, who puzzled over why children in the same family, sharing 50 percent of their DNA, were nonetheless so very different. Why is it, for example, that Harry must find an external explanation for any sports defeat when his brother Tom, in the same situation, can be so generous? After studying hundreds of sibling pairs, Schachter argued that siblings become different from each other as a way of mitigating their feelings of rivalry. Calling this a "Cain Complex," she saw that children—particularly those of the same gender and especially those born right after one another—would become different in order *not* to fight. Deidentification, according to Schachter, is a creative attempt at maintaining family harmony.[17]

Frank Sulloway, a psychologist and historian of science, compares sib-lings to Darwin's finches from the Galápagos Islands, which played such an important part in the development of evolutionary theory. All fourteen species of Darwin's finches derived from a single ancestor that had colo-nized the islands some two million years earlier. As such, they were—and still are—a stunning example of just how rich and fast adaptation can be. Sulloway argues that human siblings similarly become increasingly dissimi-lar through learning what earns attention, resources, and respect within the family environment.

"Strategies for dealing with sibling competition and for evoking sibling cooperation," Sulloway writes, "are among the principal functional mecha-nisms that govern successful adaptation within family life."[18]

Thus, differences that start out as biology are made more extreme or mod-erate by experience and birth order. This is both a biological process that affects the wiring in the brain ("neurosculpting") and a strategy for protect-ing everyone in the family.

"The concept of niches," Sulloway argues, "derives from the field of ecol-ogy where it exemplifies how different species use available resources within their environments. Family niches may be conceptualized in a similar man-ner. Siblings compete with one another to secure physical, emotional and intellectual resources from their parents. Depending on differences in birth order, gender, physical traits and aspects of temperament, siblings create dif-fering roles for themselves within the family system."[19]

Because we don't want to fight with our siblings for territory, we claim some that isn't taken. In the quest for resources, Sulloway points out, first-borns always have the easiest task. For a period of time, they have their par-ents exclusively to themselves, and however hard their parents strive in later life to be fair and equitable, they still seem to end up getting 10 percent more care than later-borns. They also typically have an IQ that, on average, is three points higher than that of subsequent children.[20] With more attention and with no sibling rival, firstborns, says Sulloway, tend to be more closely affil-iated with their parents' interests and attitudes. This makes them more con-servative and defensive of a status quo that has served them, as incumbents, very well.[21]

Middle children invariably get less attention than the first or last.[22] Younger children are less likely to be vaccinated than their older siblings, with rates of vaccination declining 20 to 30 percent with each successive child, an indica-tor perhaps of just how hard, even impossible, it is for even the best parents to be equitable.[23] Later-borns therefore face a challenge: with less care and nurture, and the conservative "position" taken, younger children have to fight harder for attention and resources. They haven't had exclusive attention from their parents, certain niches are already gone, and being smaller and less developed, they're able to do less than their older siblings. Their relative impotence forces them into more distinctive, attention-grabbing roles. They simply must diversify. And this often leads later-borns to be more receptive to and supportive of new, radical, even revolutionary ideas. It may also force them into more collaborative roles, since most later-borns learn early on that they are stronger through alliances than in isolation.

Sulloway has tested his theory against a vast amount of historical data, examining scientific revolutions from Copernicus to Newton and Darwin. In each case, he says, the new radical positions were adopted and promoted by later-borns and the more conservative (even extremely conservative) positions were taken by firstborns. He makes the same argument to explain the political fault lines of the French Revolution: firstborns adopted a more conventional and moderate politics, while those who were younger siblings promoted radical action. Bringing his research up to date, Sulloway identified the same trend in the history of major league baseball. Analyzing sibling pairs who played in the majors, including Joe and Dom DiMaggio and Cal and Billy Ripken, Sulloway found that it was the younger brother who more often tried to steal bases.[24]

The birth-order argument remains controversial, but deidentification does not—and there are some striking examples of it, none more so than in the family of Ralph Nader. Each of the four Nader children decided to study a different part of the world: Shafeek took North America, Claire laid claim to the Middle East, Laura focused on Mexico and Latin America, while Ralph, the youngest, was left with China and the Far East; between them, they had the world covered. (Apparently they felt that Europe didn't need any of them because it was so well taught in school.)[25] Similarly, the rock group Kings of Leon comprises three brothers: Anthony Followill, who sings lead vocals; Ivan, who plays drums and percussion; and Michael, who plays bass guitar. Their cousin Cameron fills in on vocals and plays guitar. The group is named after their grandfather, and that sense of serving or honoring something bigger than any individual is key to their success.

It's striking that sibling rivalry is so renowned a phenomenon, with its own terminology, while collaboration between siblings has been less studied, even though it can be so productive and creative. Many families develop both immensely gifted individuals *and* collaborators. The Wachowskis, who made the films *The Matrix* and *Cloud Atlas,* the Marriott brothers who founded their eponymous hotel chain, sisters Klara and Johanna Soderberg who created the group First Aid Kit, the Greenwood brothers of Radiohead, the Brontës, the Wright brothers, the Emanuels, and many many more unknown but effective sibling collaborations testify to the capacity for families to produce energetic collaborators for whom success neither demands nor produces dominance or exclusive success. That siblings can work together successfully doesn't mean that they do so quietly, passively, or obsequiously—quite the opposite. Wilbur Wright said that one of the things he loved about his brother Orville was that he was a "good scrapper." They argued fiercely and often—but in the service of a project they owned together.

"From an early age, I think we all had some sense of a shared story," Tony Bicat tells me. "Mother was the center of it. She created this household. The purpose of it was to provide my father with a place to work undisturbed. And because he was an artist, there was a sense that that was what we were all here for. There was this really strong sense that they worked together to create the home in which we all lived."

Tony is the eldest of three siblings. Looking at all three today, it's clear that they're related. It isn't just the shared features—the curly hair and warm, deep-set eyes. They all have a calm, thoughtful pace to their language and an open and obvious sense of curiosity about each other and about the world. That all three children grew up to work in highly collaborative art forms—theater, film, and music—is scarcely surprising: they've been learning how to work with other people all their lives. Listening to each of the Bicats describe their childhood, what's striking is that there was no struggle for dominance and winning was not an issue. Tony, a filmmaker and playwright, knows that he was his mother's favorite—the others agree—but nobody seems to mind very much, perhaps because each sibling had his or her own niche.

"Tina and I played the piano and the violin," Tony recalls. "But when Nick arrived, it was just clear from an early age that—well, if he wasn't a prodigy, he was certainly very gifted. If there had been a contest, it would have been obvious that we couldn't compare—so there was no contest."

"I'm the youngest in the family, and I was never terribly good with language," Nick Bicat recalls. "But I could always win my older brother's respect with my stunts: throwing myself from the first-floor window or downstairs. Later on, of course, the music helped too."

Today, Nick Bicat is an award-winning composer. He's written music for Hollywood movies, the London Chamber Orchestra, the Royal Shakespeare Company, Philip Ridley, David Hare, and Howard Brenton, from TV versions of *A Christmas Carol* to the steamy melodrama *Lace*. His work couldn't exist without collaborators, and he received deep early lessons in collaboration at home.

"Tony was the oldest, and he knew more than me about just about everything. He was sharp and witty and perceptive. I wanted his approval, wanted him to like what I did, would want him to laugh. I wanted him to like my music."

In between the two boys was their sister, Tina.

"Tony always had a story—that was his thing, and he used us where appropriate," Tina remembers. "Nick was very musical, and I made things: props and costumes. I made the pictures come alive. It was set quite early, how we played together. It was probably helped by the fact that we had a lot of space—a big garden—and while there were grown-ups around, I don't remember them being with us. They were always there to step in and help us, if we needed it. But most of the time, we just got on with it."

Tina has gone on to work as a designer with some of the world's most improvisatory and collaborative theater groups—Punchdrunk, Ockham's Razor, and Spiral. For the Bicats, deidentification provided a rich early foundation because each child contributed something important and unique to the group. Each had a niche and a unique capability that no one could take away. That made participation safe. They don't describe a childhood free from conflict—money was always scarce, and tensions abounded—but they learned early on, Tony says, to respect one another's territory, and they became very good at negotiating among themselves.

That capacity has continued throughout their lives. When their father died, the siblings convened to manage his collection of paintings, a responsibility they discharge together to this day. In their professional lives the Bicats have sometimes collaborated with each other, but more often with others. Each has had triumphs and failures, but what has characterized their careers is a sense of freedom and of fairness—a sense of being both supported and independent.

This isn't about happy families as such. For the neurologist Robert Burton, the critical contribution that siblings make to early childhood is that they teach a fundamental life lesson that starts in the family but ultimately extends to all human relationships.

"You're not alone," Burton tells me. "If you have a sibling, you aren't alone—in the sense that you aren't abandoned, isolated. But also, you're not alone in the sense of Narcissus: there *is* more than just you in the world. And while this can feel terrible, it also contributes an important sense of camaraderie. It means learning the value of sacrifice, learning you can lose the argument and survive, you can express yourself and be original: those are all very necessary aspects of social understanding."

For a long time, it has been so fashionable to see life as one long competition from the cradle to the grave that any other narrative has been dismissed as trivial, sentimental, or irrelevant. That so puzzled and annoyed primatologist Frans de Waal that he would devote his forty-year career to exploring how far competition dominates the lives and behaviors of our primate cousins, chimpanzees and bonobos. Chimpanzees are of particular interest, he says, because they care intensely about power—but power isn't the only thing they care about. After a fight, they have elaborate reconciliation rituals because they value relationships and appreciate that they need to be maintained. Chimps, bonobos, wolves, birds, hyenas, and dolphins all learn to repair conflict and to reconcile differences, behaviors that, de Waal writes, "would be superfluous if social life were ruled entirely by domination and competition."[26]

Primates demonstrate clear awareness that they need help to accomplish their aims and can't do much singly. They're adept at building coalitions and mediating conflict, and they show a distinct preference for prosocial choices. In one of his most famous experiments, de Waal showed that chimpanzees dislike unfairness and in some circumstances will reject rewards if they aren't shared equally.[27] Even in the unlikely setting of a game theory experiment, apes collaborated when they needed each other. So too did children between the ages of two and seven, prompting the question as to what happens later in life to the ability to collaborate. Many of de Waal's experiments have provoked outrage from economists, who simply can't accept that competition and self-interest don't prevail. Nevertheless, his work has accumulated evidence that we have evolved behaviors to avoid the detrimental effects of extreme competition because doing so has given us a sustained evolutionary advantage.

Diane Wilson and her sister, my father and his brothers, Tim the TV producer, the many siblings I've talked to who confessed to but avoided reliving the misery of sibling rivalry—all testify to the impoverishment of lives ruled by competition. Unable to trust, needing always to win, seeing success only in the failures of others—these were habits engrained early that, like the kitten's eye, left a pattern of being and behavior that could not be repaired. But the Naders, the Bicats, the Wachowskis, and all the millions of siblings who do move beyond competition find in each other a source of solidarity and definition.

We have equal capacity for both collaboration and for competition. Which of these gets attention and reinforcement depends on us, our families, and the society we inhabit. In the last fifty years of Western culture, competition has proved the dominant, insistent trope, reinforced by an ever-expanding library of books, tools, apps, classes, personal coaches, and any number of scorecards to make us bigger, tougher, meaner, more successful competitors. Inhabiting a culture caught up in a testosterone-fueled feedback loop, we've been persuaded that if we aren't top dog we must be underdogs, if we aren't winners we're losers. What's striking in its absence is any equivalent urging to hone our collaborative gifts. We know they're in there—we just don't make much effort to refine them. Opting to compete rather than to collaborate is a choice, however, not an evolutionary inevitability, and a choice that incurs high costs, not just for our family relationships but for the friendships, organizations, institutions, and world that we create.

What does this mean for Harry Hobbs? Will his hypercompetitiveness abate with time? Will the conflicts that exhaust his parents slowly but surely teach him how to be part of something bigger and more meaningful than himself? It's hard to tell.

Last year Harry, after being encouraged to apply, won a place at Eton. "No one in the family went there," Alice tells me. "We have no connections; we just thought we'd give it a go. But when he learned he'd got in—that he'd 'won,' so to speak—there was a strange look on his face: 'What have I done?'"

CHAPTER 2

Making the Grade

Few tragedies can be more extensive than the stunting of life, few injustices deeper than the denial of an opportunity to strive or even to hope, by a limit imposed from without, but falsely identified as lying within. We inhabit a world of human differences and predilections, but the extrapolation of these facts to theories of rigid limits is ideology.

—STEPHEN JAY GOULD, *The Mismeasure of Man* (1996)

Just off of Kendall Square in Cambridge, Massachusetts, stand three office blocks so newly refurbished that you can tell by looking through the windows that they're only partially occupied. With shiny steel and gleaming marble, they are just another piece in the grand 3-D jigsaw that is the campus of the Massachusetts Institute of Technology. In contrast to the flashier buildings of Frank Gehry, Steven Holl, and Fumihiko Maki, however, 700 Technology Square stands out as a workhorse—the place where hard problems get solved without fanfare.

Up on the third floor, Charles Shubert presides over a project within the Office of Educational Innovation and Technology. Shubert looks more like Father Christmas than a nerd: a large, rotund man with a warm, benevolent gaze, he has a laid-back Midwestern style and a very dry sense of humor. To say that he is a master of understatement would understate just how droll he can be. But appearances notwithstanding, Shubert and his team are tackling tough challenges: how to take advantage of large-scale computing systems and bioinformatics to advance the understanding of microbial ecology.

It isn't just the science that's hard. The simulations that Shubert and his team build use huge amounts of processing power, multiple computer systems, and a variety of computing languages. Yet the software must be accessible and usable by cutting-edge scientists whose research needs are far from simple to understand, never mind address. The layers of technical collaboration implicit in this work are legion: languages, disciplines, systems, infrastructures, knowledge levels, and personalities all combine in various permutations, giving Shubert's projects maximal complexity.

But even more remarkable than the sheer difficulty of these projects are the people responsible for producing them. It's not easy finding people who can effortlessly work across and translate between cutting-edge biology and bleeding-edge technology. Ivan Ceraj, who leads the project, is an economist from Croatia. He says that most scientists can't do computer programming at this level, and most computer programmers can't do biology at this level. If you do find people who can do both, often they can earn a lot more money elsewhere.

Key to the team are Shubert's "finds": talents he has unearthed in unlikely places and of whom he is inordinately proud. Like Shubert, Justin Riley comes from Missouri, and if you didn't know that, you might guess: a tall freckled man in his mid-twenties, Riley has brown hair, a sharp nose, and a relaxed gait that convey the ease and informality of a farmer. Riley was glad to leave Missouri; he just had no idea he would end up at MIT.

"I really struggled in math when I was thirteen, fourteen," he tells me. "I'd get a C or a B if I was lucky. I was a nerdy kid and liked tinkering with things. But I had no idea about science or any sense it was something I'd want to do."

In the early days of computing and the advent of the Internet, Riley had fun breaking computers and fixing them. He taught himself how to build websites and earned a little money that way. After high school, he went to Missouri State University with no idea of what he would do. He was really just going through the motions of college.

"I had read about people connecting computers to do cool stuff. That aspect seemed a lot of fun," he tells me, laughing. "In my spare time, I decided to check it out and ended up building a student project, 'HoToTo'—a silly name meaning half bear, half man. My friends and I went to a warehouse auction selling off really old equipment—we were really just experimenting. Four or five of my buddies sat on the floor, took the computers apart, put them all together, blew a few circuits, but got them going and installed Linux. It looked like a monster mounted on hardwood planks."

One day Shubert, who was home visiting his family in Missouri, decided to drop into MSU, where he knew the dean of sciences. In the corner of a computer lab, he spotted Riley and asked what he was up to. They talked for a while, Shubert wandered off, and Riley gave him no more thought. The next day the dean told Riley how much Shubert had enjoyed the conversation; would it be all right to forward his contact information?

"I knew he was from MIT, so of course I was interested!" Riley recalls. "And over the course of the year, Charlie worked hard to get me here. I started work at MIT before I'd even finished my degree! Fortunately for me, it turned out I love to program, but before I came here I had done very little. I was really worried about my qualifications; I knew very little scripting. I knew some loops and had played with writing in C, just working through a book. Chuck and Ivan threw me into the deep end with Java. Looking back, I'm actually still rather shocked that I got to come here! If I'd gone to the bathroom at the wrong time, I might never have met him, never got here."

Shubert was thrilled with Riley's work, not just because it was excellent but because it validated something he'd always believed: that there's more talent in ordinary places than most people ever imagine or see. And when he started looking for it, he found it. Riley's colleague is Sarah Bonner; Shubert found her working as an administrative assistant and trying to finish college. She wasn't having a good time: a reputation for being argumentative had earned her a fair amount of opprobrium from her peers.

"Then Charlie took me out for lunch and asked me if I'd like to be a software developer! I said, 'You realize I don't code—I've just done a few PERL scripts.' But he said no, he wanted to teach me, and he had a grant that would let him do that, as long as I didn't mind minority money. I said I didn't mind any money as long as it was green."

She later learned that Shubert had been watching her for a year; he was impressed by how hard she worked and how prepared she was to stand up for herself. Those were the qualities he sought. Bonner says of herself that she liked to "MacGyver" things—a term derived from a television hero who could solve complex problems with everyday materials, mainly duct tape and a Swiss Army knife. That combination of smart thinking and pragmatism was just what Shubert needed, and found, in Sarah Bonner.

"It's hard for me to talk with grandeur about what I bring to the table until I go to conferences and talk to senior developers and I am just astounded by what they don't know. Charlie says I bring a special ability to be a user and a coder and to not feel uncomfortable disagreeing with him. Before I ask a question, I like to know the possible answers so I can be prepared for the conversation. So we have very thoughtful conversations here. We're not just poking each other back and forth; it isn't a contest."

Justin and Sarah weren't star competitors in the current education system; they weren't expert at, or even interested in, guessing the right answers. But both had retained a love of learning and exploration that Shubert prized.

Nothing in their schooling suggested that they would one day be working at one of the world's most prestigious universities, or that Justin would author a paper about software published in *Nature*. The competitive education system wasn't what got them to MIT. That they had the potential to succeed is clear now, but what saved them, in the end, was luck. Imagine if Riley had gone to the bathroom at the wrong moment, or if Bonner hadn't been argumentative. Charlie—a most unlikely fairy godfather—happened to notice them, happened to help them, and happened to be in a position to change their lives. But for most children, success hinges on being able to compete at every stage of their educational career. For their parents, failure is a constant, imminent, and terrifying threat.

"What happens if the kids don't play the system? If your child goes to the wrong school, he will be scuttling coal somewhere," Betsy Rapoport tells me. "They've been given a life diagram—go to the right school, then you will get the right job, the right amount of money, and then you'll be happy and get promoted and move on straight up to the top!"

She's laughing, but she's put two children through the New York State education system and now she coaches many more through the college application process. In the kids she works with, and their parents, she sees the sense of emergency that characterizes their thinking about education as a permanent crisis.

"These kids have been competing since they were two! They start being coached and tutored at the age of three to get into kindergarten. *Kindergarten!* They have parents breathing down their necks, telling them that if they don't get into this nursery school, they won't get into the right elementary or middle school—then high school will be a disaster, their lives will be ruined. It starts young, and it just gets more and more intense."

Parental panic has reached epidemic proportions, prompting the emergence of a subgenre of books aimed at advising, sometimes moderating, but also sometimes inflaming parents who find themselves in a state of fear and trembling over their children's education. Whether you take Amy Chua's *Battle Hymn of the Tiger Mother* as a joke or an instruction manual, the book's prescription for high achievement clearly touched a nerve in the American psyche.

Anxiety about the need to succeed has been running high for decades, but the global economic crisis, together with high levels of youth unemployment, have turned that fear into self-perpetuating hysteria. If well-paid jobs are few, then a lustrous educational track record is crucial, with the risks of failure high and the costs of underachievement deadly. Slowly but surely over the last twelve years, the United States has overtaken Europe in its youth unemployment rate, with over 26 percent of Americans between the ages of twenty-five and thirty-four jobless. And young workers are the only age group with lower wages in 2013 than in 2000.[1] As the Internet, robotics, and globalization have eliminated entry-level jobs and, with them, the chance of working one's way to the top, a top-tier education appears to be the sole surviving means of getting ahead. You can forget the backroom-to-boardroom romance; now it is school and school alone that spells the difference between triumph and disaster.

Every response to this panic has proposed some form of competitive marketplace for education in which kids compete against kids, teachers against teachers, and schools against schools in a frantic bid for excellence. New charter schools were supposed to stoke market competition, threatening failing schools into upping their game. But as competitive marketplaces are wont to do, this one has prompted the schools to try to game the system, choosing and keeping the most motivated students while "counseling out" those who don't make the grade.[2] What competitive strategies have never done (but which all of the highest-achieving educational systems accomplish), is raise everyone's boat. Instead, competition stokes panic and a desperate sense that every student is on his or her own, left to hack a solitary path through a dangerous educational jungle.

Parents make strenuous efforts to ensure their children's success in the fight. Living in Boston, I encountered two parents who, on learning that one primary school used the game Red Light/Green Light in its selection process, devoted hours to training their five-year-old daughter in the game. I've known parents who preferred to send their child to a school *not* strongly associated with mathematical achievement in order that their mathematically zealous child would stand out. One father considered sending his son to a school he believed to be inferior on the grounds—for which he proffered data—that a high grade point average mattered more to colleges than the quality of the education the child had received. Other parents, more prosaically, simply employ tutors to coach their children, often late into the night, to keep them from dropping out of their GATE (Gifted and Talented Education) classes.

On top of these strategic academic decisions is the equally strategic choice of sport and musical instrument, with much soul-searching around which might look most distinctive on a résumé: Does the harp look more distinctive than the saxophone? Might it be easier for a boy to gain a school orches-tra seat with the piccolo?

Once in school, pupils are quickly sorted by the GATE exam into those who are promising and those who, apparently, are not. Whether or not gift-edness can be measured seems in itself doubtful. Experts can't agree on reli-able tests, and evidence suggests that the tests (taken by children as young as four) miss at least one-third of the most gifted students.[3] Moreover, the test preparation industry skews results: to ensure high marks, tutoring compa-nies like Bright Kids NYC coach children on topics such as spatial visualiza-tion and serial reasoning, with workbooks and hours of parental tutoring.

"Every time these tests change, there's a lot of demand," Bige Doruk, founder of Bright Kids, says. She doesn't believe that test prep, coaching, and classes corrupt results. "It is not a validity issue, it's a competitive issue. Parents will always do what they can for their children."

In just five years, between 2007 and 2012, the number of New York chil-dren who qualified for gifted and talented kindergarten places *doubled*. Nobody believed that this increase was due to a sudden influx of uniquely brilliant kids; instead, it was the result of the competitive efforts of parents and their kids. As one consequence, the ERB (Educational Records Bureau) test, one of the leading tests, was rewritten in 2013—but no sooner were the revisions published than new workbooks and classes came on the market. The inflationary impact of tests and test prep has led some schools to prefer assessments by psychologists, but this has prompted some parents to try to secure inside information on which of the assessors has a reputation for giving kids an easier ride.

Tests aren't the only way of dividing children at an early age into win-ners and losers. Tracking, also known as "homogenous groupings," separates pupils into classes that progress at different speeds. The educational ratio-nale for this is that some children pick up math or reading faster than others; the quick learners shouldn't be held back by the slower ones, who should be allowed more time. The kids absorb a simpler message from tracking: you're either quick or you're slow, academic or non-academic, a winner or a loser. Explicitly or implicitly, children are sorted as surely as Harry Potter was by the sorting hat at Hogwarts. Intrinsic to tracking and school selection is the notion that the innate qualities of a child can be seen and served, that those qualities are already there and that someone, somehow, can identify them. In the world of Harry Potter, it's magic. In real life, it's admissions officers, résumés, and exams.

"By the time kids get to high school," Betsy Rapoport tells me, "they have been tracked for years. If they are kids of savvy parents, they will have figured out that taking electives drives the grade point average down, so they will have been discouraged from taking art. They might love art—be really talented—but now the whole focus is on tactics: What gets the grades and the GPA up? Which are the best or easiest classes to do well in? What teachers grade easiest? So then you find those classes are all full of really driven kids—or the children of very strategic parents. They don't really mix with a cross-section. Later on, of course, it means they'll all be competing against each other for the same colleges."

All of this strategizing is well intentioned—no one should be surprised that parents want their children to thrive. But few children are thinking, at the ages of five, ten, or even fifteen, about the longer-term earning potential of their résumé. They're busy growing up, making and losing friends, and finding out who they are and what they like as their minds wander like cats from passion to disinterest. The gross disconnect between lackadaisical kids and laser-focused parents generates explosive frustration: if the kids can't motivate themselves, then we need to supply the motivation, and to that problem the inevitable solution proffered is—competition. After all, the trope runs, it's a hypercompetitive world out there. There's no moment too soon for kids to face the race that is life. So competition cascades throughout education: children competing for places and exam results; teachers competing for exam results (which may have an impact on their pay); schools competing for a place in the magazine and website listings that identify the institutions that promise to produce winners. And if children run faster in a race, the argument runs, won't everyone study harder when competing against one another? Isn't turning education into one giant multi-athlon the key to Olympian achievements for young minds?

That competitive mind-set informs both No Child Left Behind and The Race to the Top, two federal initiatives that are desperate to raise educational standards. Both treat education like a competitive marketplace, and both put all their faith in testing—even though fewer than one out of four Americans believes that this strategy has improved or is likely to improve local schools.[4] A 2009 bipartisan effort to draw up a Common Core similarly banked on testing, giving rise to concerns that with so much emphasis on reading and math tests, teaching anything else—science, literature, history, civics, and the arts—would fall by the wayside. Linking teachers' pay to test results disgusted parents and teachers alike, all of them well aware that this would turn pupils into great test-taking machines but would in no way guarantee the deeper learning—self-motivation and discipline, social and emotional skills, collaborative, communication, and creative talents—that their parents sought for them. The idea broached in some states that good grades might be rewarded with cash or McDonald's vouchers similarly failed to inspire.

The problem here isn't that sprinters won't be motivated by promises of medals; they will. But learning to think mathematically, to love words, to decode a map, or to design a good experiment requires a different order of thinking and a different order of motivation. What we know from at least half a century of research into human motivation is that extrinsic rewards—rankings, prizes, grades—crowd out intrinsic drive. Apparently, we can be deeply motivated by only one thing at a time, not by many things at once. And hard, short-term rewards—money, medals, prizes—tend to crowd out the longer-term, self-generated drive to learn.

This is so counterintuitive that we persist in believing that the way to motivate kids (and adults) is to offer them rewards. The landmark experiment that suggested otherwise was conducted forty years ago by Edward Deci and Richard Ryan. Ever since their original work was published, different versions of it have been tested and retested, without any significant challenge: the findings remain robust.

In the original experiment, nursery school children were divided into three groups and given the opportunity to draw. Children in the first group were promised a reward: if they drew, they'd win a certificate. Those in the second group were told nothing—but were surprised by a certificate when they had finished drawing. The third group of children just drew and received nothing for their labors.

Two weeks later, the children were again confronted by paper and pens. Now the question was: which group would *want* to draw? The group that had initially been promised a reward was the least engaged: why should they draw when there was no certificate on offer?

Similar experiments have been conducted with different ages, tasks, and rewards, and in different industries and cultures, but the results don't vary. Whether it's grades, stars, certificates, money, or trophies, "virtually every type of expected tangible reward made contingent on task performance does, in fact, undermine intrinsic motivation."[5]

Subsequent experiments (involving adults as well as children) tested the impact of external rewards on creative thinking and problem-solving. Princeton psychologist Sam Glucksberg found that people who were asked to solve a problem that required some ingenuity and were offered a cash incentive to do so took longer to come up with an answer than people who were not offered a cash reward. Many other experiments have drawn the same conclusion: the expectation of an external reward—be it a grade, a prize, or a burger voucher—impoverishes the richness of thinking that creativity requires.[6] Moreover, genuine critical thinking and innovation require that the mind be allowed to wander, to try out answers that don't work, to test concepts, and, crucially, to make mistakes. All of this is directly discouraged when the focus of learning is on exams and results.

As early as 1950, the eminent American psychologist Joy Paul Guilford had challenged his professional colleagues with a question: Why was there so little correlation between education and creative productiveness?[7] Guilford made his name by developing psychometric studies of intelligence in which he made a critical distinction between what he called "convergent" and "divergent" production. Convergent production, he argued, involves finding a single solution to a problem; by contrast, divergent thinking requires bringing as many solutions as possible to the surface. The former is fundamentally about following rules, whereas the latter is inherently creative, imaginative, and exploratory. At MIT, Sarah Bonner was a classic divergent thinker: always seeking multiple solutions and exploring alternatives. Although this may have made her argumentative—she could see more solutions than many of her colleagues—it was also exactly what made Charles Shubert so eager to recruit her. Yet our educational systems specifically reward convergent thinking while inhibiting divergent critical and creative thinking.

Two psychologists, Teresa Amabile and Beth Hennessey, rose to Guilford's challenge and devoted decades of work to experiments that explored the connection between creativity and education. They concluded that there are five ways in which education can *kill* creativity: having children work for an expected reward, focusing pupils on an expected evaluation, deploying plenty of surveillance, setting up restricted choices, and creating competitive situations. These practices all typify the education systems and policies we currently deploy.[8] We say we want motivated, creative students—but we opt for methods and structures known to undermine both.

When parents, with the best intentions in the world, race to get their children identified as gifted or talented and to have that status proven with test results, they exacerbate the problem. What we know is that interest *precedes* talent, that it isn't fixed but highly susceptible to encouragement, development, kindness, and patience—of the kind that Charlie Shubert provided for Justin Riley and Sarah Bonner.

In his book *Give and Take,* Adam Grant describes an outstanding teacher of accounting, C. J. Skender, who is so good that Duke University and the University of North Carolina have to share him. Because his students are successful, people think he's a great talent-spotter. But this is exactly what he is not. Skender's students succeed because he cares, sets high standards, and, as one student wrote, "sees the best in his students."[9] His secret isn't competition—it's interest. When kids are interested in something and can pursue it without threat of failure, they are far more likely to develop their talents and to experience the joy of expanding their own capacity. But critical to that process is a climate of safety where mistakes don't matter and are just a normal part of learning.

By contrast, an education system marked, like an obstacle course, with tests and evaluations turns learning into a commodity; permeated with the fear of failure, such a system's capacity to inspire is profoundly circumscribed. How students respond to the pressure of exams varies wildly and bears no relationship to capability. Instead, it appears that our genes significantly determine who loves exams and does well on them.

The COMT (catechol-O-methyl transferase) gene regulates the amount of dopamine in the prefrontal cortex in the brain, where we make decisions, plan, and resolve conflicts. One variant of the gene slowly removes dopamine; another variant does it fast. Dopamine levels increase with stress; enough helps you rise to the occasion, but too much becomes overwhelming. So students with the slower variety of COMT typically find it easier to think if they are not under stress. Those with the faster variety may seem a little laid-back, but under stress, they cope better. Scientists distinguish between the two genetic stress responses as the difference between "worriers" and "warriors," and their key point is that both types excel, albeit in very different environments. Hence, the paradox that hardworking students may fall apart in exams while the ones who never handed in their homework on time ace tests. What exams reveal most clearly is not intellectual or creative capacity—they just tell you how good you are at exams.[10]

The research into COMT was primarily conducted in Taiwan, which has traditionally placed great emphasis on a single exam, the Basic Competency, taken by children when they are fourteen. Applying their genetic insights to real-world testing confirmed the hypothesis that this kind of high-stakes test identifies great exam-takers but is less helpful in building or identify-ing intelligence. After 2014, Taiwan will no longer require the exam. Instead of sorting, educational policy now emphasizes raising attainment levels for everyone.

Of course, tests can help teachers determine whether students are keeping up, how much they have retained, and what they still don't understand. But standardized testing associated with external rewards—be it stars, grades, medals, or college places—turns learning from something that should be intrinsically satisfying into a transaction: do the work, get the grade. The product is prized over the process. With eyes so firmly focused on the exter-nal reward, students lose their sense of meaning and joy in their work. We produce expert exam-takers when what we ought to develop is a love of learning.

That observation may appear terribly sentimental, but it really isn't. Apart from sounding like a worthwhile ideal, what is the value of a love of learn-ing? Why don't we just teach kids what they need to know to get jobs and get on with their lives? The problem is that no one knows what they will need. The world is changing so fast, and industries come and go with such speed, that it is impossible to predict what the toolkit of the future will contain. Twenty years ago, it might have been reasonable to assume that knowing shorthand, being able to run a printing press or do electrical engineering, mastering the arcane information structure of the law, or being adept at pro-totype packaging were important skills, but today these skills are redundant. Bosses type for themselves, newspapers are fast disappearing, no one uses typewriters, domestic appliances last forever or can be replaced cheaply, software is taking over the work of paralegals and 3-D printers will take care of everyone's prototyping needs. Even doctors, lawyers, and journalists must face the fact that much of their work is being replaced by machines. As the machinery for invention and manufacture gets cheaper and the software to run it becomes easier, much old-fashioned expertise carries few kudos and even less job security.

In Charles Dickens's *Hard Times,* the schoolmaster Thomas Gradgrind insists that facts, "nothing but facts," are the fundamental and essential building blocks of education and a profitable economy. But facts don't have the currency they used to when everyone can look up anything on a phone. Moreover, many of the facts that today's researchers work with didn't exist when they were in school; the Human Genome Project and the Large Had-ron Collider built by CERN (European Organization for Nuclear Research) have revolutionized (and rendered obsolete) knowledge that a decade ago looked essential. Even medicine, that most hands-on of intellectual skills, will be profoundly altered, and careers will be disrupted, by emerging technologies such as tele-medicine and robotic medical devices. To survive in this new world our children cannot possibly be expected to leave school with all the skills or knowledge they will need. So we must aim to have them leave school with a capacity and appetite for learning and divergent thinking that will stand them in good stead their whole lives.

This capacity is what Justin Riley and Sarah Bonner have—but it isn't what competitive exams deliver. Subtly and often unintentionally, exams teach kids that there is a right answer that wins the reward. Everyone gets this message. While decrying exams and citing timetable pressures, teachers focus on teaching to the test and—implicitly or explicitly—encourage their students to learn to the test. Offered additional or mildly oblique supplementary material, what's the response? "We don't need to know that, it's not on the test."

You can't blame the kids; theirs is an intelligent, rational response to a structure in which rewards drain motivation. And teachers whose pay derives, even in part, from exam results are caught in the same trap. At a time when we badly need to develop imagination, creativity, and the intellectual initiative that generates new ideas, competitive testing is tailor-made to do just the opposite: it cultivates a talent for playing it safe, a tendency to second-guess, and a belief that there is such a thing as the right answer.

What exams do with magnificent clarity is deliver clear, objective results that enable schools to see who's top and who's bottom of the class. The vast array of exams to which we subject our children does nothing to develop their intrinsic motivation, but it does allow schools to identify winners and rank them. Since college applications routinely request (but don't require) class rankings, many schools provide them. A running grade point average makes it simple to rank students, and some schools even post the rankings on hallway bulletin boards. Even for the winners, there's a nasty social side effect when GPAs are made public: everyone knows that it is crowded at the top.

"My daughter was ranked number four in her class," according to one New York mother who doesn't want her name, or her daughter's name, to be used here but who does want their experience to be known. "For most of high school, she'd been in the top five. And in her junior year, she was struggling with a math project, so she went to one of her classmates—also in the top five—and asked for some help on a math project."

Her daughter takes up the story.

"The top five are particularly conscious of each other. And it was weird, because the three guys ahead of me were very math and sciency and I wasn't. I think they sometimes thought I couldn't be that smart. But anyway, I asked one of them to help me—and he wouldn't!"

She paused for a second.

"He said his mother had told him not to because it might jeopardize his ranking."

High school students are always full of stories about key textbooks being hidden in school libraries and bulletin board notices strangely disappearing. What rankings do—naturally—is pit students against one another. How could rankings *not* have this effect? There's only so much room at the top, even in percentile rankings. As such, rankings teach exactly the wrong lesson for life: for me to win, you must lose. Teaching children, who are born with collaborative skills, that success is a solo activity is poor preparation for their working lives, but the lessons sink in fast and deep. No wonder Yale graduate Alexandra Robbins compared high school to a game show: "Education is no longer about a learning experience; it's a game of *Survivor* where kids are strategizing to work against each other and beat the system."

Deci and Ryan, the psychologists devoted to studying motivation, identified ways to increase intrinsic motivation: positive feedback that encourages the desire for a sense of competence; optimal (not impossible) challenges; freedom from demeaning evaluations; and critically, a sense of autonomy. People—both young and old—are intensely motivated when they feel that they have some choice about when and how they work. The work becomes theirs. On a trivial level, this was demonstrated in industrial experiments in which the simple power to decide when to switch lights on and off made workers more productive. But on a more sophisticated level, Deci and Ryan's work shows how important it is for students to feel that they are working for themselves, toward goals that they own—not their parents, not their teachers, and not the state. That doesn't mean parents and teachers and schools can't help; their positive encouragement, guidance, and unexpected rewards are invaluable.

But this is why rankings can't work. They deliver too many demeaning evaluations and present impossible challenges. And the competitive parents focused on rankings fundamentally undermine their children's sense of autonomy.

Competitive pressures and threats don't solve these problems because failure necessarily overwhelms success—the amount of negative feedback is always larger than the positive. Not everyone can win—not everyone can be in the top 1 percent, or even the top 5 percent. But just about everyone can absorb the lesson that they are bound to lose—which makes them increasingly less willing to try. "In schools," Deci and Ryan write, rather glumly, "intrinsic motivation becomes weaker with each advancing grade."[11] The cost of rewarding the top 1 percent is the steady demotivation of the remaining 99 percent.

Getting the right grades and class ranking is just the beginning of the college application process. The $4 billion test and test preparation industry is another feature of the arms race that characterizes our education system. In recent years, head-to-head competition between the ACT and SAT has stimulated regular test redesign, but both are still poor predictors of college performance, underpredicting for girls, overpredicting for boys, and doing badly overall for low-income students.[12] Even parents who dislike the whole business—because expensive test prep advantages those with the money to pay for it and has nothing to do with real learning—find themselves caught up in the educational arms race in which they don't want their children to be left behind.

"I did get sucked into test prep for both my kids," Betsy Rapoport confesses. "I wasn't proud of it. I just thought: this is a game. So I sat both kids down and said: 'I don't like it, but you have to play it. So I'm signing you up for test prep even though it's odious.' It's all about resources—if you have the money for Kaplan, you have an advantage. And you may not like it, but you don't want it to be *your* kids who don't have it."

Nowadays, Rapoport says, she coaches kids in their college applications "for penance," trying to help students who may not have the same resources her own kids had.

"There weren't résumés when I applied to college; now it's huge. The intent was to encourage your kids to try a wide range of experiences. But instead, what you get are highly 'constructed' résumés, and you can tell in an instant that they've been designed by the parents, not the kid. One young woman, I look under 'Hobbies and Interests'—it says 'fluent in Italian and Spanish,' and I know it is not true. Do you want her to walk in and do an interview in Italian? Have you thought this through? That it isn't ethical and isn't true. But some kids are afraid to speak out against their parents! Another résumé said the kid was an amateur photographer when really, he just took pictures on his phone occasionally. It reeked of résumé padding. Kids are so afraid, they have come to think that where they get in is the all-defining feature of their lives—but all they've done so far is school!"

The essay, Rapoport says, is the one place in a college application where students can truly express themselves. But by the time they come to write it, many have lost the ability, or the will, to do so.

"I love the essay because it is about you being you—or it should be. But you can tell in an instant when parents were involved; I have rarely encountered a teenager who had command of a semicolon. So I say to the kids: 'I know you think the big shiny brass ring is where you get in. But you need to learn to speak with your own voice. That's the prize! Can you speak with your own voice?' But the whole educational process has taken that voice away."

Talking to parents across America, the recurrent tone was one of shame and anger. Otherwise fair-minded parents regularly felt ashamed that they felt obliged to use any advantage to tilt the playing field, whether paying for test prep or ransacking personal networks of friends, families, and even the most distant acquaintances in search of strings to pull. Nobody felt the system was fair or rational enough to trust; everyone felt they had to use any trick they could find to help their child. And that, in turn, made parents and their children angry—angry that competition had trapped them into behaviors and emotions they despised.

"One kid I worked with," Rapoport tells me, "burst into tears because she wanted to get into Washington University and her best friend—as a lark—added it to her application and got in! It was just horrible, and it ruined their friendship. It's just a nightmare, with everyone comparing offers and some kids made to feel their lives are over, finished.

"It's even worse where the school populations are quite homogenous; there you get real head-to-head competition. I remember one girl, she was so accomplished and amazing, and she said to me: 'Betsy, there are fifty just like me in high school.' She didn't feel unique or special. She was applying to all the same places as her friends, and she knew it was a zero-sum game: if she got in, her friends wouldn't. If her friends got in, she wouldn't."

Another parent, who didn't want to be named in order to protect his daughter, told me a story about his child's college application that I have heard repeated across the country.

"Susan was a fantastic student—worked hard, played hard, good at sports and languages, you name it. A kabillion Advanced Placement courses. Volunteering. Musical instruments. The all-time perfect two-page résumé. And there were so many places for her to apply—I kept telling her that she was lucky to have choices! But she decided that what she wanted, more than any-thing, was to get into Brown. It had to be Brown.

"Then some of her friends applied to Brown too, and she came home—it was like she had been betrayed. How dare they 'ruin' her chance? When early decision letters came through, all her friends got acceptances and she didn't. All those kids—100 percent got into their early decision colleges and Susie didn't, and she was so miserable. 'Why did I have to be a white girl from Westchester?'

"Then, when she didn't get into Brown, she was just completely devas-tated. She sobbed in my arms for days. Rejection felt like an indictment of all her hard work, as though she'd worked so hard for nothing. If the reward is everything and you don't get it, well, it has lost all its value."

As learning has become a commodity, the luxury brands are the Ivy League and top-ranked colleges. That's what the grades, after all, are for: winning a place at a top school whose prestige is expected to deliver entry into Amer-ica's elite—or at least the ranks of the fully employed. Here too competitive ranking systems are crucial, but they mostly work in the strangest way. To become a top-ranked college requires having the largest number of appli-cants for each available place. In other words, the more students who are rejected, the higher up the rankings the college goes, its reputation soaring on the disappointment of others. It behooves colleges, therefore, to solicit applications from as many aspirants as possible, even if they are completely unsuitable. Having the pick of the crop is great for the colleges, even if it isn't great for kids.

In many ways, the relationship between student and college has come to resemble the sadomasochistic dependency of a drug dealer and an addict. To maintain or increase applications, the colleges have to attract Nobel lau-reates to their faculties and build fantastic athletic facilities for their sports teams and luxurious student accommodations for their residents. That way more students will want to apply and fail to get in—so the college ascends the rankings. There is no encouragement in this system for colleges to spend less money, so as competition for students increases, so does the cost of attending college—with the inevitable outcome that American student debt has hit record highs of over a trillion dollars, a sum greater than national credit card debt but far harder to write off through bankruptcy proceedings.

Where once the American ideal rode on the idea of education as the engine of social mobility, today the rising costs of education, coupled with stagnation in incomes, prevent it from fulfilling that function. Places in elite institutions are increasingly reserved for those with the funds and the extra test prep to get there; the rest must be prepared to take a big gamble on big debts, with no guarantees as far as employment is concerned: at the beginning of 2013, around 48 percent of recent college graduates who were lucky enough to be employed were in jobs that didn't need a college degree.[13] As tuition costs have risen at rates from 15 to 40 percent, Oregon Democratic senator Ron Wyden attempted to introduce his Know Before You Go Bill, designed to force colleges to publish both the full costs of attendance and students' employment prospects. The intention was to warn parents and students of the debt they might incur, but the proposal also reflected how far education has come in being viewed as nothing more than a product for which the consumer is entitled to a clear, unambiguous price tag.

With parents under unparalleled financial pressure, it's no wonder students feel that they have no choice but to get those grades any way that they can. So when Steven Roderick, a smart, gentle, twenty-four-year-old student started at the University of Massachusetts at Boston, he was dismayed to find himself getting Ds and he knew he had to do something fast. He'd heard about Adderall, an amphetamine prescribed for attention deficit hyperactivity disorder (ADHD), and knew the drug was pretty easy to get. So he hoped that might be what he needed to get better grades.

"The first time I took it, I wrote a paper for an astronomy class that was out of this world. I could not believe it—I was so inspired it made me want to be a doctor!"

Adderall is a Class 2 controlled substance; its users can become dependent, needing higher and higher doses, and it has been compared to the drugs used in sports: "Adderall has become to college what steroids are to baseball: an illicit performance enhancer for a fiercely competitive environment."[14]

"I went from Ds and Fs to straight As. But your brain adapts, you have to increase the dose, and by 2011 I was up to forty-five milligrams. I started to feel Adderall was my best friend and my worst enemy at the same time."

Because he couldn't sleep, Roderick was prescribed Ativan, a powerful sleeping pill. But then he got locked into one drug to focus and one drug to relax. His need for Adderall increased—eventually he was taking 120 milligrams. He would then come off of it, take Ativan, and sleep for days. His anxiety levels rocketed; the drop of a pin, he said, would make him spin around. Although he nearly completed his university course, ultimately he had to withdraw because he could not make it to enough classes.

"Look," Roderick reflects, "I am in a culture that constantly justifies the means to an end. So how do we persuade people not to take it? All you hear is how impossible it will be to get a job when you get out, and you are going more and more into debt, and you think without this I won't be top of the class."

With big external rewards dangled over their heads like so many swords of Damocles, students like Roderick sacrifice all intrinsic engagement in their subjects. All they hear, from parents and policymakers, is about grades, university places, awards, and prizes. So, naturally, that's what they focus on: the educational commodities needed to move onto the next stage of the contest. It's the product, not the process, that matters. And if you can't win the game, you may as well game the system.

At Stuyvesant High School in New York, academic achievement is social currency. With four Nobel laureates as alumnae, the school has a terrific reputation for science, and it's a tough school to get into. But once there, students start to realize that everyone around them is pretty smart too. How can they compete? It is easier, and often tactically more astute, to cheat than to waste time on subjects they don't care about or don't intend to take beyond school. Kids post homework answers on Facebook, hide formulas up their sleeves, or photograph tests to email to their friends. The school is intensely competitive—its students aiming for Harvard, Yale, MIT—and failure is so unacceptable that winning at any cost seems preferable. In a school newspaper survey, 80 percent of students admitted to cheating.

"It becomes kind of a numbers game," says Elias Weinraub, eighteen, who is now at Washington University in St. Louis. "It was kind of addictive, in a bad way, in a sick way."[15]

One teacher began to see the same homework answers so often that she started to ask students to handwrite their work, hoping that would discourage them from copying off the Internet. The school has also had cases of students devising pencil-tapping codes and sending answers to each other via cell phones. One survey of forty thousand American high school students found that 59 percent had cheated on an exam; Rush Kidder at the Institute for Global Ethics estimates that, by the time they get to college, 95 percent of students have cheated in one form or another.[16]

Having obtained a goal by cheating, students don't kick the habit. At the beginning of 2013, Harvard College forced "somewhat more than half" of a class of 279 to leave after the largest cheating scandal in memory. They were asked to withdraw when a number of exam questions featured identical answers on a take-home exam—identical to the point of identical typo-graphical errors. While many commentators expressed astonishment at finding cheating so prevalent in elite institutions, in reality this shouldn't be surprising at all. Having fought so hard to get into these schools, students will do anything to stay. It is a chastening thought that, the more elite the school, the less the students may be driven to enjoy their education for its own sake.

This behavior isn't unique to Stuyvesant or Harvard or the United States: cheating represents an escalating problem the world over. In May 2013, South Korea had to cancel its SAT exams after a cheating ring was discov-ered among students trying for US universities. In England, it's estimated that cheating incidents have risen 50 percent over the last four years. Cheat-ing has become so widespread that administrators everywhere depend on software to address the growing problem.

"It's ironic that technology—which has certainly made cheating easier—is also the best way to eradicate it," Jason Chu tells me. "But the scale of the problem is immense, and it's global."

Chu works for Turnitin, which makes plagiarism detection software that is used in 126 countries where coursework has to be checked to ensure that it hasn't been copied, wholesale or in pieces, from the 24 billion Web pages, 300 million archived student papers, and 120 million articles from 110,000 journals, periodicals, and books that sit in the company's databases. The software is constantly being refreshed and updated to block the new ruses students devise to find ways not to do the work. The good news is that stu-dents have apparently become better judges of high-quality sources to steal from; the bad news is that there are more "cheat sites" aimed at secondary school students than ever before. And they're getting better at covering their tracks.

"What we've found is students try to circumvent our system," Chu tells me. "They will take a paper written in English and change the font or cer-tain characters to Cyrillic—our algorithm can't identify Cyrillic—so we have to stay quick on our feet. We're wise to this. Or they will change some of the words into images and submit that. It all requires so much effort—they could just do the work!"

Chu started off his career as an academic; he believes passionately, he says, in critical thinking. And once kids have to submit their papers through Tur-nitin, he says, they learn quickly that they must think for themselves. They learn better how to think about and use original content and how to give credit where it's due. Although there's a utilitarian aspect to the business, what excites him about it is that it helps, in a strange way, to return education to its original purpose.

"It isn't that students don't know that plagiarism is morally wrong; they do—even if they think it is a victimless crime. But the real problem they have is that students are not thinking about the process. They are only ever just thinking about the results. We have perpetuated this, with our emphasis on assessment. We have told students that what they are 'earning' is a grade. You do this, you get that. Their reward isn't doing the work. Their reward isn't thinking, or learning to think. It's the grade. It's all about the grade."

Online teaching doesn't promise much better. The technology is necessarily oriented toward right and wrong answers; MOOCs (massive online open courses), while offering the allure of democratized education, largely depend, for assessment, on standardized tests and automated marking. In other words, to succeed you have to know the "right" answer. And unsurprisingly, services like WeTakeYourClasses.com and BoostYourGrades have grown up to enable others to take an entire online course for you; a mere $700 guarantees at least a B grade.

"The whole idea behind liberal education used to be about building moral integrity and character," Jason Chu reflects. "That's all gone. It's a tremendous shift that has happened, that emphasis on results. It's just swept everything else aside. You do this, you get that."

It's an enduring lesson. For several years, I taught a certificate course in entrepreneurship in Boston for MBA graduates. My students were at the end of a very long educational food chain. They'd successfully fought their way through high school, college, and business school, in each case passing tests and doing everything that was expected of them. When they came to my course, they had chosen to be there, using their own time and their own money. But at the outset, what they most wanted to know was how I would grade them.

I was astonished. I was teaching these students how to start their own businesses—an activity in which grades could not be less relevant. True, many of the students, rather than founding a company, might go to work for a start-up. But no investor or employer would ever ask what grades they got on my course. How could these ostensibly innovation-loving, risk-taking adults care about grades so much? Because that's what they had been trained to care about their entire lives.

I'm always amazed, wherever I teach, at how long it takes to coach my students away from trying to identify what they think is my "right" answer and to encourage them to seek their own answer. It clearly isn't what they're used to. Teaching international MBA and MSc students in Britain isn't so different. Much of their work depends on coursework, and well beyond the academic course of their program, it is this that they find most challenging. One MSc course depends entirely on the quality of team collaboration— but invariably at least one team falls apart and fails completely because its members simply cannot work together. When I explain to them that a best-selling business book, *Give and Take,* makes a persuasive case that the most successful people are the most generous, they don't believe me. And when I explain that it was written by Adam Grant, a professor from Wharton Business School, famous for being the meanest, toughest, most quantitative business school on earth, they're frankly incredulous. These students, like their American counterparts, have fully internalized the concept of success as a solo achievement that takes no prisoners.

American panic about education often contains a subtext: if we don't get our act together, the Asian economies will overtake us and the United States will lose its dominant position in the world. Consequently, Asian educational systems are often thought to hold the key to higher levels of attainment: if only we could get American students to be as driven, as patient with rote learning, as obedient as Asian students, then surely we could maintain the status we've enjoyed for the last one hundred years. Nevertheless, in Singapore, often pointed to as a beacon of competitive educational success, learning for rewards has more recently come to be identified not as a solution but as a huge educational problem.

"We don't think that kind of education will be useful for the future," Dr. Thiam Seng Koh confides in me.

He runs St. Joseph's Institution, one of the oldest schools in Singapore. It's a traditional boys' school, started by a Catholic priest in 1852. When I visited, the students were all in bright white uniforms, and the place was run with military efficiency. The school has O levels and rankings and publishes its overall exam results. But while many commentators imagine Singapore's schools to be run along extremely conservative, even old-fashioned lines, appearances (and stereotypes) can be deceptive. St. Joseph's traditional exterior masks some very radical thinking.

"The old kind of education just helped kids work to a formula," Koh continues. "But the problem is that once there is no formula, our kids are very weak. So we need to know when to change, when to adapt, when to realize the formula isn't working. That isn't what our current system does. Our top students can do it, but we need our average to do that at a much higher volume. If the average guys are just working to the formula, we will be dead in no time. The world is just changing too fast. If we prepare boys only for exams, we have failed.

"Several years ago we were trying to move from exams as the sole criteria for success. So we went to New York for inspiration. To our horror, they'd gone in the other direction! They were trying to move to where we are, and we are trying to move to where they are! Standardized tests won't solve this problem."

The first day I visited St. Joseph's was an open day, and I was taken all over the school. It was ninety degrees outside, and bagpipes were playing, but that wasn't all that surprised me. In the center of the school, I came across science projects developed in collaboration with Harvard's Art|Science team. The idea of the projects is to realize breakthrough ideas in the space where arts, sciences, and engineering meet. Working in small groups, the students collaborate on "seed ideas," all of which aim to address a major need or opportunity in culture, industry, or humanitarian engagement. The core idea of these projects is that they are autonomously led and developed by students, not by teachers.

"Art|Science provides a different context. The teachers see that the boys *are* capable of thinking. If you allow students to take ownership, they learn how to think creatively. You make a lot of mistakes, and that is good learning."

The challenge posed by these projects is that they don't offer, or aim at, correct answers. They aim to provoke divergent thinking. Nobody knows whether the proposals will work or not, so the students who work on them learn to tolerate high degrees of ambiguity.

"In this work, there's a lot of debate, rebuttal, disagreement. It is uncomfortable for us," Koh concedes. "But it's important. It's important to give people—students and teachers—safety, the leeway to make mistakes and not pay for it. You need students to challenge you to get innovation and creativity. So how to do that here? The only way the boys learn how to work well together is to do it, to learn how to have the arguments, how to stretch the question until they can find some answers. The Art|Science projects are hard, and they're not traditional. So they are ..." Koh starts to laugh, "... they certainly are challenging."

"This year the students wanted to raise funds for Myanmar. But they hit a snag: the Ministry of Education doesn't allow schools to raise money for foreign countries." So Koh told the students to figure out a way around that problem—which they did by finding a local mission that helps Myanmar. Only by making them solve their own problems, he insists, will kids get the thinking skills the twenty-first century requires.

Although Koh describes himself as a maverick, he says that what he is doing at St. Joseph's is a very carefully managed experiment. He's gone carefully and slowly to dismantle some of the structures and expectations that, he believes, militate against collaboration and creativity. Of these, the most contentious was his determination to eradicate streaming.

"We used to have a talent class and a non-talent class. It was all academically banded. So then we mixed it up, and we saw no drop in academic achievement. Nor were teachers unduly stressed teaching a variety of students. What we gained was self-esteem, the willingness to try and not give up."

All of the top Singapore schools used to compete to take the top students, who would go on to compete for government scholarships and eventually become permanent secretaries. That isn't the world Koh is preparing his boys for.

"Traditionally, the top 3 percent will go to Raffles Institution. We used to play in that league, but now we don't want such a narrow band of students. So we don't play that game. Going forward, we want the school to be more accessible to a wider range of students. Some of the boys here will go into government or end up running large organizations. But the kind of policymaking and decisions you make when you grow up will be different if you can appreciate that not everyone moves at your pace. If you go to a top school, you're surrounded by top people and don't learn how to work with people not on your level."

None of this experimentation means that the boys of St. Joseph's Institution don't take their learning seriously; they do. But along with knowledge, they're learning profound life skills.

"Many of the boys have no idea what they want in life yet. That's okay. I tell them that any scores just measure a point in time; they don't say who you are or how good you are. But I also tell them that they are not competing against one another. It helps them through difficult times because they learn to help each other."

This isn't an abstract experiment for Koh; his own son goes to the school, so the father has to practice what he preaches.

"He can't stand biology, so he dropped it. There was a ruckus in the class-room: what signal are you trying to send? But that *is* the signal I am trying to send! Now he's enjoying himself. He has more free periods, he plays his guitar. He can make some of his own choices."

Koh may be a maverick, and his changes at St. Joseph's may be an experiment. But he's grappling with a question that is deeply interesting to Singapore's government, which is avidly watching the results of Koh's experiment. When I met with the minister of education, Lawrence Wong, he readily acknowledged that grades and targets can't deliver the levels of creativity and collaboration that the country needs. Koh's experiment is important because the government sees that masses of rote learning, more tests, and submissive traditional teaching methods will not create a dynamic and adaptable workforce. Using a new approach called "Teach Less, Learn More," Singapore educators are trying to put more white space into school timetables in order to enhance art and music offerings and develop more curiosity and a love of play.[17] In a country described by its own leaders as formal and wary of dissent, there is a refreshing recognition that the modern world needs adults who are fearless in exploration, comfortable with ambiguity, and bold in taking risks—and that no one can do any of that in later life if they never learn to do it in school.

While Koh may have been disappointed by his experience of US education, in fact Western education reform has been tremendously varied—and some of it is working. If Massachusetts were a country, its eighth-graders would rank just below Singapore in science and math, even though up until the early 1990s science and math achievement was dismal. What's most striking about reforms enacted in 1993 was what they did *not* contain: no threats of school closures, no vouchers for private schools, no merit pay for teachers, and no threat of removing tenure. Instead, more money was made available for schools, together with the insistence that everyone—not just a gifted few—would graduate competent in algebra. Teachers were given more freedom to improvise curriculum, but the expectation was that everyone could and would achieve.

One of the most inspiring recent examples of great learning derived not from contests, prizes, or exams but from a project pioneered by two British schoolteachers. Blackawton School teachers Dave Strudwick and Tina Rodwellyn, mentored by Beau Lotto, a neuroscientist who works with London's Science Museum, were convinced that children *are* scientists: curious, investigative, and full of good questions that they are capable of answering. Working with twenty-five eight- to ten-year-old students, they brainstormed questions about bees. Many of their first questions had already been answered by research published in recent scientific journals—that's how good and relevant the questions were. But then the kids hit on a question that had not been answered yet: How do bees choose which flowers to go to for foraging? Is it color or location that matters most? "Knowing that other animals are as smart as us means we can appreciate them more, which could also help us to help them," the children reasoned.[18]

Working with their teachers and with Lotto, the children were encouraged to think of their experiment as a game, or a puzzle. So they designed and built a game of colored Perspex circles and sugar water, which they put (together with a lot of bees) inside a Norman church near their school. The experiment was designed to test whether it was the color or the placement of the sugar water that most drew in the bees.

The children observed the bees in multiple conditions, recorded their observations, and analyzed their results. They concluded that bees are very good at solving puzzles and that they can learn collaboratively and from their mistakes. The children also succeeded in getting their experiment and its findings—written in their own language, not academese—published in a scientific journal, *Biology Letters*. This was the first-ever peer-reviewed paper published in which all twenty-five authors were primary school pupils who wrote in their own language. (The paper begins, "Once upon a time....")[19]

But perhaps most important of all, the children had learned to think like scientists and to enjoy it. There were no prizes, but there was great learning, fun, and a sense of accomplishment. "Before doing these experiments we did not really think a lot about bees and how they are as smart as us," the students wrote. "We also did not think about the fact that without bees we would not survive, because bees keep the flowers going. So it is important to understand bees. We discovered how fun it was to train bees. This is also cool because you do not get to train bees everyday. We like bees. Science is cool and fun because you get to do stuff that no one has ever done before. (Bees—seem to—think!)"

The Blackawton bees project was provocative and inspiring because it showed the degree to which young children can do high-level reasoning and problem-solving, without stress or exams, for the sheer pleasure of thinking. The project assumed that the children had the capacity and enthusiasm to learn and created the conditions in which they could do so with a result that represented a huge intrinsic reward. I first heard about the project when one of the young students gave a presentation: she was confident, excited, and proud. The experience had meant far more than any certificate, it had drawn in all the children, and it hadn't required any losers.

That is the kind of critical thinking that the PISA (Program for International Student Assessment) test is designed to capture. Every three years, a random assortment of five thousand fifteen-year-olds gather to do—yes—another round of exams. But these tests are different. The students can't pass or fail, they will never learn how they've done individually, and there are no prizes. The PISA test attempts to benchmark educational achievement in 87 percent of the world's economies.

PISA was the brainchild of Andreas Schleicher, an amiable official with the Organization for Economic Cooperation and Development (OECD) who is far jollier than you might expect of a German statistician. He started to design PISA in 1997, when OECD countries were clamoring for reliable insight into how well their respective educational systems were performing. The test wasn't designed to audit knowledge but to gather data around students' ability to apply what they learned. Not one to set himself easy goals, Schleicher also wanted to ask students about their motivation, their beliefs about themselves, and their learning strategies and to put some hard numbers around some of the most intractable questions in education: Is there a relationship between spending and outcomes? How critical is class size? Are our schools adequately preparing young people for the challenges of adult life? Are some kinds of teaching and schools more effective than others? Does sorting work? What characterizes a successful educational system?[20]

The first exams took place in 2000. When the results were published a year later, the German government bayed for Schleicher's blood. The data he had collected dealt a severe blow to the national ego: for reading and literacy, Germany was below the OECD average, and PISA also showed that student achievement in Germany, a country that prided itself on equality, was more correlated with family socioeconomic status than in any other OECD country. Germany's tripartite system, which ranked children and channeled them at age ten into one of three types of secondary school, effectively limited achievement.

"Sorting doesn't work," Schleicher said with a smile when we met in Edinburgh. He has personal experience of his statistically based conclusion: as a child, he'd been told in no uncertain terms that he "wasn't *gymnasium* [high school] material." That was his first inkling that trying to choose winners is counterproductive.

"Teachers routinely overestimate the influence of social background. That leads them to give up on too many children. There's no trade-off between equity and excellence. None. The top-performing school systems are the ones that do a better job of educating *everybody,* not the ones that just try to choose or find the few. The association between social disadvantage and low educational achievement is strong—but it is not inevitable."

Schleicher was well protected by his employer, so he didn't lose his job. But Germany wasn't the only country to be dismayed by his findings. The United States, the richest country in the world, was only average in literacy and below average in mathematics and science; subsequent tests have shown no improvement. The United Kingdom did somewhat better than that, coming in seventh in literacy, eighth in math, and fourth in scientific literacy. Luxembourg, which ran the most expensive educational system, lurked just barely above the bottom of the list.

But amid all the bad news were startling surprises. Chief among these was Finland, which ranked first in reading, third in science, and fourth in math. In all the subsequent PISA tests, Finland has remained the top-performing European nation. But those first results were as surprising to the Finns as to the rest of the world.

"We really had no idea at all how well we were doing," Pasi Sahlberg tells me. "I'd like to be able to say that we'd worked it all out. But that really isn't what happened."

In the 1960s, 90 percent of Finns had completed only seven to nine years of schooling, and university graduates were rare. A widespread recognition that this posed a big risk to the nation as a whole led to a remarkable series of reforms. Central to all of these reforms was an unwavering commitment to the idea that education had to serve the whole nation. This might seem obvious, but it isn't. Former British prime minister Margaret Thatcher, for example, famously believed that "nations depend for their health, economically, culturally and psychologically, upon the achievement of a comparatively small number of talented and determined people."[21] If you believe that, then you want to identify those talented people early and develop them—in which case, competition early and often can work well to produce and promote the winners. But the Finns quite explicitly rejected this approach, because they thought that the country could not afford to waste any of its human talent; the challenge of moving the small country swiftly from an agrarian to an industrial economy was too great. So the reformers demanded the collaboration of *all* political parties, together with the teaching organizations: education was simply too important to become a political football.

Today Finnish students don't take standardized tests until they are eighteen, and while they get written assessments, they don't get grades. That means that teachers can't compare, or rank, students. Neither can the students themselves—or their parents. Finnish schools are not inspected; Sahlberg himself was Finland's last chief inspector of schools in the early 1990s, before politicians decided to eliminate the process. Without league tables or streaming, none of the data or tools a competitive person—parent or child—might need to compare schools or children are available.

"We invented Angry Birds—so it's not that Finns aren't competitive," Sahlberg laughs. "Our TV is as full of competitive games as England's—maybe more! But when it comes to education and the culture, there is really no room for trying to see education as a competition. Finnish parents define learning as developing the individual: sharing, helping, doing things together, and being part of the community rather than trying to do better than your neighbor. So that's why we have no school rankings."

Sahlberg started out teaching in Finnish schools; now he makes his living studying education around the world and trying to understand what has made the Finns' experiments work. What he won't accept is that his compatriots are in any way immune to the allure of contests.

"We can make a competition out of anything—for fun. But we just don't think it's the way to inspire a love of learning. We focused on equity and cooperation instead of choice and competition. What does high-stakes testing do? It narrows the way that children think, so it discourages risk-taking. It makes kids frightened. That's not good thinking—and it's boring!"

Sahlberg doesn't believe for one moment that there's anything uniquely Finnish about the success of the country's education system—and he eagerly dismisses arguments that the Finnish example is anomalous.

"People say to me that, oh, it's easier in a small country, but Finland is the same size as Scotland, Connecticut, or Massachusetts. They say it's ethnically homogenous, but we have three native languages, 5 percent foreign-born citizens, and 10 percent non-Finnish-speaking citizens. The diversification of Finnish society since the mid-1990s has been the fastest in Europe!"

Some Helsinki schools have large numbers of refugee immigrants, but this doesn't seem to faze their teachers. It's more effective, they argue, to focus on children's minds than on their backgrounds.[22]

"Many people assume Finland has been able to perform so well because we make kids stay in school longer or have a lot of homework—so when I explain that school days are shorter compared to almost any others and that our kids don't do too much homework and there is little competition, many people do find it hard to understand."

On the cold sunny morning when I visited the Aurora primary school in Espoo, I was expecting a gleaming new building, with shiny new equipment and lots of noise. That wasn't what I found. Instead, I saw a small cluster of concrete buildings, with a sparse playground. It looked a little bleak from the outside, but inside the school was warm, quiet, and calm. Students padded about the corridors in their socks while, in the staff room, teachers made coffee, read newspapers, and did jigsaw puzzles. Marimekko mugs, a few computers, Angry Birds balloons, a mishmash of comfy chairs, and quiet laughter filled the space. For a Monday morning, there was a lot of energy in the staff room.

Amid the teachers stood Martti Helstrom, the school head. Gray-haired and sporting heavy glasses, he'd recently returned from a trip to Graceland, where he shot a movie about Elvis on his iPhone. I guessed that his green shirt, with a big black guitar on the front, was a souvenir. As I sat drinking coffee, everyone smiled at me, Martti signed paperwork, and we talked about his twenty-three years running the school.

"We are such a small country, we can't afford to lose any child. So it's our job to understand the children, find out how they learn, where they're having difficulties. Everyone learns together, but they learn at their own pace. They can stay as long as they need or move as fast as they want.

"The parents trust us for many reasons, but because we don't select who comes here, the school is not the enemy. It's very ethically demanding if you have power, so I think it's good we don't have power. Parents can choose which school they send their children to, but almost all of them just send them to the nearest one because they know we will look after their children. We won't let them fail. Of course, it helps that we have a great deal of autonomy, that we can organize the curriculum and the school day in the way we think best suits the children."

Teachers in Finland command enormous respect. The job is one of the most admired and popular in the country, and in opinion polls being a teacher is rated more highly than being a doctor, architect, or lawyer. All must have a master's degree, and few cite salary as their incentive. They're skeptical of standardized tests, and many teachers say that if they lost the freedom to determine how they teach, if they were subjected to external inspection or performance-related pay, they would want to change jobs.

In the course of their teacher training, the very first quality looked for in trainees is empathy: the warmth and understanding of their pupils determines whether they stay the course. When their training is complete, it is assumed that they will continue their own education—through further degrees and collaborative research carried out with colleagues or with teachers from other schools. Funding for all of this professional development is planned to double by 2016.

Sahlberg calls standardization "the enemy of creativity." Without standardized exams, the schools themselves cannot be ranked. Instead, they are encouraged to work together through school improvement networks to share ideas and solve problems together. That collaboration not only generates new projects but also continues and expands every teacher's professional learning. And all headmasters teach.

"The teachers themselves are very against performance-related pay," Helstrom tells me, "because it destroys the idea of cooperation. And we don't need that kind of motivation. We need motivation—everyone does—but it must come from within. We think the main task of school is to create as many possibilities as possible for every child to succeed today. If you have that feeling of success, you feel taller."

Student achievement in Finland is assessed. Students get report cards, but each school designs its own, so report cards aren't comparable across schools. Regular national assessments are also carried out by sampling about 10 percent of the school-age population. Individual schools can choose to take the same test and compare themselves against national benchmarks. But participation is voluntary, and results aren't published. Without any high-stakes tests in Finland, very little influence from central government, and no school inspections, teachers and schools can maintain their autonomy.

Later that day, I sat in on a class of eight- to ten-year-old pupils who were watching a presentation about how rainbows occur. The classroom was furnished with a piano, a fish tank, and a model village the children had made for a school movie. Normally there were seventeen students in the class, but a few were out with flu. As the presentation became rather intricate, a number of children stood on their chairs to get a better look. The teacher watched as she told me how hard it could be sometimes not to intervene.

"It's much better than a test; if you can explain something, then you understand it. We tried this, getting the children to explain how you convert fractions to decimals, and I nearly lost my courage! But we persevered, and after about twenty minutes they got it!"

During a seventy-five-minute "siesta" in the middle of the day, students could choose extracurricular activities. One drama group played the game Park Bench—but in English, for my benefit. They weren't angels—"Get a life," one said, while another suggested, "Your mother's on fire"—but when the teacher had to leave the room, they organized themselves into a dance exercise.

Outside in the cold morning sunshine, a fierce football match was raging, and I interrupted a young teacher who was reading.

"They are learning," she said, "but we also are learning. All the time. They have to learn about science and math and languages, but we have to learn about them. Who they are, how they can do their best."

"Don't you ever get frustrated, angry, disheartened?" I asked.

She laughed. "Well, everyone has their bad days. But you know, no, not really. If you love your students, you just persevere. You know they can do it. You just have to learn how."

"Love" isn't a word I'd heard used very often in schools, but everyone I talked to at Espoo used it, sooner or later. No one thought of teaching as a transaction but apparently as a lifelong relationship. But love? When I visited a high school, I asked the head, Riitta Erkinjuntti, about it.

"Yes," she said, "why not? 'Love' is a word you hear here also. The teachers know the students and trust them. When I discuss with them, even one who has behaved badly, I think, 'You are so important to me, I am worried about you.' You have to love your students."

Her school—Meilahti in Helsinki—specializes in arts and design. Most of the high schools have specialties, and it is on this basis, not rankings, that students choose them. Design plays a significant role in the Finnish economy, and not just Marimekko and Iitala: many Finnish designers have defined the look that we now call modern. From Meilahti, students will go either to university or to vocational schools. The system is designed to be porous so that students can move between the two and keep doing so for as long as they want. During their time in high school, every student gets two hours a week of career guidance from a counselor, who helps them think through their options and where they want to go next.

"We believe in all the children," Raila Pirinen says. A warm, enthusiastic woman, she is both a career counselor and a teacher trainer. I stayed with her during the school holidays, when she was still working quite cheerfully.

"The very best will get there, but we don't want to lose anyone. If they need help, they get it for as long as they need it. We have a very strong desire not to produce anxiety among the children. You don't make good decisions when you are afraid. And we want them to make good decisions."

The intrinsic motivation that the early reformers aimed to develop must have stuck because Finns continue in education for a very long time. Although education after the age of sixteen isn't compulsory, fully 93 percent of Finns complete education sufficient to gain them entry to higher education, and more than 50 percent continue in some form of adult education.

"I see my students all the time—they never really leave me!" Riitta Erkin-juntti laughed. "Even after they've left, I'll see them in the city, or they will come back for a visit. It's wonderful to learn about the jobs they're doing now, the amazing things they're learning about the new technologies, new ways of making things. They keep learning, and I learn from them!"

Public opinion in Finland is opposed to ranking and league tables, and with the gap between Finnish high- and low-achievers the smallest in the world, parents seem quite content simply to send their children to the nearest school. Since many schools finish early in the afternoon, children can walk home and play for the rest of the day.

"We trust the system because the teachers are good and they are very well educated," Carita Orlando tells me. "It's better now, I think. When I went to school, it was less free, and we were a little afraid of the teachers. But things are more relaxed now, and the children, they're pleased to learn."

Orlando has two children—Eric, fourteen, and Erica, twelve—in the local school. We met one afternoon, after school, in their warm, comfortable modern home. Eric was upstairs, working on a server he had built; Erica was playing with a friend. The spring day was rather chilly; otherwise, they'd have been outside. One of the great things about the school timetable, their parents told me, was that it was seasonally adjusted so the kids always had some outdoor time when they got home.

As we started to discuss school systems, I had to explain to Carita and her husband Greg what ranking is; the concept seemed weird to both of them, and they couldn't understand what benefit it could bring. Like parents around the world, they both wanted to see their children do well in school, but seemed bemused by the idea that one child's progress might have to come at a cost to other children. They were by no means unambitious, for either their children or themselves. Greg Orlando ran one of the bigger hotels in downtown Helsinki, and Carita started and managed her own accounting firm, though she also made time to serve as a school governor.

The Finnish people aren't angels, and their schools aren't perfect. Like other countries, they've experienced school shootings, and there are always some kids—not many but some—who just don't make it. The impact of socio-economic background can't be erased, but it's striking that this educational success story hasn't been achieved by making the school day or year longer, by increasing homework, or by raising the numbers or thresholds of exams. And it hasn't created a competitive marketplace for schools or teachers or students. So far, Finland has studiously avoided the corporatization of education—with its methodologies of bureaucracy, targets, inspections, and benchmarking—and regards it as a threat. But the fundamental reason why Finland (like Korea) does so well, PISA's Andreas Schleicher says, is that its schools educate everyone: Finnish educators don't accept that for there to be winners, there must be losers.

"The goal of PISA," Schleicher says, "wasn't to create a competition between countries, but to get the insight we needed to enable countries to improve. And many have done that: Korea, Shanghai, Poland, Singapore, even," he adds ruefully, "Germany."

"And we have learned very basic lessons. We know now that money alone won't buy you great education; money explains only about 20 percent of the outcome. We know that early streaming isn't associated anywhere with better overall performance. That the most successful systems aim at, and succeed in, raising achievement for everyone, not for the few. We know that there's no relationship between countries' educational attainment and performance-related pay as long as teachers are paid decently. And we know that no education system can ever exceed the quality of its teachers."

If education is about creating a workforce, Finnish employers aren't complaining. I spoke to recruiters and managers at accounting firms, hotels, and high-tech businesses. If they have any concerns, it is that their workers may be overeducated for some of the jobs they offer. But in a world that increasingly prizes intellectual over physical property, Finland is remarkably productive for such a tiny country. In 2005, Finland had the fourth most scientific publications per capita of the OECD countries, ahead of the United States, the United Kingdom, and Germany, and was above-average in number of patents per capita. Richard Florida, assessing the technological and innovative capacity of the world's leading nations in 2011, gave Finland the top spot.[23] The way to prepare pupils for a more competitive economy, Pasi Sahlberg argues, is to have less competition in their schools.

I thought there was one other important dynamic that I saw at work in the Finnish schools I visited. I saw it in the Espoo classroom as well as in the bright white Meilahti lunchroom where I ate alongside the teachers and students. The meal was everything you'd expect of school food—wholesome but uninspiring. So it wasn't the food. It was a power dynamic.

Finnish teachers regard themselves as students. In every conversation I had with them, they discussed what *they* were learning, what they had yet to find out and so were researching. Like the teachers in the Blackawton bee project, they exuded and shared their curiosity. Encouraged to continue their education, to collaborate on research, and to invent improved teaching methods, they saw themselves as students every bit as much as the children they taught. As a consequence, in their own minds and in the minds of their students, they didn't occupy a position of dominance, masters selectively handing down scraps of information to the deserving few. They didn't see themselves as defensive gatekeepers, umpires, or scorekeepers. Instead, they walked together with their pupils on a lifelong journey in which they all were continuing to explore, make mistakes, and learn.

That's what we all want for our children: a creative, courageous mind-set that long outlives the short seasons of exams and tests, that is resilient when making mistakes, ingenious in responding to the world's changes, and generous in working alongside colleagues. We'd like to hope that our children's futures do not depend on getting into the right school, knowing the right people, trouncing friends, cheating, doing drugs, or being lucky enough not to go to the bathroom at the wrong time. And we hope they will have a love of learning that lasts.

"My drive," Justin Riley told me when we met at MIT, "isn't about school. I like building things, just the idea of starting from nothing and making something that's useful to other people. I want to do that over and over again—like a roller-coaster ride. Once you have that moment, you want another."

CHAPTER 3

The Morning After

Any competition junkie would have overdosed during the London Olympics. Every comparison, every statistic, every victory was used to draw meaningful conclusions about Britain, globalization, athleticism, nationality, ethnicity, history, geography, color, design, weather, and clothes. In the midst of a horrible summer and a hideous economy, good news abounded, and it all had to mean something. Leading many of the euphoric headlines was a recurrent trope: haven't the girls done well? In 2012, 4,847 women had participated in the Olympics, 121 had taken medals, and of those, fully 77 were gold.

It was, to be sure, some kind of sea change, not just in Britain but around the world. After all, in 1908 male competitors had outnumbered females by 53 to 1. Forty years later, that was down to 10 to 1, but now, in 2012, women had just about achieved parity: of the 541 athletes, 262 athletes were female, and this was the first Olympics in which every participating team included women.

More remarkable than the numbers, though, were the victories. That the United States led the medal table didn't make anyone blink. What astounded those who chose to notice was this: US *women* topped the medal charts. For the first time in anyone's history, American women outperformed the rest of the world *and* they outperformed American *men*, winning 58 medals to the men's 45 and bringing home 29 of the 46 golds.

This was—and is—remarkable. After all, these Olympics results are contradicted by what a mountain of academic literature says about the performance of women. Experiment after experiment shows that women don't like to compete, that they perform worse under competitive conditions, that they won't volunteer for tournaments. Ancient stereotypes play into this perception: women are kinder, gentler, meeker, more sociable, more collaborative.

Women stayed back in the cave looking after offspring while their aggressive male partners went out hunting and killing. Women lack testosterone, a history of victory, bloodlust, the killer instinct. Everything that makes them so adorable—being nurturing, maternal, loving—is also what makes them fail.

Heads of corporations, looking at the level of female participation in the Olympics, must have been baffled and confused. In their world, the supposed lack of innate competitive drive has been used to excuse the failure to get women into top jobs, to pay them top salaries, and to appoint them to boards of directors. It isn't that women are less capable (although some people, like former Harvard president Larry Summers, would still have us think so), it's just that they lack the competitive zeal to fight their way to the top.[1]

The belief that women must be innately uncompetitive has sparked some curious thinking. A flurry of experiments in the last five years have attempted to match risk-taking with menstrual cycles, trying to prove that women are only really competitive once a month during their fertile phase. From an evolutionary perspective, this would make sense because the willingness to compete would increase the probability of conception and the quality of offspring.[2] Alas, double-blind randomized experiments pulled the rug out from under this idea.[3]

The Cambridge Centre for Gender Studies organized a discussion of gender differences and brought together some of the world's leading academic authorities on the question: Deborah Cameron, an expert on language and communication; Elizabeth Spelke, who had been appointed by Harvard to apply some real science to Summers's speculation; Simon Baron-Cohen, renowned for his definition of autism as "the male brain"; and Robin Dunbar, the evolutionary biologist. Theirs was a serious and well-informed debate, but most thought-provoking of all was their conclusion: the men decided that yes indeed, women are different. The female scientists could not identify any fundamental cognitive or developmental differences between men and women.

This conclusion might have been surprising, but in a way, it wasn't. When examining competitiveness, the same dichotomy had also appeared: female social scientists didn't see a significant difference in competitiveness while male scientists did. A great deal of this could be explained away by the often razor-thin margins of difference, by complicated experiment design, or by subtle differences in what was measured. But amid all the noise, one clear note started to resonate: women are less likely to choose a competitive reward structure. Given the option of being rewarded for work completed or being rewarded for how far they had outperformed their peers, women more often chose to be rewarded for their work alone. Those who did choose to compete performed just as well as men, especially over time.[4] So it wasn't that women couldn't compete—they simply preferred not to.[5]

And no, this can't be explained away by their caring, loving natures. Linda Babcock—an academic who made her name proving that one reason women are underpaid is because they don't negotiate for more money—postulated that women might be deterred from negotiation not because they lack competitiveness but because they believe they'll lose. When she did the experiments, she discovered that her hypothesis was right: women pay a higher social cost for initiating pay negotiations than men—but only in the eyes of men, who judge them more harshly. Attempting to negotiate for higher compensation has no effect on men's willingness to work with men, but it has a significant negative effect on men's willingness to work with women. So the desire not to attempt the competition of a salary negotiation might not represent anything more than world-weary realism. Maybe, Babcock's research dared to suggest, women don't avoid competition because they are innately uncompetitive—but because they expect to lose. And they are right.[6]

Into this fraught field waded a brave, imaginative, and eclectic behavioral economist, Uri Gneezy, an Israeli-born academic with huge enthusiasm for hard problems and big questions. When we met one bright morning in California, he clearly had a big appetite—for breakfast, for new ideas, and for learning about new industries. What makes his work so engaging is that he loves doing or watching experiments in the real world: how to price wine was one of his more entertaining forays. Though he's as easily sucked into game theorizing as any of his peers, unlike many academic economists, he brings to his findings a quality of real-world scrutiny that's rare and refreshing. One of his most widely cited papers, "A Fine Is a Price," dared to challenge the role that money plays in human motivation. Having taken the beating heart of finance into his hands, he was unlikely to be tentative when it came to the gender wars. Instead, he brought a uniquely grounded, genuinely curious mind-set to that debate.

Reviewing all the literature around men's and women's attitudes to risk and competition, he concluded that there are differences—though they're not as big and obvious as many people seemed to think—and that many, if not all, of these differences are socially determined. In many studies, the fact that women were more risk-averse than men was interpreted as a lack of competitive drive, but Gneezy wasn't so sure; perhaps, he speculated, women simply lack confidence in their ability to win. Maybe competitiveness isn't an innate, irrational drive; it might be a considered calculation determined by environment and by culture.

Gneezy thought of a wild and wonderful way to test his theory. If competitiveness is socially determined, would women be more confident in matrilineal societies, where women do hold power, than in patrilineal societies, where they traditionally lack power? It wasn't, of course, very easy to find a matrilineal society—the world has very few of them—but Gneezy located one: the Khasi in northeast India.[7] Here family life is organized around the grandmother. The youngest daughter never leaves home, and eventually she becomes the head of the household while the older daughters set up their homes nearby. Husbands join their wives' families, they have no property, no authority, and no social roles of real importance. By contrast, Gneezy also looked at the Masai of Tanzania, to whom wives are said to be less important to a man than his cattle and whose men, if asked how many children they have, won't count their daughters.

For Gneezy, this was a long way from Israel, where he grew up, or San Diego, where he now works. But with characteristic aplomb, he designed an experiment that could be easily understood and carried out by both the matrilineal Khasi and the patrilineal Masai. It was important that the task be easy to understand and not depend on any specialized talent or physical ability, so it involved nothing more complex than tossing a tennis ball into a bucket. Put into competing pairs, each team was asked whether they'd like to be rewarded per successful shot or by the number of shots by which they outperformed their opponents.

Neither culture proved especially gifted at the ball toss: participants hit the bucket only about one-quarter of the time. But the heart of the experiment was in these findings: in Tanzania more Masai men than women chose to compete, while in India more Khasi women than men chose to compete. Moreover, somewhat to Gneezy's surprise, the Indian women turned out to be more avid competitors than the African men. In other words, coming from a culture where they were accustomed to success and power, women were more willing to compete.

The experiment may be about tribes and peoples that seem very remote, but the findings are realistic. It makes perfect sense not only that both men and women are competitive, but that both men and women are more likely to wish to compete in circumstances where they believe they can win. The reason why women in many corporate and political environments don't put themselves forward is not that they're biologically programmed to be decorative or weak, but that they are shrewd judges of their chances of success. "It is evident," Gneezy mused, "that while many well-performing females hurt themselves financially by shying away from competition, poorly performing males also hurt themselves by embracing it."[8]

At work, assessing the chances of winning can seem reasonably straightforward. In the pursuit of sex, love, and marriage, however, it's much subtler. "I always think that, to get a guy, I have to be drop-dead beautiful, a bit of a minx, clever—but not too clever," Clare tells me. She's a rising executive in an engineering firm: smart, accomplished, and comfortable working with men all day long. But she's careful about how her competence comes across when she's out on a date.

"I want to be confident—I mean, I am confident, but you have to be careful not to come over too strong. If it's a first date, I guess you could say I'm cautious, watching the signals: just how much of me can the guy take the first night out?" She giggles nervously. "It's really tricky, because you want to impress the guy, but you're careful not to make him feel small."

When I asked single men what they did to attract women, a similar element of gamesmanship surfaced. Rob is in his early thirties and works in media. He has two brothers, both of whom are married with kids, and he's conscious that his family is, as he says, just waiting for him to follow suit.

"I know my family expects me to bring home a gorgeous woman—because that's what my brothers did. So, on the one hand, I'm thinking my wife-to-be has to be even better than my sisters-in-law. On the other hand, I'm also thinking, do I have what it takes to land a really fabulous woman? And it's really complicated these days, because you have to have everything—it's exhausting! The body, the mind, the job, prospects, empathy, the … well, you know … everything."

Rob's diffidence, he tells me, isn't just prudery. He doesn't want to come across as too tactical, too premeditated. But he confesses that he thinks about his dating life in competitive terms, viewing not only his brothers but all other men as his competitors. The writer and therapist Stanley Siegel is less bashful about the way this plays out.

"There isn't a man who hasn't compared the size of his penis to other men in the locker room or at the urinal, a sizing-up that leads to either a prideful smile or a sense of inadequacy," Siegel writes. "It's the shame that's coined a catchphrase: 'I'm a grower, not a shower.' One handsome, straight, young man told me, 'Men think about their penis at least ten times a day.' How often have men worried if they are going to measure up, literally, when getting naked, with a new partner's previous lovers? Will a grin or a smirk greet the bared private part? And when it's two men about to have sex, isn't there always that moment of anxiety when they wonder whose dick is bigger?"⁹

Siegel's daughter Alyssa—also a therapist—agrees that size haunts many of her male clients. "There isn't a man with whom I've discussed this who hasn't measured his penis and then gone online to see how his size stands up against others. I think the insecurity comes from a deep sense of male competition that's inbred in our culture. Most men fear they will not be able to attract and keep a mate. Will she fantasize about another man and leave me for someone better endowed?"¹⁰

In one year alone, the market for Viagra and Cialis in the United States was worth nearly $4 billion. As Viagra goes off patent, pharmaceutical companies are rushing to develop testosterone treatments. Even though misuse of the hormone causes blood clots, tumors, infertility, and liver damage, clinics offer testosterone treatments as a lifestyle option—one that may enhance a man's sexual mood and appeal.

Although these treatments have focused on men (and have largely been developed by men), it's become clear that sexual appetite is no less important for women. Nor is this a recent phenomenon: after the sewing machine, fan, kettle, and toaster, the fifth electrical appliance approved for domestic use in 1901 was the vibrator; fifteen years later, they were selling better than toasters.¹¹ Reams of research in evolutionary biology and modern sexuality confirm that women's sexual appetite is just as intense as men's and that women are just as prepared to spend very large amounts of money to attract a partner. Worldwide, the breast implant industry—despite recent horror stories—is worth over $1 billion a year. It's impossible to avoid the vast numbers of models and celebrities whose breasts, hips, lips, and faces have been augmented and decorated, all in pursuit of irresistible physical attractiveness.

Physical endowments, however, aren't always enough, and different assets can substitute for what's missing on that front. All of the men and women I interviewed about their search for a mate insisted, sometimes apologetically, that they would not take seriously a partner who didn't make a financial contribution. Unemployed actors, musicians, and artists were regularly cited as ineligible. In China this preference is even more overt: if a man cannot buy property, he will struggle to find a mate. In a society where men significantly outnumber women, men invest ostentatiously in property to improve their prospects, but this just pushes prices up, making romance and housing an even higher-stakes game. Some observers have compared the property/partner chase in China to the peacock's plumage: an eye-catching but ungainly attraction that is a struggle to wield with aplomb.[12]

The idea of sex as a contest runs throughout human history and mythology, from Greek gods to Jane Austen to Bridget Jones. Men compete with other men whose physical, professional, or financial assets may outweigh their own. Women compete with other women who may use intelligence, attractiveness, or cunning to outmaneuver them.

"A while ago, I was out with friends," Clare tells me, "and there was this guy—very handsome and single. He showed a certain amount of interest, and over the course of the evening we went to another bar and then a club, and I remember noticing that two other girls kept tagging along. And I remember thinking, "I am going to put a stop to that. I'm not seeing them having that." It was just a bit of fun, but I was determined. I did find favor in this situation, but it came with a certain amount of bitterness from the other two. That was definitely a competition. I pretended to notice nothing but did what was needed to win."

She paused for a second with a rueful smile.

"If you're not winning, it feels despondent. I run from the front. I like winning. If I think I'm not going to win, then I withdraw, because I don't want to lose."

According to psychologists David Buss and Cindy Meston, women have sex for 237 different reasons. They haven't yet turned their attention to men, but their reasons may not be so very different from the ones Buss and Meston cite for women: women have sex because they're bored; because they want to get closer to God, make their partner feel good, punish a partner who has hurt them, impress their friends, or hurt their enemies; as a form of barter for gifts; and because they're looking to boost their self-confidence or cure their headaches.[13] Women often see and even describe their sexual partners as trophies, prizes, belt notches. For many, winning an attractive partner is a race that must be won in order to gain admission to the winners' circle.

Listening to young adults talk about the dating scene today is both funny and sad. Clare and Rob, both in their early thirties, work hard at their careers and at their social lives; both concede that success at work is easier to manage and strangely less stressful. The Saturday night ritual—going out on a date or with a crowd of friends—feels like a requirement. Strategizing what to wear and how to act, sizing up the prospects, judging the likelihood of success, all of it sounds like hard work. And assessing new opportunities is a skill.

"For me, that's the hardest part," Tom tells me. "You see someone attractive and you want to get to know them, but then the question is: will they be interested in me? Sometimes I have this game I play: how long will it take before she mentions a boyfriend, partner, fiancé, husband? The shortest it's ever taken? Twenty-five seconds! On some level, I guess I still feel like a fourteen-year-old on the edge of the school disco: you want to be part of the fun, but you don't want to risk looking like an idiot."

Tom's was a rueful, not a hearty, laugh. A handsome man with a good media job, he's had his share of disappointments. And like everyone else talking about the pleasure and pain of sexual competition, eventually he adopts the metaphor of markets.

"You listen for those cues, the references that say: 'I am not on the market. I'm taken. Spoken for. Reserved.' You listen because you don't want to feel foolish and you also don't want to waste your time having a really long conversation with some girl who's going to waltz off the minute her guy walks through the door."

"The market. That's what I hate—the idea of being in a cattle market. You see that at university immediately," Mary says. A beautiful young woman with long blond hair and a steady, warm gaze, she recounts her experience at the University of Exeter with a mixture of hurt and disdain. The residence halls commanded different prices: the ones with the designer bathrooms, double beds, and three-course meals were a great deal more expensive than the cheaper and older accommodation she had chosen.

"People were definitely sizing each other up as potential partners. And I met a guy my first night. He was wearing a hoodie advertising a ski resort I'd been to. So we got talking about skiing, and after ten or fifteen minutes he asked me where I was living. When I told him which hall I was in, he just said, 'Nice to meet you,' and walked away! I was quite shaky. I hadn't realized just how ruthlessly people were pairing up."

Everyone I've talked to—from teenagers to retirees, gay and straight, married and single—describes with fear, loathing, and humor the agonizing difficulty of competing for a partner. The fear of humiliation, private or public, is intense. The dreams of success are wild and often hopelessly unrealistic.

Much of the time everyone is pretending to be having a lot more fun than they really are.

"Saturday night," Penny groans. "That awful feeling: if you have somewhere to go, you have to spend what feels like the whole day getting ready. And if you don't have anywhere to go—God, you are such a failure. Maybe you've had a hard week, you'd really like to curl up, watch a DVD. But it feels so pathetic and doomed, and you think, 'If I have one Saturday like this, I'll spend the rest of my life like this until I'm some crazy old woman found dead in bed with cats one day.' So you dust yourself off, stick on the eyelashes and totter down the stairs in shoes you can barely stand up in because...." She suddenly stops. A long pause follows as the momentum of her description suddenly runs out of steam. "I don't know why. I really don't know sometimes. Just—because."

Penny works in a large accounting firm in London. She's well paid and one day expects to be made a partner in her firm. She has already far outstripped the professional success of her parents; her father was a schoolteacher, and her mother looked after the family and did occasional substitute teaching. Penny is proud of her achievements, and her parents' pride in her is important. But she feels increasingly trapped by the feeling that somehow that's just not enough.

"It's not like being in accounting is the most sexy, romantic thing in the world." She roars with laughter. "I mean, 'I work in accounting' isn't exactly the most lascivious opening gambit you've ever heard! So you almost feel you have to work the other side even harder: 'Look, I have a sense of humor!' 'Look, I can wear sexy shoes and tight skirts. If I take my glasses off, I'm really human!'"

Disappointed and exhausted by too many fruitless Saturday nights, Penny turned to Internet dating. Here she hoped to "cut to the chase" by working through the data to find the perfect match. Her friends had tried it, and she hoped she would more quickly find a great companion.

"But guess what? It's all competitive online too! To be judged by a photo against all these other women ... it's a pretty fearsome experience. I'm not a conventionally attractive woman, but all the others have the model pose down pat. And the men on the dating sites—some in morning suits, some at the top of a mountain looking fantastic, one in his cycle helmet after a triathlon. It's just very formulaic and quite intimidating."

Clare, Rob, and Penny have all had good relationships with different partners; they also all describe themselves as "still looking" and, when pressed, acknowledge that what they seek is someone to marry. However much contraception, women's rights, and sexual liberation may have separated sex and marriage, they still remain quite tightly coupled in the popular imagination. Helen Gurley Brown's 1962 shocker *Sex and the Single Girl,* while full of instruction for satisfying sex, nevertheless insisted that the whole point of premarital sex is to learn how to choose and become the perfect spouse. Gurley still maintained in the 2004 reissued edition that premarital sex is practice; her book teaches women both how to be great lovers and find sexual satisfaction and how to discover what they like and need in a man. But marriage is always the end game.

That the wedding is the prize is a theme remorselessly trumpeted throughout popular media. Celebrity magazines are full of photo spreads documenting the great day, while even a drama as smart and insightful about women as *Sex and the City* nevertheless felt compelled to end the series with the protagonist safely married off to a rich and handsome man. Although the series had taken big risks in its portrayal of sex and female friendship, leaving Carrie Bradshaw single was somehow too radical a step to take.

Reality TV contests like *Take Me Out, Dinner Date, Girlfriends,* and *The Millionaire Matchmaker* routinely position sex or weddings as the ultimate prize. In *The Bachelor,* muscle-bound men fly planes, wield power tools, race motorbikes, win triathlons, repair houses, and love puppies, all as a way of proving that they have the physical, financial, and emotional resources needed to be great providers and fathers. Those personal, physical, and financial assets endow them with the right to choose from twenty-five gorgeous, available, seductive women for their "perfect fairy-tale ending." Reversing the format, *The Bachelorette* features beautiful, perfectly groomed, athletic, balletic, and shopaholic women who are endlessly empathetic, sensitive, and cunning and who get to choose their "Prince Charming" from among twenty-five eager, determined, and physically robust men. Success on these shows is simple: a proposal of marriage is the way you win. Although most of these relationships break up once the cameras disappear, the one that did result in a real wedding—series 13 of *The Bachelor*—was broadcast on American television as though it were an event of national importance.

The British have no need for such artifice. The idea that a big, expensive wedding is the ultimate victory celebration is nowhere more explicit than in the overheated narrative that accompanies all royal courtships. Never mind that, in the case of Princess Diana, the fairy-tale turned into a cautionary tale. When "Waity Katie" successfully pursued and captured Prince William, she was publicly applauded for her strategic patience and duly rewarded with her prize wedding. The message these epic weddings send is not easily dismissed.

"When I was twenty-eight, I went out with a man, and I absolutely loved him and he loved me, and we decided to get married," Imogen tells me. "This was me achieving what I wanted; it was absolutely all about the wedding. The minute we got engaged, my parents were thrilled, and we all went into overdrive, and it got bigger and bigger and bigger, and he was absolutely horrified! And I was spectacularly jilted. It was a horrible experience, so public. You tell people you're getting married—and then you have to tell people you're not getting married. It took away a very romantic young girl's dream: being the chosen one, the perfect day. It felt such a huge failure."

Evolutionary biologists argue that all species are driven to reproduce and that, in our pursuit of sexual partners, we are simply doing what all living things do. Some go further, maintaining that war originated in the sexual contests that were common when man was still polygamous. Monogamy, therefore, is the basis of a stable and civilized society. (This is why some politicians continue to believe that tax breaks for married couples—an ongoing cash prize—will confer some kind of social benefit.) But framing the pursuit of a sexual companion as a contest puts disproportionate emphasis on the prizes: the gorgeous partner and the big wedding.

Although it's too early to tell, it seems quite plausible that the same competitive narrative may frame gay marriages too. All of the gay men and women I talked to insisted that the gay dating scene is not so very different. Some sleep around a great deal; others settle down. That it is now safer to be open and honest about one's sexual orientation makes the dating scene less dangerous and less secret. The demand for gay marriage has been, first and foremost, a demand for equality: to have the legal rights and tax privileges enjoyed by heterosexual couples for decades. But with the legalization of gay marriage, gay weddings may also begin to attract the same climactic hysteria long associated with "the big day" for heterosexual couples.

"I think that marriage is still seen as the goal of a lot of relationships in the LGBT community," Cindy tells me. "To get that piece of paper. It is a status symbol, and it gives you permission to exit the marketplace. Of course, we don't know yet what the divorce rate will be. But it's certainly true that getting married, getting the certificate, is seen as an achievement."

That weddings continue to be a big deal is clear from their price tag. The average cost of a wedding runs at around $28,000, which is more than half of what most Americans earn in a year. In New York—the most expensive place in America to get married—the cost hovers around $65,000. As a consequence, one-quarter of newlyweds start their married life encumbered by debt they've taken on to pay for the celebration. But they aren't thinking about the future; they're marking their victory.

"There's no doubt," David tells me, "that I saw it as crossing the finishing line. I got married when I was forty-two, and on the one hand, it meant I was retiring from the race. That was a relief! On the other hand, I remember thinking all I could hear was the sound of doors closing. But I think there is this sense that you've won: landed the trophy wife and all that. I remember saying I'd waited so long because I was choosy, and there was some sense from my friends that, wow, I'd had some good innings, really played the field—and was still virile enough to land a prize! So yeah, it was kind of triumphant."

"I think David was really proud of me," Sarah recalls. "I was ten years younger than he was and, in those days, very slim, very pretty. And I was proud of me because I'd really decided he was the one. I'd strategized and planned and made sure this time it worked. Because I'd had other boyfriends who hadn't worked out, and I was determined this time it would.

"I remember on my hen night, sitting around with my girlfriends. Most of them were married, not all. But we got to talking about what our husbands, boyfriends earned—comparing salaries and prospects. And I sat there feeling very smug. It had been a chase, and I had run it as carefully and as tactically as some people run marathons. So on the big day—the church, the dress—that was it. I'd won!"

Sarah and David's wedding pictures tell the same story: proud parents beaming alongside a visibly triumphant bride and groom; you can almost hear the cheering. But now they both think that that was the problem.

"The day after the wedding was strange," David recalls. "It just felt like the morning after a big party. I woke up thinking I should feel different. But I didn't. A little hungover maybe. But that's all."

"I never really thought beyond it," Sarah says. "Get your guy. Get the babies. That's it. That's what I did. And then I was sitting at home thinking, 'Now what? I'm young and I'm smart and I'm still pretty and what do I do now?'"

It's easy to dismiss the emphasis on big weddings as a purely middle-class phenomenon, but in fact it runs across classes, cultures, and countries. And in the competition for mates, it isn't even the only prize. In many communities where marriage is rarely thought of, the big prize is a baby. I saw this firsthand in a Nottingham community where many of the young women I met expected and hoped to have babies soon after leaving school. Girls as young as fourteen talked easily about how many babies they wanted and whether it would be better to have a girl first or a boy.

"You want your baby-father to be handsome," Beth tells me. "Because you want a good-looking baby. You keep your eyes open, and you definitely don't have sex with anyone who's ugly. Who'd want an ugly baby? So when I look at guys, that's what I'm looking for: someone really manly, strong. That way, I know I'll have a pretty baby."

Beth is a pretty young woman; she says her father was handsome too. He's not around anymore, but that doesn't bother her because most of her friends don't have fathers at home either. She's an energetic, resourceful young woman, bubbly and alert. Did she ever, I wonder, consider not having babies?

"I might. I might not. But you'd have to have a plan, something else you really were going to do. Otherwise, there's no jobs around here, what do you do? No job. No money. No baby—what a loser!"

For Beth and many of her friends, having a baby is a sign of reaching adulthood. For many of the men in her community, fathering a child is a sign of virility. Some boast of all the children they've conceived; their high score demonstrates their potency.

The problem with framing sexual conquest as a competition is not only that it is dehumanizing but that it focuses attention on the result, with little or no thought about what comes afterward. Just like learning and exams, the immediate reward is more highly prized than the long-term process. While everyone's imagining the headline, the excitement, and the drama, there's little recognition that cute cuddly babies don't stay that way for long. Once all the excitement wears off, the hard work of raising children offers very few prizes. Similarly, after the big wedding day come the long years of life together.

After their wedding, David and Sarah had two children and got a dog. David worked long hours as a management consultant, and Sarah worked part-time in medicine. Like many couples before and since, they both struggled to balance their jobs and their family life. But the real issue between them became power.

"David earned at least twice what I did, he paid for all our vacations, and he bought the house. So I felt I had to make it up somehow: doing the ironing and the cooking. After a while, of course, I resented it. So what happened is, I just thought, 'I do the work here, it's my house, my kids.' I just claimed the territory and thought, 'You have all the money? Well, at home I have all the power.' If David wouldn't contribute, then I'd make sure he couldn't contribute. So he was useless with the kids, never knew where anything was. He competed with money. I competed with competence. We definitely kept score."

Life at home, they both acknowledge, became one long battle. They became "champion bickerers" and routinely attempted to outperform one another. If David had a success at work, Sarah made him feel useless at home. If Sarah arranged a fantastic birthday party for one of their children, David complained about the bills he would have to pay. Looking back now, Sarah says she realizes she had made it inevitable that he would cheat.

"I wouldn't let him win at home, so of course he had to win somewhere else. So he had an affair at work. I can't believe I didn't see it coming. Work was where he was successful. Of course that was his choice—he didn't have to do it. But I can see why he would."

Sarah and David now live separately. When I asked David what role competition had played in the breakup of his marriage, he was thoughtful. At first he dismissed the idea, but later in our conversation he came back to it.

"We are, I guess, both competitive people. I've always won. The affairs I've had—I guess you might call them conquests—in some ways they were just a continuation of my bachelor days. But I also think that, if I couldn't win at home—and Sarah, let's be quite clear about this, wasn't going to let me win—then I just took my game somewhere else."

Adultery isn't uncommon. Although, understandably, it's hard to measure, academic research suggests that spouses put a great deal of effort into "guarding their mates," and they do so because most have experienced what is called "mate poaching." Two of the leading "benefits" are revenge and conquest.[14]

Emily Brown is a marriage therapist who sees in her consulting room the infidelity that psychologists study in their labs. What she sees is that poaching is almost always about power.

"Adultery is a form of competition," she tells me. "It is a way of saying, I am not getting enough of something—maybe sex, attention, love, success—so I can justify having an affair. If you bring that win/lose mind-set into relationships, it is devastating. The inability to admit to mistakes can be a problem too. These small elements of competition just create a wedge that slowly pulls people apart. A lot of men still struggle if their wives are very successful. Not all, but a lot."

Recent academic research confirms Brown's experience. When Kate Ratliff and Shigehiro Oishi designed experiments to test how a partner's success affects self-esteem, they found a distinct gender difference. "Men's implicit self-esteem was lower when their partner succeeded than when their partner failed, whereas women's implicit self-esteem was not affected." They are careful to point out that these findings pertain to Americans and are more variable among European and more diverse groups, suggesting that the attitudes uncovered by their results derive significantly from social norms and aren't inevitable.[15]

That sexual contests are also power struggles is nowhere more luridly illustrated than in the relationship between the writer Ayn Rand and her acolyte Nathaniel Branden. Twenty-five years her junior, Branden was completely smitten when he was welcomed into Rand's circle of admirers and evangelists. (There's even a suggestion that in changing his surname from Blumenthal to Branden after meeting her, he was attempting to amplify his affiliation.) An avid devotee, Branden was initially excited and flattered by the prospect of an affair with Rand; as long as their respective spouses both knew and at least tacitly agreed, the relationship seemed entirely consistent with their belief that a moral life is the pursuit of rational self-interest. The unacknowledged sexual tension the affair introduced into their respective marriages even seemed to spice up those marriages somewhat.

But it soon slowly became clear that what might have begun as a meeting of minds and bodies (as Branden describes it) was really a struggle by Rand to dominate all aspects of her young protégé's life. To maintain his allegiance to her Branden had to be unfaithful to his wife, cuckold Rand's husband, dedicate all his time, energy, and thought to her work, and lie to his friends and colleagues about a relationship that Rand insisted be kept secret. In other words, he had to subjugate himself entirely to the mind and body of Ayn Rand. At first this was exciting—she was famous, and he was besotted by her ideology. But the relationship became an existential contest: Who was more important? Whose ideas mattered most? Who was the dominant actor in a tangled web of love, sex, business, and money?

As Branden grew in age and confidence, his discomfort with Rand's dominance, his subjugation, and what he called "a life of lies and deception" became unbearable. Everything he gained—Rand dedicating *Atlas Shrugged* to him, her permission to evangelize her work in an institution bearing his name—was a gift bestowed by her. When the competitive strains of the relationship blew it apart, they competed for supporters, followers, and copyrights. Rand saw everyone as an enemy or an ally. That the relationship was doomed by its competitiveness was clear to Branden only much later in life.

"Competition corrupts the natural pleasure and joy of what we are doing. It takes the joy out of work, out of life, if you succumb to it. It is anti-life."

Now in his eighties, looking like a snowy-haired Clint Eastwood, Branden still recalls his affiliation with Rand with some excitement. Her picture is on the wall of his Los Angeles study, and he cites his memoir—*My Years with Ayn Rand*—as one of his favorite books. But he doesn't believe that her zealous belief in free markets appropriately relates to personal and sexual relationships.

"I competed with Ayn and her understanding of human psychology, and that was a mistake. I wish I had handled it differently. She was too competitive, too narcissistic. I didn't see that then. You can't love someone and compete with them."

He stopped and stared at me for a long time, his piercing blue eyes watching intently for my response.

"It was a great adventure. She was a sorceress of reason. But reason isn't love. Love isn't winning an argument."[16]

"I think it does depend a lot on whether there's some element of fairness in the relationship," therapist Emily Brown tells me. "One couple I worked with, she was the big money-earner and he was the financial treasurer of a church, earning very little. But they both really loved their jobs. And you are seeing this a lot more, where the woman is the major breadwinner. So it can work. But the couples I know where it does—they really work at it."

In 40 percent of American homes, women are now the major breadwinners.[17] In Britain, the figure is closer to 25 percent. What makes these marriages work is the sense that they are working together on a shared project, what Glenda, a mergers attorney, calls "the us."

"My husband and I both work for 'the us,'" Glenda tells me. "That's why, if he makes a bed, I don't say thank you—because he hasn't done it for me. Maybe I think this way because I used to be a project manager. I might say, 'Good job!' because he's done it for us, he's done it for the household. We all benefit from the work that we all do."

Glenda and her husband have a sense of a joint enterprise to which they both contribute the skills and income that they have. What's critical, she tells me, is that both give their best. It is impossible to be treated as an equal at work if you aren't an equal at home—and that's measured not by income but by commitment.

In my own marriage, there have been times when my husband has been the sole breadwinner and other times when I've far out-earned him. We simply both agreed at the outset that we would do the work we loved and live on whatever it brought us. At home, we work hard—sometimes perhaps too hard—to be scrupulously fair in sharing child care, chores, and time to do what we want. Earning extra income doesn't buy extra privileges.

One of the advantages that gay couples have, Cindy tells me, is that you can't tell who is the major breadwinner and there are no traditional assumptions. When Cindy and her partner Beth first met, Beth supported them both while Cindy started her business. Once her business was thriving, Cindy became the major earner. The fact that no one knew and that nobody made assumptions was, she says, quite liberating.

"Nobody knows. And we don't care. We swap leads. That doesn't mean there's no anxiety attached to it—but there's a lot less social pressure about what the relationship looks like to other people. You can change places without a lot of social grief. In that sense, marriage shares a lot of properties of collaboration: you share the wings."

After being, as she puts it, "spectacularly jilted," Imogen spent ten years living alone. But she still wanted to get married and have children. When she met James, they married quickly, with a beautiful church service and "a very homespun jolly reception" that, she says, put the wedding in its place. It wasn't the culmination of a race but the beginning of a lifelong project.

"The wedding is so powerful in our culture," Imogen says. "I still had vestiges of that, but it's just one day and it's the beginning, not the end! The idea of the perfect day is so dangerous. But now I felt no obligation to turn up as a meringue! I wanted to turn up as myself—it must be terrifying for young men when this apparition turns up looking nothing like they have ever looked before!"

Both in their forties, James and Imogen had their first child a year after marrying and their second child two years later. Slowly they came to see their family as the ultimate collaboration: work that they shared and that meant they had to find ways to live together.

"We came from very different backgrounds," James says. "I come from

Salford, from quite a rough place where you have to defend yourself. And Imogen came from nice leafy Buckinghamshire. My family, there's a lot of conflict, a lot of shouting. That doesn't happen in Imogen's family—they talk about their feelings a lot, but they don't shout."

Imogen felt that she had to understand better where James was coming from, the kind of emotional language he was accustomed to. James had to learn that shouting and storming off aren't the only ways to resolve conflict. They both think that they had to change a great deal.

"I think it's about becoming a changed you. You're still who you are, but you grow and change," James tells me. "I'm not me anymore in the sense that I was when I was a teenager or in my twenties. But does that matter? I think the idea that people are fixed, that they don't change, is just bizarre. Of course I've changed. That's what you do. It's not about growing older. It's about growing."

"I agree," Imogen says, "though I think, for women, the loss of self in the early years is quite staggering. With two young kids, you do feel shoved to the edge of your own life. But then you work your way back again. Because of my family, I feel much more me, a richer version of myself."

Imogen continued to work as a journalist, but James grew increasingly discontented with his work managing a local law firm. As his frustrations grew, the two of them decided to start a business together. The company makes and distributes savory and sweet crumbles; James is the cook, and Imogen—in between journalism assignments—does sales and marketing. They both say that they really appreciate the other's abilities.

"The things James does, I can't do," Imogen says. "Incredibly organized, attention to detail. He has such a methodical approach to cooking—which is why he can do the work of two people. I could never do that!"

"People want to talk to Imogen and to buy from her," James insists. "Because of her journalism background, she's happy to cold-call. Selling is about understanding the other person, and Imogen is good at that and I'm not."

They don't always agree about everything. Both like to get their own way, and they experience the irritations that most couples would find familiar: James spreads his work materials all over the house, while Imogen doesn't load the dishwasher to James's satisfaction. What wins the day, they say, is who cares most.

"I do all the decorating because I care about it," says Imogen. "He trusts my judgment and doesn't care that much."

"I can be quite bossy," James admits. "But in a lot of areas I cede my power to Imogen because I trust her and know she's good at so much. I'm less concerned because I know she wields power wisely."

Theirs is a strikingly practical conversation. Both James and Imogen have each other's measure, and they're highly committed to each other. Winning isn't on the agenda of either spouse. As good a marriage as theirs appears to be, however, it is increasingly a minority lifestyle.

Today more than half of American adults are single, and roughly 31 million live by themselves. Single households, as a consequence, are more common than nuclear families, multigenerational families, or shared homes. And the majority are not young or old but middle-aged. Worldwide, Sweden tops the list with 47 percent of households being singletons.

This new trend has led to significant hand-wringing on the part of politicians and sociologists. At the very least, it has provoked a housing crisis, with more people wanting their own space. But when author Eric Klinenberg set out to explore the causes and consequences of this unparalleled phenomenon, what he found was not a wasteland of lonely spinsters and misanthropic bachelors. For many, living alone was a cyclical condition, not a permanent one. Moreover, people living alone were socially more active than those who lived with each other; singletons created and enjoyed a thriving public culture.[18]

"When I was at school, I joined the National Youth Choir," Carol tells me. "And the friends I've made there, I've kept throughout my life. And lots of them have got married and had kids. And I haven't. I've gone out with a lot of guys—I still do. But I think of my friends as my family. They're the people I turn to if I need something. And they're the people who contain all those memories of me over time."

Carol stays at home on Saturday night when she wants to, goes out with friends, or Internet-dates when she feels like it.

"My best friend Rebecca, she and I have very similar taste in men, and we have gone out with the same person, at different times! He was called Nigel, and he had the biggest penis either of us had ever seen in our entire lives. And he had a girlfriend at home in Manchester and cheated on her with both of us. What's lovely is that he is long gone, but we have this wonderful friendship. And we have never had any rivalry between us."

Another singleton, Ben, says that he does sometimes envy what he calls "the power of two": joint mortgages, the ability to live in bigger houses in nicer areas because of two incomes. But he loves his independence and friendships and the time that he has to devote to them.

"I live on a very friendly street, and I know everyone and everything about everyone. And it's great. My neighbor across the street, Sara, she's getting on a bit, and I'll take her to her hospital appointments, call in on people if I haven't seen them for a while. I look after people on my street—and they look after me, feed my cats when I go away, water the garden. I have a much richer social life than any of the families here because I have the time to spend with people. And I like to think I'm part of the glue here that makes the street a community."

The singletons in Klinenberg's book, together with many I've known and interviewed, don't see sex as a prize or social life as a contest. Instead, they enjoy shifting between their roles as friends, colleagues, godparents, uncles, aunts, nieces, nephews, and neighbors. How we live, together or apart, with or without offspring, need not become a socially determined contest. It will, however, require very high degrees of social relatedness: people who are good at helping each other, sharing needs and burdens, asking for help, and acknowledging mistakes.

Legally and technically, men and women, living alone or together, can have children now with or without marriage and cohabitation. That may take some of the heat out of the social contest. But bringing up those children to feel safe, secure, and able to form relationships with the people around them will always be an inherently social and shared act. As one single parent said to me, "I'm on my own, but I'm not alone. I have all these connections—to my son, his friends, their parents and teachers, and his grandparents. And in a way, the more different we are, the harder it is to compare or compete. You need everyone to help."

For all their lightness of touch, the so-called comedies of Jane Austen are tales of high-stakes contests in which failure is too terrible to think or write about. In Austen's world, women without resources faced a catastrophic future, threatened by poverty, homelessness, desertion. Marriage and offspring feel like everything to Austen's heroines because they were everything. Today, the changes wrought by modern reproductive technologies and new social mores—individuals can live with or without marriage, with or without children, alone or together with partners of their own or the opposite sex—have lowered the stakes in what used to be a very high-stakes game indeed. There's more time for individuals to experiment and decide today, and there are more choices.

But the challenge of making and preserving connections, teaching, inculcating, and then honing the social skills required to be part of a wide rich society, has become greater than ever. Young people who have been taught to compete at every turn are poorly equipped at the outset of their social and sexual lives as the loosening of sexual, family, and social structures puts greater pressure on them to build and maintain structures of their own. We've only just begun to think about what that means for young and old adults. What we do know is that this challenge confronts men and women everywhere. At home. At work. Equally.

CHAPTER 4

Angry Birds

At the end of the nineteenth century, if you had been looking for a society characterized by competitiveness and social mobility, Norway would not have been your first choice. A stolidly conservative place, its greatest artist, Henrik Ibsen, so hated his country's stultifying conventions that he spent most of his productive life abroad, creating a new theater aimed at exploding traditional ideas of hierarchy and dominance. While he secured the relative quiet of self-imposed exile, Ibsen's homeland seethed with debate about social status, power, and influence, and it was there that the subject of competition found its first systematic analyst.

Thorleif Schjelderup-Ebbe was born in 1894 in Oslo (then known as Kristiania) to two successful and wealthy sculptors, Axel Emil Ebbe and Menga Schjelderup. As a child, he was talented, adored, and spoiled. Educated at home by private tutors, every summer he and his parents would leave the city's heat for a country house some fifteen miles away. From the age of six, the boy occupied himself by making friends of the farmyard chickens. He would spend hours watching them, giving them names, and avidly noting how they related to one another. When the family returned the following summer, Thorleif would immediately recognize all of the older chickens and correctly identify the newcomers.

So engaged did the boy become that eventually he persuaded his mother to buy him a dozen chickens of his own. In the winter he would travel out to visit them; in the summer he would spend all day observing them. Thorleif had no interest in what they produced—eggs didn't matter to him. What captivated the boy was how they communicated. At the age of ten, he started to draw diagrams that accurately portrayed the status competition he was beginning to discern.

"He began to write down his discoveries about the hierarchy among them," his son Dag later recalled. "There were these triangles and, a strange thing, one of my father's laws, is this hierarchy: triangular, quadrangular, any kind of angle. Chicken A may be the master of B and B may be the master of C, then you would think that A would be the master of C but by some quirk it's possible that C may be the master of A. It works in all kinds of rotations depending on when the chickens first met, how it happened then. Or if a chicken gets sick, it is reversed. He started to write that down."[1]

This wasn't a childhood fancy, and Schjelderup-Ebbe didn't grow out of it. He continued to monitor his chickens when he enrolled at the University of Oslo to study zoology, and in 1921 he published his thesis on hierarchies among flocks of hens. It is to Schjelderup-Ebbe that we owe the phrase "pecking order" (*hackordnung*).

All of the chickens, Schjelderup-Ebbe noted, wanted to be the first to eat. But the same one always succeeded; he called her "the despot." There was always just one despot, and she pecked all the rest. In a flock of seven hens, three got to peck four others, one got to peck two, one got to peck one, and a solitary hen got to peck no one. So the privilege of pecking and eating descended until the bottom hen got the least amount to eat and was, he wrote, "very nervous because of the number of pecks she received. I had the impression that she tired herself out in a constant attempt to avoid punishment and to get enough food. In contrast, the despot, who chased others from the food or the nest and who was never bothered by anybody seemed to feel very well."[2]

Pecking orders, as Schjelderup-Ebbe mapped them, are always vertical. Being at the top bestows huge privileges—more food, more safety—and being at the bottom is perilous.

"A grave seriousness lies over the chicken yard and hens exhibit much anger and fear," he observed. The pecking orders weren't stable, and the chickens were never peaceful. Rebellions broke out, and older chickens were particularly vulnerable. When new hens were introduced into the yard, incumbents invariably enjoyed an advantage and would fight to defend their primacy. They would also eat more than they needed to, consumption being a badge of power. But at all times, every hen understood the social structure: "There are no two hens in the same group that do not know exactly who is 'over' and who is 'under'.… The social structure is in the chicken's blood; it is exhibited by young animals when they grow up, regardless of whether or not they have been raised apart from the older chickens. In other words, the tendency to social structure is inherited rather than learned."[3]

But while Schjelderup-Ebbe's analysis of social relations among chickens proved astute, his ability to understand the behavior of humans proved sadly less successful. Initially taken under the wing of Kristine Bonnevie, the first woman professor in Norway, his mentor was, according to Schjelderup-Ebbe's son, "very domineering, high in the hierarchy."[4] The two scientists fell out when Bonnevie concluded that a well-written article ridiculing her could only have come from Schjelderup-Ebbe. Deaf to his protestations of innocence (the article later turned out to have been written by one of Norway's leading novelists), Bonnevie withdrew all support and cast her protégé out of the academic nest.

"You don't need the job," he was told. "You have money."

But like most scientists, money wasn't what Schjelderup-Ebbe wanted. He craved the respect of his peers and a position within the academic hierarchy. That was denied him by his Norwegian colleagues. Restless, he traveled all over Europe, publishing and teaching where he could. His paper "Fortgesetzte biologische Beobachtungen des Gallus domesticus"—"Biological Observations of *Gallus domesticus* in Its Daily Life"—was published in German in 1924 and would prove the seminal work in the study of social behavior in animals. But that cut no ice with Schjelderup-Ebbe's Norwegian peers.

"They said, he has made a name for himself in Germany, he's not the kind of person we like here," his son recalled. "So they found a way of preventing him from getting his doctorate. It was most unfair."[5]

Schjelderup-Ebbe continued to cast his net wide, writing children's stories and poems, studying mathematics, chemistry, the intensity of fragrance in flowers, and the difficulty of getting old seeds to germinate. Producing over one hundred scientific works, he kept searching for his place in the academic hierarchy, but to no avail.

"In about 1955," his son recalled, "he got a letter from Konrad Lorenz and Lorenz said, your work has been a great influence on my work—my father was there before him! Then, in 1973, when the Nobel prize was given to three scientists (Konrad Lorenz, Karl von Frisch and Nikolaas Tinbergen) for their work in ethology, I said to him, you should have had this! After all, he founded the word pecking order. My father is the one who discovered it."[6]

Throughout his childhood, Dag remembered, his father kept a scrapbook, cutting out and gluing in articles that reported on his work. Having been passed over for recognition so often and so firmly, he cherished every mention and every professional membership. At his father's death, Dag Schjelderup-Ebbe gave the scrapbooks—ten volumes of them—to the university that had refused to honor him. Poor Schjelderup-Ebbe: the man who had so keenly recognized and mapped hierarchies and power struggles never learned how to use his insights to his own advantage.

But his legacy was immense. Thorleif Schjelderup-Ebbe gave us not only the concept of pecking orders, which we apply to this day, but the very idea that we all compete for status and that this has a discernible impact on our behavior—on how we act and whether we flourish.

Most of the time, like Schjelderup-Ebbe's chickens, we create and discern relative positioning implicitly—and we do so with surprising speed. Social hierarchies spontaneously emerge in children as young as two years old, along with the biological systems that process information about social ranking.[7] The first person to map behavior in humans with the same kind of rigor that Schjelderup-Ebbe brought to chickens was Harvard's Robert Bales. He observed groups of people from behind one-way mirrors, trying to assess just how positions of dominance were determined. Bales noted that, while groups of people coming together for the first time might all start as equals, almost instantly, as with chickens, there is "a drift towards inequality of participation." That drift starts to separate and segment people into roles and ranks and to define different social relationships in the group. Just as the incumbent hen is more likely than the newcomer to dominate, so in a group discussion the first person to speak is the one most likely to start building a reputation and a position of dominance. Other members of a group quickly start to adopt distinct roles or niches. One may become a specialist in advancing ideas, another a "chronic objector." Some are great at keeping the peace or releasing tension. Others gain respect, while a few are just well liked. But in almost no time at all everyone has a role and a rank. Usually, Bales concluded, the best-liked contributor comes second or third in the hierarchy. "It is not impossible," he wrote, "for the man ranked at the top in ideas also to be best liked, but apparently it is difficult."[8]

Bales paid keen attention to the ways in which dialogue creates hierarchy, but more recently it has become clear just how much social ranking occurs even before a word is spoken. Gaze and eyeline alone may assert dominance: those who look directly into your eyes before they speak and continue to do so after they've finished may, regardless of content, assume a more dominant position than those whose gaze moves on quickly. In experiments where all indicators of status were fastidiously removed, academic researchers found that all of their participants reached conclusions about relative rank before any conversation began.[9]

Body language communicates almost instantaneously and remains immensely influential even in circumstances where thinking should matter more than physique. In the hypercompetitive environment that is Harvard Business School, Amy Cuddy was well aware of a pecking order in her classroom: the despots stretched out in what she called a "high-power" pose, occupying a great deal of space. By contrast, others with a "low-power" pose would curl up, shrink into themselves, almost seem to disappear. She was pretty sure that these different poses weren't correlated to intelligence, but she worried that they might start to correlate to grades. So she wondered whether changing their body language alone could alter the perceived status of quieter students, whom, she felt sure, had much to offer. Might it be possible, she asked herself, to "fake it till you make it?"[10]

When she tried changing the postures of these students, Cuddy found that there were too many circumstances in which conspicuously high-power poses were uncomfortable or inappropriate for them. So she tried something more subtle: if students adopted high-power body language *before* a critical social evaluation, might they still come across as more powerful? Cuddy designed an experiment in which, just before a simulated job interview, students would adopt high-power poses for just two minutes in private.

What she found was pretty remarkable. The students who adopted physically powerful body language for just two minutes raised their levels of testosterone (the dominance hormone) by about 20 percent, making them feel more powerful. Moreover, their levels of cortisone (the stress hormone) fell by about 25 percent. Objective observers of the simulated interviews—who did not know what they were looking for—assessed the "high-power" students as having more presence and being more compelling and more attractive.[11] Simply acting powerful, in private, was enough to convey status to strangers.

Our sensitivity to power and rank is immediate, unconscious, and persistent. But just as influential as visual cues is the voice. At Kent State University, sociologist Stanford Gregory discovered that, below the audible frequencies in the human voice, there is a low hum, at around 0.5 kilohertz, that we all, quite unconsciously, discern. That hum conveys social status. Watching and listening to the sound waves of Larry King interviews, Gregory found that the more powerful the guest—George Bush, Elizabeth Taylor, Bill Clinton, Norman Schwarzkopf—the more King adapted his low hum to meet theirs. But when he interviewed less powerful guests—Garrison Keillor, Spike Lee, Dan Quayle—their lower status prompted them to adapt their voices to King's. The lower-frequency signal of the human voice, Gregory concluded, communicates much more than just pitch—it communicates power.[12]

Gregory went on to test his research against nineteen televised American presidential debates. In each one, voice alone proved to be both an indicator of dominance and an accurate predictor of the popular vote.[13] Margaret Thatcher was famous for having dramatically lowered her voice when she became prime minister, but that was part of a conscious effort to diminish her femininity. What Gregory identified was something different: the unconscious, virtually inaudible signals of status that we all receive and interpret.

Accents, too, convey position, with Southern and Ivy League accents going in and out of fashion. And where you shop, whether Safeway for the thrifty or Whole Foods, which is reassuringly more expensive, contains a status message that customers understand and endorse. Even frugality can convey prestige: your homegrown organic veggies can burnish your environmental credentials when placed alongside someone else's supermarket frozen carrots.

When I lived in London and worked in broadcasting, three questions could triangulate your position in the pecking order with pinpoint accuracy: What do you do? Where do you live? Where did you go to university? Answers to these questions identified class, income, and prospects—everything anyone needed to know about your social status.

These differences used to be denoted by class—as so perfectly articulated by John Cleese, Ronnie Barker, and Ronnie Corbett:

CLEESE: I look down on him because I am upper-class.

BARKER: I look up to him because he is upper-class, but I look down on him because he is lower-class. I am middle-class.

CORBETT: I know my place....

CLEESE: I have got innate breeding, but I have not got any money. So sometimes I look up to him.

CORBETT: I still look up to him because, although I have money, I am vulgar.

These days, however, pecking orders are less stable and inherently more volatile. Those with money may lose it overnight; those with jobs may lose them overnight as well. And we all belong to more than one pecking order: a clerk at work may be a lay minister in church, while a bank executive may feel, in the company of artists, that he has nothing of interest to contribute.

The competition for acceptance, attention, and admiration is never more intense than during adolescence, when identity can feel fragile. A fascinating observational study of high school students mapped their pecking orders to try to identify whether social competition might be implicated in teenage smoking. When the researchers interviewed the kids, every one of them, without prompting, described which of their friends were on top, falling, moving up, in the middle, at the bottom, or cast out. Quite voluntarily, they described their social world as inherently vertical and they could "recognize, differentiate and label their peers in terms of status, prestige and popularity." From the information they received, the researchers could map the teenagers on the same diagrams, with the same accuracy, as Schjelderup-Ebbe had applied to his chickens.

Pecking order and smoking were closely linked. The largest group of smoking teenagers were the "top" girls, who took up smoking, the researchers concluded, because it made them stand out as self-confident and independent. But what was most intriguing about this study was its identification of where the stress levels were greatest. Being in the middle offered security; those girls were least susceptible to social pressures when it came to smoking. The positions in the pecking order that experienced extreme stress were at the top (those who were afraid of losing the prime position) and the bottom (those who were afraid of dropping out entirely).[14]

Competitive pressures manifest themselves in different ways in different eras. Smoking, promiscuity, intelligence, energy, violence, lethargy—all these behaviors have been fashionable at some time as young people strive for status and identity. This competition is pervasive and constant and can become addictive. In her brilliant memoir *Wasted*, Marya Hornbacher described the social contests to be thin.

> Starving is the feminine thing to do these days, the way swooning was in Victorian times. My generation and the last one feign disinterest in food. We are "too busy" to eat, "too stressed" to eat. Not eating, in some ways, signifies that you have a life so full, that your busy-ness is so important, that food would be an imposition on your precious time.[15]

When Hornbacher attended a boarding school for gifted, artistic teenagers, her giftedness as a writer was immediately obvious. But her talent was not enough to protect her from status contests within the intense community of the school.

"When you get to school," she tells me, "everybody has talent, and you are a fish among fish. On the talent front, you're trying to compete for a limited number of positions. As adolescents, we took that at such a literal level. If I don't make it, I am *nothing,* so I have to make it. At the level of appearance and weight at Interlochen and Choate and Cranbrook, the girls are profoundly in competition with who can have the perfect body."[16]

For Hornbacher, starving allowed her to rise in the pecking order; succumbing to temptation—eating—meant humiliation. Even when she ended up in the hospital, what she calls her "competitive vanity" didn't stop; it escalated. Eating disorders, she tells me, become a kind of endgame in which the most successful die.

"That is how you win. Being on units where people said, 'I had a heart attack when I was fourteen.' 'Well, I had one when I was twelve. I watched a girl die.' 'Well, I didn't die when I did that. I had liver failure and I was okay...."

Hornbacher was gifted, determined, and lucky. She had true insight and, at some point, decided to live. She realized, she says, that starving to death was "completely stupid and chicken-shittish of me." What makes Hornbacher remarkable isn't her anorexia but her insight. Eating disorders have the highest mortality rate of any mental illness. Five to 10 percent of anorexics die within ten years of contracting the disease; 18 to 20 percent will be dead after twenty years, and only 30 to 40 percent ever fully recover. And this isn't just a problem for girls: an increasing proportion of those suffering from food disorders—currently some 15 percent—are male. Moreover, one unexpected consequence of other ethnicities acquiring more wealth and status is that now men and women of all races compete to lose weight. Eating disorders in China, once unknown in that country, are now deemed to be at US levels.[17]

To Hornbacher, the cost of this social contest is twofold. First, there is permanent physical damage, such as heart damage and infertility. Second, there is invisible damage from the way extreme social competition concentrates so much energy and attention on the individual that it kills the ability to collaborate. With so much emphasis on self, thinking about, appreciating, or connecting with anyone else becomes impossible for the person with an eating disorder. For Hornbacher, the competition to be the best at starving imposed a form of tunnel vision that shrank her perspective and stunted not just her physical but her imaginative growth.

"At Interlochen, creativity was fundamentally disabled by competition. The competitive nature of the school deadened that collaborative spirit.

There's an equation people make. If you are in a constant state of competition, you know how you'll win, how you'll get to the top of the tree. But you can't do anything else. There's no room, no capacity for anything, anyone else."

Extreme competition, of the kind Hornbacher describes and experienced, is fundamentally antisocial because self-interest overwhelms concern for anyone else. Such extreme individualism becomes uncreative because it can't see or respond to others. And because competing for status easily becomes addictive, Hornbacher says, it drives you to greater extremes, compels you to take bigger and bigger risks. This is the dark side of empowerment: if you can be or do anything—if the game of life is yours to win or lose—then losing must all be your fault.

"The real world makes me feel impotent … a computer malfunction, a sobbing child, a suddenly dead cellphone battery—the littlest hitch in daily living feels profoundly disempowering," Ryan van Cleave wrote in his memoir *Unplugged*. "Playing *World of Warcraft* makes me feel godlike."[18]

A gifted writer and a thoughtful teacher, van Cleave conformed in no way to the cliché of the nerd or the anorak. Yet he became addicted to computer games, sometimes spending up to sixty hours a week playing them. He had a dream job at an American university and a pregnant wife whom he loved. But nothing in his real world could possibly deliver the unalloyed sense of achievement he derived from computer games.

"Being a winner, you have to have incredible self-esteem, and I thought I was getting it through the game," van Cleave tells me. "Also that satisfaction—the OCD in all of us—of accomplishing a task. That feeling of completion and pleasure. The games are built so that the reward system continuously offers you carrots and better carrots so you feel like you are winning. And then there are leader boards so you have a public, worldwide arena for your achievements. People know who plays with the best group, who is best in the group; people are very aware of them. They're much clearer, much more absolute, than anything the real world delivers."

The games and the status he won felt so rewarding that van Cleave neglected his wife, his newborn child, and his working relationships. The status of the virtual world felt infinitely more empowering than the havoc he was leaving behind "IRL" (in real life). The game gave him intrinsic rewards ("I did better today than yesterday") and external rewards ("Everyone can see how great I am") in a way that the real world never could.

Van Cleave's addiction wasn't accidental. It was very deliberately cultivated, as all computer games are designed specifically to play on our hunger
for rewards and status.

"As a games designer, competitiveness is a crucial element. In single-
player games, you want to be able to boast to your friends. In multi-player
games, your score is where everyone can see it."

Noah Falstein is an engaging enthusiast, a veteran of the games industry. Tall and balding, with a small graying goatee and piercing brown eyes,
he exudes intellect and critical thinking. Perhaps what is most surprising
about him is his calm: he may build adrenaline-inducing software, but quiet
reflection is far more his own style. Falstein was one of the first employees at
Lucasfilm Games, where he was instrumental in crafting many of the rules
and language now standard in online and computer gaming.

"Addictive cycles are kind of dismaying," he concedes. "There's a fine line
between pleasure and addiction in many things. Games are treading that
line, and we designers will confess that we look for ways to make games more
addictive. It's one of those ethical dilemmas we have big discussions about.

"The games all have compulsion loops. It's a really disturbing term, but
we build them in, and it makes games really good. We use a hill-climbing
algorithm: Start with a low skill and challenge level and increase it gradually.
If you increase too slowly, you wander into boredom; if you increase the
skill level too fast, they give up. In games we draw it as a vibrato, a wavy line.
You get a break and an extra challenge. Brain research suggests it works like
physical training—glucose depletion and recovery. Don't give it every ten
seconds—mix it up! Sometimes there will be big rewards after three hours.
People become game widows. They're hanging on because they don't know
when there might just be a big reward, and they have to have it."

In his quest for status, van Cleave was as addicted to winning as Hornbacher had been to starving. Indeed, he was so concerned about winning
that he forgot everyone else: after seven years of dedicated gaming, his wife
threatened to leave, his kids hated him, and his career hung by a thread. He
had spent real money buying swords and armor for his avatar and used up
irreplaceable time trying to secure esteem and success. With huge difficulty
and discipline, he pulled himself back into real life, where he has stayed ever
since, chastened and mildly in awe of how far he went.

"I am deeply relieved to be out of it. Because there was no reason for it to
end; you can play *World of Warcraft* forever—and I think, at one stage, that's
what I might have done, might have wanted to do! My wife had no confidence I'd ever be able to quit."

What van Cleave and Hornbacher both discovered, and nearly sacrificed their lives to, was the insatiability of status contests. Because the rewards are all relative, because there will always be someone who's done better, won more, achieved more, satisfaction cannot but prove elusive. Social psychologists call this the "hedonic treadmill" and are quick to point out that it never makes people happy.

Running software companies during the Internet boom, I saw the hedonic treadmill play out on an epic scale. I watched with fascination as many people around me became suddenly very rich. At first, their cars got newer, bigger, and more expensive. Then they invariably moved house and often got a newer, younger wife. Yachts came next. Then, for the few, a plane. Then a better plane. My own standard of living was improving fast too, but what I came to understand (which I had not known before) was that there was no ceiling to this hierarchy. Status is always relative, never absolute.

"I can show you billionaires in their fifties who are still trading because they don't want to fall behind. They have a huge fear of losing day to day, and they want to wake up every day feeling that they are going to win, just like any athlete."

Michael Karp is the obsessive managing partner of Options Inc., which is primarily an executive search firm. Karp made his name advising banks and hedge funds on how much to pay their employees. When companies decide how to allocate their bonus pool, it's Karp they will call to find out what their competitors are paying.

Karp himself—talking fast and furiously, glancing at his Blackberry, tuning into conversations outside in the hallway—is insatiable. As we sat in a glassed-in conference room full of hard edges—polished, green marble table, black leather chairs, glass doors—he was eager to describe the raw energy on which his business runs.

"Relativities—it's massive. Comparison with each other? Massive! That's why we are in business, because we know who makes more. That's what we do. We talk to people all the time. Where are you? What are you making? We have all that information. So when a client comes to us and wants to know what to pay—we can tell them how much more they're going to have to pay to get the people they want."

On the day we met, the *Wall Street Journal* had just published a story about the top five hedge fund managers of 2012.[19] Karp was excited; he knew them all, and he knew just how they'd respond.

"'Course they'll be thrilled. Except the ones that aren't there—they'll be pissed! But I know those five, I know how they made their money; it's all sub-sub-prime! They're all watching each other. They all want to know: What's the other guy doing? How's he making his money?"

Karp pounds his hand into his fist and talks furiously. Next to him sits Jessica Lee, an elegant tall Asian American who analyzes data about pay and bonuses from all over the world.

"Anything human is relative," says Lee. "Pay has become—the curve is steeper. When I look at compensation for traders, before 2008 you would see the midpoint and the average within the same range. Now a whole range isn't helpful anymore. Following the crisis, you have more losers and fewer winners.

"It is excruciating to go through what four thousand people have earned and to silo them into specific categories so you can analyze and compare them," says Lee. "It's excruciating because you could be a senior vice president at one bank and director level at another bank, and so the titles may be different but still they are direct competitors. It's very labor-intensive."

Lee perseveres with her excruciating work for two reasons. The data is a valuable product—by so meticulously picking through the numbers, Lee makes it possible to do side-by-side comparisons between individuals, organizations, responsibilities, and productivity. The result is an annual report that Options sells for $11,000 a copy. Moreover, when Options itself wants to recruit someone, knowing exactly what everyone else earns gives the firm more power in pay negotiations. Options is not the only organization that collects data on compensation—there is a whole industry of compensation consultants—but it does so more comprehensively than most of its competitors. Karp does it compulsively.

"I have loads of competitors—Egon Zender, Spencer Stuart, all the big guys. They've all been around longer than I have, they're bigger than I am. But I never stop working. Today's Wednesday—I've already done two black-tie dinners this week. I have four more—and it's only October. November, December, big black-tie months. I'll talk to everyone, give everyone my card. We never stop. We're 24/7. That's how we get the data, and that's how we win."

What matters most about money—and forms the basis of Karp's hyperactive business—is relativities. Absolute amounts do not, in themselves, bestow status. For that, you have to be confident that you are getting more than the next guy. This is why pay becomes an insatiable issue: what matters isn't getting enough but getting more.

But winning delivers social status only if it is visible to people who know how to read the signs. While a great deal of charitable giving may be altruistic, it isn't only altruistic. It is also a public proclamation of status, as meaningful as appearing on *Fortune*'s lists of the richest people in the world. Donors don't just want to give; most of them need to see their names carved on the walls of buildings—which is why naming rights command such a huge price tag.

"I think that the honors system shouldn't be ignored in this context. That has been a powerful motivator for some people in the way they behaved. If they made huge amounts of money and could use the charitable side of the company—their ultimate aim was status, recognition, in England it's a peerage. It is a very powerful driver."

I'll call the speaker Russell Stevens, because he doesn't want to be identified. A punctilious, mild-mannered man, he enjoyed a highly successful career in financial services. But after thirty years, he walked away, disgusted by the widespread mis-selling of mortgages and insurance products to people who didn't need them and couldn't afford them. What drove such aggressive selling, he says, wasn't greed or anything to do with shareholders. From his vantage point, the desire for bigger and bigger profits was driven entirely by senior executives' desire for personal prestige and social status. If you made enough money and gave enough—visibly—to charity, then a peerage would surely follow.

"They were *all* honored," Stevens says of his former bosses. "Status was a very powerful driver: gongs, titles meant an awful lot, and I know it influenced the way my boss and all his colleagues operated. Certain charities we sponsored, certain meetings and facilities given to different organizations, quite significant amounts of money involved in that. And it worked! I'm not saying they didn't care about the cause—sometimes they did, sometimes they didn't. That's what lay behind a lot of bad moves: endowments, subprime, you name it. You have to generate the revenue to earn the status to get the visibility to get the gong. It only works if it is public, which is why none of this was ever anonymous—that wouldn't have served the purpose."

Stevens is angry about an industry that he used to be proud of, but which he feels has been taken over by individuals who use companies entirely for their own ends. What drives them, he insists, isn't ambition; they have no higher purpose or inspiring goal. They merely seek social dominance for themselves. Stevens is a gentle dissident, speaking without personal rancor or grievance. But the hunger for visible superiority, he feels, has fundamentally hijacked entire companies and institutions.

Sir James Crosby, Sir Fred Goodwin, Lord Stevenson, Lord Browne: it is striking that the major business failures of the last ten years have come from corporations whose heads—and figureheads—were ennobled, some of whom remain so to this day.

"More than money," Stevens tells me, "people wanted to be part of the club. The Club, if you get my meaning. If you were in any sense an outsider, if you started to question activities, you rapidly became excluded. That is the most powerful part of competition—I don't want to be left behind."

All social systems—be they organizations, industries, or countries—have hierarchies, formal or informal, implicit or explicit, and they may be very steep or relatively flat. Just how steep an organizational hierarchy is has come to be known as the "power-distance index."

This term was coined by a Dutch academic who studied organizations rather as an anthropologist might. For forty years, Geert Hofstede (and more recently his son) had the unique opportunity to study a vast multinational corporation, IBM, to identify how the cultures of its organizations varied from country to country. Did behavior and values really change from place to place, and if so, what characterized the differences? To be able to think about the work, Hofstede defined the salient characteristics that show how a culture works. One of these was "power-distance," which he used to describe the steepness of a hierarchy and the emotional distance between those who have power and those who do not. What Hofstede discerned was the imbalance in power relationships that Schjelderup-Ebbe and Bales had studied years earlier. But Hofstede sought not just to observe and diagram this imbalance, but to measure it.

Today you can follow the Hofstedes' findings wherever you travel, using a handy iPhone app, CultureGPS: the higher the score, the steeper the pyramid.[20] The US power-distance rating is 40; the United Kingdom is rated at 35 and Canada at 39. Analyzing countries like France (68), Russia (93), China (80), and Malaysia (104), Hofstede saw that in these societies, wealth, power, skills, and status invariably go together. The powerful enjoy great privilege and often come from the same families. Their societies are characterized by economic inequality (often bolstered by the tax system), and the exercise of power depends on social or financial dominance. In societies like this, you can predict that doctors will typically be treated as superiors by their patients and teachers will be regarded as gurus handing down knowledge. Power-distance typifies most working and personal relationships, and corporate pecking orders typically mirror the social hierarchies of the countries in which they are based.

"In the large-power-distance situation," Hofstede wrote, "superiors and subordinates consider each other as *existentially unequal;* the hierarchical system is based on this existential inequality."[21] Leaders in these kinds of organizations are typically autocratic; when they do well, they're seen as good fathers. Visible power matters both to them and to their employees; their expensive cars confer vicarious status.

You can describe a great deal about a culture—whether of a company or a country—by observing the distance between the powerful and the powerless. That distance always carries a cost, and the greater the distance the higher the social costs.

In the 1970s, when Michael Marmot conducted his famous studies of over ten thousand Whitehall civil servants, he showed that those at the bottom of pecking orders experienced the greatest stress and, with it, worse health outcomes.[22] Men in the lowest grades of work—such as messengers and doorkeepers—had death rates three times higher than those of men in the highest grades. Although some of this difference was subsequently explained by lifestyle choices—diet, smoking—those alone did not explain away more than one-third of the increased heart disease rates in lower-grade workers. Power-distance had a direct impact on their physiological and psychological well-being. Power protected the mighty in quite real, physical ways, and distance left the powerless vulnerable and exposed to physical risk.

More recently, fMRI studies have refined this work, confirming Marmot's finding that stress is worst at the bottom—but only in a stable hierarchy, like Whitehall in the 1970s. When social systems become more volatile and subject to greater change and reorganization, as has happened recently, then, just as with the teen girls, the stress concentrates at the bottom and the top. Dominant people fear losing position; subordinate people fear being cast out altogether.[23]

What's more, we all have a remarkably acute sense of where we stand. In a study that examined the relationship between socioeconomic status, stress, and health, participants were shown a ladder of ten rungs and asked to indicate where they placed themselves in society. Their *subjective* sense of where they stood turned out to be a better predictor of stress-related health outcomes than any objective data about them.[24]

This finding has clear costs as far as health care is concerned, but it also has implications for our ability, individually or in organizations, to capture and use the productive creativity we are each capable of. Very steep hierarchies convey a severe, implicit, and constant social threat: the shame of falling down or out. The pressure that these cultures exert on individuals makes it very difficult for them to think. And that is something we have known—or should have known—for over one hundred years.

The field of psychology rarely produces what it is confident enough to call laws. But that is exactly what happened in 1905 when two scientists, Robert Yerkes and John Dodson, got together to study stress. Using what they called "dancing mice," they put their subjects into a nest box wired with electricity. The box had two doors, one white and one black. Using a slight electric shock, they asked, could they teach the mice to discriminate between the two doors? Yes, they could; in fact, the creatures' learning increased with the intensity of the shock.

But then came the second and more complex version of the experiment: would the same hold true when the mice had to discriminate between black and gray, a more subtle distinction? The results here resembled a bell curve. The mice learned well with a mild shock, but far less efficiently with an intense shock.[25] These findings became known as the Yerkes-Dodson Law, which states that stress can enhance learning on an easy task, but it will impair learning on a more difficult task.

We've only recently begun to understand why Yerkes-Dodson has achieved the status of a law. Any complex task requires a lot from your brain: working memory, executive processing, decision-making, and divided attention. But stress specifically impairs the functioning of the prefrontal cortex, where we do our thinking, and of the hippocampus, which is responsible for coordinating all the different mental activities required to solve a problem. So when we feel deeply threatened, we may have all the mental capacity we need, but we just can't quite pull it all together.

Hierarchies reinforce what those at the top have, but also what those at the bottom lack. Sendhil Mullainathan, a Harvard economist, and Eldar Shafir, a Princeton psychologist, call the latter a "scarcity mind-set," and they have documented the degree to which it creates tunnel vision, narrowing perspective and shortening time horizons. The anxiety provoked by a sense of scarcity is enough, they argue, to lower an individual's IQ by as much as losing a night's sleep, which in itself is worse than being over the legal alcohol limit.[26]

The high stress of steep hierarchies makes it both harder to think and riskier to dissent. In most organizations full of smart, informed people who have been recruited and trained at great cost, the biggest problem is surfacing the knowledge that they have. Research into organizational silence shows that most executives have information, issues, or concerns that they never voice, either because they fear retribution or because they hopelessly feel that whatever they say won't make any difference. We've seen this play out repeatedly in scandals in the Catholic Church, in banks, and in insurance companies—organizations full of knowledge that no one dared articulate. The steeper the hierarchy, the harder it is for an individual to be heard, for knowledge to surface, and for debate to take place. This is just one reason why academic Marianne Jennings included "fear and silence" as one of her seven signs of ethical collapse in organizations.[27]

The costs of steep hierarchies are therefore extremely high: not only are health outcomes worse for individuals, but there is less creativity, innovation, and productivity, and even less credibility, for the organization as a whole. And there is another cost, one that is harder to see but critically important: good ethical judgment. Moral and ethical questions are, of course, particularly complex. We know that they are cognitively very expensive and that, when people are tired or distracted, ethical distinctions are some of the first that they fail to make. So it isn't surprising to see that high-power-distance environments, which are stressful and threatening, are associated with higher levels of corruption.

When Hofstede compared his data with Transparency International's Corruption Perception Index, he found that exporters from countries with a higher power-distance index paid more bribes. They had both the power to do so and the comfort of knowing that no one around them would protest or stop them. But what we also see in all walks of life, from school to high finance, is that when people feel under competitive social stress, when their backs are against the wall, they are more likely to cheat. Hypercompetitive people in particular are associated with poor ethics because, for them, winning is so critical.[28] In social systems where the difference between success and failure is acute, in steep hierarchies with maximum power at the top and none at the bottom, fixing the game can seem safer than playing it. And even those who might wish to change the game find it impossible to be heard. Whistleblowers emerge from large, steep hierarchies because silence is pervasive and speaking up is dangerous and rare.

As corruption is exposed in institution after institution—from schools to churches, sports organizations to financial services—we have to ask ourselves how responsible we are for creating the conditions in which this was bound to occur. Competitive social orders make winning simultaneously more important and riskier than ever before. The stakes go up, but security disappears; stress increases, and our ability to think declines. We find our-selves trapped in a compulsion loop of our own design: the more competitive a society, the steeper the hierarchy and the greater the inequality—which in turn makes the competition more ferocious.

This problem of power goes some way toward explaining some of the aber-rant behavior observed in very powerful people: the sexual exploits of Dom-inique Strauss-Kahn, John Browne lying under oath, or the sexting antics of Anthony Weiner. Power makes people feel more confident, more likely to view other people as a means to their own ends and more entitled: after all, as winners, they deserve prizes. Academic research has further found that those with power are more likely to act in ways that disregard conventions, morals, and effects on others and that power is a predictor of sexual harass-ment because it disinhibits aggression.[29] In just the same way that firstborn siblings show less refined social understanding—because they can get atten-tion without it—so more powerful people often demonstrate less social finesse because they think they don't need it. Status, pay, and power create a sense of imperviousness, which is exactly what Anthony Salz's inquiry into Barclays Bank found: "Hiring the best talent in a highly competitive interna-tional market (and during a bubble period) ... pay contributed significantly to a sense among a few that they were somehow unaffected by the ordinary rules. A few investment bankers seemed to lose a sense of proportion and humility."[30]

After four decades of research, Hofstede has concluded that his power-distance index is becoming more polarized; steep hierarchies are getting more vertiginous as economic inequality has become more pronounced.[31] "Increases in wealth may reduce power distances but only if and where they benefit an entire population," Hofstede wrote in 2010. "Since the last decade of the twentieth century, income distribution in some wealthy countries, led by the United States, has become more and more uneven: wealth increases have benefited disproportionally those who were very wealthy already. This has the opposite effect: it increases inequality in society, not only in eco-nomic terms but also in legal terms. This kind of wealth increase therefore also *increases* power distances."[32]

While it's been recognized for a long time that government policy in both Britain and America has led to a concentration of wealth at the top of the pecking order, the theoretical justification has been that the wealth would trickle down. This, after all, seemed to be the gist of Adam Smith's argument that even though the rich are driven by self-interest, they are also "led by an invisible hand to make nearly the same distribution of the necessaries of life, which would have been made, had the earth been divided into equal portions among all its inhabitants, and thus without intending it, without knowing it, advance the interest of the society."[33] On that basis it is argued that, if you cut taxes for the rich, they will spend their additional money and this will trickle down into society, creating jobs, which create more spending and thus generate growth, making everyone better off. With its ancient pedigree, "trickle-down" economics makes intuitive sense (even if the term was coined by a comedian, Will Rogers). The only problem with trickle-down economics is that it turns out not to be true.

When economists Thomas Piketty, Emmanuel Saez, and Stefanie Stantcheva studied the real numbers over a period of fifty years in eighteen OECD countries, they found that lower tax rates not only failed to promote growth but created greater inequality. Allowing the rich to get richer was associated with greater income inequality, not faster growth. "Lower top tax rates," they found, led to "top earners [bargaining] more aggressively for higher pay." Their gain wasn't everyone's gain, it was someone else's loss, and lower tax rates didn't promote growth but rather exacerbated inequality.[34]

The costs of this inequality, as Richard Wilkinson and Kate Pickett demonstrate in *The Spirit Level,* are pervasive and profound: poor mental and physical health, weaker communities, higher crime rates, increasing obesity, poorer educational achievement, weaker friendships, and greater violence. Students who live in states with greater economic inequality are more likely to search for help with cheating on exams or try to buy term papers.[35] Steep hierarchies and inequality break the social contract, separating those with power from those with no power at all. What holds true for countries pertains to any unequal social group, whether it is a corporation, a charity, a club, or a gang. Extreme hierarchies—rich/poor, powerful/impotent—undermine and disable the social stability they purport to preserve. As competition widens the gulf between winners and losers, aberrant behavior proliferates; smoking, anorexia, plastic surgery, lying, cheating, mis-selling, insider trading, and corruption become the by-products of ferocious social competition.

Even Pope Francis (who must know about power-distance firsthand) has acknowledged that trickle-down, "which has never been confirmed by the facts," doesn't work but contributes to inequality.[36] But there are societies that already know this. Hofstede also analyzed countries characterized by low power-distance, such as Finland (33), New Zealand (22), and Austria

(11). In these societies, skills, wealth, power, and status do not invariably go together. Power is based on expertise, and the tax system is designed to reduce income differentials. Political and social power come not from dominance but from the ability to secure the participation and collaboration of others.

In these societies, patients treat doctors as equals and students treat their teachers as equals. Education is seen as depending on two-way communication, and teachers expect to see initiatives coming from students. This is strikingly observable in the Finnish schools, where teachers and students alike are learners. Equally, in companies characterized by low power-distance, employees aren't afraid of their bosses, they are prepared to speak up, argue, and acknowledge mistakes, and they typically prefer a more consultative style of decision-making. The emotional distance between managers and workers is far smaller. In organizations like this, smart leaders don't turn up in fancy new cars or planes.

While high-power-distance cultures have become more extreme, their low-power counterparts have become yet more gentle. Hofstede relishes a story about the king of Sweden being unable to pay for goods in a store when he found himself with a checkbook but no identification. Only when citizens came to his rescue, using their coins to identify him, was the shop assistant willing to accept the king's check, but not without first taking note of his address. We may think that the association of wealth with status is inevitable, but it isn't.

The power-distance spectrum that Hofstede analyzed in such detail shows that human pecking orders aren't fixed; they reflect and enact particular values at a particular time. Our love affair with competition, the belief that contests will identify and elevate the best, has produced a social structure that not only fails to deliver prosperity but afflicts us with its opposites: volatility, stress, corruption.

But we don't have to live in the chicken yard. Many great projects succeed not despite their lack of a power structure but because of it. Mike North is one such super-collaborator. By day he works as the chief technology officer of NukoToys, which combines real-world toys, like playing cards, with computer games such as *Monsterland* and *Animal Planet*. For most people, that would be enough, but Mike is a driven individual and he is always looking for more ways to use and extend his knowledge. So he volunteered to work with Reallocate, a nonprofit that brings together engineers to solve humanitarian problems.

"Engineers," North tells me, "are the people who design and build the world; they want to create things and do good. But in the last few decades, if you are a good engineer, you get promoted and become a manager and you never do engineering again! And engineers really miss that. So they come into Reallocate to get back to hands-on work, creating something very tangible. That's meaningful in a way that just being part of a corporate ladder isn't."

At Reallocate, North was approached by a charity, MiracleFeet, which helps children born with a clubfoot. Could Reallocate's engineers help solve one of their problems?

"The kid in Nicaragua comes in to see the doctor," North tells me. "He's eleven, he's traveled with his dad, and that meant riding a horse for three hours and a bus for six hours. When they see the doctor, he says, 'You have to come in every week for six weeks.' Well, that won't work! You need something he can take away, understand, and use by himself. You can't go in and impose technology; that never works."

To solve the problem, North assembled a team of Reallocate engineers at TechShop, a workshop open to anyone who wants to make something. When you join TechShop, you get access not just to great tools but also to the rich wealth of knowledge that belongs to the people who work alongside you. TechShop's founders believe passionately that inventors have to work openly together to learn from each other and grow. For North's project, TechShop brought in Autodesk, which provided the team with prototyping software, and Objet, which has 3-D printers that can be used to make product models. Without hierarchy or structure, everyone piled on to produce a foot brace for kids so easy to use that repeat visits to the doctor aren't necessary. Sharing their tools and their ideas, the team quickly solved the problem.

"The final, working Miracle Brace is a twentieth-generation product," Mike tells me. "But that's why we needed help and why we had to have facilities like TechShop. The old big, corporate, hierarchical engineering model is too slow, too expensive, and it doesn't use the expertise of the people who are going to be living with the final product. Talk to people, understand what they want, prototype as fast as possible, get help and advice and insight from *everybody!* That's how you find your road."

When they thought they were done, North traveled to Nicaragua to test the Miracle Brace on real children. And that was when he realized the power of collaboration: it had taken him beyond self-interest to a place where he could see, and serve, others.

"It didn't all hit me until I was there and I had this magical moment," North says. "All these tools and people came together to help this person I never even knew existed. This is truly life-changing. You realize life is greater than your own."

Most TechShop projects start with entrepreneurs who hope their ideas will spawn profitable companies. But everyone who wants to work there must contribute to the open innovation that is so critical to its spirit. The machines are great—but the contributions of experienced designers, engineers, and craftspeople make the difference.

In some ways, the physical creation of the Miracle Brace was the easy part: the talents of Reallocate, the facilities of TechShop, and the resources of AutoDesk and Objet made that feasible. The hard part of any collaboration is getting everyone generously and selflessly to work together. With no power to make anyone do anything, how did North get his disparate team to work together well enough to make a product that actually worked for people they'd never met?

"I think it helps that you don't have any formal authority—no title, no status," North insists. "Part of communicating as humans—that's what we're working on—is you have to be able to open up as a person."

North now runs a program to help people learn how to design for developing countries. One part of the workshop teaches participants how to be clowns—more Cirque du Soleil, he says, than red noses. It may sound weird, but the kind of communication necessary to collaboration is about replacing power with humanity.

"That's what a clown workshop is," North says. "Open up, be vulnerable, draw in your audience so you can communicate on an emotional level. Drop the PowerPoint; be equals. Community, a sense of communication: that's everything."

North is a highly inventive individual. He invented Reallocate, he was one of the inventors of the Miracle Brace—and he still has a full-time job making toys. But what strikes me most is how inventive he has been in his thinking about how people can work together without formal power structures. Collaborative projects can descend into compromise, conflict, or chaos, but developing a shared sense of vulnerability is a powerful starting point. Clowning together reduces distance so that sharing gets easier and differences—in disciplines and know-how—become assets.

Hofstede always argued that an empowered workforce requires less supervision, but even he might have underestimated just how far that could go. Crowdsourcing—the open call for all or any ideas to solve a problem—is used increasingly to tackle problems as wide-ranging as diabetes, software glitches, and market research questions. It began not with the Internet but with genealogical research: in 1942, the Mormon Church asked its members to provide information about their family backgrounds. But new technology has made it easier, faster, and cheaper to ask for ideas, information, feedback, or funding from a global array of experts and amateurs. Funding platforms like Kickstarter and content platforms like Quora and Media eliminate the distance that often submerges knowledge and insight: anyone with a contribution to make—money, a good idea, past experience, know-how—has a role to play, and unfettered feedback and joint learning are the only rewards for sharing. Like TechShop but usually without face-to-face communication, crowdsourcing is all about tapping the worldwide expertise that often lies buried deep inside corporate pyramids and providing opportunities for brilliant ideas to surface regardless of title or power.

The rise of collaborative networks capable of everything from software and drug development to car-sharing, house-sharing, and personal lending—the so-called sharing economy—has attracted a lot of attention because of the technology it deploys. But the software is not the point. These companies use technology to solve coordination problems, but more importantly, they've captured the public imagination, grown, and succeeded because they speak to the human impulse to connect to one another and share. The software doesn't create that desire, it merely responds to it, while the success of the businesses testifies to the ubiquity and power of mutual interests.

All of the crowdsourcing companies reduce or eliminate the cultural, institutional, and geographic hierarchies that stunt learning and limit experience. The growth and success of these forms of crowdsourcing derive from the fundamental recognition that the best way to develop a new idea or to do great work isn't by hanging on to it for credit, but by sharing it in return for great feedback and contributions. The technology of crowdsourcing might be new, but it responds to a deep human desire to help.

"The way you succeed here is by helping each other. That's really the key value: contribution." Sheona Barlow has worked for W. L. Gore in Dundee for twenty-six years, since she left school at the age of seventeen. She had a summer job as a receptionist but asked so many questions about everything that the plant leader suggested that she study electronic engineering. Eventually the company put her through four years of coursework at the local college, then Open University modules toward a master's of science degree in manufacturing and technology. Along the way, she had two children and worked on all kinds of different projects. What she didn't get was a title.

"At Gore," she explains to me, "it isn't really a pyramid. You work alongside your colleagues and communicate directly. You do your best for them; they do their best for you; everyone works hard. That's it. The most important thing you get isn't a title; it's the recognition and respect from your peers."

Newcomers, like Barlow twenty-six years ago, get sponsors who show them around the organization and try them out on different teams until they find a project they want to work on—and people who want to work with them. The emphasis is on cooperation and autonomy, not rank. People like Barlow thrive in this environment because they're internally motivated—Barlow clearly loves learning—and because they help their colleagues. Although Gore is a large global company, with revenues of some $3 billion, getting to know people there isn't hard because each business unit is limited to a few hundred people. This is an organization deliberately designed to have the lowest possible power-distance.

When Bill Gore founded the business in 1958, his years of working for DuPont had persuaded him that he wanted to do things differently. He didn't want a hierarchy, and he loathed bureaucracy; instead, he sought to create an organization built on trust and collaboration. He believed that people go to work each day to do a good job and want to do the right thing by themselves and by their peers—in other words, that they can be trusted.

Gore's work is the design and manufacturing of high-tech devices. The company has a stellar track record for innovation, having registered over two thousand patents for medical devices, polymer processing, and electronics. Although Gore is famous for Gore-Tex® Fabrics, used to waterproof boots and fabrics, most of its revenue comes from inventing and manufacturing small numbers of highly complex, custom-designed products that often sit inside other gadgets. The Rover that landed on Mars contained cable assemblies and materials made by Gore; mobile phones and airplane black boxes also contain sophisticated technology invented and manufactured by Gore associates.

The company ascribes its remarkable innovativeness to its culture. Everyone can take time to develop their own projects and ideas and can invite others to help them. This freedom is alluring; young associates are warned not to take on too much because what's most highly prized at Gore is each associate's ability to honor his or her commitments.

At Gore, associates are expected to share ideas early and widely. Just as Mike North did so effectively at Reallocate, instead of hanging on to a project in order to defend credit and power, Gore associates are encouraged to put their ideas out where colleagues can see them, add to them, refine them, and challenge them. If an idea elicits no interest, that says a lot. If it provokes debate and discussion, that says even more. Whether or not people want to contribute to an associate's idea depends a lot on how much they like working with that person and how generous and helpful he or she has been to others. None of this has anything to do with how power is wielded in a formal hierarchy. One of the questions engineers with new ideas are asked is: "Who will want to celebrate with you?"

Elixir guitar strings provide a classic example of the Gore process at work. Dave Myers, a Gore associate working on cardiac implants, spent some of his time playing with PTFE, the long molecule that is the water-repellent in Gore-Tex. An avid cyclist, he wondered whether coating his bike spokes with PTFE would repel some of the water and grit that slowed him down. It did—but the market of cyclists eager to shave fractions of a second off their time wasn't big enough for a mainstream product. So Myers applied the same thinking to his other pastime: playing the guitar. Guitar strings go out of tune because of the sweat and oils they absorb from the hands that play them. Might PTFE prove just as successful in repelling those? When he found that it did, Myers called a meeting, and associates gathered to help him develop his new product idea. With a large market for an innovation that represented a significant improvement over existing strings, Elixir guitar strings became an industry standard.

As Barlow showed me around the Dundee plant, the atmosphere was one of relaxed and quiet deliberation. This factory—spectacularly clean and full of concentration—is as far from a black satanic mill as it is possible to get. The pool of work sits on shelves, and it is up to each individual to get it done and move it through the system. Coordinators keep work flowing through, and they check to ensure that no one is struggling. It's easy to ask for help. On the wall is painted a quote from Bill Gore: "Our success, our very survival, depends on having created a society, a family of teams."

Leaders do exist at Gore, but they aren't appointed—they emerge. A leader is defined as someone who, when he or she calls a meeting, people choose to turn up. Barlow became known as a leader because she was great to work with and was a terrific team builder. That capacity emerged naturally; Gore doesn't send people to business schools.

"Leading by example is key," Barlow explains. "We have had examples of leaders who've come in from other companies, from hierarchies, and they think they can direct people and manage them, and the associates say: 'I don't think so.' If a leader thinks the position alone will make people follow, they're wrong. It's all about earning the respect and trust of your colleagues."

One of the few titles in the company belongs to the chief executive. But even this appointment follows the same logic: to run the business, you must have earned the respect and support of the people around you. So when the previous CEO retired, associates were invited to nominate someone they would be willing to follow.

"We weren't given a list of names—we were free to choose anyone in the company," Terri Kelly explains later. "To my surprise, it was me."

Kelly has been with the company all her working life. A mechanical engineer, she started out working on military fabrics. Like all the other associates, she initiated projects that gained traction—and others that never did. But she achieved the CEO role by earning the trust and respect of Gore associates over time. She is a leader only because people choose to follow her.

Key to these relationships at Gore is scale, the rule that no business unit can be more than two hundred people. This makes the relationships and commitments between associates close and personal. And while accountants might argue that this is inefficient, Kelly argues that the benefits it bestows—ease of communication, trust, reciprocity, and innovation—easily outweigh any cost. Gore has never had a single year of losses. This is a cash-rich company where, after three years, associates can become shareholders. After fifteen years, they may trade their shares in or continue to hold them. On retirement, associates receive the cash value of their shares—shares in W. L. Gore don't leave the business.

When he designed his company this way, Bill Gore believed that people are innately collaborative and he was prepared to put his money where his mouth was. Fifty-five years later, Gore continues to be a powerhouse of innovation without having had to alter its remarkable culture. Competition and pecking orders don't explain its success—but their absence might.

Some of the most successful companies in the world deliberately and thoughtfully cultivate the flattest hierarchies they can. Some do so because their founders believe that this drives higher levels of creativity and collaboration; in others the refusal of power is based on the recognition that there is always more knowledge and insight within an organization than at the top.

"I was just signing checks one day and I thought, 'Why am I doing this? I didn't buy these things. I don't know why we needed them. Why do I have the power to do this? It's stupid.'"

Chris Rufer is the founder and CEO of Morning Star, one of the largest producers of tomato-based products in the world. If you're eating ketchup or pasta sauce in the United States, the chances are that you're consuming some of the billion pounds of diced tomatoes or tomato paste that come out of Rufer's company every year. You won't notice that—Morning Star won't be on the bottle—and you won't find anything distinctive about the product. Except the way that it is made.

Rufer is a handsome man, even charismatic. But his own leadership was what bothered him. He thought long and hard about the process that ended with the check in front of him. Between needing something, getting it, and paying for it, a lot of people, rules, and authority intervened. Mulling over some of the core tenets of business—like "the buck stops here"—Rufer decided it was all wrong. Instead of hierarchy and dominance, why didn't companies concentrate on two fundamental ideas: freedom and responsibility? Everyone who worked for him, Rufer thought, should have the freedom to think about how to do their work and the responsibility to figure it out with their colleagues.

"One day, Chris passed around a draft of some of the 'colleague principles,' as he called them. About twenty-four of us sat around in a trailer and talked about it," Doug Kirkpatrick recalls. "We weren't quite sure what it would mean, but I didn't see any downside to it. People should be closer to their own decisions. So we thought it was worth a try."

Producing a billion pounds of tomato products through a decade when prices were mostly falling was difficult and risky. Nevertheless, Rufer introduced—and the whole company developed—a process they call self-management. Morning Star has no hierarchy and no employees. Instead, it has colleagues and colleague principles, chief among which are: a responsibility to make things happen; an agreement to tolerate different values, tastes, moods, and methods; and a commitment to direct communication and negotiation. But the two most profound guiding principles are that everyone must keep their commitments and no one can use force. No one has power *over* anyone else. Dominance is denied.

The Morning Star factory, a maze of pipes, turbines, pumps, and valves outside in the roasting California sunshine, looks more like an oil refinery than a kitchen—and it's just about as dangerous. The roar and smell of the place is overwhelming as pristine hair-netted sorters pick out sticks, worms, and rattlesnakes from the truckloads of fresh produce delivered to the factory every day. Tomatoes are 95 percent water, so every batch has to be cooked, evaporated, and filtered at 212 degrees Fahrenheit until it is a perfect 31 percent solid, sterile enough to be stored outside for years. The lab where samples are tested for color, pH, and bostwick (how thick and viscous the paste is) looks like a pharmaceutical plant. Nothing moves quickly except the tomatoes on a conveyor belt; all the people are quiet and methodical, going about their business without bosses.

The air-conditioned control room monitors the evaporators sitting outside in the hot sun. An array of screens allows a team of just three engineers to manage every stage of the process. Hans has been with Morning Star since 2002. Shaking hands with Hans, a big, solid man, feels like grabbing a brick. He is, his colleagues tell me, a top-notch mechanic; he's also a taxidermist and children's clown in his spare time.

"We have a lot of freedom here. We practice self-management like doctors practice medicine," he tells me. "That doesn't mean we get everything 100 percent. It means we try to keep getting better."

Previously, Hans worked in the navy, where he liked the clarity that came with hierarchy. But at Morning Star what he enjoys is that everything *isn't* explicit.

"Here is fun, because knowledge is the leader; you find the person with the most knowledge and together you make decisions. So you're always learning. In the navy, everyone just took care of their one position. Here I man the plant. My colleagues man the plant. If there's a problem, everyone will run to it. Everyone is always learning, building their knowledge. We all just want to do what needs to be done better."

Standing in beige overalls, and often glancing at computer screens behind him, Hans regales me with the details and nuances of producing such a vast quantity of tomato paste and the constant efforts to become ever more efficient.

"Every winter, we come up with new projects—ways to be more efficient or to improve the machinery. We can bid for money for capital projects, and then the people who know most, or will be most impacted, they decide if it's a good idea. If we have the money, then we vote on whether it's worth it.

"Today we're low on tons—trucking hasn't delivered, so we've had to slow down. So we want to figure out how to make that smoother. We want to go fast. It's wasteful otherwise, and we can't 'ketchup'!" Hans has obviously made this joke many times, but his delight in talking about his work remains palpable.

"We all do lots of psychometric tests—like Myers-Briggs—because we all want to understand how best to work with each other. You have to understand the next person to get alone with them. I'm an ESTJ, and everyone knows it. It's great because everyone learns how to deal with each other."

Doug Kirkpatrick, who worked with Rufer in the early days of Morning Star, now runs the Self-Management Institute, which attempts to explain and evangelize the learning developed by the company. He readily acknowledges that it can be hard for outsiders to understand how to navigate the company; without the titles of a formal hierarchy, buyers and vendors can find it difficult to know quite who does what.

"But what they find is that working with us is like working with a partner. We aren't out to screw them. We work the same way with our customers and vendors that we do with each other. We want everyone to be responsible, to hold to their commitments, and to understand each others' needs."

Kirkpatrick also concedes that this kind of low-power-distance culture doesn't work for everyone.

"Some people have been hired who understand what we are doing at an intellectual level, and they'll profess agreement. But at some point they decide, 'I can have my little island of hierarchy and I'm going to set myself up as king of the hill and work around this self-management stuff.' But the culture just overwhelms them, because everyone here understands they don't have to be dictated to! So when that power play fails, that's the beginning of wisdom: that person either gets it or leaves. Nobody here can fire anyone—but anyone can request that someone leave."

When it comes to pay, the company doesn't benchmark against its competition. Employing about four hundred people, Morning Star pays an average salary of more than $90,000 and offers a wide range of benefits. Its chief attraction, however, lies in employees' ability to gain the respect of their peers and the opportunity to learn.

"If you're living up to your colleague commitments," Kirkpatrick says, "you'll get a cost-of-living increase. If you think you've earned more because you've created some innovation or you can make a business case, there's a team that will consider it. Or projects you've come up with, you can come and talk about it. You are a self-managed, independent businessperson here, so if you want something above and beyond, you can make the case."

Kirkpatrick acknowledges that running a big, complex factory twenty-four hours a day with four hundred people, high temperatures, and significant danger isn't easy. But it works. The team that mans the factory built the factory. They take pride in running it and improving it. And no one has a boss.

"I don't think anyone here feels that they work for Chris," Kirkpatrick says. "They work for each other, for the process, for the knowledge. It is a huge jugular paradigm shift. Especially if you are used to a command-and-control hierarchy. You have to relinquish that power intentionally."

Reluctance to give up power is how Kirkpatrick explains the fact that, notwithstanding his evangelism, few companies have emulated Morning Star. Many are keen to learn, but most lack the courage to abandon status and dominance. Not so Eileen Fisher, who has slowly but steadily over the last ten years handed over leadership and ownership of her clothing company to the employees. She has done so in part because she appreciates that doing so ensures the company's longevity, but also because of a profound commitment to collaboration between every part of the business. The transition hasn't been without its challenges—fabric designers weren't used to talking to finance people, and decision-making could be slow. But having learned how to make space, accord respect, and listen to one another is now how the company explains its exceptional success. In the fashion industry, which is characterized by big egos and power plays, this is remarkable—as is Fisher's regret now that she named the company after herself. After all, she tells me, the company is really all the people who make it work.

In Chicago, it was fully fourteen years before the software firm 37Signals hired a manager, its earlier reluctance driven by a desire to give everyone in the company maximum freedom and responsibility. In North Carolina, Nucor Steel trains all its employees to be leaders and to think of leadership as a form of service to others. New managers aren't expected to issue edicts, dominate meetings, or create task forces, but to listen, share, and learn together. The company does no performance appraisals but lists every one of its seven thousand employees in its annual report: a powerful way of articulating where productivity really comes from.

In South Africa, Paul Harris brings a fiercely egalitarian approach to one of the most highly regarded financial institutions in the country, FirstRand Bank. He does so because, just like Gore and Rufer, he is convinced that the only way to get the best from people is to know what is really going on—something that's virtually impossible inside steep hierarchies. He's so committed to these principles that he wrote them down in what he calls his management credo.

"I work *with* people; they do not work *for* me. I am obsessive about understanding market trends and the business and how we can improve it. Therefore, I try to talk to anyone, because everybody has something to offer if they are given a chance. My attitude is that I have never learned anything from someone who agrees with me. So I welcome alternative views and new ideas—however crazy, because to get a good idea you must discard lots of bad ones. This way I harness the collective wisdom of the organization.

"I believe that the more power you give away the more you have, because when people are trusted and empowered, they take ownership and will not let you down. I judge people by their ability and confidence to come up with new ideas. To express their views irrespective of whether they conform or not to conventional wisdom. Progress depends on new ideas and challenging the status quo. I judge management by their ability to harness the wisdom of people below them and thereby empower them. Not by the number of people they control but rather about the number they liberate."

FirstRand is known across southern Africa as an innovator and a trusted resource. As early as 2000, the bank introduced eBucks, an electronic payment system that brought buyers together, led the introduction of electronic banking, and pioneered the use of cell phones for financial transfers in Africa. Yet when you talk to Harris, it is to the energy and enthusiasm of his people that he consistently pays tribute. What drove them? What drives him? The desire to do something better.

These are all big, complex, creative, and successful businesses that have eliminated or reduced pecking orders in order to liberate the human capacity for creativity and innovation. They flourish by reinforcing the social bonds between people, eschewing the competitive forces that kill creativity, and embracing those that enhance it: fairness, autonomy, freedom, debate. Their example challenges us to reject the extremely high costs of inequality and hierarchy and understand that they aren't a necessary evil but a cost imposed by people whose idea of winning requires unsustainably high levels of loss.

Escaping the stressful addiction of pecking order competition isn't simple. There aren't as many companies like TechShop, Gore, Morning Star, Eileen Fisher, 37Signals, and Nucor as there are people who would like to work in them. The economic crisis has left many people stranded in organizations where they feel they have no choice but to compete to survive. And many manifest a form of Stockholm syndrome: having spent so long a time in these environments, they persuade themselves that they're great. After all, if you've made it to the top through a highly competitive system, it's most unlikely that you will find fault with it.

"Competitiveness was all the time in me," Karl Rabeder recounts to me. "I tried harder, so all my employees had to try harder too."

Rabeder is a tall, birdlike German whom I met on a beautiful, clear spring day in Mallorca. As we sat out in the sunshine, he told me the story of having been raised by a grandmother who always imagined that she would be free if she had more money, more land, more everything. He absorbed that lesson from her, he said, and it pervaded the gift business that he started to build in his twenties.

"I all the time compared myself with the maximum possible. All the things that I thought were possible I wanted to reach and get. It was more or less hopeless. Goals like doing in Austria what I did in Germany—a market ten times bigger—and then we could do the whole of Europe and then the US and then maybe buy a private jet! I asked myself the wrongest of all questions: what is possible? Not: what do I really want? Asking the question gives you a thousand answers, and following those, you lose yourself."

Rabeder's business grew and grew. Was that, I asked him, because he had been a good boss?

"No. Because I did not really see my employees. I didn't see their personality. To be a good boss you have to realize what the work means to everyone. Sometimes I was hard on them, sometimes tolerant. But I tried to turn them into copies of myself. I never knew who they were."

When I first met Rabeder, I wondered whether he would be reluctant to talk about his past, the business that had made him wealthy. But he didn't mind at all, describing it like a foreign country that had been interesting to visit but even better to leave. He had spent the first half of his life, he told me, doing nothing but comparing himself, his company, and his numbers to those around him, always checking where he stood in the pecking order. But that had never taught him to think for himself.

Eventually, in 2009, Rabeder became so unhappy that he sold his company and founded the nonprofit organization Credit, which aims to reduce poverty in South and Central America. In February 2010, he announced that he would donate his entire fortune, including the profits from all of his properties, his car, and his businesses, to his charities.

Today Rabeder has homes nowhere. He rents a small flat in Mallorca and camper vans elsewhere. He runs seminars for people who, like him, want to escape the insatiable pursuit of status and rank and privilege. He is astonished, he says, at how many people languish in the same dilemma: desperate to escape the addiction of competition and to find the freedom they once imagined winning would bestow.

"I now live the maximum freedom I could find. I have friends around the world. A girlfriend. And my freedom. I always thought of myself as a bird who had decided to live a human life. And now I'm free—free as a bird!"

When visiting companies like TechShop, Gore, Morning Star, and Eileen Fisher, I heard the same two words over and over again: trust and freedom. Being trusted gave people the opportunity to think for themselves, to make and learn from mistakes, and to reach out for help. Trust was both what they got and what they gave. And freedom was the reward: not life on a beach or endless parties, but work enriched by others and the social capacity to connect to people without fear, intimidation, or distance. They had escaped the chicken yard.

CHAPTER 5

Keeping Score

Nations have a sense of global pecking order every bit as fierce as the pecking orders among individuals. So in 2000, when Sydney hosted the Olympic Games, the Australians found themselves the butt of many British jokes. Singled out for scorn was the design of the Games medals, which featured the Roman Colosseum. Didn't the ignorant Aussies know the difference between ancient Greece (where the Games were invented) and ancient Rome, where the famous arena stood? As imperious journalists mocked their hosts' lack of a classical education, they conveniently overlooked the fact that the medal design wasn't Australian and had been in use—without comment—since 1928.

To be sure, the design was anomalous. But that it had survived so long was no mere pedantic oversight. The great arena has long been the model for every Olympic stadium since the Games were revived in 1894. Its iconic shape resonates with tradition: throughout Western history, it was in places like this that spectators were entertained by competitors fighting for their lives.

Historians today still can't quite agree on the exact details of the entertainment displayed in the Colosseum; they don't even know whether a "thumbs-up" meant live—or die. The fragments of historical record that remain are centuries apart and don't add up to a single coherent explanation of how and why the building was used. Only one account of a gladiatorial fight survives, a poem by Martial in which the two combatants are so evenly matched that the crowd demands that both be given honorable discharges.

What we do know is that the Roman games were phenomenally expensive, both in financial cost and in lost lives. When the emperor Trajan celebrated his conquest of what is now Romania, he did so with 123 days of shows in which 11,000 animals were killed and 10,000 gladiators fought. Seating was in strict social pecking order, with the richest and most powerful at the front and the poor and disenfranchised high up in the back. Most exhibitions contained a political subtext; the slaying of crocodiles, for example, represented dominion over Egypt. Shows put on by aristocrats were straightforward attempts to gain popularity—not far removed from the aims of politicians and corporate sponsors today. The Colosseum divided opinion; while attendance was usually high, not everyone approved of its spectacles. Seneca, in particular, found the slaughter pointless and corrupting.[1]

Lacking a conclusive account of the building, writers throughout the ages have had the perfect opportunity to construct their own interpretations. Byron found the "gladiators' bloody Circus" a noble wreck, Dickens was glad that the Colosseum was ruined, and Mark Twain mocked it as the birthplace of tawdry entertainment. Only Ridley Scott seems to have imagined it as a place of unbridled courage and outright heroism. For most people, the Colosseum is a daunting, deadly place where competition and entertainment met in a merciless exchange: win and live, or lose and die.

Perhaps the historical anomaly of the Olympic medal was overlooked for so long because the site reflects our ambivalence about intense physical competition for high stakes. To enthusiasts and romantics, elite sports represent the height of human achievement, the glorification of the body and of mental discipline. To spectators, it is showbiz: corporate entertainment or a day out for the family. For others, it represents cruelty, exploitation, and suffering.

Since 2004, Olympic medals have become historically more precise, if poetically less resonant. One side features the goddess Nike with the Panathenaic Stadium, home to the first modern Games in 1894; the image on the obverse is left to the discretion of the host country. What can't be designed out of existence, however, is the huge cost that high-achieving athletes must pay to delight the public. What looks effortless isn't just effortful: like their Roman predecessors, the competition of elite athletes requires that they put their lives on the line.

There was nothing brutal, grim, or romantic about the University of Bath's sports training village. When I visited in the spring before the 2012 Olympics, its glass and steel felt more like an airport than a gladiatorial arena. With high ceilings bathed in sunshine, and swarming with young, healthy, free citizens, the place hummed with energetic intent. Less athletic spectators could watch Olympic aspirants in training while more sociable undergraduates congregated at the café. The food on offer wasn't noticeably healthy, but it was fuel.

Amid the students and coaches sat a quiet young man, eating a sandwich and reading. When he looked up, it was his eyes that drew me in: so dark they seemed to have no whites at all. He wasn't and didn't want to be the center of attention; he was keeping himself to himself. This was Dai Greene, world hurdles champion and a favorite for a medal in the 400-meter hurdles at the Olympics.

Greene is from Wales, and he hadn't come to Bath for the architecture or because the university had the reputation for offering a great social life. He was there to train.

"This is the highest track in the UK," he told me. "You can't beat it for wind and rain. If I can go through this, I can go through anything. I enjoy pushing myself. My mum says it is character building. If I train in crap weather, I can run anywhere."

With his quiet voice and lilting accent, there was nothing superfluous about Greene. At six-one, he was lean, taut, and self-contained. Born in Felinfoel near Swansea, he didn't know many people in Bath; his family and his girlfriend were all back home. He said that everyone was "friendly enough," but the truth was that he didn't have much time for friends. He was in Bath to train six hours a day, six days a week. Nothing else counted.

"What gets me through training is to win medals."

As a boy, Greene had wanted to play soccer—his hero was Ryan Giggs—and he played for Swansea City at the age of thirteen. In his teens, he contracted Osgood-Schlatter disease, a painful condition caused by stress on the tendon attaching the quadriceps muscle in the thigh to the front of the tibia. The disease typically strikes during adolescent growth spurts, but some studies maintain that half of its incidence is provoked by sporting activity.

But Greene loved sports, discovered he had a gift for hurdles, and wanted to go to university, he said, "to prolong the agony." His first big success came in 2005 when he won silver at the European Athletics Junior Championships, with a personal best of 51.14 seconds. The following year he qualified for the senior tournament, but things started to go wrong: injuries and epilepsy caught up with him.

By now, Greene was so dedicated to his sport that, rather than let disease get in the way, he decided to come off of his epilepsy medication and try to control his condition through hard work, determination, and a highly disciplined lifestyle. That wasn't an easy or obvious choice for a young man in his twenties, but Greene was starting to develop a steely determination. In 2007, at the European Athletics U23 Championships, he took the gold medal with a new best—49.58 seconds—despite an ankle injury.

"I had to switch my coach because my training was very one-dimensional and I kept breaking down," he recalls. "Then I moved to Bath, but I still wasn't improving. It was a very dark time. You start to question what you're doing: Are injuries normal? Is everyone getting them? But all the injuries I had were because I was improving so fast—some elements just got left behind."

A year later, in 2009, he set a meet record and a personal best at 48.62 seconds. He led the European rankings for the first time. As Greene explained: "When you watch the 400 hurdles, it looks pretty easy. The guys seem to take it in their stride—that's what the top guys do. But there are 150 strides that are all preplanned, and if I am slow going into one stride, then I've lost two- or three-tenths of a second going in, two- or three-tenths going out. You have to make sure everything is spot-on and you feel 100 percent."[2]

"In athletics," Greene tells me, "you have got to train every day. When things are going well, you think it's easy. And I love pushing myself hard. I'll do an afternoon's training and be absolutely shattered. But I've gone through so much. There's nothing you can throw at me I can't handle."

Greene's mother works as a care assistant in a primary school; his dad is a bricklayer. He says that they work every day and the house is always clean; he has grown up in an atmosphere of quiet dedication. When he talks about his parents, or about his younger brothers still at home, they feel a long way away. When Greene talks about mental toughness, it doesn't feel as though the injuries are all that's on his mind.

Like every athlete, Greene has to balance events like the European championships that bring prestige with the events that bring in money. Physically, no one can do everything on the calendar, so athletes have to decide what matters more: prize money or medals. For Greene, there's no contest.

"I'm not motivated by money at all. In 2009, when I decided to come here, I was living off of ten thousand pounds a year. It is nice to make money because it makes life easier, but training comes first. For me, it's the titles and the medals. They are the highest accolades in sport."

For Greene, competing isn't personal. He knows who his competitors are, but he doesn't pay them much attention. If you look at other people, he thinks, you just get distracted; also, you don't want to give your competitors that edge or the mental support they could get from knowing you're paying attention to them.

"There's only a few seconds—maybe just one second—between first and second place. So you can't give any sign of weakness. It's an intimate space, the call room. I remember one guy, before a race, talked about his flight getting in late, and I thought, 'You're just making yourself feel better, giving yourself excuses.' Twenty minutes later, I beat him. You have to act invincible."

It was impossible not to be moved by Greene: so many setbacks, so much discipline. Beneath his calm understatement, there was so much going on: the determination to overcome his injuries, to control his epilepsy, to stick to the lonely, isolated regime—and to win at the Olympics. That determination filled his life. He focused so exclusively on the seconds and hundredths of seconds that determine the difference between winning and losing that nothing else seemed to exist for him. Every choice he made was defined by whether it contributed to, or detracted from, his goal. While the rest of us might watch our lives unfold day by day, Greene's life was something that wouldn't exist for him until he could look back on it.

"The Olympics are the ultimate, because they are only once every four years and there aren't that many you can take part in during your lifetime. So you don't have many chances. To win one—you just imagine yourself winning, on the podium, listening to the national anthem. It must be the greatest feeling on earth!"

It must be, because the cost for athletes like Greene has been very high. Years of injuries. Years of solitude, running in the cold, the wind, the rain. Years of going home alone each night to watch television, go to bed, get back up, and do more of the same. Years of nothing but thinking about time, the hundredths of a second, the tiny irreducible difference between success and failure.

In January 2012, Greene suffered another injury. It set back his training schedule, but it didn't deter him. In July he was made captain of the British Olympics athletics team after achieving a personal best—47.84—in a Diamond League race in Paris. After seven years of training, he had stripped 3.3 seconds from his time.

At the London 2012 Olympics, it was easy to imagine Greene's victory, but watching the 400 meter-hurdle race was agonizing. Greene had sacrificed so much to be there, and hopes were running high, with observers constantly referring to Lord Burleigh, who'd last taken gold for Britain in

1928. As Greene stood poised in the blocks, he looked wound up tight—and suddenly tiny.

Just fourteen-hundredths of a second—a time gone before you can say it—stood between Dai Greene and his Olympic medal. When the race was finished, he panted on the ground, staring at the results board, willing the numbers to come right, grimacing when they did not. It was, everyone said, such a fast race. Finishing fourth meant no medal, no podium, no national anthem. Nothing. Only later, in tortuous interviews, came praise for the victor. And plans for Rio in 2016.

"The records get faster every year because the training methods, the technology, and the facilities just keep improving. In the next twenty years, you think the records must start to plateau—there must be a point where it stops—but they're still just going up and up. Faster and faster. And every year, there are so many more competitors...."

In the excitement and euphoria that surrounds the Olympic Games, it's easy to forget the simple fact that most participants lose. Out of the 10,820 athletes who took part in the London 2012 Games, only 962—8.8 percent—took home a medal, and 9,858 athletes went home with nothing but memories, souvenirs, injuries, and debt. Greene was one of the lucky ones. His training was funded by the Wells Sports Foundation, and because he's in a relatively high-profile sport, he received a great deal of attention and popular support. For most athletes in most sports, none of this is available.

Studying the world's top athletes, the US Track & Field Athletes Association concluded that five of its top ten athletes earned less than $15,000 a year—derived from prize money, grants, and sponsorships. That figure did not take into account income from part-time jobs, but neither did it include the costs of agents' fees and health insurance. Sprinters and marathon runners stand to gain the most: world leaders with name recognition may get shoe contracts, appearance money, prize money, and health insurance, all adding up to some $400,000 a year. But when you turn from runners with international name recognition to those who are only within the top fifteen in the world, those numbers halve. An American marathon runner in the top twenty to fifty might take home $25,000 in a year.

For the very top hurdlers with international name recognition, the earning potential can reach around $150,000 annually, while 50 percent of those who are consistently top ten in the world earn between $30,000 and $100,000 before tax and agency fees. For jumps, throws, and heptathlons, the numbers are lower still, and for race walking there's really no income at all.[3]

If your sport is more obscure—say, skeleton sled racing or the kayak slalom—there is little or no sponsorship available, but the training regime, just like Greene's, requires total dedication and most of your time. For every Michael Phelps—a stupendous achiever in a globally popular sport—there are dozens of athletes dedicating just as much of their lives to a sport where the earning potential of a lifetime career is negligible.

The Olympics, of course, are supposed to be about glory, not money. But looking at data for US athletes, it is clear that even popular sports like baseball and football offer little to the vast majority of their amateur players. In men's and women's basketball, there is just a 0.03 percent chance of becoming a professional; in men's soccer, just 0.04 percent of players turn pro. In football the rate is 0.08 percent, and in baseball, which offers the most professional opportunities, only 0.60 percent of high school players make a professional team. In no sport do the chances of a professional career reach even 1 percent.[4]

Darren Heitner used to be a sports agent but left the business, disillusioned by how hard it is for any but a few to make a real living.

"The promise seems so great, but it's an illusion. It's common for most players not to make it to a major league. So minor league players are on a forty-man roster, and they will make one to two thousand dollars a month—less than they might make, say, waiting tables. They do it because they imagine that they will get drafted into the majors—but 90 percent of them will never have a day in the majors. So they have to survive on their signing bonuses.

"The average career in football is, maybe, three and half years—in other words, most players never make it to a second contract. In basketball the average career is about four years. There the contracts are for two years, with options on the next two years. So most of them don't make it to the second contract either. And the first contract isn't worth much money—especially after taxes and fees and all your costs.

"In baseball, players can be drafted out of high school. They're more valuable because they're younger and the teams hope they can develop them. So the kids sign onto a team with a six- or seven-figure signing bonus. Five, six, seven years down the line, when it doesn't work out, the organization doesn't value the player, he leaves and enters the real world with no qualifications, no real education, with nothing."

In 2011 and 2012, the Knight Commission on Intercollegiate Athletics proposed reforms that were intended to protect players' education, either by offering stipends (which was rejected by most schools) or by linking teams' revenue shares to educational performance. These good intentions were subverted when a community college, Western Oklahoma State College, began offering such cheap and easy courses that just $400 and two weeks of easy study could earn athletes three full-semester credits.[5] Heitner says that good agents insist on contract clauses covering university tuition or a bonus for education so that the athlete has the chance of earning college credits in the off-season. But plenty of players don't have the clause or don't commit much time to their schooling because, convinced that they're the best, they think they won't need a backup plan. When you are entirely focused on winning, a plan B isn't what you think about.

"These players grow up around enablers," says Heitner. "It starts with parents being gung ho about their kids, telling them how great they are. Then they go to competitions at a very young age. They may really be the best in their local scene. Then their coaches tell them: 'You're the best I've ever seen'—and they may be right! But it's not a local business, it's a global business. We've got great footballers coming into the game from Samoa! In baseball, so many of the major leaguers are from Venezuela, Japan, Dominican Republic. So it's a rude awakening when the competition expands to the rest of the world and your talent isn't quite what you and your parents and your coach thought it was."

All competitive athletes will tell you that they are driven by love of the sport, not a desire to make money. But there are real costs to this passion, including loss of the time to learn to study, to make friends, to have a life.

"At the age of fifteen, I was doing nine training sessions a week. Up every morning at 5:00 AM, swimming four mornings a week, five evenings a week. My exams didn't turn out as I wanted—there was no time to do the work because I was at the pool whenever I wasn't at school. People thought I was insane, but I just loved it."

Erin Jeffries doesn't come from a sports-oriented family, but her parents supported her when, to their surprise, they discovered they had a daughter who was one of the fastest swimmers in England. Every morning her mother Tish also would get up at five to drive ten miles to the university pool, sit and plan out her working day while her daughter trained, then drive home and go to work. The regime was tough on both of them—and not just logistically.

"It was hard for her," Tish recalls, "to compete against her friends. There was one girl she was friends with, and she could not beat her. Erin was the better swimmer, but it was as though she couldn't risk the friendship. When the girl got ill and was off training—no problem winning the race. But when she came back, well, it was tricky. It's hard to want to beat your friends."

"When I was training at Bath," Erin remembers, "I had no time for a social life. I didn't really form the friendships I might have if I had had the time. I was always swimming, training. I think it must have been quite annoying for the friends that I did have: that I was just never around."

Erin looks like a swimmer: tall, lanky, alert. She swam long distances—800, 1,500 meters—because, she said, she had the endurance, not the speed. It wasn't inevitable that Erin would go to Loughborough—she didn't quite have the grades to get in—but her coach helped her, and she won a coveted spot at the United Kingdom's leading sports university. The commute got shorter, but the day was just as intense.

"Monday, Wednesday, Friday: Get up at 5:00, training at 5:30–7:30, back by 8:00, breakfast, lectures at 9:00, maybe three in a day. Lunch. My day revolved around eating and swimming. Do work in the afternoon. Then training at 5:00—land training, two hours swimming. The other two days, training was just in the evening. Then Saturday sessions would be race pace. It was very competitive between all of us. Sunday a day off. Maybe I'd go out once every two weeks—not as much as the others.

"When I won a race, it was the best feeling—doing a time you've never done before. But when I lost a race, it was horrible, heart-crushing. When you do a time off of your best, when people like your friends beat you, it's hard to see them afterwards. I didn't want to talk to anyone. I was very emotional, and I'd end up crying."

Coming in fifth in the country in the 400-meter medley, Erin started to lose heart. Exhausted and frustrated, she began to realize how much she was missing: time with her friends, time to study, time to think. Perhaps if she were a sprinter, she thought, she wouldn't be so tired all the time—but she didn't have the build for sprinting. As she talks about this time in her life, she is nearly in tears, remembering the hope and frustration, the exhaustion and the expectation.

"If I thought I'd make the Olympics, I would have continued. But I'm sure I would have quit soon after that. The main thing is, I wanted to get a decent degree. I wanted to feel that I could have some kind of career afterwards. I wanted to have a life before it was too late."

In the middle of her third year, Erin stopped swimming. It was an agonizing decision; while she was making it, she avoided her friends, her coach, anyone who would try to persuade her one way or the other. But now she feels she made the right decision just in the nick of time.

"Your whole life is centered around swimming. When that's taken away, you wonder, 'Who am I?' When I stopped swimming, I felt lost for a few months. But then I got a good degree and realized how close I'd come to not getting anything out of university. I was so glad I'd stopped and used the chance to study. I don't regret it now at all."

Two of her friends persevered. Kate didn't make it to the Olympics, and Rich, a friend since childhood, was 0.004 seconds off the qualifying time, so he couldn't go either.

"It was a massive blow to his career, not making that tiny amount of time. Maybe he had had a bad night's sleep or been ill a week before. You could have trained for the last four years—and you just miss it. It's all for nothing."

Erin doesn't swim anymore; she just can't enjoy it. Although it's hard for her to relive the extreme ups and downs of her swimming career, she's emphatically relieved that she stopped when she did. After graduating, she traveled all over the world—France, Switzerland, Australia—and although she worked everywhere she went, she said her real purpose was to retrieve the years of growing up that she had missed. The years when all her friends were building relationships and careers, partying, experimenting, learning who they were: she wanted to snatch that experience before it was too late.

What Erin was responding to—and acting on—is a well-understood psychological phenomenon. The cognitive capacity of the human brain is quite constrained, and there are hard limits to the amount of information we can process at any given time. Similarly, it appears that we can be motivated by one thing at a time, not by multiple aims. Assaulted by too much information, or too many motives, our brain acts like an editor, choosing what gets in and what gets left out. Extreme focus on a single goal creates tunnel vision that excludes anything extraneous to the goal. In true life-or-death circumstances, this kind of focus is valuable. But what works well in the short term proves impoverishing and depleting when it becomes a lifetime habit.

The logistical and intellectual demands of elite sports crowd out everything else, incurring a cost that goes well beyond any financial risk. Just when young people are exploring, finding out who they are and what they want from life, athletic competition represents an exclusive demand—sucking out every last bit of time, attention, energy, concentration, and enthusiasm in their lives and leaving behind what can feel like a vacuum.

"You spend so many years working towards your particular goal to become an Olympic champion," heptathlete Denise Lewis recalls. She had won gold at the Sydney Olympics—but the experience of winning wasn't what she had imagined.

"And when you achieve that, there is this sort of emptiness, this void. You just don't know what to do with yourself.... There was just this 'What do I do now?' moment.... You're back on your own in a bus traveling to the athletes' village. It's half past one at night, and the world just seems a big place and you're just very much on your own."

Retiring from her sport at the age of thirty-three, Lewis had focused on her athletic goals for so long that she no longer knew who she was. As she explained in 2012, "I just felt like, 'Who am I? What do I do? How will I call myself?' The worst moment for me was when you have to fill out any form and you have to put your occupation. And I used to just tap my fingers thinking, 'What am I?'"[6]

Andre Agassi says that sports stop you being who you are. He is rare among elite athletes, not just in having been able to play dazzling tennis, but in having written an autobiography that goes far beyond the conventional lists of prizes and scores. His remarkable book, *Open,* tracks his agonizing journey before he stopped playing tennis and could finally be who he was. What makes Agassi's book so unusual is his account of his dawning sense of who he might be and his gradual recognition of the people, processes, and vested interests that stopped him from claiming his own identity. He came to hate tennis because it prevented him from becoming who he really was.

"Tennis is noncontact pugilism. It's violent, *mano a mano,* and the choice is as brutally simple as it is in any ring. Kill or be killed. Beat or take your beat-down. Tennis beatings are just deeper below the skin. They remind me of the old Vegas loan shark method of beating someone with a bag of oranges, because it leaves no outer bruises."[7]

When, after the 2012 London Olympics, Sebastian Coe brought out his memoir, *Running My Life,* critics were quick to point out how little personality the book conveyed. It wasn't just that the narrative was dull, but that there were hardly any other people in it. Coe's mother, her death, his wife, their divorce, his adultery—none of this gets much attention or provokes any insight. But Coe's story, banal as it might be to read, is not unusual. I spent most of one summer interviewing Olympic aspirants, and one thing became monotonously clear: their absolute focus on their goal eliminated everything else in their lives. It wasn't just that they didn't have time for other things—friends, reflection, a social life. They no longer had imaginative capacity for such things either. Such extreme focus—on scores, times, numbers, measurements—had made it impossible for them to think in other terms. That's the bruise you can't see.

The visible scars, of course, aren't trivial; Dai Greene's many injuries, for instance, aren't unusual. While we might naturally associate sports with health and fitness, at the elite or professional level sports are more commonly connected to injury and long-term health problems. At the University of North Carolina at Chapel Hill, Frederick Mueller was an enthusiastic sports coach, but now he is the director of the National Center for Catastrophic Sport Injury Research.

"Before I started, we had lots of catastrophic injuries, and a lot of rule changes were designed to prevent them. But recently the emphasis on winning has really taken over sport at all levels, and that has created these problems. Nowadays second place means you're a loser, and that puts athletes and players under a lot of pressure."

Mueller collates data on fatalities and serious injuries in all sports, and his research has been instrumental in reducing death from head injuries and heat stroke in American football. Yearly reports show a rising concern about head injuries in soccer. But all the sports he studies—cross-country running, soccer, field hockey, water polo, basketball, ice hockey, swimming, wrestling, volleyball, gymnastics, skiing, pole vaulting, baseball, softball, lacrosse, track, tennis, rowing, horse-riding—are associated with fatalities, near-fatalities, and serious injuries. Most of these injuries derive from the sport itself, but some, such as heat stroke during football tryouts or the fatalities caused by trying to make weight in wrestling, are clearly caused by the drive just to win a spot on the team. It is extremely sobering to read these reports on deaths and catastrophic injuries caused by poor, often unqualified coaching combined with the youthful desire to win.[8]

"You see parents fighting each other and coaches who have no training at all. And everyone wants to win! These kids don't have any time off, and they're playing all the time and having minor injuries and overuse injuries, and the parents are pushing that. Some of the injuries I've seen, the kids won't tell coaches if they're injured because they don't want to lose their spot, their scholarships—even parents are involved. With concussion, some of these kids will have problems for years afterwards."

Concussion is a fact of life in today's sports world, with high-contact sports like boxing, soccer, and American football proving most dangerous.

During a single season of football, a professional American football player will receive over one thousand blows to the head and face a 75 percent chance of concussion. This risk of head injury doesn't just reflect the nature of the game; it is the direct result of wanting to win: 78 percent of concussions are sustained during games, not practices. Mueller now compiles an annual survey of football injuries: in 2011 he found four fatalities directly caused by football and twelve fatalities indirectly caused by heat stroke, blood clot, or heart attack. In the National Football League (NFL), offensive and defensive linemen have a 52 percent greater risk of dying of heart disease than the general population.

One reason for that higher risk is that linemen are getting bigger. More mass means more force, which makes collisions ever more dangerous. Every year since 1942, football players have been getting heavier, with a cumulative average weight gain of one hundred pounds. And that's not all muscle: 97 percent of NFL players are estimated to be overweight, with 56 percent of them obese.[9] This makes them highly susceptible later in life to heart disorders, higher blood pressure, and metabolic disorders like diabetes.

But while they're still in the game, one recurrent problem Mueller sees is that they will do almost anything to stay in it. Rule changes have attempted to manage this—professional players suffering concussion must be cleared by an independent neurologist before returning to the field—but players often won't tell their coaches that they're experiencing signs of head trauma: loss of consciousness, visual disturbance, headache, memory loss. It is for that reason that Mueller recommends that a physician be present at all games and practice sessions—something some teams do and can afford to do, but many do not.[10] "Without adult intervention in concussion management," one researcher concluded, "youth sports can become a demolition derby."[11] And while it might be tempting to put this down to American hypercompetitiveness, Science Daily, the journal that published their paper, also reported that in the United Kingdom most football teams don't follow international guidelines on concussion, and only half seem to be aware that they exist.[12]

Knowing what the sport could do to his body was one factor in John Moffitt's decision to quit the game. After nearly twenty years playing for the Seattle Seahawks and the Denver Broncos, Moffitt was troubled by poor sleep and disturbed vision. "They're merchandising human beings," he said when explaining his sudden decision to retire. "I don't want to risk health for money."[13]

Between 2011 and 2012, six retired NFL players committed suicide. After their deaths, autopsies revealed that they had been suffering from a form of dementia called chronic traumatic encephalopathy (CTE), a disease it is now thought derives from multiple concussions. One of these tragic cases, Dave Duerson, shot himself in the chest so that his brain would be left intact for future study; he bequeathed it to the Boston University School of Medicine. Since Duerson's death in 2011, the BU researchers have studied the brains of thirty-five football players and found that thirty-four of them had CTE.[14] More recently, it has become possible to study the brains of players while they are still alive. UCLA researchers studied the brains of five living football players and found that all five were living with CTE, whose symptoms include memory loss and depression.[15] Whether the disease is specifically linked to concussions or multiple aspects of football make it a dangerous sport remains ambiguous. Football, after all, as Michigan State coach Duffy Daugherty once said, isn't a contact sport; it's a collision sport. And that has led some observers to wonder if the game itself, and the players' desire to win the game, isn't the heart of the problem.

"Calling the head-injury crisis a concussion crisis made it sound as if it stemmed from how the game is played, not from the game itself," sportswriter Jonathan Mahler ruminated. "It doesn't take a concussion to damage the brain. The routine plays, the beautiful plays, the most purely football plays—they all could be causing brain damage too. That's a reality nobody wants to acknowledge, because if football's problem is indeed existential, if the game doesn't *have* a crisis but *is* the crisis, the future of football is in more peril than anyone thinks."[16]

Recognizing, at last, the link between concussion and football, the NFL in August 2013 agreed to pay $765 million to more than four thousand retirees and families of players who had suffered advanced dementia and the long-term effects of head trauma. But football is not the only sport characterized by serious injury and fatalities. Baseball has three to four deaths every year. The most common source of concussion for female athletes is soccer, with a 50 percent chance of concussion.[17] And after football, the most dangerous sport in America, says Mueller, is cheerleading.

"Cheerleading accounts for more injuries than all other girl sports put together," Mueller says. "It is fiercely competitive. They start them really young, they travel all over the country and put in hours and hours in places that aren't safe, with coaches who have no professional qualifications. And of course, the more spectacular stunts—flips and twists twenty-five feet up in the air—are the riskiest."

Laura Jackson was just fourteen when she went for her cheerleading tryout. Eager to win a spot on her high school team, she took a running start across the gym floor before launching herself into a flip. She can't remember what went wrong, only that she landed on her neck, turned blue, and couldn't breathe. She had broken two vertebrae in her neck, and the bones pinched her brain stem. Today Laura is quadriplegic—and an active campaigner for cheerleading safety.

"Cheerleading has changed completely from what you might remember at school," Mueller tells me. "It's a high-stakes sport now, with a fiercely competitive organization. In many schools it isn't considered a sport, so there aren't any rules or regulations around how many hours you can practice." Mueller also points out that cheerleader stunts "are almost always performed on hard surfaces. So when they go wrong, the results are catastrophic." Over thirty thousand American girls end up in emergency rooms every year with injuries sustained during cheerleading. The sport is not inherently dangerous; what makes it so damaging is the extreme to which the participants are being pushed—and pushing themselves—to win trophies.

Fueled by competitive drive, athletes now court dangers only recently discovered. Researchers at the University of Leuven examined the heart muscles of triathletes and marathon runners after a race. They expected to see hearts in peak condition, but what they found instead was that the athletes' hearts had changed shape, and that the function of the right ventricle (which pumps blood into the lungs) had become "severely dysfunctional." The hearts of some of the athletes returned to normal, but some did not, with MRI scans showing signs of heart scarring.[18]

Although the sample size in the University of Leuven study was small, the medical director of the London Marathon, Sanjay Sharma, thought that it had to be taken seriously. "My personal feeling is that extreme endurance exercise probably does cause damage to the heart in some athletes," Sharma said. "I don't believe that the human body is designed to exercise at full stretch for as long as 11 hours a day, so damage to the heart is not implausible. The potential for such projects is enormous considering the colossal increase in participation rates in endurance events such as the marathon. The long-term conclusions of the authors may appear preposterous to some, but could prove to be the retrospective 'elephant in the room.'"[19]

The promise and romance of money and glory drives athletes hard. It always has. But today the certain knowledge that for every one of them who wins a spot on a team, a place in the race, there are hundreds more who would like to be there makes the competition more intense. And as if that weren't stressful enough, the more thoughtful contenders know that they don't have much time to win. There's no time for second chances, so they'd better make it while they can. Taking seven years to shave three seconds off of his time could make sense for Dai Greene if he had all the time in the world—but he knows that he doesn't. His whole life is run against the clock and the calendar.

Gymnasts usually retire by the time they are twenty. Track and field athletes typically retire in their thirties. A few players push into their forties, but for the most part sports are a young person's game. If retirement comes early to most athletes, it also comes as a shock. Sports may provide a great metaphor for life, but aren't very good training or preparation for it. Many athletes, in retirement, confront the vacuum that Denise Lewis so eloquently described: they feel lost, without an identity, without a plan, and without the structure, colleagues, or social support provided by less competitive careers. They've retired much earlier than their contemporaries and are often depressed, disillusioned, and disoriented.

In a 2011 study of Olympians, a team of Swedish and Australian researchers talked to medalists about their transition out of sports. Thomas (none of the participants were identified), who had won a medal in a combat sport, tried to become a coach. He found it hard, he said, because it involved too much self-sacrifice to the interests of others; he had only ever thought of himself. Now he found that there was a difference between being a sportsman and being a person.

"If you quit and you retire from sport, you can't only think like this and you are not alone anymore, and it's not only going on success or that you win. You are living with other people and you have to socialize or whatever. It's a bit more complex."[20]

Finding an identity and learning to think about other people, Thomas said, was the hardest thing he'd ever done—much harder than winning his medal. "You can win one time, two times. But one day it gets you. And that's one part of it that got me at the [second] Olympic Games.... What happens if you fight and you lose and you don't have the recognition? You commit suicide or what? You have to find something else."

Michelle, who won in team sports, suffered from depression and anxiety when she left sports to become a teacher. "In [my sport] you would be training for some intricate little skill that you want to improve or perfect and you had constant goals and you had constant reassurances that you were doing the right thing." Michelle had spent her whole life being a perfectionist, aiming at measurable, short-term goals. But in teaching, perfection wasn't attainable, goals were ambiguous, and there was never an absolute victory. Tunnel vision proved poor preparation for life's complexities.

Retiring professional athletes miss the simple clarity of winning or losing. Scott Tinley, one of the finest triathletes in the world, continued to compete, he says, for far too long. On retirement, he felt lost, depressed, confused. He worked through his disorientation by interviewing over two hundred fellow athletes about their transition to retirement. He wrote his book, he says, as a form of healing. Quoting baseball pitcher Sandy Koufax, Tinley feels that "an athletic life is a self-liquidating life."

Everyone Tinley interviewed missed the scoreboard, the applause. He cites statistics: the suicide rate among former NFL players is nearly six times the national average; the divorce rate for professional athletes after retirement is 60 to 70 percent. And only the very lucky few have earned enough truly to retire. Most have to reinvent themselves in a world that they don't know and for which they're often ill equipped.[21]

"The careers are really short," says former sports agent Darren Heitner. "Many athletes go broke, not just because they're from poor backgrounds or don't spend wisely. You can't live your whole life on your signing bonus— even if you manage your money well. And with no education, it's really hard to find other opportunities. If you want to do TV and *Dancing with the Stars,* then you have to be a big name, have the right contacts, the right agent, the right relationships—the pool of athletes chosen is just so small. There's no way you can live off of sports for the rest of your life. A Usain Bolt, a Peyton Manning maybe—these are profound exceptions. But very, very few can rest on their laurels for the rest of their lives."

Time, for professional and elite athletes, is highly concentrated; so much depends on the short term—the minutes, days, and weeks—that there's little room or time to look further ahead. The tunnel of their tunnel vision is strikingly short. Ironically, it is the extreme brevity of their careers that often makes athletes that much more determined to win and to win now. In 1984 a physician and biochemist named Robert Goldman asked 198 elite athletes a question: would they take an undetectable drug that guaranteed them a gold medal if they knew it would also kill them within five years? Fifty-two percent said that they would. Goldman repeated the survey every two years for the next decade, and the results didn't budge. This came to be known as the "Goldman dilemma."[22]

In 2010, forty-eight professional American football players were asked similar questions. Asked, "Is a good chance of playing in the NFL worth a decent chance of permanent brain damage?," 53.6 percent said that it was worth the risk. And in response to the question "If a star player were concussed, would his colleagues want him back on the field?" half said that they would. As one respondent put it, "When the adrenaline is pumping and it's Friday night, the selfishness comes back and I'd want him to come back."[23]

In 2009 some bright Australian researchers asked themselves just how peculiar this dilemma is: perhaps we would *all* willingly make these kinds of trade-offs. They surveyed 250 people who were not elite athletes; of these, only two were willing to make the Faustian pact. The study's authors concluded that athletes, to reach the elite level, "must display a singular focus and desire to the exclusion of other life-affirming activity."[24]

Many psychologists see the athlete's hypercompetitiveness and extreme focus as a form of masochism, in which physical pain helps to obliterate the psychological suffering of earlier childhood trauma. Others see it as a form of narcissism: an unquenchable hunger for attention and applause. Rare is the athlete to whom victory is unimportant, who is playing the game for the sheer joy of it. The point of the game now is to win.

"The athletes themselves are paid to win, and they like to win," says Don Catlin, doyen of drug testing. "They don't want to take drugs, but the drugs work well, so they have to decide, 'Will I stay drug-free or not?'"

Catlin virtually invented the drug-testing industry in the United States in 1982. Working at Walter Reed Hospital, he developed tests for cocaine and street drugs. By the time he moved to UCLA, it had become clear that the United States would need a world-class drug-testing facility for the 1984 Los Angeles Olympics, and Catlin was asked to start it.

"There was no anti-doping industry in the US at the time—none," he recalls. "Good funding was available, so the department chair's eyes bulged! And I never really turned back. It was exciting."

Although his job is to find ways to catch athletes cheating, Catlin has a lot of sympathy for the pressure that they're under—and that they put themselves under.

"Life is tough for an athlete. It's rare for them to do well, and most of them have no backup plan. Olympic athletes aren't so well off; they'll make money if they win a gold medal and if they're in a high-profile sport, but not otherwise. Silver or bronze—it's nothing. They cut their education short. Everything—school, friendships—is bypassed in favor of sport. They do the best they can, but there's a lot riding on them.

"If you're Mark Spitz, that's okay—he won seven golds! Or in the old days, ten to twenty years ago, if you were an East German, you might get a car, an apartment! Athletes don't know much about chemistry, but the doctors and chemists and trainers—they know! The cost is so high, the athletes need to get a lot out. I admired those who stayed clean, but it's really hard to fault those who do drugs: the winning margin is *so* close, and yet that tiny difference makes such a big difference to their lives."

Catlin lives in the midst of a perpetual arms race. Every time he designs a reliable test for a new drug, a murky group of chemists, trainers, and agents find a way around the test or invent a new performance-enhancing substance. It doesn't matter that many of these are life-threatening; the Goldman dilemma shows that the majority of athletes don't care. As the potential gains and the number of competitors both increase, the doping problem grows. The World Anti-Doping Agency, the US Anti-Doping Agency (USADA), the Australian Crime Commission, and the UK anti-doping agency all agree that the use of human growth hormone and peptides is on the increase and that testing is not keeping pace; although the agencies estimate that at least 14 percent of athletes use banned substances, only 2 percent are ever caught.[25] Nor is the problem confined to professional sports; because these substances are easy to get, amateur and sub-elite athletes are using them too.

Erythropoietin, one of a class of drugs more popularly known as EPO, is a case in point. Widely implicated in the now ruined career of cyclist Lance Armstrong, EPO is a dangerous drug. In 2008 a major review article reported that, when used to relieve anemia after chemotherapy, it increases the risk of death. Other studies implicated it in tumor formation, and a 2010 study connected it to strokes and heart attacks.[26] By anyone's definition, this is a risky drug, especially when administered by individuals who may not have any interest in long-term effects. Yet Catlin says that it remains the drug of choice—because it works. And because you can easily buy it online.

For the goal-focused athlete, doping represents a horrible choice. It's often presented as a real-life example of game theory, although, for the athletes concerned, it's no game at all. If everyone is doping, you can't win without drugs. If no one is doping, you improve your chances if you dope. The only condition under which not doping is the best strategy is when you can be completely confident that no one else is using a stimulant—and that condition rarely arises. Many researchers in the field, looking at the numbers revealed by the Goldman dilemma, have concluded that doping is now endemic, infiltrating every sport and major event. And some athletes agree.

"Have I ever cheated in sport?" Will Carling, former England rugby captain, wrote. "Of course I have, in fact I am so sad I still do in order to beat my kids! How sad is that! But it is ingrained, not the cheating, but the need to win! And hence on a serious level, I look at these guys who have been exposed and wonder would I have been any different?"[27]

And it's all for us. Sports are big business, representing some 2 percent of global GDP.[28] It's an entertainment business that draws crowds and headlines with bigger, faster, longer, more dramatic attractions. The races get longer, the games grow more fierce, the linebackers get bigger, and the serves break new records. We don't want to think that tennis players may need to be shot through with cortisone just to get onto the court for our entertainment. We don't want to consider that, as linebackers get bigger, their chances of heart disease increase. We like to imagine that we are watching the triumph of the human spirit when in fact we are highly likely to be watching the ingenuity of the criminal mind.

"It's not cheating if everybody's doing it," was how Victor Conte explained it.[29]

In 2004 Conte was arrested for running the Bay Area Laboratory Cooperative (BALCO), which supplied performance-enhancing drugs to top-flight Olympic athletes, boxers, cyclists, football and baseball players, and some of the most famous names in American sports, including major league baseball players Barry Bonds and Jason Giambi and Olympian Marion Jones. The scandal plunged a stake through the heart of the idea that sports competition is fair, that it brings out the best in people, and that it wisely and generously rewards the virtuous and hardworking.

"The Olympic Games are a fraud," Conte insisted. "It's almost like, what I'm here to tell you right now is that not only is there no Santa Claus, but there's no Easter Bunny or Tooth Fairy either in the world of sport. I mean, the whole history of the Olympic Games is just full of corruption, cover-up, performance-enhancing drug use. It's not what the world thinks it is."

Conte claimed that he had created the drug program for Marion Jones that led to her five medals at the Sydney Olympics, that he'd done similar work for her then-husband, Tim Montgomery, enabling him to break the 100-meter world record. The BALCO scandal exposed how deeply steroids, EPO, and supplements had penetrated American and Olympic sports. Conte felt that "his" athletes had no choice, that drug-testers were always behind, and that the athletes' desire to win was so strong that they didn't care about risk.

Sending Conte to prison may have sent a message and caused new testing regimes to be developed for virtually every sport. But it hasn't stopped the role of drugs in sports becoming a persistent leitmotif in sports coverage. The biggest one-day drug bust in sports, in August 2013, in which thirteen Major League Baseball players were suspended for violating anti-doping rules, suggested that little had changed. And much to his surprise—and disappointment—Don Catlin has stayed busy.

"I thought it would be simple," Catlin laughs. "You find a drug, you just need to know its retention time and get a sample of it. I thought I could clean it up in about five years! I had no idea of the magnitude of the problem."

As the problem grew, it became Catlin's lifelong passion. He was at the London 2012 Olympics, overseeing the testing lab there. As in Beijing, 4 percent of athletes were caught doping, but only 4,686 tests were administered, so no one will ever know the full scale of illegal drug use at the London Games. Nor is it clear how far anyone wants to know the truth. For the Olympic organizers, doping presents a dilemma: testing everyone is expensive and time-consuming, and the more you do the greater the risk of catching so many athletes that the Games might lose their romance.

"The challenge never stops," says Catlin. "Drugs with drugs inside. Masking drugs. Growth hormone is hard to detect. Genetic manipulation may prove impossible to detect. They're always trying to get ahead of our knowledge and understanding."

Travis Tygart was head of legal affairs at the US Anti-Doping Agency when BALCO unfolded; the scale of that scandal appalled him. He feels that the BALCO case revealed not a few athletes gone wrong, but an entire ethos that had been corrupted. Cheating by doping, Tygart believes, was just the worst manifestation of the desire to win at all costs.

Among all the athletes involved in BALCO, Tygart tells me, "none ever felt good about cheating. They all knew it wasn't right and couldn't justify or live with it."

Tygart grew up playing sports; as an adult, he coached school teams. But what he loved when he was growing up had changed profoundly, and he wanted to understand what had happened to sports. With that in mind, he commissioned the report "What Sport Means in America," a sobering reflection on what competitive sports have become.

"The footprint of sport on society is large," the report found: three-fifths of American adults were involved in some kind of sport, and one-quarter were actively involved. But cheating was also pervasive: one in five admitted to having bent or broken a rule, half knew someone who had broken a rule, and of those who had cheated, virtually all (96 percent) said that they knew others who had done so. Sports volunteers, participants, and fathers of children age eight to seventeen admitted bending or breaking rules at the highest rates.

Most striking of all was a contradiction. Americans *said* that what they cared about most in sports was fun, fair play, integrity, self-discipline, patience, and a sense of community. What did they care about least? Winning and competitiveness.

But when asked what sports in fact reward, the answer was: winning and competitiveness. In other words, the idea of sports—games that teach important life lessons—is great, but the reality is completely different: sports do indeed teach lessons—just all the wrong ones.[30]

"We saw kids taking supplements," Tygart recalls. "Two-day workouts and year-round seasons were becoming common. One parent of a fourteen-year-old inline roller skater—not even a money sport or an Olympic sport—his father had hired a trainer and put him on one of the most sophisticated programs of human growth steroid that we'd come across. We talked to the kid: he was just doing what his dad told him to do. The parents were just so over-the-top win-win-win. They weren't that far from pushing drugs—on their own kids!

"The culture gets more competitive and extreme: 'Win at all costs!' 'I'll do anything to get the scholarship.' The erosion of family dinners and vacations at the expense of driving kids to practice and tournaments is just terrible. And it really made us think: What do we want out of sports? Do we want an ethos that is all about winning at all costs, trampling the competition, breaking the rules? Or do we want something more meaningful?"

The sense that sports had lost their way fueled Tygart's mission to clean them up. For over two years, in the face of three death threats from unknown sources, he pursued the investigation into Lance Armstrong, doggedly accumulating the evidence that finally stripped the cyclist of his Tour de France medals and of his reputation.

Doping is the biggest, most visible sign of sports gone wrong. But if winning is all that matters, then the huge costs of elite and professional sports can seem acceptable. Just like commoditized education: if the product, not the process, is all that matters, then the drugs and the cheating don't matter. The problem, for Tygart, doesn't lie in the sports themselves, but in society's idolization of winning athletes and of athletic competition.

"We have so overvalued winning," Tygart concludes. "We focus too much on the minority. Does it make sense to focus exclusive attention on a tiny group of winners? Common sense says no, and so does our research. When you focus exclusively on winning, that overshadows all the other good attributes in taking part."

It's important to recognize that Tygart is himself an avid sportsman. He loves sports—just not what they have become. And while it would be comforting to think this is just an American problem, in the United Kingdom two-thirds of children say they feel pressure to cheat in sports because of a "win-at-all-costs" culture, and more than one-third say that they feel no remorse when they do cheat.[31]

Steven Baddeley is director of sport at the University of Bath's Sports Centre, where Dai Greene and many other Olympians trained. Baddeley played badminton at an elite level in the 1980s, but in the winter after the London Games, when asked to participate in a public debate on "Would you let your child be an elite athlete?" he adopted the opposing position.

"I believe passionately in sport," Baddeley tells me. "But elite sports are different. They're bad for kids physically. You have to push yourself to the limit, and the body will break down—if it doesn't, you aren't working hard enough. The research in badminton showed that 70 percent of the under-sixteen squad had stress fractures in their back. That's bad for you. When you do sport, you will lose. The good thing is that it teaches you to deal with failure. But teenagers, very few of them have the emotional resilience to deal with it, which is why you get lots of bad behavior from teenagers in sport."

Watching everyone from children to professionals at Bath Training Village has given Baddeley a sharp perspective on the role that sports play—or could play—in all our lives. Much of the problem, he says, starts with clubs that compete for talent at earlier and earlier ages.

"The clubs are competing against each other; they're picking kids early in order that they *not* go to other clubs. How do you pick out five-, six-, seven-year-old kids? Can you really say they're talented? It's ridiculous. But they get them to specialize—far, far too early. That's where the injuries come in. It isn't for the kids; you get tennis clubs picking kids just so they won't go into football."

The very idea that some kids "have it" while others don't offends Baddeley. Although his focus is on sports, his views echo those of teachers who believe that childhood should not be a time when kids are sorted, but rather when their energies and enthusiasms find opportunities to unfurl.

"I avoid the word 'talent,'" Baddeley tells me. "Young people have potential, and the idea that some eight-year-olds are more talented than others—I just reject it. Everyone's potential isn't the same—some are taller, and that helps in basketball. But many more would have the same potential if they were just given the opportunity."

The standard argument for paying so much attention to elite sports, and putting so much money into them, is that they will inspire the rest of us—that watching the Dai Greenes, Denise Lewises, and Michael Phelpses of the world sends us all out onto running tracks and into swimming pools. But a systematic review by the *British Medical Journal* found no evidence that the Olympic Games increase sports participation. In the United States, Tygart would love to imagine that the Olympics send a nation onto the running track, but that isn't what he sees. In fact, the implication of the USADA's research is that the emphasis on winning and winners is what propels people *out* of sports. Eighty percent of American children give up sports by the time they're twelve; the overemphasis on winning means that if they can't win, they quit.[32]

"From a revenue standpoint," Tygart tells me, "capturing TV space for elite competition definitely draws viewers and revenue dollars. But we haven't seen any proof that that alone builds more participation in the grassroots level that leads to a lifetime involvement in sport."

Trickle-down doesn't work in sports any more than it does in economics. Focusing resources, rewards, and celebrity on the top few doesn't help anyone, including, as we've seen, the athletes themselves. Using competition to identify the best and then using the best to inspire the rest turns out to be a great theory; it just doesn't work in practice. Instead, the message received is that sports are only about winning, and if you can't win, then you may as well not bother. Examining the 2000 Sydney Olympics, a study sadly concluded that the only pastime that was more popular after the Games than before was watching TV.[33]

No one argues with the idea that sports can provide a rich experience that teaches fairness, fun, the joys of community, and collaboration. But the pastime has been hijacked by an obsession with competition, with winners and with winning. Could it ever be possible to get back to the original dream in which games are "played," not "fought"? At USADA, Travis Tygart commissioned a second report to identify ways to repair the wreckage he saw all around him. If the problem wasn't sport per se but what sport had become, was there any chance that sport could regain its original and crucial playfulness?

Tygart's report, "True Sport," talks a great deal about what sport could and should be and about the values it ought to demonstrate.[34] While bad sport provokes lying, cheating, violence, delinquency, and alcohol and drug abuse, true sport could be a source of improved health, higher self-esteem, creativity, and problem-solving; it could also reduce the incidence of eating disorders, obesity, depression, and suicide. The report's eloquent plea to return play to games even suggests that healthy participation in sports can improve academic outcomes. For that to happen, however, a lot has to change.

Parents and coaches have a big role to play. Just as Finnish schools do so well by challenging themselves to make all children succeed, and Jamaica produces great runners because everyone runs, so both Baddeley and Tygart believe that the central focus of sports should be on encouraging all children, not just the winners. Crucial to this change is "to stop and remind ourselves that in sport, like so many other areas of life, experiences can be as important as outcomes."[35] In other words, the score is not the point. Kids drop out of sports because there's too much competition and not enough fun; the game isn't a game anymore. Winning needs to take a backseat—and stay there.

More important than early talent spotting is the development of an intrinsic love of all sport. There is no relationship between early development and later success, and while most athletic directors saw specialization only increasing, the report insists that it is dangerous. Children who specialize too early risk the disappearance of their childhood and becoming "socially handcuffed." Athletes who specialize experience more pressure to succeed, have fewer meaningful social interactions, and suffer more overuse injuries. Ninety-eight percent of athletes who specialize at an early age never reach the highest level of sport; they're more likely to burn out. Instead, teachers and parents should encourage kids to play many different sports and to develop a love of the game—not a need to win.

Coaches are vital role models, and USADA is critical of how untrained and unqualified most school coaches are. They have the potential to inspire and develop young people, but they need to know what they're doing, physically and emotionally. Coaches themselves were self-critical, with 78 percent of them identifying the inappropriate behavior of coaches as the most serious problem facing sports today. Few coaches know enough about safety, physical and emotional development, training, or conditioning—but all of them feel huge pressure to win. The report argues strongly that coaches need professional training and qualification.

Parents need to change their game too. "When child athletes feel that their parents are supportive and positive and emphasize mastery and enjoyment, they are more likely to display concern for opponents and grace in losing. They also are less likely to trash talk or whine and complain about the coach or their playing time. Children of parents who create anxiety about failing and emphasize winning are more likely to engage in poor sport behaviors than children whose parents encourage enjoyment and self-mastery." Some sports organizations have put in place codes of conduct—for parents.

Underneath the "True Sport" report runs a subtle but profound subtext. Sports embody social and political values, in London and New York as surely as in ancient Rome. Sports are both an influence on and a reflection of who we are.

> In a climate in which corporate executives fabricate financial records, citizens evade taxes, professional athletes commit felonies or engage in immoral behavior, college football coaches are caught in recruiting scandals, colleges prefer students with athletic prowess over academic achievements, and university coaches are paid more than the president of the institution ... cheating and unethical behavior appear to pay off, or at least go unpunished in many cases. This breeds an environment in which only "chumps" play by the rules.
>
> If we let the desire to win run rampant and unchecked through sport, then we will continue to see the transgressions among athletes, coaches, and fans mount. If we cannot save sport from an obsession with extrinsic rewards, then where will our children turn to learn the lessons that true sport offers? And is our nation well served by a citizenry that learns to prize winning and extrinsic rewards at any cost as the values held most dear?[36]

After retiring from cricket, Mike Brearley, widely regarded as one of England's greatest cricket captains, trained and practiced as a psychoanalyst. To many, this seemed a surprising leap, but to Brearley himself it was a perfect fit—and not just because cricket has always been regarded as the most cerebral of games.

"Sport gives you the license to compete," he tells me, "just as analysis gives you a license to say what you think. We need those safe places that are set aside from the everyday business of life."

As we sat in the warm, comfortable front room of his Chalk Farm house, surrounded not by sporting memorabilia but black-and-white Miro prints,

Brearley was keen to explain that sport is not, should not be, the same as life. Its chief value is, or should be, its safe distance and difference *from* life.

"I have had one or two male patients for whom sport has been important. It allows inhibited people to show off their skills, to be flamboyant, allow disinhibition, and create real engagement. People are really present to each other, and it's very enlivening. At its best, it is absolutely body-to-body, eyeball-to-eyeball, and a lot is revealed and allowed. But it is not quite life; it's to the side of life. This is what makes psychoanalysis and sport the same. They're both full on—but slightly 'as if.' You are not the patient's father or mother, but 'as if.' That's an illusion that is allowed. It's through that artificiality that you can get to some of these things in life. But it isn't the same as life."

Sport, however, has become a ubiquitous metaphor and mental model for success in all walks of life. And in just the same way that the gentle illusion of sport has become corrupted and distorted by competitiveness and winning, the same costs—tunnel vision, excess, and cheating—can be seen in businesses that take modern sport as their mental model.

"I just wanted to win. It was just about me and my goal, nothing to do with anyone else. I was completely focused on my own strengths. I was there to win—that was my focus."

Melody Hussaini sounds like an athlete, but she isn't. She was a contender in the seventh series of *The Apprentice*. The show makes much of the metaphorical connection between sports and business, with episodes often structured as races in which contestants have to clear hurdles. Challenges start as team sports, but ultimately the game is all about the soloists: the apprentices who can beat all their so-called colleagues to the prize. The overarching message of the show is that business is just like sports: vicious, antisocial, with one winner whose success is achieved only through the defeat of all competitors.

When she took part in the show, Hussaini displayed many of the characteristics of competitive athletes: tunnel vision, rigid determination, a focus on self to the exclusion of others. The show's editors made much of the fact that, at the end of the first episode, she toasted herself; this became a recurrent theme throughout her appearance. She was both lauded for her drive and mocked for her inability to listen to others, use their talents, or recognize their experience. Hussaini was eventually "fired" because her determination to win had made her such a poor collaborator.

"I kept wanting everyone to know I deserved to win. A lot of that was edited to highlight my desire to win—but I did say those things, of course I did. I have a fighting spirit. When I was a child, I used to walk around saying, 'I am going to be successful.' In life, you're competing with six billion people. You can't worry about everyone."

Hussaini has fully absorbed the message that success is a solo, individual act, requiring a total focus on self. Even if she doesn't train for it as determinedly as Olympic aspirants, she has adopted their internal focus. When I drove to meet Hussaini, I couldn't find her house. I phoned for directions, but she couldn't give them. She had always got home, she said, using her GPS. She had no idea where I was or what landmarks I might look for. Lacking any imaginative capacity to see what it might be like for someone *not* to know where she lived or how to get there, she was at a loss to describe her own surroundings.

A combination of maps, phone calls, Internet searches, and my husband eventually got me to Hussaini's front door. Later, as we talked, she perched next to a muted television screen that covered one side of the sitting room. Although it was hard to talk as the gaudy images of E! flashed across the room, it seemed never to occur to Hussaini that anything might distract my attention away from her. What emerged was a bizarre, often contradictory collage of disconnected ambition.

"I would like to be on the top of the Rich List. I want it. But this can drive people to the point where they forget what they are trying to achieve. Competition for its own sake is a dangerous time-waster and a dangerous thing. It can breed pure greed. That's why I just focus on the destination."

Hussaini runs a social enterprise aimed at giving young people the skills they need to abjure crime and to get into jobs. It seems a curious route to the Rich List. There seems to be no coherent project or sense of how she might meaningfully connect to the world at the heart of Hussaini's drive. All she wants, to the exclusion of all else, is to be a winner.

Hussaini has energy and intelligence. But she can't connect with other people because she can't see them. Like many hypercompetitive people, her goals resist all connection to, or recognition of, the complexity and value of other people. That her business has no employees, only far-flung associates, reflected, and contributed to, the sense she conveyed of being on her own.

But Hussaini's idea of leadership isn't eccentric or even unusual. *The Apprentice* is predicated on the belief that success for one requires the defeat of everyone else and that business is just a matter of keeping score. After all, only one person can win this game show, and only by making everyone else lose. Entirely consistent with this image of success are the show's hosts, who position themselves as master manipulators and umpires. *The Apprentice* makes for hyperbolic entertainment, purveying an impoverished, decrepit image of business success as requiring acts of short-term, quick-fix domination. And it's not alone. With their hyperactive commentators and scrolling stock prices, the TV channels that focus on business now resemble nothing more than the sports programming from which they're obviously derived.

Just as the true value of sports has become corrupted and distorted, the application of the competitive sports metaphor to business and leadership has warped and misaligned individuals and organizations otherwise replete with talent and promise. The tunnel vision that athletes need to achieve their goals—the kind of extreme focus displayed by Dai Greene, for instance—may work for well-defined and immediate goals achieved by individuals. But most of the work we do can't be defined by a momentary measure; it critically requires imagination, mental flexibility, and sustained creativity of a kind that the rigidity of tunnel vision specifically disables.

A competitive mind-set may help us hit tomorrow's sales target or get through the week's monotonous tasks, but it's a terrible way to manage complex projects over the lifetime of a business. We know that vast business enterprises depend for their success on networks and systems of thousands of highly collaborative, interconnected creative people; rationally, we recognize that one individual alone won't determine success or failure. But the absolute focus on self that athletic prowess requires—and that the former Olympians found so hard to shake off—stands completely at odds with the collective nature of business achievement. Nevertheless, the athletic image of leadership as an act of solo heroism has proved persistent and potent. Magazine covers sporting the rugged profiles of business leaders and the motivational life lessons of CEOs (strangely akin to athletes' memoirs) perpetuate the same trope: the heroic soloist can and will save the day, single-handedly. Ambitious organizations just need to pick winners.

Academic researchers have long puzzled over the myth of the CEO as heroic soloist. One study of 111 chief executives analyzed photographs of the CEO in annual reports, the CEO's prominence in company press releases, the use of the first person in interviews, and overall compensation. They concluded that the more prominent the chief executive was by all these measures, the more dynamic and grandiose the company strategy, the larger the number and size of acquisitions, and the more extreme and volatile the stock performance.[37] Outsize expectations of the leader put pressure on him (or, occasionally, her) to make more dramatic decisions and adopt a more hyperbolic profile.

Ambitious acquisitions offer a great shortcut to widespread publicity and applause. Depending on whose research you credit, the failure rate for mergers and acquisitions lies between 50 and 80 percent. But these moves persist because they make individual leaders look dynamic, decisive, tough, and (when they're completed) victorious. That they are regularly written about as head-to-head contests between two hypercompetitive CEOs only sharpens their drama and enhances the charisma of the winner.

Tyco was a sure bet—once—because it was run by the most aggressive CEO in America. GE, a vast multinational conglomerate, was apparently run by just one man: Jack Welch, author of *Winning*. BP, likewise, depended wholly on the genius and foresight of John Browne, who, in his "inspirational memoir from a visionary leader," drew up a chart aligning columns of world events, BP events, and events in Browne's own life as though they were all of equal significance. Meanwhile, Paris-based Compagnie Générale des Eaux promised to transform itself from a successful water utility into a global media and entertainment business purely because of the towering will of just one man—Jean-Marie Messier. That the company had no relevant assets or capabilities, and the CEO no experience of the media business, didn't matter: heroic leadership alone would effect the transformation. Messier sometimes referred to himself as "J6M." Four of the 'M's stood for "Moi-Même, Maître du Monde": me, myself, master of the universe. He was saying overtly what the rhetoric around leadership often suggests: that superheroes can do anything, win any race, clear any hurdle.

Like superstar athletes, superhero CEOs warrant extravagant pay and lavish surroundings. When Merrill Lynch CEO John Thain had his office redecorated with its notorious $35,000 commode, or Tyco CEO Dennis Kozlowski boasted of his $15,000 dog-shaped umbrella stand, these props were not just pecking-order symbols: they were the just deserts of the heroes who singlehandedly guided their company's fate. Only when the businesses failed did these props look extravagant; before that, they merely symbolized the faith that others had bestowed on their leaders.

We believe in stars. This belief in heroic leadership emerges every time a company hits a crisis. Instead of examining systemic issues, the cry goes out for a messiah who will singlehandedly compel transformation. Thus, in 2009, when America's automakers were in trouble, a "car czar" was called in—Steve Rattner, a man with no background in the car industry. Rattner knew at once what needed to be done. Consulting Jack Welch and headhunters, he hired a new CEO for General Motors. Clearly one man would turn around a vast, complex business. Being a heroic soloist himself, Rattner would know another one when he saw one: Ed Whitacre, former CEO of AT&T.

"His reputation was for toughness," Rattner wrote about Whitacre. "I remembered having once read a *Business Week* story that described him killing rattlesnakes on his Texas ranch (he would pin down the snake with a stick and crush its head with a rock). His flinty image was reinforced by his lean, six-foot-four frame, his full head of gray hair, and his laconic speech."[38]

Although he'd never worked in a manufacturing business in his life, Whitacre got the job; clearly he had what every heroic soloist needs. Rattner writes admiringly of Whitacre's first meeting with his new team:

> "I'm used to winning and have no intention of seeing that change at GM." The GM executives, unused to this sort of bluntness, were impressed, and so was I. It was superlative leadership as I had always imagined it.

Whitacre went on to star in GM's television commercials; what the ailing business needed was for customers to see that it now had a dynamic leader. But after ten months on the job, Whitacre lost interest and quit. He had apparently never wanted to stay a day longer than was needed, and clearly killing snakes and appearing on television were all it took to engineer a complex turnaround. Those who stayed for the long haul viewed Whitacre's glory as akin to a rooster taking credit for the sunrise.[39]

The romance of the heroic soloist is seen nowhere so vividly as in the hagiography surrounding Steve Jobs. If you were to believe much of what's been written about him, you might imagine that Apple had little need of its large workforce: Jobs apparently did it all. The truth, as usual, is more subtle: when Jobs had outstanding collaborators—Steve Wozniak at Apple, John Lasseter at Pixar, Jonathan Ive at Apple again—his businesses thrived. But when he was on his own at NeXT, without the creative conflict those brilliant peers offered him, his venture foundered.

It isn't that leaders don't have an impact; they do. The problem is that the leadership of any organization is infinitely more complex, subtle, and contingent than any race or soccer match. Companies can't be saved with a single kick or by shaving a second off completion times. When we worship outstanding performers, we infantilize everyone else, conveying the message that everyone can—even should—be passive in the face of towering ability. In just the same way that focusing on elite athletes discourages sports participation, the focus on business leaders as winners conveys the dispiriting message that others don't count. Instead of galvanizing and surfacing the rich talent that always exists within organizations, solo superheroes are expected singlehandedly to work miracles. That is, of course, why they fail.

Loaded with superhuman expectations, CEOs develop their own form of tunnel vision: working exorbitant hours to the exclusion of everything else in their lives. Jack Welch, running GE, wrote romantically about the long hours he kept and the weekends when he could go into the office and work with his team. John Browne, asking himself why he didn't retire earlier from BP (before his reputation was ruined by a false witness statement), concluded that nothing outside BP was as exciting or as highly valued. When work excludes all other aspects of life, the reality checks, questions, and discontinuities that we all need to test our thinking simply vanish; there's no time for them. Despite overwhelming evidence that long hours produce fatigue that clearly, and physically, damages our ability to think, heroic soloists imagine that their only chance of meeting outsize expectations is to work all the hours that they can stay awake. Like the athlete who ignores injuries, they're oblivious to the science that connects fatigue with biased judgment and rigid thinking.[40]

Corporate workouts incur their own injuries. Following up on Michael Marmot's research on Whitehall civil servants, Finnish researcher Marianna Virtanen examined the long-term impact of working very long hours and came to two startling conclusions: working eleven or more hours a day at least doubles the risk of depression. And those working fifty-five hours a week or more begin, in their middle years, to suffer cognitive loss—that is, their performance is poorer when tested for vocabulary, reasoning, information-processing, problem-solving, creativity, and reaction times. This level of mild cognitive impairment in middle age also predicts earlier dementia and death.[41]

And just as in elite sports, careers at the top are very short. Although no two studies can agree about the average tenure of chief executives, it currently hovers around five years and has been falling steadily. CEOs don't last long in the top spot, not just because the expectations are too great and the business environment dauntingly complex, but also because the mental model of leadership that derives from sporting success—the super-athlete, the star player—lacks the subtlety, complexity, collaboration, and time that true achievement requires.

Nevertheless, when CEOs get the top job, many do just what elite athletes do: focus single-mindedly on the score. Share price becomes the single, simple measure by which winning or losing is defined. So pervasive and single-minded has the obsession with stock price become that most people now believe that every company has a legal obligation to prioritize stock price above all else. This is not true.

Lynn Stout, professor of corporate and business law at Cornell, is feisty and furious about the degree to which a willful misunderstanding of the law has led boards and executives to succumb to what she calls the "myth of shareholder value." The law concerning corporate behavior, she says, comes from one of three places: a company's charter, national law, and case law. None of these, she argues, requires maximizing the share price as the overriding responsibility of a company or its directors. Indeed, she says, most of our corporate problems can be traced back to this flawed idea.

The myth of shareholder value derives chiefly from neither lawyers nor businesspeople but from economists—primarily Milton Friedman first, and then William Meckling and Michael Jensen. Friedman argued that because shareholders "own" the corporation, the only "social responsibility of business is to increase its profit." That is not only a non sequitur but also, Stout argues, wildly inaccurate. Shareholders don't legally own a corporation: it is an independent legal entity that owns itself. And directors are not "under any per se duty to maximize shareholder value in the short term, even in the context of a takeover." Case law—in this instance, *Air Products Inc. v. Airgas, Inc.*—found that disinterested and informed directors can ignore today's stock price in favor of the long-term interests of a business.

When economist Michael Jensen and business school dean William Meckling, in the most widely cited article ever published in a business academic journal, proposed that executives be seen merely as agents of the shareholders, Stout found that the law did not agree with them. They had failed to capture the true economic structure of public companies, their purpose, and their stakeholders.

"The problem is that they read the law wrong and they read business wrong," Stout tells me. "And if that weren't enough, there is a notable shortage of reliable results showing that shareholder primacy actually works better." In fact, there is plenty of evidence to the contrary, showing that companies whose governance requires more shareholder involvement actually do worse. The idea that corporations should be managed to maximize shareholder value has led to "reforms" over the past two decades that give shareholders more influence over boards and make managers more attentive to share price. The results are disappointing at best. Shareholders are suffering their worst investment returns since the Great Depression.[42] The population of publicly listed companies has declined by 40 percent,[43] and the life expectancy of Fortune 500 firms has plunged from seventy-five years in the early twentieth century to only fifteen years today.[44]

In her book *The Shareholder Value Myth*, Stout argues that the myth has become so pervasive that even though it isn't true, many CEOs and corporate directors believe it is. (So, strangely, do many corporate critics.) Most, when pressed, confess that they don't really know what the law requires, so they assume the share price is how they are measured.[45]

Belief that shareholder value is a legal requirement gave rise, Stout says, to a second aberration: the linking of executive pay to the share price. Although there is no evidence that performance-related pay delivers superior performance (and a lot of evidence to the contrary), many public companies have been eager to hold their executives to account by tying their remuneration to the company's stock market valuation. In doing so, they may have hoped to counter increasing public disgust at high salaries and bonuses. But the effect of performance-related pay has been to create tunnel vision of just the kind that athletes demonstrate: an absolute focus on short-term price goals that are often entirely at odds with any organization's long-term vitality.

A company's share price is, at best, a very weak indicator of its strength or value. Does anyone seriously believe that, in the course of a single day or week, despite no changes at all to its operations, a company genuinely becomes 1, 3, or 5 percent more valuable? Even Fisher Black, one of America's leading economists, conceded as much when he said, "The price is more than half of value and less than twice value."[46] What he meant is that a company valued at a hundred dollars might be worth fifty or two hundred—and it might also be on the brink of either implosion or explosive growth. None of this is revealed by its price.

Pressure to maintain numbers is cited as the first of Marianne Jennings's "seven signs of ethical collapse" because it makes management focus on the wrong things.[47] Numbers also inspire what Lynn Stout calls "fishing with dynamite": quick, brutal strategies that create a lot of value instantly, even if they wreck opportunities for the future. This, she argues, is what happened within BP, where pressure to cut costs led employees and contractors to ignore standard safety procedures. Many companies that cut jobs, training, and research and development fish with dynamite insofar as they're trying to make the numbers look great without any concern for the long-term health of the business or the environment in which it operates. Ornate tax avoidance strategies similarly may save money during a CEO's brief tenure while destroying the company's long-term reputation.

Nevertheless, the allure of the stock price is that it represents a nice, simple score by which the CEO and the company directors can measure their own achievement. Stock price determines their place in the market just as visibly and publicly as if it were their seat in the Colosseum. Shareholders and pension funds, investing for the future, might want company leadership to consider the long-term health of a business, but that isn't how CEOs are measured, so it isn't what most focus on. The single metric of the stock price becomes so critical to a sense of status and of success that managing it can become the company's core competence and the CEO's main focus.

Jack Welch, CEO of GE from 1981 to 2001 and for many years the champion of shareholder value, became highly expert at managing his numbers. In forty-one out of forty-six quarters, he hit his forecast to the *penny*, missing it five times by two cents and twice by one cent. The chance of these earnings not being "managed" is statistically implausible. Similarly, Microsoft met or beat its market forecast for forty-one out of its first forty-two quarters, missing just once by a cent. This is what Roger Martin, dean of the Rotman Business School in Toronto, calls "gaming the game."[48] To the degree that we conduct business as though it were sport, we must expect it to share the same aberrant behaviors.

Years after retiring from GE, Jack Welch changed his mind, declaring that, "strictly speaking, shareholder value is the dumbest idea in the world."[49] Like many bad ideas, however, it had caught on, not least because it seemed so simple. Nevertheless, keeping score takes time and attention. It's impossible not to notice that, while Microsoft was so busy becoming expert at this game, it failed to notice the emergence of the World Wide Web or to develop new technology for databases, computer games, or mobile computing—all vast new areas of innovation. If the score is all that counts, then just like grades at school, the outcome is prized over and above the process required to achieve it.

This privileging of outcome over process is real and observable on a daily basis. I ran companies for CMGI during a time when its price was climbing steadily, and there were days when you knew how the stock market was doing without looking at a computer monitor: you could feel the adrenaline in the air and hear the excitement in the voices of employees who should have had their minds elsewhere. But just as you can't judge the long-term health of a football player by the number of points he scores, so you can't tell anything about the long-term health of a company by its share price. CMGI crashed as fast as it had risen, and it wasn't alone. Of the sixty companies extolled in Jim Collins's *Good to Great* for their cumulative stock market returns, at least eleven have since gone from bad to worse.[50] Scores don't tell you everything, but like the shadows on the wall of Plato's cave, they are easily mistaken for the real thing. The compelling simplicity of the stock price distracts and detracts from the reality that is more complex and demands more effort.

Not all companies work this way. For many, success can neither be captured in a single score nor achieved by any one individual. The work of the company starts and remains a collective, creative activity.

"Profit is not the main driver—it is the result of what you do. No financial person will ever run this business because they bugger up more businesses than they ever help. If you were a cricket team and you were sending someone in to open bowling or batting, the last person you would send would be the scorer."

Hugh Facey is as tough-minded an industrialist as you will find anywhere in the world. His manufacturing business, Gripple, has offices in Sheffield, Sao Paolo, New Delhi, Chicago, and Strasbourg. The company makes a vast range of suspension devices for hanging lights, heating components, fences, and pipes. A spin-off company, Loadhog, produces weird and wonderful new packaging products. Both companies have won prizes around the world for innovation, design, and engineering. Portly, gray-haired, and with bushy eyebrows through which you can just discern sharp eyes, Facey describes himself, somewhat disingenuously, as a "simple Yorkshireman." But there's nothing simple about the way he thinks about business and leadership.

"I started my first business in 1989, and I sold it in 1992. And I thought at the time that it was wrong that I got all the benefit of the sale and not the staff—because they had grown the business with me. And I thought then that there just had to be a better way."

Far from relishing the prospect of owning his company outright and reaping all the profit and the glory, Facey was determined that everyone who worked at his next business, Gripple, would own part of it. Over the years, he has adapted the company structure so that now everyone who works there owns shares in it. Facey doesn't have an office; his desk sits alongside the rest of the staff in a wide, bright open space inside a red-brick Victorian

gun works factory. As Facey showed me around, he pointed proudly to slo-
gans painted on the walls, with messages empowering people, creativity, fun,
energy.

"This was them, not me," he insisted. "The staff did all of this. They're the
ones who have all the ideas. Business is about ideas, not about the bottom
line. I find that the more we think about the ideas, the better the company
does. And ideas don't come from accountants—scorers—they come from
the people who make the products or the people who talk to the customers.
You can only get ideas from people."

At Gripple, 25 percent of all sales come from products that did not exist
four years earlier. Ninety-two percent of its output is exported. The emphasis
throughout the business is on innovation, creativity, and problem-solving.
LoadHog, the container business, was spun out of new ideas generated
inside Gripple. The company also runs a small innovation lab where Facey
and others in the company mentor and nurture young inventors from the
local university. The long-term life of a business can never be guaranteed by
a share price but only by the ability of the staff to invent new products that
people need and want.

"We started making all our own wire rope a few years ago. All the gripples
used rod rope to hang things—ducts, lights—but they were stiff, and wires
aren't. So we thought if we could make wire, it's more flexible, you can hang
things diagonally. Turns out too that the carbon footprint is one-sixth of the
rods. And now we don't have to depend on the Chinese."

High levels of innovation are no guarantee that the business will avoid
hard times; in 1996 everyone had to take a pay cut. The next year, however,
everyone had an even larger pay increase. The point, says Facey, is to listen
to people and make them feel responsible for their work.

"Challenge everything. That's what we do here. We have no HR department and no buying department. They're all bullshit, they get in the way and
don't let businesses run. If people own the business, why would they ever
buy something not good for the business? We believe in letting our people
get on and do it. There's one job description, and it's the same for everyone:
if the ball is falling, catch it. Same for me, same for everyone."

When I ask if he ever has to fire people, Facey laughs.

"We never have any trouble recruiting; people have heard of us. If somebody joins and doesn't fit in, they usually just take themselves off because
they're not happy here. What would the signs be? Turning up late. We have
no time clocks, but everyone knows what needs to be done, and if you

weren't pulling your weight, weren't working hard—well, you just wouldn't fit in, would you?"

Facey is clear that the long-term prosperity of the business depends not on his genius but on the commitment and creativity of every single staff owner. Every year he has been giving away 5 percent of his ownership so that, ultimately, the company will be owned by the people who work there. He has no ambition to be a heroic soloist—quite the reverse. Facey is passionate and committed when it comes to the power and potential of everyone else.

"Everyone here is always looking for the next idea, the problem we can solve. So we encourage people to come up with ideas. One was called a terralock. One of the US guys said there was a problem with the levees in New Orleans and Florida. So we designed something for them, and now we have an order for a million dollars. We didn't have that product last year, but now we're talking of it becoming a major product over the next two years. We are going to launch eighteen products this year. People should come to work and have fun; that's how you get ideas. Not just by keeping your eye on the boss and waiting to be told what to do."

Contemplating retirement, Facey has restructured the company so that it can't be sold; he insists that it must sink or swim, do or die. Success for Facey isn't about him. It isn't about the balance sheet. It isn't about defeating competitors, lavish acquisitions, or dramatic exits. Gripple doesn't exist for any other reason but to invent great products that in turn generate jobs that last.

"I've no time for the big bonuses, the bonus culture. Here, when we do well, everyone's investment in the business is worth more—that's your bonus. And the better we do, the more we can do. That's a huge reward too."

Under its new structure, every owner within Gripple has one vote—"me and the cleaner," according to Facey—and they decide how the organization works. "If they're going to bugger the business up, it's their own business," he insists. "The role of capital in this business is to be the servant of the members of this organization—the servant, not the master. That's the way it should be."

Like many employee-owned firms, solvency and growth are the goals, not revenue numbers or quarterly earnings. Proponents of these businesses argue that these goals—focusing on meaningful improvement, not simplistic or arbitrary targets—are exactly what makes them so successful.

"Forty percent of our profit goes to every single member of the staff. The rest goes to internal investment: more training, more R&D," Terry Hill tells me. "We want to look over the horizon and see what's coming, in new technology, in new architecture. We spend more on R&D than anyone in our field."

Hill works for Arup, a global structural engineering firm responsible for some of the world's most complex and inventive buildings, such as the High Roller coaster in Las Vegas, the National Aquatics Center and the Bird's Nest stadium at the Beijing Olympics, the Marina Bay Sands resort in Singapore, and the Millennium Bridge in London. The firm gets these assignments because it operates at the cutting edge of structural engineering; in 2013 Arup launched a microalgae facade in Berlin aimed at seeing whether algae could simultaneously shade and power a building. The firm is exploring biological bridges, detachable homes that can travel with you, and the houses that will be needed in 2050 when 75 percent of the world's population lives in cities. This research, says Hill, is feasible only because the firm doesn't have shareholders, isn't in any kind of race, but is committed to just three things: excellence, honor in the way people treat each other, and what he calls "reasonable prosperity"—by which he means that anyone wanting to earn a huge salary can go elsewhere. The sheer complexity of Arup's projects requires high levels of collaboration, which require equally high levels of trust. That level of trust was engineered into the company through its ownership structure.

By giving the firm to the staff, Ove Arup effectively disinherited his children. He did so because he believed passionately in doing socially useful work in pursuit of quality and because he wanted people to join hands with others who thought likewise. Money, he argued, was a divisive, not a unifying, force—but with everyone an owner, that sense of mission would be shared in real and tangible ways every day.

"We don't waste time managing analysts' expectations, we don't have to mess with any of that," Hill says with pride. "We just build things. If anyone here is working on a problem they don't know how to solve, they can post a question on the intranet and in twenty-four hours they'll get an answer from someone somewhere in one of our offices who's solved that problem. We share knowledge and build trust, because we help each other and grow—personally, professionally—together. And most of our people—75 percent—stay, so our growth is their growth. Even through the recession, there is not one year we have not grown."

With 11,000 employees in 42 countries, Arup's accumulated knowledge is immense. Asked to build riding stables for the Beijing Olympics, one Arup staff member needed help figuring out how to cope with 2,500 horses that would be jittery after being flown around the world. "You can imagine the effluent!" Hill laughs. But it turned out that another Arup staff member had worked at the Jockey Club in New York and could pitch in. Why, Hill asks, wouldn't everyone help when they all stand to benefit from the firm's success?

Arup is a flat organization, designed not to create or worship super-stars; Arup believed that stars are manmade illusions that mystify thinking. Instead, he built a firm designed to succeed because everyone in it counts and becomes an owner from the day they start. If there is a pecking order, it changes constantly: Hill was amazed, in his first year, when the person he had been working for on a Nigerian project later offered to work for him. But that flat structure builds trust, both between staff and with clients. Arup is famous for never taking bribes, and this reputation greatly simplifies its worldwide business dealings, according to Hill. And because everyone is an owner, the chances of people staying silent are virtually nil: if anything, the fact that everyone has a voice sometimes slows down decision-making. But even that has advantages because choices that take a long time—like whether to enter Japan—are also given a long time to work: ten years in the case of Japan. Most architectural firms last just one or two generations; Arup is in its fourth. The company isn't aiming to cross a finishing line but to keep growing and learning and building.

Hill and Facey know that employee ownership alone is not a panacea for all business ills, but what inspires them and the people they work with isn't a life-or-death struggle against competitors but a lifelong contribution of human ingenuity to a community of colleagues whose lives are enhanced by the work and the social relationships they share. It is a very different model from the cortisone-enhanced death throes of Andre Agassi's last tennis match, the extravagant and self-serving acquisitions of Jean-Marie Messier, or the intricate financial filigree of GE.

Gripple and Arup aren't exceptional, of course. In the United States, half of all employees are involved in some form of employee ownership. Many of the world's most successful and global businesses—Zeiss, Huawei, Tullis Russell, Publix supermarkets, and W. L. Gore, as well as many of the start-ups in Silicon Valley—are run this way. Even private companies that started out wholly owned by their founders can change: after twenty-five years, Eileen Fisher has allocated 32.5 percent of the clothing company she founded to her employees in the belief that this will make it more sustainable, collaborative, and creative. So far, she says, nothing has proved her wrong.

My own experience of working in employee-owned firms is that they change fundamentally the way people in them think about their colleagues and about themselves. You need fewer rules because trust is high; after all, if you own part of the company, you don't need anyone to tell you not to waste money or time. You don't require rewards to encourage you to support co-owners who are floundering, and you don't need prizes to remind you that customers are critical. Above all, when anyone wins, everyone wins. The creativity of Silicon Valley can't entirely be ascribed to the fact that most employees own shares in their companies—venture capitalists or founders typically dominate decision-making—but from my own experience, I know it changes the social contract: how people think and feel about the way they work together.

Employee-owned businesses fundamentally change the focus and relationships of the people who work in them. When everyone is an owner, the pecking order isn't a pyramid but a network. Because people relate to one another as peers, with equal passion and commitment, they bring the full richness of their differences to the problems and challenges they must confront. And if this provokes a lot of conflict, then just like siblings who must learn to mediate each other's needs, the organization gets very good at energetic collaboration.

A walk through the Gripple building bears no relationship to spectator sports or to gaming the game. Instead, the place hums with human creativity and energy of a kind no score can capture. Success in business or in life is not determined in a few seconds, in a few minutes, or even in a business quarter. We cannot measure progress in scores or tables or statistics. Life is both rich and confusing because it is full of ambiguity, change, uncertainty, and ambivalence. It's very slick to talk about life as a game, but in our heart of hearts we know that it is infinitely more complex, both more exciting and more boring, constantly fleeting, persistently changeable, incriminating, and forgiving. If it is a game, then it is never won and never truly lost.

Back in Bath, 2013 got off to a good start for Dai Greene. He did well in early races and was running without injury. He's still focused and motivated, intent, he says, on capturing Kriss Akabusi's British 400-meter hurdles record. He has support: Akabusi would like to see him succeed. He likes Greene, admires his discipline, and wants the title to go to a worthy athlete.

Akabusi himself is something of a rarity: a sportsman with a rewarding and happy retirement, running his own business and coaching executives. Of all the athletes I ever asked about winning, it was Akabusi whose answer has most remained with me.

"When you win, you have two feelings. In the moment, there is euphoria, a substantiation of what you've done, a getting there. But after three or four hours, it's disappointing. Is that it? All over. The whole year geared to a race and it's done. The euphoria doesn't last longer than the drug testing. You're getting your old man out, peeing in a bottle, and it's back to reality. You start to wonder why you put yourself through all that and exposed yourself to losing. What I didn't know then—what I know now: you get much more joy down the road, like now. You get life; that's much better than winning. I get more joy out of life now."

PART II

The Case of the Purdue Chickens

CHAPTER 6

Only the Impresarios Thrive

Winning at all costs comes at a price; collateral issues of rivalry, arrogance, selfishness and a lack of humility and generosity.
—ANTHONY SALZ, with Russell Collins,
Salz Review: An Independent Review of Barclays' Business Practices, 2013

In the summer of 1951, *Harper's* magazine gushed over "an unrestrained, dramatic race involving a dozen of the largest American drug houses, several leading foreign pharmaceutical manufacturers, three governments and more research personnel than have worked on any medical problem since penicillin."[1] What was all the excitement about? The prospect of manufacturing cortisone.

Cortisone is a steroid hormone that reduces pain and inflammation in muscles, joints, and injuries. Today it is used to treat everything from eye disease to arthritis. It is what Andre Agassi injected during his final days on the tennis court. But in 1951 cortisone wasn't easily available; it had to be extracted from cattle bile and cost $200 per gram (equivalent today to some $2,000). Everyone knew that this could be the miracle drug for arthritis and inflammatory disease. Newsreels showed helpless arthritics, after a single injection, bounding onto the dance floor and regaining their youth. Expense wasn't the only problem. Sourcing enough cattle bile required slaughterhouse animals in volumes no one could contemplate. So the race was on to find a way to produce cortisone artificially, at a price and on a scale that would enable it to fulfill its vast therapeutic and commercial promise.

The underdog in the race was Syntex, a tiny chemicals company in Mexico that was pinning its hope on making cortisone from Mexican yams. Leading the effort was Carl Djerassi, a pioneering, Viennese-born American scientist who had patented the world's first antihistamine. Djerassi was—and is—hypercompetitive.

"We were the underdog because we were tiny, because we were in Mexico," Djerassi recalls. "And we were up against the big guys—everyone wanted to synthesize cortisone. So yes, it was a race, everyone knew it was a race."

Today, at the age of eighty-nine, Djerassi is as engaged and amused by the competitiveness of science as ever. With a mass of white hair and a white beard, he may look like an athletic Father Christmas, but he is a mischievous and challenging interlocutor. Not for him the romance of science as the pure pursuit of thought; to him, it is and always has been a fierce contest.

The intensity of the race to synthesize cortisone wasn't just about making money. The challenge contained several particularly knotty chemistry problems. Anybody who solved them stood to earn what was, for scientists, more important than money: the accolades of peers. That could only be achieved by being the first scientist to publish the solution to the problem in the *Journal of the American Chemical Society* (*JACS*). Establishing priority through publication was how the race would be won.

"Science," Djerassi tells me, "is like the Olympics—but without silver or bronze. You come first or you are nowhere. We have to document the priority, that we got there first.

"Sure, there's joy in the discovery," he wrote in his autobiography. "But that's not why you're doing it. Let's take Hillary. He wanted to be first to climb Everest. If he'd only wanted it for the sake of doing it, he could have gone with his Sherpa, who had been sworn to secrecy, taken no photos, and climbed down again, telling no one. That would be pure mountain climbing. But that is not what he did. And that is not how we do science."[2]

Djerassi's main competitors were led by Robert Burns Woodward, professor of organic chemistry at Harvard and blessed with a bigger team, more resources, and superior infrastructure. In the days before overnight delivery and the Internet, being based in Mexico put Djerassi at a severe disadvantage. Because scientific journals took weeks to arrive, he couldn't keep abreast of new findings that might move his own work forward. So he persuaded a former classmate, who had just moved to Harvard, to phone through any research relevant to their work. Better still, he recruited a mole—nicknamed Flash—to spy on Woodward's progress.

By June 1951, Djerassi's team had succeeded: they had made and tested synthetic cortisone from yams. With mounting excitement, they rushed to write up their results and to establish their priority. With no overnight delivery, they had to trust their precious manuscript to air mail delivery by propeller plane. Once it had gone, there was nothing to do but wait. With astonishing sangfroid, Djerassi went off to explore the pre-Columbian ruins at Palenque.

When he got back, an alarming telegram from Flash greeted him:

Woodward finished cortisone Thursday. Writing note title Total Synthesis of Cortisone. Leaving nothing to imagination or intelligence of reader. Observed on his desk note quote tell Bliss, Gates says hold journal day or two unquote. Don't know importance of this. Arranged with Fieser publish same time. Suggest change your title.[3]

Just a few weeks after Djerassi's success, the Harvard team too had reached the same goal. Like Djerassi, they wanted the publicity—and priority. "Hold journal day" in Flash's telegram referred to the date on which the news would be published. So whose account would appear first? Normally, every scientific article has to go through a lengthy review process, but the telegram implied that review might be waived for the Harvard team. Djerassi didn't know where he stood: Had his own report been accepted? Was it in the process of being reviewed? Suddenly, being the underdog was not motivating but infuriating; just about everyone making the critical decisions about publication came from Harvard.

"It was impossible not to brood over the overpowering quasi-incestuous influence the Harvard chemical establishment had," he later wrote. "For a few days, a wave of paranoia overwhelmed us. Though a gringo chemist, I suddenly felt like a native Mexican—misused and discriminated against by Yankees up north. Even now, four decades after the event, I can still feel my adrenals respond."[4]

In the end, four articles about the synthesis of cortisone appeared simultaneously in the August 1951 edition of *JACS*, even though Djerassi's report had arrived in the editors' office on June 22 and Woodward's had not arrived until July 9. Infuriated, Djerassi felt that his competitors had "gotten away with murder." His only compensation was a huge picture in *Life* magazine over which he gloated: it featured him with his team, grouped around a giant yam.

"We were two weeks earlier!" Djerassi insists to this day. "What difference does it make? To the world, to science, to patients? But we were first!"

Winning the race didn't turn out quite as Djerassi or anyone else expected: neither the Syntex nor the Harvard synthesis of cortisone was ever used on a single patient. While they had all been frantically competing with each other, two scientists working for the pharmaceutical company Upjohn had invented a simpler, cheaper solution.

What the race did achieve, however, was to put Syntex on the map as a company that knew how to synthesize hormones. And Djerassi's next project changed the world: synthesizing norethisterone, he made the first female contraceptive and is known, to this day, as "the father of the pill."

Djerassi is often charged with having precipitated a sexual revolution and divorcing sex from love. But within the scientific community he is more controversial for the frankness with which he describes the competitiveness of science. Nearly into his tenth decade, he openly acknowledges that he is still competitive—"*very* competitive," he says—and insists that his colleagues are no different.

"Some scientists furiously deny this, but that's just hypocritical bullshit," Djerassi insists with relish. "It's a mixture of poison and nourishment. Science can be most collegial and at the same time most brutally competitive. And your brutal competitors are your colleagues. You are dependent on them and compete with them—but brutally."

Djerassi has been criticized by his fellow scientists for, as he says, washing their dirty linen in public. In several novels (which he calls "science-in-fiction") he describes the often desperate, sometimes comic antics of scientists so intent on gaining recognition, priority, and prizes that they perpetrate all kinds of deceit. Sexual infidelity, stealing, changing data, lying—Djerassi even has one character who changes her surname from Yardley to Ardley to ascend the alphabetical list of authors. *Bourbaki's Gambit* describes the perpetration of a scientific fraud to get revenge; the more memorable *Cantor's Dilemma* shows how far scientists will go to win a Nobel Prize. The books are clever and comic, but Djerassi is quite outspoken about the degree to which the culture of science displays occupational deviance.

He is also more relaxed about it than many scientists. He has won his fame as the father of the pill, secured his priority in synthesizing hormones, and retired (albeit unwillingly) from Stanford. But for scientists still in the fray, the competitiveness of science is an increasing source of anxiety and alarm.

From an economic perspective, the world of science has a tournament structure: fostering intense competition by amplifying small differences in productivity (like two weeks) into large differences in recognition and reward. Tournaments take the high achievers produced by competitive school systems and turn them into ferocious contenders who imagine that, if they don't act like divas and superstars, they'll be accounted losers. According to economic theory, tournaments are supposed to bring out the best in individuals and force the best work to the surface, but even economists now concede that tournaments have perverse outcomes. These are especially costly in an activity that depends on collaboration—like science.

"We had two groups of scientists, both looking for a particular gene for rheumatoid arthritis. One group was in the US, and the other was in Sweden. And they were in a race! They found all the families and generations of families that had the gene, but they had a problem: each team's group was too small to be statistically important. Neither team could generate sufficiently meaningful data. Their competition had divided the field into two parts, neither of which was large enough to count. They both had to have the numbers!"

Vijay Kuchroo almost giggles with the perversity of the situation he describes. The Samuel L. Wasserstrom Professor of Neurology at Harvard's Center for Neurologic Disease, he has seen this scenario more times than he likes to remember: great science, immensely clever scientists, stymied and stalled by their professional rivalry.

"They had to share their data or no one would have anything with any validity," Kuchroo tells me, still astonished by the stalemate. "In the end, my colleague David Hafler brought them together. He said he should get the Nobel Prize for this—not for science, but for peace: it was so difficult to get these groups to work together!"

As we sit amid the sprawling and lavish buildings that constitute Harvard's medical establishment, Kuchroo thinks intently about the role that competition plays in science. Now in his fifties, with a mass of salt-and-pepper hair, he brings to his work the same youthful enthusiasm he had when I first met him twenty years ago. He is known to work all hours, to be relentless in rethinking problems, and while that could make him sound like a bully or a bore, he is neither. Immensely well liked and highly regarded, Kuchroo has a personal gentleness in his manner that belies his formidable focus.

"Science, you know, it sounds so abstract. Much of what we do is so abstract. But it is also terribly personal. It's not about a product or an institution. It's *you*. It's *your* name on the paper, it's *your* work. A lot of scientists take it so personally, and you get—in extreme cases—you get suicides when people turn out to be wrong. It's just very, very personal."

Kuchroo recognizes that such intense identification with work has its benefits, but lately he has been more concerned with the problems it provokes.

"The problem of credit—who gets the credit for the work—is very difficult. Everyone wants the credit, and that can make people very solitary and very competitive."

Kuchroo isn't just talking about ego. Credit, to an academic scientist, is the currency of progress. Research has to be published in order to gain recognition. Every published article builds a scientist's professional résumé, and the number of times it is cited by other scientists indicates the importance of the author's contribution to the field. A steep pecking order of professional journals determines prestige: publication in high-impact journals like *Nature* or *Science* can make a scientist's name or even, in China, earn an author a house. It is customary for most scientific papers to credit multiple authors; the first-named author has done the most work, and often the last-named author is the sponsor and supervisor. But having too many authors on a paper diminishes everyone's luster, so the competition for authorship is critical—careers can depend on it.

"If you have ten postdocs," Kuchroo says, "some may be disproportionately the backbone of the lab. They provide the ideas, open discussions, and they should get credit—but this is often not the case. It is the person who sees what the idea could be and brings it to fruition that really matters, but often the authors in the middle may have been the backbone of that idea."

Kuchroo worries about this because having a lab full of rivalrous scientists is profoundly counterproductive. He has seen that in his own lab.

"Five or six years ago, I had a lab filled with some of the best people I ever had. But they had no common purpose. You could see it: the tissue culture room was trashed. No one cared! No one talked to one another. Everyone was working hard, but they weren't producing anything. Competition really was taking its toll."

Part of the problem was that everyone seemed to feel the need to behave like a master of the universe—even the ones who didn't honestly feel that way about themselves. Kuchroo recognized that a few motivational speeches would change nothing and that ratcheting up the competition was likely to make things worse rather than better. Instead, to boost the creativity his lab was losing, Kuchroo took an unusual step. He employed a psychologist, Kerstin Lagerstrom, from the Karolinska Institute.

"Vijay had told his group that I was coming and we were going to work together on team development," Lagerstrom recalls. "I'd say that 60 percent were eager to work with me, 20 percent were just wondering what it was all about, and 20 percent didn't turn up.

"That some didn't turn up—I'm used to that. But to ignore it was telling.

One of them, he was thinking that talking about team is rubbish. 'I will make my science, and I have no need of a team.' Some of them had other priorities, thinking, 'Why spend time on this? I'm too busy. My time is expensive.' Some of them were curious and frightened. What would happen? You could hear that."

Her affiliation with the Karolinska Institute, Lagerstrom tells me, helped her to get the scientists' attention; the Institute's committee awards the Nobel Prize for Medicine. That commanded respect even from Harvard researchers. But what struck Lagerstrom most of all was that everyone who turned up seemed to work as an individual, deciding his or her own timetable and priorities. She also felt that there were far too many egos in the room.

Lagerstrom asked the group to consider three animals: lions, owls, and St. Bernard dogs. Which one, she asked the lab members, do you feel like? After designating a corner of the room for each animal, she asked the scientists to go and stand with their fellow animals. And she watched as they observed each other—how many in this corner, how few in that one.

"There are men there thinking about being lions who are not. You put them in three corners. They can see, 'My God, in this team we have too many lions. We have just two dogs. What does it mean?' And all these owls are standing about. Everyone stopped for a second."

Lagerstrom asked each group to explore the characteristics of their animal, their positive and negative attributes, and then to present their animal to the others. All the time, she watched as the scientists collaborated, discussed, and puzzled over the exercise.

"So they are talking about the animals all the time. After ninety minutes like this, they are so in these animals, they can talk about them. They think they aren't talking about themselves—but of course they are! We have all these animals in this room, and every animal is necessary for this team."

Getting the scientists to discuss how the animals related to one another defused personal tensions and released a deeper conversation about how collaboration works. But then Lagerstrom asked the scientists to fill out a questionnaire about their own work habits. Suddenly, sharp contradictions emerged: how people imagined themselves was strikingly at odds with the way that they really worked. They thought they were leaders or collaborators, but for the most part they all worked as soloists.

When the group broke for dinner, Lagerstrom noticed some of them phoning their missing colleagues to tell them they should turn up the next day.

Over the two days that she spent with them, Lagerstrom helped the scientists to see two important things: First, their behavior in the lab got in the way of the very achievements they sought. They might imagine themselves to be collaborative, but in fact most of them were isolated and uncommunicative. Second, they came to see that a productive working environment needs all three animals. Lions, she explained, defend the group and bring out the best in people. Owls do most of the thinking and the work. The St. Bernards are more interested in other people than themselves; they are the glue of the group, but become despondent and passive if there isn't enough action. The group only works when all three can contribute fully.

"The message from me," Lagerstrom continues, "was that *everyone* has to think about how they can improve their communication with everyone else. Everyone needs to get feedback so that the team can become better. And everyone—not just the leader—needs to take responsibility for that." Collaboration is just that: co-labor.

For Kuchroo, the experience revealed that collaboration has to be designed, not assumed. He had hired too many owls who thought they were lions—meaning that he had hired a lot of young scientists who wanted to be superstars and thought that the way to achieve star status was to act like prima donnas. But this was futile because, if they couldn't or wouldn't share, they could achieve nothing. And he needed to have more than one lion in the lab because that would foment debate, which would encourage everyone to speak up.

"The scientific discipline requires collaboration," Lagerstrom observes, "but the system rewards soloists. And they think it's productive, but for science as a whole, it's just the opposite."

This isn't just a matter of personalities. Many institutions are predicated on the belief that competition surfaces the best talent and that combining the top talent produces the strongest, highest-achieving teams, departments, organizations. They often cite the theory of natural selection to explain why this must work. Since nature is constantly selecting the best for breeding, thus creating resilient, productive species, surely what great teams need is to combine talents honed and selected by competition. This interpretation of Darwin is more than a little simplistic and, when applied to teams, throws up significant problems.

William Muir teaches and researches population genetics, and he wanted to understand, in practice, how natural selection really plays out in groups. Perhaps because he works at Purdue University, he chose to explore this by investigating how to breed the most productive chickens.

Chickens, as we know, have always lived in flocks, and in the egg industry they're typically kept in groups of nine to twelve. Seeking to increase egg production—the marker of a successful flock—Muir designed an experiment. In the first instance, he simply identified the most productive groups of hens and observed them as they bred freely. Then, as a contrast, he selected the most productive individual hens and used them to breed the next generation of hens. What, he wanted to know, would prove the most productive method: the free flocks or the super-hens?

After six generations, Muir compared results. The free flocks were still full of plump, fully feathered hens, and egg production had increased dramatically over the course of the experiment. But the second group, the supposedly super-hens, was shocking. After six generations, only three hens were left; the other six had been murdered. The three survivors were nearly bare of feathers, having plucked each other mercilessly.

When the evolutionary biologist David Sloan Wilson reported this experiment to some of his colleagues, showing the slides of the ragged super-hens, a professor came up to him exclaiming, "That slide describes my department! I have *names* for those three chickens!" It turned out that her department had adopted the policy of promoting individual high achievers purely for their individual accomplishments, and the results had proved just as catastrophic as Muir's.[5]

Yet many imagine that dream teams must contain the largest number of superstar soloists—that, after all, is what a tournament structure delivers. But collaboration is a great deal more subtle than that, and disciplines that depend on it, like science, find that the very qualities they need are undermined and undervalued by the system they depend on. Competition is supposed to produce the best scientists—but it also produces behaviors and attitudes that undermine the work.

Over the last decade, the tournament, which has always been the model for scientific achievement, has become strikingly even more cutthroat. In part this is because there are more scientists than ever. While governments demand ever more science graduates, the truth is that the scientists we already have struggle to earn a living in a vocation they love. The competition for resources militates against the collaborative relationships on which original science depends.

"Throughout most of its history," writes David Goodstein, vice provost at CalTech, "science was constrained only by the limits of its participants' imagination and creativity. In the past few decades, however, that state of affairs has changed dramatically.... What had been a purely intellectual competition has become an intense struggle for scarce resources."[6]

Every principal investigator who runs a lab produces, on average, at least ten PhD graduates, each of whom must then find a postdoc position before qualifying to run his or her own lab. But nowhere are scientific budgets increasing by that order of magnitude. The chances, therefore, of getting a position and funding for research decrease even as recruitment increases. So perverse is this system that one professor has referred to biomedical research as "a Ponzi scheme," claiming that "we are selling our incoming graduate students a bill of goods."[7]

Principal investigators have no interest in changing this. The more postdocs they can get (and the cheaper), the more work they can generate. An oversupply of postdocs makes them pretty cheap, and there is no evidence that earning a PhD increases your lifelong earning capacity. The cost in money and time means that young scientists never catch up financially to their nonscientific peers.

"There's a lot of dead bodies, out of my lab anyway," one scientist acknowledged.[8] "There are going to be kids that aren't going to make it. I know they're not going to make it, but I'm going to lie to them. I'm going to say, 'Well, you might get a PhD.' And I know that their chances are probably one in three."

Science is inherently and necessarily a collaborative and accretive act. Every new finding builds on earlier work; hence Newton's famous statement, "If I have seen further, it is because I have stood on the shoulders of giants." Each discovery, large or small, positive or negative, opens up avenues for subsequent exploration or shuts off dead ends. On a formal level, that's what the scientific journals that so haunted Djerassi are all about: not just staking a claim to priority but disseminating the information required to enable other scientists to take the next step. On an informal level, discussion, debate, the exchange of knowledge, and mistakes allow everyone to do more considered work and to avoid duplicating errors. That is how science, as a system, is supposed to work.

But it all falls apart when the sharing stops. That's why Kuchroo was so concerned by the behavior in his lab: without discussion, work can't progress. Scientists are haunted by the fear of being scooped, of finding out that work in which they've invested years has been duplicated elsewhere and published first. That fear makes them stop doing the one thing that makes science productive: talking to one another. Fear generates silence, which stops creative work in its tracks. In 1966, 50 percent of 1,042 scientists said that they felt safe talking about their research; by 1998, that number had fallen to just 14 percent. "Secrecy," researchers John Walsh and Wei Hong wrote, "is strongly predicted by scientific competition (measured as concern over having one's research results anticipated)."[9]

"I'm always wary of submitting grants to study sections," one scientist acknowledged, "because it's not unknown for them to take your ideas, kill your grant, and then take and do it. And I think all of us have either had that happen to them or know somebody who had that happen to them."[10]

Scientific conferences, which are supposed to be a maelstrom of collaboration, have become instead a standoff of defensive, rivalrous researchers more afraid of being scooped than being discovered.

"I presented my dissertation to an international conference," one scientist recalled, "and the topic was on ethical decision-making by nurses. A number of famous nurse-ethicists came up and asked if they could have a copy of my paper, which wasn't published yet.... And I talked to my postdoc group and our mentor, and they said, 'You're not going to send it, are you?... You're a fool if you do.'"

"I presented posters for an academy meeting," another scientist confided. "And then a few months later, I saw an article almost the same. And I said, 'What's going on?' So I look at the time the paper was submitted. It's almost the same time, you know? I don't like to say anything, but it was almost identical."

"And you thought they were just taking pictures," his colleague commented.[11]

The oversupply of ambitious science graduates has produced a crisis of expectation in which legions of ambitious young scientists identify all peers and potential collaborators as rivals. And that has consequences that scientists now call "normal misbehavior": secrecy, sabotage, data "cooking," and culling.

Secrecy easily morphs into misrepresentation when scientists feel that the only way to protect their work is not to share their findings in full. In the rush to publish and establish priority, they omit crucial details so that their fellow scientists can see their results but won't quite be able to reproduce or challenge them. At its worst, data editing can change the picture completely. One scientist reported being asked to "shave" the last two data points off of her results since they seemed to undermine the impact of her conclusions. But without the full data, other investigators could neither understand nor build on her work.

Scientists regularly talk about gaming the system by promising more than they know they can deliver, eking out results in three papers where one would have been more coherent, or cutting corners in the rush to publication. The process of peer review—the vetting of research reports by colleagues—has come in for increasing scrutiny and criticism because getting published is so critical to scientists' careers and reputations. Just as Djerassi feared that his Harvard competitors might be shown favoritism, so today scientists anticipate that the work they submit to peer-reviewed journals may be rejected or intentionally stalled by reviewers who are also their rivals. The same fears apply to grant applications. It isn't uncommon for grant reviewers to dismiss an area of research, arguing that it is unfruitful, in the hope of doing the work themselves.

This "normal misbehavior" isn't new. In the days before science brought any financial or institutional rewards, journals were created specifically in order to establish priority; that was the only prestige that science had to offer. But the promise of status introduced a motive for fixing the game. Writing in 1830 on the "Decline of Science in England," Charles Babbage identified forms of scientific misconduct that he called the "trimming" and "cooking" of data. He also lamented the prevalence of "pleasers": scientists so ambitious to be elected to the Royal Society that they always conformed to prevailing views, never risking argument or debate. Since Babbage's time, however, pressures on scientists have only increased, not just because of the overabundance of scientists but also because of what has come to be known as the "Matthew effect."

The name, coined by sociologist Keith Stanovich, refers to the biblical passage Matthew 25:29: "For unto every one that hath shall be given, and he shall have abundance: but from him that hath not shall be taken away even that which he hath."[12] As applied to real life, this means that winners tend to attract more benefits to themselves, thus perpetually putting themselves in a stronger position to win yet more. Just as in sports, where a few gold medalists get the commercial endorsements, professional sponsorships, top coaches, and premium facilities and the rest fight over scraps, in science the Matthew effect is seen to reward the top scientists with well-paid, secure jobs, excellent facilities, and more postdocs than they can handle. They also find it easier to get their research funded and published and are routinely asked to discuss their work at conferences around the world. Meanwhile, the rest must compete furiously for marginal visibility and scraps of funding for research that is underresourced. In some countries, it is even government policy to focus on so-called centers of excellence, leaving the rest to die by the roadside. The problem with the Matthew effect in science isn't that it is unfair; even scientists themselves don't seem too perturbed by issues of justice. What bothers them is that it doesn't produce great science.

Science is accretive and incremental but also, to some degree, random. That is to say, it requires a large number of small insights to produce a transformative event. Very small discoveries can be disproportionately important because, without them, the next step can't be made. But scientists don't know what those small bits will be, and they particularly don't know where they will come from. One classic example of this is the invention of polymerase chain reaction by Kary Mullis, a scientist described to me variously as a "surfer pothead" and a "combative but competent chemist." He described himself as a "a generalist with a chemical prejudice."

In 1983 Mullis was working for Cetus Corporation, a young biotech company in Emeryville, California. He described his work—duplicating DNA—as repetitive, slow, and boring. Driving to his weekend cabin one Friday night, contemplating an experiment that he knew wouldn't work, Mullis had an idea that he thought could radically improve DNA duplication.

"For the next few weeks I described the idea to anyone who would listen," he wrote later. "No one had heard of its ever being tried; no one saw any good reason why it would not work; and yet no one was particularly enthusiastic about it. In the past, people had generally thought my ideas about DNA were off the wall, and sometimes after a few days I had agreed with them. But this time I knew I was on to something."[13]

He was indeed on to something. Mullis's invention of the polymerase chain reaction (PCR) is widely credited with having made possible the revolution in genetics that followed, and in 1993 he won the Nobel Prize for his work. But no one would have picked Mullis as a high-achieving scientist to back. He didn't have a raft of publications to his name or a famous sponsor, and he wasn't working in an elite scientific institution. And much of the scientific understanding that was required for PCR had been lying around for years.

Stories like this in science (and there are many) acquire a semimythological status because they illustrate the degree to which you can't pick, or plan, winners. "Identifying the top 10 percent," wrote one journal, "is impossible without a crystal ball or time machine."[14]

That is what makes the Matthew effect dangerous. If it were possible to pick winners, concentrating resources on them might make sense. But since we can't, the concentration of resources on the few—any few—reduces diversity and productivity and amplifies risk. Science relies on having many eggs in a very broad array of baskets. But the Matthew effect in science reduces the baskets, the eggs—and the surviving chickens. It also creates a very steep pecking order.

I've never met a scientist who, when asked about a Matthew effect in science, did not immediately confirm its ubiquity, to the detriment of science overall. Young scientists see how the game is played, and what they learn can be corrosive: every colleague is a rival; every collaboration poses a threat. Confronted by the stark realities of modern science, every researcher competes in the race to become a publishing star.

At the turn of the millennium, one such star was Jan Hendrik Schön. A shy German physicist working at Bell Labs, he had just turned thirty when he started to attract attention. He'd had a shaky start after arriving in America; like many a young scientist, he worried about job security, his data weren't good enough to publish, and he was on a short-term internship. But then his data began to improve. Working on ways to turn nonconductive plastics into semiconductors or even superconductors, Schön was doing research that held immense promise for computing, for laser technology, and for nanotechnology. One Princeton scientist said that Schön's work "defeated chemistry."[15]

Schön was a classic owl: shy, retiring, and more inclined to work alone than in a large research group. For visa reasons, he had to keep returning to the German lab where he'd done his PhD and where he continued some of his research. So, although he was an avid basketball player and affable sportsman, his work was mostly solitary. That didn't hurt his reputation, which, if anything, was enhanced by his isolation. Schön was said to have "magic hands," and although he had the occasional collaborator, much of his behavior reinforced the mystique of the brilliant young loner.

He was working at Bell Labs at a particularly stressful time. Between the 1950s and 1970s, the lab had had the reputation for being the most fertile lab that had ever existed: it had produced seven Nobel laureates and was credited with the invention of the transistor, the laser, information theory, UNIX, and the C++ computer language. But by the time Schön arrived, the lab was owned by Lucent, whose share price was falling. Senior managers felt under pressure to cut costs and to generate big wins that would prove the relevance of its research and justify the lab's continued existence. Schön's work fit the bill: brilliant science with immediate technology applications. And every one of Schön's papers, published in *Nature* and in *Science,* increased the lab's intellectual prestige.

Celebrated as one of MIT's "Innovators Under 35" in 2002, Schön was credited with having produced

> single-molecule transistors whose electrical performance is compara-
> ble to that of today's best silicon devices but which are hundreds of
> times smaller.... Schön's clever design established Bell Labs as a leader
> in the race. But Schön is not interested in simply reinventing the tran-
> sistor.... He also helped devise the first electrically driven organic laser,
> which could mean cheaper optoelectronic devices. The soft-spoken
> Schön recalls being "very surprised" by how well his molecular tran-
> sistors worked. But it won't be a surprise if Schön helps transform
> microelectronics.[16]

When Schön's mentor, Bertram Batlogg, was due to move to Switzerland, Schön asked a colleague whether he should follow. No, said the friend, he should stay put. If he moved with Batlogg, his mentor would get too much of the credit, and "Hendrik," he said, "you're the star."[17]

Over the next two years, Schön published paper after paper. The scientific world was agog. Bell Labs was thrilled with its superstar, while the leading scientific journals competed so fiercely for the privilege of publishing his new work that they reduced the time they took to review it.[18]

As Eugenie Samuel Reich recalls in *Plastic Fantastic,* Schön's work was so exciting that physicists around the world sought to reproduce his effects in order to understand them. To do so, they had to be able to replicate his experiments. When they couldn't, they blamed themselves, assuming that their techniques were inadequate, their materials were subpar, or their equipment was faulty. When Joe Orenstein at Berkeley tried and failed to get Schön's results, he said he felt "like a clumsy oaf."[19]

At the University of Minnesota, Alan Goldman, one of the world's lead-ing authorities on superconductivity, and one of his postdocs, Anand Bhat-tacharya, hoped to surpass Schön's discoveries. After trying for nearly a year to reproduce Schön's results, they had gotten nowhere. Bhattacharya wrote to Schön, asking for help; he hadn't written sooner, he said, because Schön was such a star. Schön answered their questions, but still nothing worked. The postdoc grew increasingly frustrated as work that was supposed to last just two or three years stretched to five.

At the University of Delft, Ruth de Boer's PhD research, based on Schön's findings, seemed to get nowhere too. Nearly in tears, she considered quitting. In Florida and in Japan, scientists had the same experience. No one published anything because negative results aren't deemed to be findings—and no scientist wanted to broadcast failure. "Just because you don't understand the science," one investigator commented, "doesn't mean it's wrong."[20]

By 2001, Schön was on a "publishing rampage"—he published seven papers in November 2001 alone[21]—and speculation abounded that he would win the Nobel Prize. As Schön became more famous, he also became more isolated, preferring to eat alone or to hang out with German-speaking researchers working in areas different from his own. Any criticism of Schön's work was dismissed as competitive jealousy.

Superconductivity and nanotechnology were becoming such hot topics that *Science* started publishing some of Schön's work on Science Express, a website designed to fast-track new scientific discoveries. But as the publications accumulated, so did the questions. The data looked too smooth; there wasn't enough "noise"—random data that didn't fit. And many of the effects that he described even Schön himself couldn't explain.

By the beginning of 2002, Schön was being pestered by mounting questions prompted by his work; his colleagues tried to persuade him to publish more detail so that other scientists could replicate his findings. He couldn't. But while some members of the scientific community were skeptical about his ferocious productivity, just as many were dazzled by the new scientific celebrity. During a talk at Princeton, he was challenged by professor of physics Lydia Sohn, but she soon fell silent, feeling no sympathy in the room. As she left, another faculty member asked her pointedly how many papers *she* had published in *Science* or *Nature* recently. Schön and his colleagues "were golden people, you couldn't say anything," was how Cornell's Paul McEuen described them.

The sheer volume of Schön's work had aroused McEuen's suspicions. On May 9, 2002, he worked through the night comparing Schön's data in different papers. Over and over again, even though Schön claimed to be using different materials, the data were identical. "This stuff is fake," McEuen concluded the next morning. Too many of the graphs were too similar; there wasn't enough noise or mess to prove that different experiments had generated their own results.

For at least four years, Schön had been doing science backward: identifying what it was scientists hoped to find and generating the data that looked as though he had found it. An investigation into his work found him guilty of using the data set from one experiment for numerous papers and plotting his graphs from mathematical equations, not actual results. Twenty-eight of Schön's papers have now been retracted. His PhD was revoked, his prizes rescinded, and the German Research Foundation banned him from German science for eight years. That ban has now expired.[22]

Had Schön falsified his data purely because of the competitive pressures he felt to produce? According to Eugenie Samuel Reich, who researched his story, Schön was such a pleaser that he would explain anything the way you wanted to hear it. Schön appreciated the competitive pressures around him and responded to them by producing big news in high volume. Likewise, Bell Labs wanted, and needed, the acclaim that Schön brought the lab; that acclaim strengthened its position in the scientific and financial markets. *Science* and *Nature* competed for his stunning papers, each one seeking to be the first to publish them. The scientists who knew firsthand that the experiments could not be replicated—well, they didn't want to tell anyone they had failed. Everywhere Schön looked, he saw competition and succumbed to it.

Schön's was one of the most daring and extreme frauds in scientific history. But it was not an isolated incident. Scott S. Reuben, an anesthesiologist working at Baystate Medical Center in Springfield, Massachusetts, is said to have fabricated results in twenty-one papers going back to 1996. His research appeared to provide support for multimodal analgesia: the use of nonsteroidal anti-inflammatory drugs and neuropathic agents in place of opioids for pain relief. All of his scientific papers have now been retracted. But perhaps the most daring of frauds was that perpetrated by Korea's Hwang Woo-Suk, who claimed to have cloned human embryonic stem cells.

Nor is scientific fraud limited to the so-called hard sciences; the social sciences too have had their scandals. The most notorious of these involved Diederik Stapel, a Dutch social psychologist who attracted attention when he seemed to prove that eating meat makes people more selfish and that white people are more likely to discriminate against black people when they meet in messy environments. *Science* had trumpeted that Stapel's work had profound policy implications, and he was made dean of the School of Social and Behavioral Sciences at the University of Tilburg. But suspicion was aroused when he wouldn't let students participate in his research or dissect his data. Stapel's data were too perfect: it turned out that he had developed a habit of sharing only the results that confirmed his hypotheses, fatally distorting the bigger picture. Eventually, fifty-five of Stapel's journal articles were retracted. Talking with remorse about what he'd done, Stapel cited competition as a reason, not an excuse: "There are scarce resources, you need grants, you need money.... I am a salesman. It's like a circus."[23]

One widely shared characteristic of fraudsters is that they are almost always pleasers: they are good at intuiting what's wanted and then delivering it. Their work reinforces stereotypes and expectation; far from being original or creative, they can see what will make them successful and just take shortcuts to get there. They don't need to be original thinkers; they flourish in highly competitive environments precisely because success is so clearly defined, hot topics are so obvious, and the focus (just as in sports) is on outcomes, not experience or learning.

Schön, Reuben, and Stapel and many other scientific frauds point to a larger trend in science: the alarming—and increasing—rate at which research papers are withdrawn when they prove to be fraudulent, unreliable, incomplete, or inaccurate. In October 2011, *Nature* reported that retractions had increased tenfold over the past decade, while the number of published articles had increased by just 44 percent.[24] Most scientists believe that this retraction rate represents only the tip of the iceberg when it comes to faulty, rushed, misleading work.[25]

Papers are withdrawn because they are found to contain mistakes (73 percent) or because they are fraudulent (26 percent). Although plagiarism is a concern, fabrication—making up the data—has proved to be a bigger cause for concern.[26] Online, retracted articles can be withdrawn or identified as having been withdrawn. But because that can't happen in print, faulty work can have a long afterlife: one study showed that retracted research was still being cited twenty-four years later.[27]

Retractions are symptomatic of the intense competitive pressure to produce—too much, too fast—that all scientists experience today. With too few jobs, low pay, and the severe bifurcation of scientific talent into winners and losers, the pure love of science for its own sake is easily abandoned. In one study, 17 percent of postdoctoral fellows acknowledged that they were willing to "select or omit data to improve their results." And 81 percent were willing to select, omit, or fabricate data to win a grant or to publish a paper.[28] You could call this science's Goldman dilemma: if the reward is great enough, the risk seems worth taking.

The rising rate of retractions, of course, represents a huge cost: wasted resources, wasted time, and wasted opportunity. For every experiment that is done or postdoc hired, others are rejected or never even make the attempt. The time and effort that so many gifted scientists spent trying to replicate Schön's work wasn't just wasted; it was unavailable for work that might have proved authentically productive.

Ferric Fang, professor of medicine at the University of Washington, sees the growing rate of retraction and fraud as indicative of the dysfunction of competition in science more generally. His argument isn't theoretical. As the editor of *Infection and Immunity,* Fang confronted scientific misconduct firsthand when one of his authors, Naoki Mori, was found to have manipulated data and images. Fang was so disturbed by the experience that he launched his own research project to identify how widespread the problem was becoming.

"We have found," he tells me, "that the more important the journal, the higher the number of retractions. But you get all kinds of other dysfunction: old work pawned off as new and a strong skew to positive findings. In science we are rewarding people only if they find a positive result, and that's the wrong incentive. If competition could be ratcheted down, if there were more jobs so scientists were not so desperate, things would be better. The degree of competition dictates the severity of the problem."

These aren't abstract problems for Fang. He is careful about the kinds of personalities he recruits into his own lab and tries hard to model the collaboration he feels is essential to productive science.

"I've become a lot more sensitive to recruiting collegial people. I tend to blab the minute the experiment is done! I *want* to get feedback, and I share unpublished data because it pays off: my colleagues point out things I hadn't seen. Science is a community endeavor, and it's crazy when we take individual credit."

Fang can withstand being scooped—as he has been—because he's well established now. But for the younger generation, he says, excessive competition is demoralizing, destructive, and counterproductive. Anxiety over the future, he says, is at an all-time high.[29]

"There is a very real risk that we will lose a generation of scientists. As older scientists hold on longer because their retirement plans aren't as healthy as they had expected, I see young people bailing or choosing other options entirely. So many young people have no prospects—nothing attractive to retreat to. We could accommodate a larger scientific workforce, but it would need a very different structure."

The tournament of science has generated a vast array of perverse outcomes:

secrecy, sabotage, the Matthew effect, fraud, fabrication, plagiarism, a rising rate of retractions—all of which undermine public faith in and support for science. If the collegiality and transparency on which science fundamentally depends is being destroyed by too many scientists chasing too little funding, I asked Fang, wouldn't science be better with fewer scientists? If there is such oversupply, why do governments keep calling for more science graduates?

"My sense is that science has evolved into a more aggressive, businesslike activity where scientists see themselves as small businesses competing in a zero-sum game for credit and funding. Science is a team sport, but the rewards are individual. This is a big disconnect and a huge obstacle to career paths. If funds were given to institutions instead of to individuals, then we might be able to organize things differently, have career paths and midlevel scientists. But no one wants to make a first move because they all compete with one another."

The fundamental cost to science of head-to-head competition is trust. Young researchers, competing for jobs and funding, don't trust their colleagues enough to collaborate with them. Established scientists don't always trust each other's motives. The desire to establish priority erodes a sense of common purpose. The pressures of time, money, and ego corrode the integrity of work that, if it can't be trusted, undermines public respect and understanding for science at just the moment when we need it most.

"We have big problems right now that science can solve," Fang insists. "But if you look at the needs of society and the relative number of people doing high-quality science, just 0.1 percent of the population is an active scientist, and that's not enough! The US spends twice as much *on beer* as it spends on research and development, and funding is at its lowest point since the 1960s."

You might think that the business world would know better; after all, it's often to the commercial world that policymakers look for ideas about better management and structural reform. But much of the competition in science has been imported from the business world, where executives don't know the story of the Purdue chickens and many imagine themselves to be social Darwinians, convinced that the struggle for survival is the best way, even the only way, to generate commercial fitness.

"We used to have these shoot-outs," Joe tells me. "The idea was that we'd compete to design the best concept, tagline, whatever. It was the most dysfunctional thing I've ever seen. Teams would steal briefing materials, go into databases, remove crucial information, and never put it back. At first I thought, 'This is a game. They can't mean it!' But they did mean it. And it wasn't fun."

Joe worked for one of the largest ad agencies in New York. Now a freelance creative, he doesn't want his full name disclosed because he still works in the industry. But he can't stand working in any one company for too long, he says, because the dog-eat-dog cultures are so vicious. At his last agency, Joe headed up a business unit that, like all the others, was responsible for its own profit-and-loss account. His unit's profitability determined his bonus and his place within the corporate pecking order. That, he says, had all kinds of perverse consequences.

"I had a really talented designer working for me," he recalls. "But her forte was animation, and I didn't have any animation work. One of the other teams had a great animation job, and I tried to get her involved in it. But the guy leading that team thought that if he gave it to her, she'd be off of my books and my team would look more profitable. Well, he didn't want that, did he? So he wouldn't take her—so she left. The next time we wanted to pitch a big animated campaign, we didn't have the talent we needed."

Internal competition of this kind has just the same effect in advertising and other industries as in science: no trust, no sharing, plenty of sabotage.

"A few years back, I was in a team pitching for new business," Joe tells me, shaking his head. "And the same agency had four teams, all in the same company, pitching against each other. It got so we had to take our materials home with us at night—because otherwise they'd go missing or—oops—someone spilled their coffee on a big display. Just ludicrous stuff. We communicated via private email accounts so we couldn't be hacked! I had to check that everything charged to my accounts was actually my business—because other business units used to try to move their costs into mine. It was mad! All within the same company."

For Joe, his profit-and-loss accounts and his position within the corporate pecking order were the means of keeping score and fostering internal competition. For highly competitive people, the clarity of that score and the possibility of a clear win make work more exciting. From the first time Brad Ruderman walked onto the trading floor at Lehman Brothers, he was hooked.

"I saw a situation I couldn't believe," he tells me. "So competitive as to boggle the mind! Energetic people just knocking the cover off the ball:

energy, activity, just the most amazing scene to behold."

Ruderman couldn't wait to join in, and after a friend introduced him to the managing director, he started to work his way up. It was quickly obvious to him—and to everyone else—how the game worked.

"We're all on commission," he explains, "and every day of the week, our prior day's commission would be posted on the window of the managing director's office. So every day you walk into work, your net income is posted for everyone to see. If that doesn't foster competition for someone who is already competitive, what would? Of course, that's what it's for. For someone like me, if you're not up there somewhere near the top, it's a disaster. You have to do something because otherwise, well, you're nothing."

Earning anything less than $100,000 a month, Ruderman explains, made him a loser. But if he had made $140,000 in July, then anything less than $120,000 in August made him a loser too. So every month, he needed more and more to stay in the game. This wasn't, he hastens to assure me, because of what the money could buy. It was because the money identified him publicly as a winner or a loser.

"It wasn't greed," he tells me. "It wasn't about stuff. It was about my personal scoreboard with everyone else. Sometimes there'd be three days left in the month, and I hadn't hit last month's target, so I'd push the envelope to do something not always in the best interests of my client. I lost all morals, all ethics."[30]

The business-as-sport metaphor plays its part, with many sales organizations using these kinds of scoreboards to motivate their teams. At HBOS, on Saturday mornings, if salespeople had met their targets, they were rewarded with cash. If they had failed, they got a cabbage. The ritual public humiliation, firmly segregating winners from losers, was supposed to be motivating. Instead, it was implicated in the widespread mis-selling of mortgages and insurance. Likewise, when Anthony Salz reviewed what had gone wrong at Barclays Bank, where mis-selling and interest rate manipulation had flourished, he found at the heart of the dysfunctional bank a culture that employees described as "winning at all costs." The glory of being a winner and the shame of being a loser were both so extreme that no one dared question the system. The word used least often to describe the bank's culture was "courage."

The clothing store The Limited used to run sales meetings at which high achievers sat at the front, with lower earners stuck at the back—just like at the Roman Colosseum. They called the strategy "Winning at Retail"—or

WAR for short. What The Limited, and Lehman Brothers, and other firms using these kinds of humiliating techniques don't seem to acknowledge is that these "wars" create casualties: in Ruderman's case, it was his clients and his own internal sense of right and wrong. His frantic desire to compete caused him, as he later recognized, to abandon his moral compass and chase success at any cost. The same could be said, on an epic scale, of the financial institutions still trying to unwind the bad deals they made in their rush for market share and headline profits.

Because human beings are competitive, when we are put into these tournaments, our first response is to try to win. The most obvious way many people try to do this is by working harder—which is, of course, why the tournaments are created in the first place: companies are trying to motivate the workforce to be more productive. Longer hours become another kind of arms race, both for attention—face time—and for the hoped-for productivity that more hours will generate. The problem is that the strategy backfires. Over one hundred years of research into productivity have shown that, after about forty hours a week, when we work longer we make more mistakes—and the extra time goes to cleaning up the mess we've made.

"We see it here in England and in the US, but if you really want to see long hours," Jim Brady tells me, "go to Hong Kong."

Brady worked in financial services in Asia—Hong Kong and Singapore—for years. He loved the people and the work, he says, but he didn't love the way it got done.

"We were working quite ridiculous hours—being at your boss's beck and call at 2:00 AM, at 7:00 AM. Emails in the middle of the night followed by more emails: why haven't you answered me yet? It would make headlines in the paper here if we worked people like this. You can only drive people that hard for so long. Then they crack up, they have heart attacks or they leave or they make—and this certainly did happen—they make very big mistakes. But there's this sense that if we don't run, all day, every day, someone, some competitor, will be on our tail."

Juliet Schor, in her book *The Overworked American*, estimates that, as Americans work longer, they sleep less, losing sixty to ninety minutes of sleep every night. An accumulated sleep debt doesn't just make people feel bad; it also makes them perform badly. As the brain becomes steadily more fatigued, it starts to siphon off energy (in the form of glucose) from the parietal and occipital lobes to the thalamus. The reason for this is efficiency:

the thalamus is what keeps you awake. But the parietal and occipital lobes give you capacity to think. So the harder you have to struggle to stay alert, the less able you are to do the creative, imaginative thinking that modern work most requires. That this is bad for us, we know: for instance, when the Bank of America intern Moritz Erhardt was found dead after working three straight days, the competitive pressure to put in the hours to secure the job was instantly identified as the prime suspect in his death. The harder we compete to stay in the game the less able we are to play it.[31]

For genuine creativity and collaboration to flourish inside organizations, the people who work there need to be rested, alert, and able to trust one another. But notwithstanding the physical and ethical costs implicit in pitting employees against one another, many large corporations take internal competition one step further and formalize it into forced rankings, a process by which all employees are placed in a strict pecking order so that the bottom 10 or 15 percent can be eliminated. The system was made famous by Jack Welch at GE, where every year the workforce was forced into ranks of the top 20 percent, the middle 70 percent, and the bottom 10 percent—who could be let go. Welch argued that the system was kind because it gave the bottom ranks plenty of warning that they were failing.

In various permutations, the same concept is still applied, by some estimates, in half of the Fortune 500 companies. AIG divides people into five ranks, GlaxoSmithKline into four, Lending Tree into three. Advocates of forced ranking argue that the system rewards outstanding performers. But what none of these companies seem to appreciate is that forced ranking creates levels of competitiveness and distrust between individuals that make the system uncreative—a human equivalent of the Purdue chickens.

Puzzling over the curious failure of Microsoft to develop any truly innovative technologies for over a decade, the writer Kurt Eichenwald found that every single employee he interviewed cited "stack ranking" (the company's version of forced ranking) as the most destructive process inside the company, driving out untold numbers of bright people.

"It leads to employees focusing on competing with each other rather than competing with other companies," a former software developer told Eichenwald.[32]

Top-notch developers did not want to work with other strong performers because doing so would risk their ranking. As a consequence, jobs were secure to the degree that people surrounded themselves with pleasers who would never pose a challenge or a threat. By putting all of its employees in a constant state of threat, Microsoft didn't inspire ambition for excellence but a prevailing desire for safety.

"People do everything they can to stay out of the bottom bucket," one Microsoft engineer said. "People will openly sabotage other people's efforts. One of the most valuable things I learned was to give the appearance of being courteous while withholding just enough information from colleagues to ensure they didn't get ahead of me on the rankings."[33]

Eichenwald's descriptions of the horse-trading that characterizes Microsoft's ranking process are eerily reminiscent of the same process at Enron, where it was called "rank and yank." Managers retreated into conference rooms, pulled down the blinds, and wrote employees' names on whiteboards or Post-It notes. Then the trading began: "I'll let you keep Jane if I can keep Kevin." Because a certain percentage had to fail, much depended on office politics, on fitting in and not standing out. This kind of popularity contest is a recipe for obedience and conformity: the opposites of creativity.

Forced rankings were forcefully evangelized by the consulting firm McKinsey, which argued that, in the "war for talent," only the firms most ruthless in identifying and promoting talent, while throwing the rest out, became truly successful. Subsequent research hasn't validated their argument.[34] Of the companies McKinsey celebrated, 33 percent vanished, 18 percent have proved disastrous, 16 percent have proved disappointing, 10 percent have done okay, and only about a quarter have proved the thesis.[35] Far from ensuring success, forced ranking made failure more likely. In 2013, Microsoft announced that it would abandon stack ranking—but Yahoo's chief executive, Marissa Mayer, began to adopt a similar system in a desperate attempt to boost her ailing firm's creativity.

Forced rankings are a particularly perverse form of motivation because they destroy one of our most profound motives for working, which is the desire to belong to a group. Humans are inherently social; we can do very little alone and crave the safety and sense of connectedness that social relations provide. Abraham Maslow ranked the need for "love and belongingness" in the middle of his hierarchy, testifying to our intrinsically social nature. Yet formalized evaluation tournaments threaten our relationships with all our coworkers, atomizing the society of the workplace until it's everyone for themselves.

Competing to work the longest hours would be bad enough, but the various permutations of forced rankings generate a persistent sense of threat: always under evaluation, individuals fear ostracism. What we now know about brain function suggests that this is cognitively exhausting. The brain has quite hard limits to its capacity, and energy used for one activity is unavailable for others. When we feel threatened, our brain's amygdala, constantly scanning the horizon for danger, generates fear and anxiety, sapping energy from the prefrontal cortex, the part of the brain we most need for planning and decision-making. Working under a persistent sense of threat therefore carries a cognitive cost, as fear drains our capacity to think and to learn.

Yet every company says that it wants and needs creativity and innovation, which are often correlated with risk-taking—you have to be willing to tolerate a lot of ambiguity and danger to realize an idea that no one has tried or seen before. Some businesses set out specifically to recruit people who demonstrate a high tolerance for risk. Intel has done this for years. But once inside the corporation, something strange seems to happen: risk tolerance declines, even vanishes. Intel has long puzzled over this problem, little imagining that its ranking system—called FOCAL—may have quite a lot to do with it. The people I spoke to within Intel didn't find this phenomenon puzzling at all. No one, they said, wanted to risk their standing in the rankings.

"If I'm getting arbitrarily ranked by my peers, of course I'm going to stop taking risks!" Jackie Witt tells me. "The system wasn't based on achievements, knowledge, skills: it's based on whether people like you! People that are likable aren't always the most productive or creative.

"You know the Intel mantra, Andy Grove's slogan: only the paranoid survive. Well, sure, they *survive*. But paranoia isn't a great state to do creative thinking. So what you found at Intel was that easy, compliant people moved up. People were paranoid enough to make everyone their friend—but that's where the energy went! I worked with someone there who was a risk-taker, and she was not moving up. She was very productive, not necessarily well liked but hugely effective. But she was stuck indefinitely at the middle third. But I thought her work was outstanding, original, and driven. But of course, she just left."

Witt is a seasoned project manager and highly accustomed to competitive multidisciplinary teams. Her very calm, thoughtful approach to complex projects has led her through Intel, Toyota, Genentech, Apple, Fujitsu, and even subsidiaries of GE. She says that much of her work resembles mediation: getting combative teams to listen to each other. But this work becomes difficult when there's a charismatic CEO, because everyone is vying for attention and credit.

"Turf wars. Toxic people. This kind of dysfunction can be very disheartening," she says. "It costs people jobs, bonuses, mental health. A lot of people don't feel they can walk away, so they stay feeling abused, angry, frustrated. And they didn't start that way; they started out hoping to do a really wonderful job.

"The other thing about forced rankings is that, however frequently they're done (in some companies it is every six months), they're very present. They absolutely make you concentrate on the here and now. How am I doing *today*? You can't and you don't think about the long term. Why would you? If you don't do well today, there won't be any long term. So the kind of sustained thinking, horizon gazing, imaginative speculation you need to be truly creative—it doesn't even cross your mind. You are always focused on the present threat."

Witt approaches turf wars and toxic people with knowing bemusement. But they came as a shock to Cathy O'Neil, a young Harvard data scientist known online as Mathbabe. In 2007 she left academic mathematics to work at one of Wall Street's most secretive hedge funds, D. E. Shaw.

"When I was being recruited," she laughs, "I didn't know they were specifically looking for competitive people. I was interviewed by person after person, all asking me math puzzles. I didn't know it was a contest; I kept answering them because I'm a mathematician and I love math! I think they interpreted my facility as smugness, and that impressed them. But I wasn't nervous because I didn't care that much. I just got through by sheer luck and love of subject."

When she started work, however, she was amazed by the culture she discovered.

"People didn't talk to each other! You couldn't ask for help. I was told—*explicitly*—not to ask for help. Why? Because nobody wanted to be seen helping anyone else. There were some nice people there, but if you really insisted, the only way you could ask a question was online—so that if someone decided to help you, nobody else would find out!

"There was a foosball table. You thought, when you saw it, that that might be kinda fun. But it was not there for fun. It was there so everyone could compete with each other, show off to each other. My feeling was that they got competitive people because they wanted everyone to stay in line and to define their self-worth through their banking achievement. Everyone had to acquiesce to the bonus."

D. E. Shaw was famous for attracting the brightest people it could find; former Harvard president Larry Summers (the same one who questioned women's innate ability to do math and science) had worked there for $100,000 a week. O'Neil knew her colleagues were brilliant—that wasn't in doubt. But they did not want to share anything. This made meetings quite peculiar.

"In a group meeting, you couldn't say what you were thinking. People had ideas, of course. But they'd never tell you what they were because they might be thinking of starting their own fund. And if they articulated their idea, then that would be owned by D. E. Shaw and they'd end up in competition with their own idea! So if you had a good idea, the one thing you absolutely had to do was shut up. You didn't want anyone to steal your idea—or to steal it and outperform you. So you had these meetings, with plenty of super-smart people around the table—all saying nothing."

If scientists don't share because they seek priority, financiers don't share because they want credit—and the money that comes with it. If you were a new person working in an old fund, you didn't dare contribute a fresh idea because that wouldn't attract any credit or bonus—because the fund was already in production. So you wanted to save your bright ideas for a new fund; that was the only way to get all the credit. Or your idea might be worth even more if you left and set up on your own. In the meantime, you'd better just keep your thoughts to yourself.

"Basically everyone was just your rival. You'd have to have special trust with a specific person to be able to collaborate. Every other person constituted a threat. It was very unpleasant. I think of myself pretty much as an alpha female, and I'm more than capable of looking after myself, but this was pretty intense. It was very repressed. The atmosphere of secrecy—the idea that anything of value had to be *hidden*—it was just very repressive."

O'Neil ultimately left D. E. Shaw, returning to academia and to a role advising Occupy Wall Street on better economic models than the ones she had watched collapse all around her. Nevertheless, she insisted, contrary to much public commentary, that the business models she'd seen in action *had worked*. The financial crisis came about because those business models had delivered—but only to the advantage of their designers, not to the benefit of anyone else. The economic crisis was just a version, writ large, of what she'd seen at the hedge fund: a tournament that disproportionately favored a few.

Competition, she concluded from her experience, always provides a motive for gaming the system. It doesn't promote excellence. It doesn't generate great thinking because great ideas can't spread. And it militates against anyone taking responsibility when the system breaks.

"When it's each man (or woman) for himself, then who cares about the system? Nobody! As long as I'm okay, I'm okay. I'm a winner. You're not? Too bad."

Competition values secrets, encourages a lack of transparency and the hoarding of information, and discourages the desire to share or to collaborate. As such, it can become criminogenic: producing environments that inspire or even normalize criminal behavior. No wonder academic studies have found that highly competitive people are more likely to be drawn into insider trading, which seeks to make money from private knowledge.[36]

That secrecy has two profound consequences. It creates a Matthew effect, making those who have information richer and those without the information poorer. This is visibly demonstrated in the crime of insider trading, where those who have information gain more money, more power, and thus more access to information. And that, in turn, makes the winners feel sublimely independent from, and not responsible for, the system as a whole.

That can be seen in the raft of insider trading cases brought since the financial crisis. But perhaps more profoundly, the disconnectedness of the solo winner is most visible in the choices made by traders who, as early as 2005, started to glean the consequences of subprime mortgages and the explosive derivatives market, which, to them, was the ultimate big secret. And so, instead of warning that the house might be on fire, they placed big bets on it burning down. Hedge fund traders like John Paulson, Michael Burry, and Eugene Xu felt no responsibility for the system as long as they could figure out how to use it to be winners. In the race to establish the intellectual priority of their cunning, this was too good a chance to miss. Those who gain most from tournaments have the least interest in repairing them.

Scientists don't give up easily; tackling hard problems is what they do for a living. At the Weizmann Institute of Science in Israel, the molecular biologist Uri Alon struggles daily with the challenge of creating a productive lab in a scientific culture that militates against collaboration. At times, his experience in science had been so bad that he couldn't get out of bed in the morning. Being scooped filled him with shame, and getting stalled or lost in a project was crippling. But he also loved science so much that he felt that there had to be a better way of doing it. How could he counteract the destructiveness of competition with levels of engagement and motivation that would be more creative? What motivations and processes could change the dog-eat-dog culture? He found some of his answers in improvisational theater.

Alon doesn't come across as a natural performer. In person, he's introverted and intensely serious. But the process of doing improv changed the way he thought about and did science.

"Unlike science, in improvisation theater they tell you, 'You will fail miserably. You'll get stuck.' But what happens *when* you're stuck is different. First, you expect it to happen because everyone tells you it will happen. And then, everyone shows you a lot of solidarity. They've been there too. You aren't a loser—you're one of them.

"I also learned from improv theater how to have a conversation that opens up new ideas. The central principle of improv is to say, 'Yes, and ...'—to agree and build. So if one actor says, 'Here's a pool of water,' and the other says, 'No, that's just the stage,' then the idea is over, it's dead. It's called blocking. But if instead, 'Here's a pool of water!' 'Yes, let's jump in! Look—there's a whale.' 'Let's grab its tail. It's taking us to the moon....' That way you unlock hidden creativity by building on each other's ideas."

In science, competition promotes a lot of blocking, but in Alon's lab, "Yes, and ..." prevails. This has two consequences. It broadens everyone's thinking, making every student in the lab more responsive to the others and opening up new ideas. Students feel supported and encouraged to persevere. "Yes, and ..." also creates a climate of safety, the sense that thinking can be wide-ranging and risky. Instead of competitive stress narrowing focus and imagination, solidarity and encouragement enlarge human creativity.

Creating an environment in which students expect to fail, but where they can fail safely, has made Alon's lab very creative. Working at the interface between physics and biology, he and his students made surprising and important discoveries about general principles of how biological systems like the body are designed. A rich emotional environment of risk-taking, support, and creativity put the lab on the map.

Alon can't protect himself or his students from being scooped. But what he can do is mitigate the fear and shame that accompanies the experience. He's even written a song about it, "Scoop, Scoop," which he sings, with his colleagues, anytime one of them is scooped.[37] I've seen him do this onstage too, and the impact is striking. Alon isn't a dazzling singer or guitarist— but that's the point. He's willing to be fallible and vulnerable in the service of supporting, encouraging, and motivating the people around him. If the price you pay for sharing is that you sometimes look a little ridiculous, it doesn't matter. What matters is the encouragement you provide to others.

Uri Alon is a well-published, highly regarded scientist, but one of his most widely cited publications isn't about biology—it's about managing motivated teams. It was published in *Cell*, but is relevant to any walk of life.[38] In it, he comes to three conclusions.

Productivity is a function of having enough autonomy to feel free, responsible, and proud. Threats decrease that sense of freedom and obstruct the support that every creative person needs.

Social connectedness is, in itself, motivating. In his weekly two-hour lab meetings, Alon carefully sets aside the first half hour to talk about anything *except* science: birthdays, the news, vacations. Then, when a paper is presented by a member of his lab, the group is given a role to play, as imaginary referees or brainstormers. The goal, he says, is to teach every member of the lab that they are there for each other.

But most important of all, Alon insists that the route to great innovation or discoveries is through failure, what he calls "the cloud": the part of the process where things go wrong and you lose direction. Second-guessers never make it to the cloud because they play it safe, which is why they achieve little. But truly creative people find themselves in the cloud routinely because they're exploring new territory. If, when you're in the cloud, you think about winning and losing, you stay stuck. Fear shuts down your imagination and ability to think broadly. But when Alon's students come to him and say, "Uri, I'm in the cloud," his response is, "Great! That means you're close to something important." That's when he gives the student the most support, encouragement, and solidarity.

The reason competition is so detrimental to creative work is that it severs the links between people who could help each other and because it insists on framing everything as success or failure. Time and again, talking to people who have led lives full of innovation, creativity, and achievement, I've found that their abilities come not despite failure but because of it. Alon's now highly influential thinking about science came from thinking and talking to others about being stuck. Had he concealed his sense of confusion—like the scientists who couldn't replicate Jan Hendrik Schön's results—he would never have been able to motivate himself or all the people around him.

Critical to everything Alon discusses is trust: the feeling that it is safe to explore and to make mistakes. Mistakes, after all, are how we all learn, beginning with how we learned to walk and talk—we experimented and discarded what didn't work before finding what did. But intense competition makes people afraid to make mistakes—and even more reluctant to share them. And that's dangerous.

"If you can't talk about mistakes, you learn nothing. If anything, it just convinces you that you're perfect, which is really dangerous," David Ring tells me.

One of America's leading orthopedic surgeons, Ring has become as famous for his openness about errors as for his skill in the operating room. On one occasion, he operated on a woman who needed treatment for trigger finger, a condition in which a finger gets locked rigidly into position. But Ring failed to operate for that condition; by mistake, he operated for carpal tunnel syndrome.

He immediately told the patient what had happened and did the correct operation the same day. But what startled his colleagues was that he wrote and published an article, describing how the mistake occurred. Instead of hoping no one would learn about his error, he analyzed, publicly, every step that had gone wrong: surgeons had been running late, so stress was high; the nurse had marked the correct arm but not the incision site; and the operating room had been changed, so the nurse who prepared the patient wasn't present and the nursing team changed during the procedure. He spelled out these mistakes not to apportion blame but to identify fixes; documenting the errors led to improvements that stopped them from happening again. David Ring, previously recognized as a good doctor, came to be described as a great man.

Ring now argues that the way to make hospitals safer isn't to compete for perfection but to create a climate of safety where errors can be openly acknowledged and swiftly fixed. And he's a major leader in a movement to eradicate blame and celebrate improvement. Ring says that medicine has learned a lot about the value of mistakes from the aviation industry, where everyone, at any level, is encouraged to speak up about the smallest slip. Of course, as he points out, in an airplane everyone really is in it together.

Competition isolates people, pitting them against one another, but we do better, more creative work when we acknowledge how much, in fact, we need one another. Alon's lab is more productive because its members support each other through "the cloud." Ring's hospital is safer because he doesn't think he's perfect. The excellence of the work derives from networks of support and improvement in which every contribution counts.

"Everyone is royalty."

That's the way John Abele describes the rich array of physicians, surgeons, and scientists who helped him build Boston Scientific into one of the world's leading medical device companies. In sharp contrast to the scientists who jockey for position or the CEOs who tell their stories as heroic soloists, Abele describes his business largely by telling other people's stories. Disruptive technology may have been what made the company rich, but Abele is quite confident—evangelically so—that the business derived its success from its talent for collaboration.

"A lot of people think collaboration is soft," Abele tells me. "It's a paradox. In order to gain control, you have to cede control. You have to recruit some of the people who maybe don't want to see you succeed. It's fraught with contradiction. This kind of collaboration isn't soft at all—it's very, very hard."

Critical to Boston Scientific's early success was development of a balloon catheter that could enlarge narrow or blocked arteries without surgery. The device had been pioneered by a junior physician, Andreas Gruentzig, who built early prototypes in his kitchen, using a razor, tubing, and adhesive. Gruentzig was passionate, curious, and clever, but perhaps his greatest—and least predictable—advantage was that he had little personal or professional power.

For years, Gruentzig practiced on dogs and corpses, but of course the time came when he had to try his device on living humans. To do so, he needed the help and support of surgeons, the very people whose work his device would disrupt. According to Abele, who loves celebrating Gruentzig's achievements, it was the young doctor's modesty and curiosity that won him allies.

"Instead of proclaiming that his ideas were revolutionary breakthroughs that would change medicine, Andreas referred to them as incremental advances. He was always the first to point out the deficiencies in the tools he pioneered and was constantly on the lookout for signs that they were flawed. People responded in part because of Andreas's unusual willingness to share credit for whatever was achieved."

In 1976, at an annual meeting of the American Heart Association, Gruentzig started to introduce his device to surgeons. They became so intrigued by his ideas that they all wanted to come and see his work for themselves in Switzerland. Demand grew so great that he had to use another new technology—video conferencing—to accommodate everyone. What he wanted most of all, and what drew in so much interest, wasn't to show off his device but to get ideas from his expert audience. Critical to this process, says Abele, was that Gruentzig didn't think of his device as "his," and he didn't see the surgeon community as outsiders. In the project to find a way to clear arteries without surgery, everyone was equal—including Gruentzig himself. Everyone was royalty.

The intense interest in his device enabled Gruentzig to pioneer not only his innovative catheter but also the world's first live demonstration courses—a practice now standard in medicine around the world. He did so in order to share every detail of his technology because he wanted the surgeons to understand it and to share their doubts, concerns, and ideas; he recognized that sharing would be the best way to improve the device. In addition—as if two breakthrough ideas weren't enough—he created a voluntary registry of the patients he and his colleagues treated in order to track results and share data. The very fact that everyone had access to each other's procedures put them on their mettle to do their best work.

"It's no exaggeration," Abele later wrote, "to say that the rapid sharing of experience and techniques enabled by the registry saved many lives and prevented untold complications.... And when it came time to publish papers, Andreas and his closest collaborators made sure to spread the intellectual wealth."[39]

Gruentzig was just the opposite of the scientists in Kuchroo's labs; he made headway even as he shared lavishly and refused to posture or jockey for position. His pioneering product wasn't developed for a nonprofit but for a commercial business; the fact that money was to be made from it did not impede the sharing—of knowledge, insight, data, and experience—that contributed so critically to its success. Nor were Gruentzig's collaborators saintly and selfless; Abele describes them as having big personalities, ample egos, and terrific self-confidence. Moreover, they were all rivals, and most were far more established and successful than the inventor himself. That Gruentzig had no power—to compel their attention, to demand their time, or to tell them what to do—lay at the heart of their fruitful collaboration. There was no power-distance problem because Gruentzig didn't have or seek power. What he did was inspire others to join his quest for a breakthrough procedure. He spoke to physicians' highest aims and to their professional pride and never presumed to have all the answers. His big contribution lay in keeping everyone's trust levels high.

"All the divas think they are best," Abele tells me wryly, "but what you need are really impresario skills: not putting yourself at the center of the picture but bringing everyone in. I see a lot of people define collaboration as individuals and institutions working together for a common goal. No, that's not enough. In great collaborative leadership, the job is to tweak the environment so that the sum is greater than the individuals who are contributing. This is a very different category of leadership, and it may involve sacrifices. People laugh and joke and think collaboration is some kind of feel-good enterprise, and I'm sorry, in those situations the achievement is never greater than the sum of the parts."

That the talents of collaboration are so elusive may not be because they're rare but because they're rarely taught or celebrated. Our educational systems focus relentlessly on solo achievement. In a survey of 1,824 university students given a series of mock job descriptions, any that mentioned teamwork or collaboration were specifically rejected. The students didn't want to be collaborators—they wanted to be stars. Employers were even discouraged from mentioning teamwork in job ads if they wanted to attract high achievers.[40]

The sports world celebrates and overpays individual athletes and habitually attributes success, even in team sports, to individual star players or coaches. Aping the entertainment industry, which monotonously resorts to the easy marketing strategy of turning a soloist into a brand, young people beginning their careers are told that they must be brands to sell themselves in an increasingly terrifying job market.

The cult of celebrity invariably portrays outstanding performers as superstar soloists. Worse still, the myth of the selfish, misbehaving soloist is rampant in entertainment. Ask aspiring young artists in music, film, theater, dance, or painting and they will recite for you the huge egos and trashed hotel rooms that denote success. They don't know the lamentable fate of William Muir's super-chickens either, and as surely as the young, uncommunicative Harvard scientists, they've come to believe, as one young musician insisted to me, that "it's the assholes who succeed."

This ethos is highly misleading—not just because the bulk of all work today is done in teams and we badly need people who can do this work with skill and passion, but because even with regard to the entertainment industry it's simply wrong. One of the distinguishing features of the "idols" produced by talent contests is how swiftly their glory is extinguished. The most successful artists depend on a dense skein of collaborative relationships, richly knitted and fastidiously nurtured. Nobody does great work alone, and no one survives very long if they aren't good at working with others.

Nowhere is this more obvious than in the music industry. In 2012, when Adele's album *21* won six Grammy Awards and became the fourth-highest-selling album of all time, it was easy for the press to express astonishment and delight at the brilliance of one young woman. The truth was far more interesting.

That one album used the services of over one hundred musicians, producers, arrangers, and engineers. Adding the design and marketing executives behind the album would double that number. The brand may have been focused on one individual, but the operation itself depended fully on making all the contributors work together.

"Adele is a brilliant collaborator. She wouldn't be able to do what she does if she weren't also fantastically good at working with other great people," according to producer Jim Abbiss.

Abbiss has worked with Adele since, as an unknown young singer, she brought out her first album, *19*, in 2008. He has a long and distinguished track record working with artists as diverse as the Arctic Monkeys, Bjork, Massive Attack, and The Kooks. Both as an engineer and a musician, he has spent a great deal of time in recording studios seeing how music comes together.

"Although the technology in music today means you *could* in theory do it all yourself, nobody does! And nobody does because it is always better—always—as a collaboration. Whether it's a whole ton of people like *21* or just a few people, the music gets better."

If the music industry has a reputation for slick and aggressive self-promoters, Abbiss doesn't fit the image. Thickset and wearing a plaid shirt, he looks more like a builder than a musician. He's keenly alert to the people around him and curious about places and ideas he hasn't encountered before, demonstrating many of the qualities that John Abele so admired in scientists: passionate curiosity, modest confidence, and mild obsession. He describes his job with marked understatement—he "serves" his artists, he is just a "sounding board"—and you rapidly sense that he contributes to a production only what it needs: tough love at times, reassurance at others. He demonstrates a genuine curiosity about other people, listens very carefully, and works hard to advance an idea, even in a conversation.

"Adele is very open and giving, so it's hard not to like her. That helps. Of course, she can also write fantastic melodies and songs and sing better than most people on the planet, so she can afford to be generous! But she genuinely likes people who can make the work better. She doesn't have any arrogance or worries about that."

According to Abbiss, Adele's commitment to the song is what makes her a great collaborator. She'll embrace what makes it better and reject what doesn't. Personal dominance doesn't come into it.

"We worked on a song together for her first album, *19*. This was a cover of Bob Dylan's 'Make You Feel My Love.' I thought it needed strings and suggested a string quartet. Adele had never worked with a string quartet before and wasn't sure how to use it. So I called in Rosie Danvers."

"I just got a call," Danvers recalls. "Jim said, 'Can you bring in your quartet and do some work with this singer, Adele?' I didn't know her—no one did. Jim said there was no need to do anything in advance, just turn up with the quartet. And I thought, 'Just turn up?' I was upset because every project I do, I want to do it to the best of my ability. I wasn't going to chance it. I wanted it to be fucking brilliant!"

Rosie Danvers is a classically trained cellist. She found session playing unsatisfying, so she created her string quartet, Wired Strings, in the hope of building richer collaborations with a wider array of musicians. Hers was a relatively new idea, and this unexpected opportunity with an unknown talent wasn't an obvious winner. But that didn't matter. It was in her nature, she told me, to give of her best. Eight months pregnant, she listened to the demo and set to work. The singer had, she thought, a "notably good voice." That just made Rosie work harder. Two days later, in the studio, everyone met for the first time.

"So Rosie played us excerpts, and Adele would say what she thought: she liked this, didn't like this," Abbiss recalls. "Everyone had to be quick and confident to adapt—and everybody was. Bear in mind, at this point, there isn't any money, which means there isn't any time. But in the space of three hours, everyone changed a lot of what they'd come in with, and we got great performances from everyone. The whole mood was: The best idea wins. It's not about you or her or me. The best idea wins."

As Abbiss and Danvers separately related the story, they both beamed, laughed, and smiled—clearly, this had been a great experience for everyone. Studio sessions are expensive and often stressful, but for each of them, these three hours had been relaxed, productive, creative. Danvers left the session feeling that she had achieved everything she'd hoped for when she'd formed her quartet.

"We all just left the session pumped! You're creating something *together*. It is just so much more fulfilling. Second-guessing is boring. But this time everybody contributed. And everybody loved it!"

The reference to second-guessing is telling. Truly successful artists with staying power don't choose between deviant behavior, on the one hand, and obsequious compliance, on the other. They develop the skills, nuance, empathy, and intelligence required for complex collaboration. Danvers wasn't passive in her collaboration; she wasn't waiting for a moment of solo glory (like Kuchroo's sullen scientists), nor did she look for alibis in case she wasn't successful. A fully mature collaborator, Danvers took responsibility for the quality of her contribution. Not surprisingly, she's gone on to do more work with Adele, both in live shows and on the award-winning album 21. Listen to "Set Fire to the Rain"—that's Albers and her quartet giving the song its distinctive sound. She's also brought the quartet to work with artists as diverse as Beyoncé, Jay-Z, Sande, Kanye West, Lana del Ray, and Paul Weller. The brief is usually vague, and invariably there's little time, but she's always determined to bring her best and to knit together the contributions that everyone brings to the work.

"I don't want any competitiveness in my sessions. In a traditional orchestra, the leader sits at the front, and then there's a pecking order all the way back. Forget that: everyone sits where they want. We all have to pull together, I need everyone's feedback. People like that; it gives them responsibility for the whole. It's more than just turning up. I want everyone to go away feeling they've given their best. It isn't about being chummy. It's about creating something together."

Just as in science, who gets the credit in music is always an issue. Credit has an impact on royalties, so there's more than ego at stake. But the best artists tend to be those who can appreciate the contributors who've made their work so good.

"It's important to be fair about credit," Abbiss explains, "because sometimes the smallest thing can make such a huge difference. Generosity lies at the heart of collaboration, I think. And it's striking that the artists who have real staying power ... they're all great collaborators. They know they need other people, and they welcome them and they're generous in the credit they give."

Everyone I've spoken to in the business appreciates that no great music is made alone. Reluctant to name names, every producer I asked identified bands that had talent but lacked staying power because they behaved like divas. Many of the artists in these bands hadn't started that way, but media hype and celebrity branding had turned their heads, sending them down a quick trajectory from prima donna to has-been. By contrast, the artists with sustained, meaningful careers know that they don't create in a vacuum, that they need to be provoked, stimulated, inspired by fellow artists.

This is not, of course, the message conveyed by the numerous talent contests around the world, where the focus is all on finding the single individuals whom record labels can market and replace. Music schools that aim to produce genuine musicians for lifelong careers hate these tournaments, and most musicians do too. With too much focus on personality and packaging, they say, the music gets lost.

It is impossible to have this conversation with classical musicians without, sooner or later, one name coming up repeatedly. "Lang Lang," one musician groans. Actually, lots of them groaned—and refuse to be named. But the cause of their discomfort is always the same.

"He simply doesn't listen," was the opinion of one horn player. "It is an incredible thing to say about a musician. Perhaps the worst thing that you *can* say. But he doesn't listen. He is so focused on being the top dog, the center of attention, that he really has no idea what else is going on inside the music. So of course, when he ignores us, we ignore him. The concerts are just awful. I'm amazed we don't get booed."

Although he never mentions Lang Lang, the name hovers over my conversation about music with the pianist Fou Ts'ong. Widely regarded today as one of the world's greatest living pianists, Fou Ts'ong won his fair share of competitions during his seventy-year career. But the competitive nature of music, he says, has changed.

"This competition culture is very detrimental because it is producing performances that may be technically dazzling but which are very, very unmusical. Technically there are thousands who can play the most demanding works. So they feel that they have to do something to make themselves special. But they don't need to; the composer is special enough. The performance is supposed to be about the music, not about the performer."

With his focus on Chopin, many of Fou Ts'ong's concerts are solo affairs. Doesn't that mean that he is the center of attention? How does a soloist collaborate?

"But that is what you must do!" he insists. "When I am playing, I am always playing *with* the composer. That is the important one. It is never about me. It has to be about the music. My god is the composer. I am always there only to try to communicate what the composer wants, so I am working, really, I am working for him, with him."

On large orchestral works, like a piano concerto, Fou Ts'ong always learns the entire score, not merely the piano part. It would not occur to him, he tells me, to work any other way.

"I have to have a concept of the whole piece; otherwise, how do I know what the piano is doing? Anybody who is a real musician always has the whole thing in his head, not just his part. Very often there is these days a lot of pianists with brilliant fingers, but they concentrate too much on the piano part, and you cannot play the music that way. I try to teach my students to learn the score and ask good questions. The greater the composer the more complex and varied their text. That's what I call the right approach. To try to find out the composer, to keep asking questions—that is the greatest originality."

The one place in the world where you might still expect the deliberate cultivation of star soloists is the Royal Academy of Dramatic Art (RADA), famous for the many remarkable actors it has trained: Richard Attenborough, Peter O'Toole, Glenda Jackson, Alan Bates, Anthony Hopkins, Alan Rickman, Fiona Shaw, Adrian Lester, Imelda Staunton, Ben Wishaw, Sophie Okonedo, and many more. But even here, director Edward Kemp is looking for skills and talent that go well beyond individual excellence.

"A lot of the students who apply imagine that acting is all about them. It's part of celebrity culture," Kemp tells me. "But that's not what we're looking for. We spend days with audition candidates because we want to see how they work with one another, how each young actor keys into what they're being offered by everyone else onstage. It's about what they reflect and how they respond, not just about what they do individually. Many don't understand that and come to give their big performance. But they don't do well. Not here, not anywhere really."

Just as music producers see that collaborative musicians enjoy longer careers, RADA's teachers recognize that actors who both give and get a lot from each other have richer, more substantial opportunities. Over the years that I've served as a council member for the Academy, we have periodically worried that too many students applying imagine that beauty and presence are enough. But what the profession wants and rewards are actors who are highly attuned to one another, who bring experience of life that enables them to read, interpret, and send signals with subtlety and understanding.

As I watched auditions for the 2013 class of student actors, the range of styles, ages, sizes, body shapes, accents, and approaches was remarkable. But talking with the tutors, I came to see what they were looking for: a rich (and sometimes mysterious) blend of experience (this is my contribution) with responsiveness (what I offer you is tempered and mediated by what I get from you). One candidate, Dino Keljalic, was a Serbian refugee who had fled first to Holland, then to Norway, where he'd trained as a doctor but then decided that he had to give acting a try. Tall, muscular, with dark curly hair and a sharp black beard, he undoubtedly had physical presence, but this wasn't what made him compelling.

"What's remarkable about Dino," Kemp reflects, "is that you can see that he brings understanding of other people to the actors he shares the stage with. He's engaged by them, interested in them. That's what it's about: what happens *between* people."

Earlier, Kemp had told me that identifying artists with true potential has always been difficult, not least because no one can predict how life will change them. He told me a story about an oboist at a neighboring music school whose career had stalled. Thinking she lacked the ability to forge a career as a professional player, her tutor recommended that she consider other options. She had an idea for a website business, so she set up a company, while continuing her musical training. It flourished and she did well. But what amazed and delighted her tutor was that her music dramatically improved.

"That's what makes this such a tough business," Kemp concludes. "You imagine the way to get better is to hammer away at it for hours. But it's more oblique than that. You can't do great creative work if you don't have a life to bring to it—and to the people you work with. It's about responding to other people. If it's all about you, then it's not really interesting."

In recent years, a wellspring of innovation in modern theater has come from new collaborative companies of artists—actors, writers, designers, musicians, puppeteers, and choreographers—who devise work together. The Canadian director Robert LePage speaks openly about how he creates his plays: he brings nothing, he says, but his ability to listen to what his collaborators contribute. Choreographer Twyla Tharp attributes the huge successes in her career to her collaboration with audiences. When you try to unpick who has done what in many of these theater groups—Punchdrunk, KneeHigh, Handspring, Complicite—you find yourself in the middle of a maze with no center. It isn't that everyone is doing each other's work—each brings unique expertise and discipline—but the cross-reactivity is so dense that it becomes impossible to map. None of this is possible where someone is trying to win.

Groups like this flourish by finding and developing outstanding partners. Many work together for years because finding the right blend of people who appreciate the challenge and reward of working together can be so rewarding—but also so difficult. The impresarios and producers who understand how to blend talents cultivate and nurture the participants they depend on: a flourishing flock of chickens is hard to construct and requires years of trust, mistakes, shared failure, and shared success. Ask CEOs what their biggest worry is, and they'll all say: the people. Not because they can't find great people—but because the competitive mind-set of almost everyone they recruit militates against their being great team members. Companies know that they derive greater creativity and innovation from teamwork—but what, they wonder, makes a great team?

To answer that question has required collaboration too. A team of researchers from Carnegie Mellon University and MIT started with individual intelligence tests that show that there is such a thing as "general cognitive ability"; in other words, if you're good at one thing, you're very likely to be pretty good at other things. And that general cognitive ability is a reliable predictor of a wide range of outcomes, including success at work and even life expectancy. The research team wondered, does a group equivalent exist? Is there a way of distinguishing very able teams—and if so, what are their characteristics?

They brought together sixty-three participants and gave them an architectural design test. When the volunteers worked on the project alone, their general intelligence turned out to be a good predictor of their performance. Next, they were put into groups—but here it turned out that neither the average general intelligence of the group members overall *nor* the intelligence of the single smartest group member was a good predictor of performance. Great teams couldn't be designed just using the math of intelligence tests. Moreover, factors such as group cohesion, motivation, and satisfaction didn't seem to explain the high-achieving groups either.[41]

Three factors made the crucial difference. First, there seemed to be a strong correlation between group achievement and social sensitivity. This was measured by the "Reading the Mind in the Eyes" test (the same one that measured empathy loss in the testosterone experiments). The groups whose members were better at reading faces and were more responsive to one another turned out to be more productive. Second, the underachieving teams had a few members who dominated the conversation—divas, soloists, owls. But the teams in which every member made a more equal contribution performed better. Finally, the teams that had more women did better too.

These researchers concluded that it might be easier to raise the intelligence of a group than an individual. You don't need to add super-brainy people to make a group "smarter"—that would just give you the problem of the Purdue chickens. But you do need to find team members who contribute their best but don't dominate, who are alert and responsive to everyone in the group and eager to hear what they bring. You also need to have enough women.

Collaboration matters because we know that we do better work, find more ideas, and craft more solutions when we work collectively. Although very little in our culture trains, rewards, or even seems to notice great collaboration, Uri Alon, David Ring, Adele, Fou Ts'ong, the inventions of Boston Scientific, the artistry of groups like Punchdrunk, and the productivity nurtured so carefully now within Vijay Kuchroo's lab all testify to our innate capacity to do phenomenal work together. That talent lies within us naturally, always, inherently. What we need is to build the structures and processes, the habits and relationships, that draw it out and make it grow.

On the fourth Thursday of each November, Americans sit down to Thanksgiving dinner. Almost every table sports a roast turkey and, alongside it, a dish of cranberry sauce. One of my earliest childhood memories features a sparkling pressed-glass plate holding the translucent red log of cranberry jelly. Every year we would carefully extract it so that it emerged intact, like a glistening, wobbly jewel, rimmed by the indentations of the can that had held it. Ocean Spray cranberry sauce, one of America's most iconic products, is sold to 62 million homes and made from a hard, bitter berry that grows only in North America. Like Thanksgiving itself, the cranberry represents the triumph of creativity and daring over adversity. But the story of Ocean Spray, the company responsible for the fruit's ubiquity, challenges many of America's most ideological notions of competition.

The cranberry sauce of my childhood was first invented by Marcus Urann, a Maine lawyer who had invested heavily in cranberry bogs. The berry is one of just three indigenous North American fruits (Concord grapes and blueberries are the others) and had first been cultivated on Cape Cod.[42] Observing that the sandy winds of Massachusetts Bay helped the vines to flourish, farmers in the 1820s started to layer their bogs with sand in order to produce a crop large and reliable enough to market. In the 1890s, Urann started buying up bogs, but he found that he was producing more fruit than he could sell. Since the berries didn't keep very well, he looked for a way to use up the surplus; today he is credited with being the first farmer to can cranberry sauce. Although many jokes have been made about this rare example of a lawyer's creative pragmatism, Urann's example was swiftly copied, until he found himself in head-to-head competition with two farmers: Elizabeth Lee and A. D. Makepeace. At this point, Urann did something even more creative: instead of competing with them, he invited them to join forces with him.

The name Ocean Spray was Urann's, but the company was run by all three farmers along the Rochdale principles—the governing ideas, pioneered in the 1840s, that led to the cooperative movement in the United Kingdom. Central to Ocean Spray was the idea that farmers owned the business together and that the goal of the organization was to preserve the value of their farms and the crops they produced. Instead of competing to become the biggest or most powerful, each farmer would help the others by sharing resources and know-how to expand and enrich the market for them all.

From its inception until his death in 1963, Urann operated as general manager of Ocean Spray, with Makepeace as treasurer; fundamental to the business throughout its history was the principle that the growers were the owners and ultimate managers of the business. Urann's legal expertise turned out to be particularly helpful. By cooperating with his erstwhile competitors, Urann and the new company attracted the attention of the U.S. Department of Justice. He and his colleagues reached an agreement not to run the company on competitive principles: the goal was not to eliminate other cranberry growers but to co-market and co-develop new products. A depression in agricultural prices during the First World War had generated widespread support for farmers, and in 1922 the Capper-Volstead Act had given cooperatives like Urann's additional protection for their organizational structure. They weren't combining in order to fix prices, but to develop and co-market their goods.

The sauce business thrived, as did the cranberry farms. The 1960s and 1970s saw an explosion in product innovation with the creation of bottled cranberry juice cocktail with its many extensions: CranApple, CranPrune, CranGrape. Global sales took off after research in the *Journal of the American Medical Association* showed that cranberry juice reduced urinary tract infections.[43] Subsequent research indicated that the proanthocyanidine in the berries prevents plaque formation and periodontal disease, while regular, long-term consumption of the juice can kill *Helicobacter pylori,* which causes ulcers and stomach cancer.

That the bitter little fruit has miraculous health-giving properties was, of course, sheer good luck, unknown and unforeseen by Urann and his confederates. But the way they chose to run their business was their own deliberate design and choice. Putting cooperation at the heart of the company has had consequences for every aspect of its success.

"We now have 750 farmer-owners and I work for them," asserts CEO Randy Papadellis. "I sometimes think of myself as the chief alignment officer because that's what I spend all my time doing: keeping everyone's interests aligned."

Those 750 farmers elect 13 board members who hire the chief executive. Votes are proportional to a farm's size, and there has occasionally been some tension between the big farmers and the smaller farmers. But the alignment that Papadellis talks about is firmly focused on building and protecting the long-term profitability of every single farm, large or small.

"We don't work for faceless shareholders," chief operating officer Ken Romanzi insists. "We work for third-, fourth-, fifth-generation cranberry farmers who want to keep value in their farms healthy. We know them personally; they're our neighbors. And that produces incredible pride in this company: that we aren't just making and selling 'stuff': we are using all the creativity we can find to develop and protect the farms, the traditions, and the people that depend on them."

Romanzi isn't a romantic. Before coming to Ocean Spray, he worked for Frito-Lay, where his claim to fame was the launch of jalapeño Fritos. His philosophy then, he says, was that if a product stood still, you just had to put cheese on it. But since Papadellis recruited him, Romanzi has become a vocal champion for the coop and the farmers whom it serves.

"We promise the farmers that we will take all of their crop, that nothing will be wasted, and that we will get the highest possible value for it that we can. We do that by building the Ocean Spray brand and by creating great new products. But then there's this night job we have. We start talking about crop supply, fruit supply, what form the fruit is in. And they can see they do even better if we work on those products together.

"You wouldn't have any of those ideas or discussions if you worked for Coke or Pepsi. You would just beat up on your procurement people to get the lowest price. But we procure from our owners, so we aren't trying to drive their prices down but to drive our product values up. This isn't about winners or losers, about top dogs or underdogs."

Every year the company's profits are paid as dividends to the owners, who decide how much executives get paid. Papadellis laughs when I ask him about his pay. He's not paid like the CEO of Pepsi, he says, nor is he in the market for yachts or precious gems. Nevertheless, he notes, "I'm paid well enough. The board has done well by all the employees because we do well by them."

"Until you're in it, you don't realize the difference the ownership makes," Stu Gallagher tells me. His office is full of antique cranberry scoops and spectacular photographs of gleaming red bogs. "I live around these farmers every day. They are my neighbors, and I've coached their kids' sports teams.

The whole business is just part of the fabric of your life. You don't feel like that at Nestlé, where I used to work. When we go into a new country, we aren't just another faceless American corporate giant. We have a story to tell that people around the world appreciate.

"The time horizon is endless: the children's children. If that were a private equity company, they're looking at three years. At a public company, it's a quarter. It makes my job more satisfying, meeting three or four hundred owners, the grower, the spouse, the kid, the grandchildren: they all come to the annual meetings."

Three times a year the executive team hits the road to share news about the business and hear about the crop. This is when farmers—who might otherwise be competitors—share ideas about how to tackle issues like water shortages, environmental regulation, or plant diseases. Ocean Spray's agricultural staff provides everyone with more scientific research than any one farmer could afford. Instead of vying to outdo one another, they share experience from region to region.

At Boston Scientific, John Abele believes that true collaboration is characterized by passionate curiosity, modest confidence, and mild obsession. He would be right at home in Ocean Spray's product development office, where dedication to the cranberry borders on the religious. Kathy Reilly has spent fifteen years at Ocean Spray, living, breathing, dreaming cranberries.

"Growers come up with great ideas," Reilly recalls. "I was at our annual grower meeting, and one of the growers had made his own pressed berry bars—sweet and dried berries pressed together with sauce and sugar—and said their kids love them—it was one of the best things I'd ever tasted. One grower made a salsa. So now, we have a berry bar in the works and we make a fruit salsa. We can't use all their ideas, but we test just about everything that comes our way."

Housed in a sprawling colonial mansion surrounded by cranberry bogs, the company has a relaxed and comfortable atmosphere that nonetheless shouldn't be mistaken for laid-back. Every executive I met at Ocean Spray was keenly aware of his or her responsibility to the owners and to the farms. But I found also an appreciation that creativity and innovation derive from the careful nurturing of relationships and a commitment to the long term. No one can call a meeting before 9:00 AM, during lunch, or after 4:00 PM. In the summer, everyone finishes at lunchtime on Fridays. And no one takes vacation during the harvest.

"It doesn't work without trust," says Papadellis. "That trust requires constant communication. Repeated communication. There's a lot of give-and-take. You can't just focus on a few because the structure requires that everyone counts. I report to the biggest farmers, the smallest farmers, and everyone in between. We have to make sure that at no point is anyone left behind."

Papadellis knows from bitter experience that his task isn't simple. He came into the company in 2000 as COO and immediately confronted a crisis. The farmers couldn't agree on the company's direction, so the board kept getting thrown out and, in its own turmoil, firing chief executives. The source of so much conflict was an opportunity to sell the business to Pepsi.

"They made a very big play for the company—flying in on corporate jets, making videos about us with Britney Spears, trying to show what a big deal they could do with us. But I thought there was nothing they could do that we couldn't do ourselves. And that keeping the business as a coop would keep the farmers themselves in a much stronger position. They would never have to compete for the management's attention."

In what Papadellis laughingly calls "a resounding 50.8 percent vote," the farmers decided to keep the coop. The real heroes, he says, were the 49.2 percent who agreed to support the management plan: "They gave us the space to execute, and it worked." Conflict subsided as all the farmers agreed to give Papadellis's plans a chance. Fundamentally, he concludes, for all the turmoil of the turnaround, the coop structure had worked. Conflict wasn't absent, but when it arose any resolution had to deliver not for the few but for everyone.

The experience of keeping so many stakeholders firmly connected hasn't just made the business creative and profitable. It has also taught everyone at Ocean Spray to become nimble collaborators. The company has strategic partners everywhere, with Nestlé in the United States, Gerber in Europe, and Heinz in Australia. Working for years in a company where no one person, department, group, or investor can be the superstar has imbued Ocean Spray with the habit of sharing that underpins its success: $2 billion of revenue in 2012 and a compounded growth rate, over the last decade, of 5 percent per year. The company simply couldn't achieve this success if it tried to sort farmers into winners or losers or if Papadellis and his team lost sight of the good of the whole. The company is engineered to avoid surplus and waste. There can't be any picking of winners, and there's no incentive for lying or fraud. The very structure of the business makes a Matthew effect not just impossible but undesirable. For anyone to win, everyone has to win.

That the company focuses on the long term isn't only a function of its structure. The cranberry business runs, necessarily, on a long cycle: that it can take up to five years and $60,000 per acre before a new bog becomes productive militates against short-term thinking. But so too does the design of a company where 75 percent of the owners must agree before any change can be made to the ownership structure.

Cooperatives—worker-owned but not worker-managed—are widespread in agriculture, though not (as we'll see) as widespread as they could, and perhaps should, be. And not all coops have proved wholly resistant to the siren call of Wall Street. The Diamond Walnut Company started as a coop at the same time as Ocean Spray but went public in 2005; since that time, it has been riddled with accounting issues.

On the other hand, in every country and in every industry, cooperatives are some of the world's most successful businesses, employing over a billion people. The world's largest cooperative, Mondragon, runs banks, schools, and universities. It also manufactures computer chips, sheet metal, bicycles, and washing machines and operates business consulting services and retail outlets. The seventh-largest company in Spain, the Mondragon coop has proved strikingly resilient throughout the country's economic turmoil. In 2012 the *Financial Times* awarded it a "Boldness in Business" prize for driving change; sixty years after it was started, the company's business structure was deemed innovative and inspiring. The success of Mondragon has worked to the benefit of the entire Basque region of Spain, where it is based.

The Emilia Romagna region of Italy may be an even more striking example of the social and economic power of cooperatives. Eight thousand coops are based there, employing three out of every four people and generating a GDP per capita that is 30 percent above the national average. People within the coops don't just work together; the coops cooperate with each other. To make clothing, one coop may specialize in cutting, one in dyeing, and another in embroidery, and by working together they can protect the expertise for which the region has become famous. The same cluster model applies to world-famous products like Ferrari, Lamborghini, and parmesan cheese.[44]

In the United States, the first cooperative was formed by Benjamin Franklin for the provision of fire insurance. Today it's estimated that up to 30,000 American cooperatives operate in agriculture, financial services, child care, utilities, retail, and wholesale businesses, accounting for more than $3 trillion of assets and $500 billion of revenue.[45] In 2013, Sally Jewell, the CEO of

America's largest consumer cooperative, REI, was appointed secretary of the Department of the Interior.

While there are a host of differences between coops little and large around the world, they all derive from the fundamental aim of creating business structures in which the Matthew effect is impossible or irrelevant, where success is focused on the many not the few, and where everyone has both a stake and a responsibility. They are structured specifically to eliminate the perverse incentives of head-to-head tournament competition. This structure does not make coops uncompetitive in the sense that they cannot make their way in the world. It does make them uncompetitive in the sense that nobody's success requires the failure of colleagues. They operate with a promise, not a threat.

What strikes Randy Papadellis—who worked for global, publicly traded packaged-goods companies before coming to Ocean Spray—as remarkable about the coop structure isn't so much its historic legacy as its profound fit for the future.

"I think we may be where other firms need to get to. We have a longer horizon, not focused on quarterly returns but on passing on to the next generation. We are tied into a much longer-term view than most companies. We take a more holistic view where we are committed to making sure that everyone we work with—everyone—benefits. No one gets left out. We all win or no one wins. And that's not just us, our generations, but the generations of the future."

In South Carver, Massachusetts, the 2012 cranberry harvest was particularly fine. Over several warm days in October, Gary Garretson watched with paternal pride as aquatic harvesters roamed across the water of his flooded bog. He'd made these machines himself: floating watercraft with what look like egg beaters at the prow, gently stirring the water to shake the berries off the vine. As the berries floated to the top, the pond took on a brilliant red sheen and large wooden brooms brushed them toward the shore.

"It's been fabulous. I think we are the perfect model—from the five-acre grower to the two-thousand-acre grower, we are all under the same umbrella. I can't fathom anyone who thinks that entering into a contractual agreement with big producers will be more beneficial than dealing with their brethren collectively over time. Pooling my money and my fruit with other growers, we increased the marketing ability and opportunities for success for my farm."

With his spritely white walrus mustache, Garretson stands watching as his fruit accumulates on the water. His fleece jacket sports the logo for his farm; his chest-high waders are labeled OCEAN SPRAY. He clearly feels no contradiction between the two.

"Here you are all treated the same, whether large or small. Everyone at Ocean Spray is just top-notch—they have our best interests at heart. It is difficult to get 750 people to agree on anything—it is a real challenge to be doing that. But as messy as it can be, it is the fairest and the best deal for farmers, and our success is their success."

In their different ways, Ocean Spray, Mozilla, W. L. Gore, Morning Star, Arup, TechShop, Eileen Fisher, Gripple, and the huge range of cooperatives and employee-owned firms around the world represent paradigms of successful collaboration. They demonstrate that our instinct and our talent for working together are just as strong and more productive than the competitive instinct that pits us against each another. In addition, these companies are notable for being strikingly well run by chief executives who are not lavishly rewarded and whose names and faces are not broadcast across the media. The success of these organizations is systemic, not heroic.

The most creative teams, labs, groups, and companies all represent, in miniature, societies that energetically develop trust and respect between people. Their strength and energy come not from picking winners but from providing a broad base of support for everyone to grow, give, and connect. Just as Finnish education is determined to help every single student, creative teams find courage in working with colleagues who offer generous support, challenge, insight, and human connection. In place of the tight focus on competitive goals that narrows thinking, constrains imagination, and infuses work with fear, people are creative when they can stand tall, scan the widest horizon, and dare to explore.

PART III

The Business of Winning

CHAPTER 7

Clone Wars

While many young engineers aspire to retirement at forty, Andy Hildebrand got his wish. He had spent eighteen years working on signal processing in the oil industry. Sending sound waves down below the earth's surface produced reflections that, when correlated correctly, could map what the waves hit and where. For companies like Exxon, this was a critical tool for identifying oil reserves. That the stakes were high taught Hildebrand an invaluable lesson.

"It really gave me a sense of quality that is very demanding," he tells me. "Coming from the oil industry, where people are going to spend maybe $300 million, $600 million drilling wells—you can't afford software that fails. So I have this mentality that software just shouldn't fail."

Free to pursue his dreams at the age of forty, Hildebrand decided to study music composition at Rice University. He wanted to write music for symphony orchestras, but it's tough to find full orchestras that are ready and willing to try out a neophyte's student compositions, so Hildebrand started playing with synthesizers. His software expertise came into play, of course.

"At the time, synth playing was onerous because of limited memory, which meant that you could only do loops. So I reprocessed the synth so that you couldn't hear the repeats. A friend said a lot of people needed that, you could make money doing it, but I knew there wasn't a lot of money in music. I was just having fun."

Hildebrand gives the impression of someone for whom having fun is a pretty serious motivator. Bearded, relaxed, and unpretentious, he has a talent for dabbling—and for listening.

"So I'd already sold a couple of pieces of software, and one day I was having lunch with my sales rep. And his wife was with us, and he happened to mention that it would be really nice if I could write something that would make it sound like she sang in tune. It was a pretty awkward moment; everyone just looked down at their food. But I knew right away how you'd solve that problem. I just didn't think anyone would be interested."

In 1997 Hildebrand didn't have anything new to take to a trade show, so harking back to the lunchtime conversation, he decided he'd write the software for the sales rep's wife. No focus groups, no market research. Just having fun.

"They ripped it out of my hands!" he remembers with a laugh. "I had a demo booth, and I'd pick an out-of-tune vocal, and in real time, it would be in tune. People were astounded. Not that it hadn't been done before; others had tried and failed because the software didn't work well enough. I guess there weren't a lot of well-educated signal-processing experts in the music industry! But this did work well. That's why it was a big hit—because you couldn't tell, it sounded natural, and there were no glitches."

"Dr. Andy," as he's now known in the trade, had created Auto-Tune, the world's best-selling audio plug-in, which can shift the pitch of a sung note without changing the timing of the performance. With this tool, music producers can eliminate bad, fluffed, or wrong notes; they can also change voices overall. AutoTune makes it possible for singers to produce recordings that are pitch-perfect without costly and exhausting retakes. If you think that your favorite singers have miraculously flawless voices, it isn't a miracle—it's Dr. Andy's software.

Almost every top-forty single played on the radio uses AutoTune. It sprang to fame in Cher's best-selling song "Believe," it gave Kanye West's "Heartbreak" its plangent tone, and it has been used by artists as varied as the Black Eyed Peas, Bon Iver, Miley Cyrus, Eminem, Jamie Foxx, Faith Hill, Wyclef Jean, Kid Rock, and Billy Joel. Many performers are quite cagey about whether they use it or not, preferring to sustain their myth of perfection. Because ever since its debut, AutoTune has been considered by many music lovers to be a form of cheating.

Hildebrand himself is jovially unconcerned by these accusations. Being able to correct the odd duff note radically altered the economics of recording, which now required fewer takes and less perfectionism. And using AutoTune, he says, is no different from his wife using makeup to look her best, or anyone using PhotoShop to eliminate red eye in photographs. Sure, some people go further and use it to erase the vocal equivalents of lines, crow's-feet, and double chins, but who cares? If the music gets better, surely that's what it's all about. In the digital age, music is an industry characterized by artifice, and AutoTune is just one of the many tools it uses.

Nevertheless, and much to Hildebrand's delight, AutoTune soon became a cause célèbre. Nothing sparked comment or sales more than Jay-Z's song "Death of AutoTune," which suggested that AutoTune ripped the heart out of music, replacing it with all that was phony and crass.

The indie pop quartet Death Cab for Cutie took the debate one step further by sporting blue ribbons at the Grammys as their protest against the banal uniformity that AutoTune produced. The flaws and idiosyncrasies of the human voice, they insisted, were what gave it character and shouldn't be airbrushed out of existence. The most meaningful argument against the plug-in, however, came from R&B artist Ne-Yo, who endorsed its utility—but also felt it was being misused.

"AutoTune was meant to be a safety net," he argued. "You sing and sing and sing, and you don't want to blow your throat out trying to do the same note a thousand different times. So you sing it a few good times, and you let the AutoTune catch whatever notes fall out. It's not supposed to be wings; you're not supposed to strap it on your back and jump off the building. Not: I can't sing at all so let's turn AutoTune all the way up so that I just sound like Willie the Robot. That's whacked, that's terrible. It takes all the character out of your voice. You hear it on the radio and you go: who is that? Because you have no idea because everybody sounds the same."[1]

In theory, one of the chief virtues of competition is that it is supposed to motivate people to be creative so that the marketplace will be replete with a wide variety of products—something for everyone. The desire to be better, do better, and beat the other guys should drive everyone into work determined to invent fabulous new goods and services that will attract customers and lower prices. Consumers should benefit because they have more to choose from—for less.

But this new technology allows anybody and everybody to populate the airwaves with music that is virtually indistinguishable. It doesn't make music better, it makes it all the same. Reality TV stars like Kim Kardashian, Heidi Montag, Michaele Salahi, Angelina Pivarnick, and even the desperately unmusical Rebecca Black can pretend to have musical careers only because of AutoTune; singers like Ke$ha, Amelia Lily, and Cheryl Cole don't even try to differentiate themselves from each other. Even Andy Hildebrand, who vigorously defends his plug-in, accepts that it has changed people's idea of what music is.

"People never heard the mistakes before," he says. "Lots of people didn't sing in tune at all—think of Marilyn Monroe singing 'Happy Birthday' to

JFK! But now, you cannot possibly sing out of tune. You just won't get away with it. So it has changed how people listen and what they expect to hear."

People have become accustomed to flawless, homogenous music, and so mostly that's what they get. The problem is that what used to make each singer unique has now, increasingly, been carefully and fastidiously removed. No wonder AutoTune is sometimes called audio Botox.

Although it may be exacerbated by software, the problem posed by Auto-Tune isn't, at heart, a technology problem. The theory may be that competition drives creativity, but the reality is that it produces clones. Because creativity and innovation are hard—why bother? It's so much easier to spot a success and then just copy it. That's one of the themes in Charlie Kaufman's brilliant film *Adaptation,* in which the protagonist, played by Nicholas Cage, accosts screenwriting guru Robert McKee (as impersonated by the actor Brian Cox). McKee's book *Story* and the nonstop seminars that he conducts around the world aim to teach anyone and everyone how to write a Hollywood film script. There's a formula (largely derived from Aristotle), a method (every scene must have a beat), and some standard tricks. The protagonist of *Adaptation* only succeeds when he has produced a script that cleaves limpet-like to the tired rules of the McKee system.

McKee isn't the only formula-hawker. Syd Field tells writers pretty much what needs to go on every page, while Blake Snyder's *Save the Cat*—"the last book on screenwriting you'll ever need"—tells you "how to make your story like everything else out there only different." Aspiring writers lap these up.[2]

In *Adaptation,* this kind of thinking is a joke; in real life, it's tedious. Kate Leys is one of Britain's leading script development editors. She has worked on some of the most successful British films of recent years—*Four Weddings and a Funeral, Trainspotting, The Girl with the Pearl Earring*—and with a wide range of writers and producers, from veterans who are too well known to admit their debt to her to aspirants just starting out.

"Success breeds clones. That's exactly what happens. People making commissioning decisions default to clones. They want replicants! And we in the audience feel this happening; it feels like everyone is making the same decisions."

It would be hard to find anyone with a more wry sense of humor about the film business than Leys. But somehow she has resisted the cynicism that pervades the business, and she continues to marvel at its ability to throw up insanely bad copycat ideas.

"I was once sent a script called 'Four Funerals and a Wedding'!" Leys roars with laughter. "You do think, 'Bless your heart, to have misunderstood so profoundly makes you almost endearing.' It does happen!"

What audiences want is not just more of the same but fresh, creative works that respond to and reflect their moods, times, and preoccupations. And these keep changing.

"When I worked in London at Film4," Leys recalls, "I remember coming into work after the Labour election landslide and looking at the slate in front of us, and we were all thinking, 'The world has changed; we need to rethink this stuff. What worked yesterday won't work tomorrow.' The *only* way to stack the odds is to see it as a risk. If you want to play safe, decision-making becomes conservative and becomes cloning. But you have to stand on quite a distant hill to see that happening."

Few decision-making executives in the film industry last long enough to gain that perspective, the average tenure of a studio head of production being just eighteen months.[3] So while smart, imaginative, creative people might like to take risks, they rarely seize the opportunity to do so. In part, Leys says, this is because too much money is on the table.

"Studio film execs are looking for exactly the same thing you or I would be looking for. They want original, offbeat, quirky stuff; strong voices, great stories, big ideas. It's what they do with those scripts when they get them that goes wrong. Creativity is about risk, and very large amounts of money is about *not* risk. So the moment the spend is agreed, everyone around the money begins to panic. A whole lot of people start to ask questions, like, 'Is it really, really going to work? Will people really, really get this? Is it definitely good? Shall we change it a bit? Shall we take out this weird bit, and that risqué bit, and the very bleak ending?' It can bland itself out in a matter of weeks. And then it reverts to formula."

But of course sometimes the idea wasn't even fresh to begin with. Hence, two *Anchorman* movies, three *Spider-Man* movies, four *Pirates of the Caribbean*, six *Resident Evils*, seven *Star Wars*, eleven *Star Treks*, twelve *Friday the 13th*s, and a peculiar rash of penguin movies: *Happy Feet 1* and *2*, *Mr. Popper's Penguins*, *March of the Penguins*, *The Pebble and the Penguin*, and *Surf's Up*. The film business may be competitive, but it's alarmingly easy to go to a multiplex with twenty-four screens and find nothing you want to see.

In their quest for a sure thing, many executives have been persuaded that their safest option isn't to make decisions at all, but to use algorithms instead. The premise behind Epagogix software is that with enough data on previous box-office successes, the next ones can be predicted. The software can rate explosions, violence, plot turns, love scenes, car chases, and quirky characters. Of course, the technology comes with the same problem that AutoTune provoked: tested using the same tools, the movies all turn out to be strikingly similar products. In the summer of 2013, many consumers couldn't remember which explosive blockbusters they'd seen and which they'd missed. Box-office returns were down, perhaps because anyone who'd seen one movie felt they'd seen all the rest.

The relatively lower costs of television might make a wider range of creativity more feasible, but it doesn't. When Fox wanted to launch a new channel, it didn't identify new genres, interests, tastes, or audiences. Instead, it just copied ESPN and launched another sports channel focusing on the same sports, the same teams, and the same elite athletes as its well-established rivals. Although sports coverage regularly ignores a vast number of sports and local teams, the new entrant did nothing to showcase these or to serve neglected audiences; instead, it just followed the leader.

Even new subjects recycle old formats. It's remarkable (and alarming) how similar business coverage is to sports coverage: same double-headed presentation, frenetic pace, and rolling headlines, with stock prices replacing sports scores. After *The Sopranos* pioneered dark, brooding drama, we got more gangsters (*Boardwalk Empire*), more drug-dealing (*The Wire*, *Breaking Bad*), and more men brooding on their own mortality. When *Mad Men* made the late 1950s and early 1960s appealing, *Pan Am* and *The Playboy Club* swiftly followed. And once *Sex in the City* proved that friendship was a meaty topic, *Girls* attempted to update it.

A seasoned television executive, Archie Tait has worked on dozens of TV dramas and drama series. The economics of production, he argues, require that any viable company have a recurring series of some kind—for him it was *Inspector Morse*—to cover the overheads of the business. Only once that security is set is there any chance of doing something different. One of Tait's most memorable productions, *Chimera,* caused shock and amazement when it appeared to kill off every single one of its characters in the opening episode. So radical a departure from format, he says, just wouldn't be feasible now.

"Broadcasters want to ingratiate themselves with audiences and not surprise them. In part, that's because they're all using the same market research, which asks people what they want—and they can only answer with what they know. Most people have no other way to articulate their desires. Producers and broadcasters copy style, but they rarely rise to the challenge when they see something extraordinary."

The ubiquity of formats—cooking shows, reality TV, quizzes, and talent contests—is partly explained by the degree to which broadcasters spot a success and then just copy it. It's cheaper to keep an audience than build a new one, so as long as a program gets viewers, it's economical to renew. I was involved in commissioning the first series of *MasterChef* for the BBC in 1988; I was incredulous to discover on returning to the United Kingdom thirteen years later that it was still on our television screens.

Formats persist because of the structure of the industry itself. The independent producers of these shows are usually paid only just what they cost to make—sometimes even less than that. The only way that they, and their companies, can make a profit and stay in business is to sell the format around the world. Simon Cowell's production company, Syco, can make as much (or more) money by selling the format for his talent contests than from the shows themselves. The same goes for shows like *Renovation Game, I Hate My Body, Jeopardy, I'm a Celebrity ..., Big Brother, Who Wants to Be a Millionaire,* and *Secrets of Shoplifters.* Once an audience is established for the shows, it's easier for schedulers and cheaper for producers to keep them running, around the world, indefinitely. There is no financial mileage in producing something fresh and original that can't be endlessly repackaged and resold. But when I asked Tait whether this could ever produce (or find) another Dennis Potter, he replied with, first, a stunned silence—perhaps he was amazed anyone remembered—and then a loud guffaw.

"No sequel! No format! No franchise! Are you kidding? I show *Singing Detective* or *Pennies from Heaven* to students, and their jaws drop. They have never seen anything like it!"

Tait concedes that some identical programming can emerge coincidentally from a shared sense of the zeitgeist. Two series about department stores, *The Paradise* and *Mr. Selfridge,* came out too closely together to have copied one another. Just as scientists around the world may suddenly feel the time is ripe to solve a particular problem, and Alexander Graham Bell and Elijah Gray filed patents for the telephone on the same day, so TV producers may separately identify and pursue projects that feel like they will touch a nerve. But the fact that they develop remarkably similar product isn't just a coincidence; it's also a reflection of the fact that what feels familiar feels good.

We should not be so surprised by this. Our brains have a distinct preference for the familiar. The human brain is lazy; rather than process information afresh with each encounter, it prefers to look for matches, indicators of a known quantity that do not require scrutiny. There's simply less neurological demand exerted by things that are roughly similar to what we already know—so they make us feel safer and more secure. This is the neurological foundation of bias.[4] Creativity requires divergence, but ostensibly creative industries embrace convergence with a vengeance.

Competition has given consumers years' worth of highly formulaic detective stories, medical dramas, game shows, talent contests, reality TV programs, and endless musical wallpaper. But maybe it doesn't matter; it's just entertainment. Yet the same patterns endlessly repeat themselves in other competitive arenas as well. Political campaigns, working from the same or similar market research, target the same voters and ignore the rest, even though a democracy is supposed to engage everyone. Once Apple brought out its iPhone, every other telephone manufacturer scrambled to come up with something similar—some products were so similar the manufacturers got sued. When the iPad came out, the same pattern repeated itself: quick copies that, like HP's TouchPad, were almost as swiftly withdrawn because they had absolutely nothing new, additional, or better to offer.

Nowhere is this cloning compulsion more expensive than in the development of new drugs. Although pharmaceutical companies endlessly complain about the high cost of producing new drugs, the truth is that, despite increases in research and development spending of 12.3 percent every year since 1970, these businesses aren't any more innovative now than they were fifty years ago.[5] Despite flurries of mergers, acquisitions, de-mergers, and restructurings, the rate of production of new drugs has proved surprisingly constant, creating what everyone both in the industry and in the world of academic science regards as a profound innovation problem. This is because the drug companies concentrate on "me-too" drugs.

A me-too drug duplicates the action of an existing drug, but some minor alteration allows it to be marketed as though it were a completely new therapy. So Tagamet (cimetidine), Zantac (ranitidine), Pepcid (famotidine), and Axid (nizatidine) are all brand names for histamine H-2 receptor antagonists, which means that they all treat peptic ulcers in fundamentally the same way. Any new drug that comes out—think particularly of Viagra or Prozac—is invariably followed by a clone that is different enough to need FDA approval, a patent, and marketing as though it were different, but that bestows virtually no therapeutic improvement whatsoever. The goal of these drugs is often to circumvent patent expiration or to cash in on a new market pioneered by a competitor. There is no requirement that the "new" treatment be different—only that it prove superior to a placebo.

In 2002, omeprazole, a heartburn drug produced by Astra-Zeneca, was about to lose its patent. The potential loss of the $5 billion a year the drug generated had prompted a lot of so-called innovation, leading in 2001 to the introduction of esomeprazole, which would become one of the best-selling drugs in both the United States and the United Kingdom. The two drugs are basically the same, with the marginal difference that the molecular structure of the newer drug is a mirror-image of the old one. Complex molecules can exist in left- and right-handed forms, and all that Astra Zeneca did was swap a right-handed pill for a left-handed one. There was one big difference, however: the new pill was more expensive. Ten times more expensive.[6]

Classic economic theory argues that competition will not only offer more choice but bring the price down. But that doesn't seem to be the impact of the me-too drugs. Research suggests that drugs described by the FDA as having "little or no therapeutic gain" enter the market at the same price as the old drug in the United States and at about twice the price in some other markets. Other studies of anti-arthritic pain relievers showed exactly what shouldn't happen: while efficacy was *negatively* correlated with price, toxicity was *positively* correlated with price. The more expensive clones were less effective and more dangerous.[7] The stomach ulcer treatment Tagamet went *up* in price when its clone, Zantac, entered the market, and both drugs continued to go up in price when more clones—Pepcid and Axid—came in too.[8]

Price isn't the only problem. As always in competitive environments, sharing and trust are predictable casualties. That pharmaceutical companies work on drugs so minutely related means that they guard fiercely the data collected about clinical trials. Competition is always the reason they cite for why they can't publish this material—they don't want to give anything away to their rivals. Were they not racing neck and neck down exactly the same narrow alleyway, of course, this would not be such an easy excuse, and the open publication of data would make for significant improvements in patient safety. Instead, the industry has become notorious for its reluctance to share any data, good or bad, that might leave patients, doctors, and funding institutions wiser and safer.

Moreover, while the differences between these drugs may be minuscule, they still take time, attention, and research resources. Looking at public data on the number of subjects in clinical tests—since the drug companies are loath to release data themselves about how much they spend and where—it seems to be the case that fully 80 percent of R&D spending goes toward products that do not offer any significant therapeutic improvement.[9] Selling more clones instead of finding new treatments represents a gigantic opportunity cost in time, effort, imagination, creativity, and scientific know-how devoted to me-too drugs that make no impact on human health.[10] Even as the director of the Centers for Disease Control and Prevention (CDC), Thomas Frieden, sounded the alarm in March 2013 on the severe problems with existing antibiotics ("Our strongest antibiotics don't work, and patients are left with potentially untreatable infections"), the pipeline for new antibiotics is running dry.[11] Britain's chief medical officer, Professor Dame Sally Davies, argues that this danger represents a greater threat than terrorism: "If we don't take action, then we may all be back in an almost 19th Century environment where infections kill us as a result of routine operations."[12]

While drug companies just try to copy each other, failing to lead the innovation the world needs, they also studiously avoid work on so-called orphan diseases: conditions whose sufferers aren't numerous enough to constitute a major market. Since each orphan disease afflicts a small number of people, you might think that they don't really matter. But when you add all these diseases together, they afflict one out of every ten people in total. Copycat drugs don't discriminate: they fail big markets and small ones alike.

"Our priorities are tilted by marketplace imperatives," Bill Gates told the Royal Academy of Engineering; apparently surprised to discover what he called a "flaw in the pure capitalistic approach. The malaria vaccine in humanist terms is the biggest need but it gets virtually no funding."[13]

From a doctor's perspective, this presents two problems: for some diseases there are no drugs at all, while for others there are too many and telling them apart is incredibly time-consuming. When patients come in asking for the new clone they've seen promoted on TV and in magazines, doctors feel a responsibility to proffer an informed response. Trying to make sense of an ever more crowded marketplace of approved and off-label treatments is complicated, eats up time, and increases the costs of medical treatment overall.

Copying the competition isn't just uncreative; it also leads to a misplaced sense of comfort. The mortgage market, prior to the bank bust of 2008, was full of people—home buyers, realtors, and lenders—copying what they saw around them. Surrounded by status competition, consumers didn't want to be left out—after all, if their neighbor was making money buying and flipping houses, they didn't want to be left at the bottom of the pecking order with nothing. Market competition made all the real estate agents and lenders feel the need to pile into a heated market; failing to do so would have meant a loss of market share, perhaps a drop in share price, even the loss of a peerage. The competitive desire not to be left out overwhelmed many financiers' rational concerns.

"By 2003," Michael Sarnoff tells me, "subprime lenders were multiplying and everyone knew the loans were just stupid: [lending] to people with terrible credit, no income, occupancy fraud, income fraud…. They all started throwing wood on the fire in the form of additional lending so you could lend to anybody—to a dead person! The amount of crime in the mortgage industry was just incredible."

Sarnoff is a staid, sane Midwesterner who worked—and still works—as a chief credit officer at a large Midwest bank. Even after all this time, he's outraged by what his industry has done. But he's also more prepared than many to explain just why no one stopped it.

"Subprime was about ripping off poor people," he tells me. "But here's the thing: To function as a business, we have to employ a sales force. And it was hard to recruit salespeople. There was no way on earth that we could hire, let alone retain, a single good salesperson if we weren't prepared to let them sell subprime. They stood to make huge commissions off of these deals—of course they wanted to sell them! So what were we supposed to do? Sit on our principles and watch as every salesperson we had walked out the door? To stay competitive, we had to let them sell subprime."

What Sarnoff experienced firsthand—the competitive pressure to offer salespeople whatever they wanted to sell, no matter how stupid it was—was replicated all the way down the food chain. At Countrywide, official company policy was to match any loan a competitor offered, even if it was reckless or extravagant. Ratings agencies, fighting over business (and all using the same software), didn't want to turn anything down because they'd lose clients to their competitors. Investment banks, packaging collateralized debt obligations, didn't want to bring too much scrutiny to bear or they'd lose customers. In the heat of an inflamed market, nobody kept a cool head.

One reason the economic crisis has proved so profound is that so much risk was exacerbated by the replication of the same products, the same kinds of debt, in the same kinds of institutions. Classic economic theory turned out to be wrong: a competitive market had not diversified risk but concentrated it. Competition hadn't produced variety but rather had encouraged everyone to do the same thing. When the market crashed, there were no safe havens left.

As the markets increasingly are dominated by algorithms, the chances of this kind of amplification only increase. Not only is similar (if not identical) software used to conduct trading, but analysis of markets may turn out to be more uniform than you might expect. Thanks to algorithms, future news outlets don't need journalists anymore. Narrative Science, a Chicago software company, can take market data, analyze it, structure it, and turn it into an article complete with illustrations and graphs. It looks like but doesn't quite feel like the real thing. If you've read a story lately that came out of Chicago with no byline, chances are it wasn't written by a person but by a machine. The inherent danger of this model lies in the fact that all of the analysis proceeds from certain assumptions about how markets work, producing a feedback loop that amplifies what it analyzes. People reading the articles draw conclusions that lead to trades that produce data that is analyzed according to the same instruction, which leads to more trades … and so on, theoretically forever. Instead of a functional market in which a wide cross-section of styles, assumptions, and attitudes balance one another, algorithms keep doubling down on the same old beliefs, leeching diversity out of the system.

The importance of diversity is easily seen in nature. Right now, the British landscape is being devastated by Chalara dieback, a disease affecting ash trees. In Denmark the fungal disease has already killed up to 90 percent of ash trees, and experts expect the same impact in Britain. What makes the disease so catastrophic is the lack of biodiversity: most ash trees are the same species. Safety and resilience require diversity—but that's just what our landscape and our business environment lack.

Why innovate when you can copy? The irony, of course, is that it feels less risky following the leader than being the leader—even though, as it turns out, it isn't. Convergence feels safer than divergence: people imagine there is safety in numbers. So, after the heady days of subprime mortgage and credit default swaps ended with a crash in 2008, many investors were left wandering around a market that felt like a ghost town—until they stumbled upon a dark corner of the derivatives market that they'd mostly overlooked: the commodities futures market.

This market invested in the future price of food. Before 1999, only those actively involved in growing, producing, or selling food products—farmers, millers, and companies like Kraft and Nestlé—were allowed by law to make big investments in coffee, cocoa, wheat, soybeans, beef, and chicken. Goldman Sachs created a derivative that tracked twenty-four raw ingredients—the Goldman Sachs Commodity Index—but mortgages and debt were so much more attractive as investment vehicles that commodity prices stayed relatively stable. In 1999 the law changed; now anyone could take very large positions in commodity markets. So when the tech bubble burst in 2000, suddenly real food looked a lot more interesting than virtual companies and the commodity index funds attracted a fifty-fold increase in investment.

That was nothing, however, compared to what happened in 2008. With most markets moribund, real food—something people absolutely have to have, and demand for which is tightly coupled to a growing global population—looked immensely attractive. According to the congressional testimony of institutional investor Michael Masters, in the first fifty-two trading days of 2008 commodity speculators "flooded" the markets with $55 billion: an increase in the dollar value of outstanding futures contracts of more than $1 billion a day. By July this figure had reached $318 billion.

Fred Kaufman, who has tirelessly researched this new bubble, describes the commodity market as a "sparkling new casino" where everyone wanted a place at the table.[14] Academics started to publish articles about the new market, and financial publications soon picked up the scent. The *Financial Times, Global Pensions,* the *Journal of Finance,* the *Journal of Portfolio Management,* and the *Journal of Derivatives* all analyzed, dissected, and fueled the new trend. "You had people who had no clue what commodities were all about suddenly buying commodities," one Department of Agriculture analyst told Kaufman, but that didn't matter to the brokers. Everybody wanted part of the new me-too investment vehicle.

These clones didn't bring prices down. "The more the price of food commodities increases," Kaufman wrote, "the more money pours into the sector and the higher the prices rise." Desperate to find a place that could deliver the kinds of returns they all remembered from the go-go days of the building boom, speculators who had no interest in agriculture or food at all piled on, outnumbering the true investors four-to-one.

Commentators noticed food prices going up but blamed the phenomenon on China (wanting more protein) or on the world's growing population. Others said that the price of wheat had skyrocketed because so much had been given over to ethanol production. They were all wrong. Prices weren't rising because real people wanted to eat more or because they wanted to burn greener fuel. A herd of money managers were all chasing the same derivatives. Barclays, Deutsche Bank, Pimco, JPMorgan Chase, AIG—all wanted the same products and the same returns.

As food prices started to rise, the New England Complex Systems Institute started mapping their correlations to increasing civil unrest around the world. The result was alarming: it wasn't just British and American households that were feeling the pinch. "Despite the many possible contributing factors, the timing of violent protests in North Africa and the Middle East in 2011 as well as earlier riots in 2008 coincides with large peaks in global food prices. These observations suggest that protests may reflect not only long-standing political failings of governments, but also the sudden desperate straits of vulnerable populations. If food prices remain high, there is likely to be persistent and increasing global social disruption."[15]

As Kaufmann crisscrossed the world, talking to governments, investors, analysts, and farmers about the consequences of food derivatives, he grew increasingly furious and distraught.

"The 1936 Agriculture Act limited the degree to which people not working in the industry could invest in it. But once commodities were deregulated, it opened the door to people treating food as if it weren't food. Derivatives are a classic virtuality—an imaginary construct derived from something else. So food derivatives—which do have a real impact on what real people can afford to eat—became an investment vehicle. Just like mortgage-backed securities made people forget that they represented real homes for real people, food derivatives make people forget they're having an impact on real food prices. But with food it's even more important than your home; it's a matter of life and death. But not for investors. They just think it's virtual food!"

Food, Kaufmann realized, had become financialized just as our homes had been. The more people invested in it, the bigger the bubble grew and the more people wanted in. Only this time the endgame didn't make people homeless—it left people hungry.

"If Wall Street concocted a scheme whereby investors bought large amounts of pharmaceutical drugs and medical devices in order to profit from the resulting increase in price, making these essential items unaffordable to sick and dying people, society would be justly outraged," Michael Masters testified before Congress. "Why is there not outrage over the fact that Americans must pay drastically more to feed their families?"[16] And why, he might have continued, do we turn a blind eye to the fact that what hurts Americans can kill those who live in less affluent parts of the world?

That the market for food has become so explosive an issue and so dangerous for the world is significantly a function of the concentration of invest-ment in commodity derivatives. If only one or two institutions or traders were interested in it, we might deride their values but not be threatened by their choices. But with all the major financial institutions—including pen-sion funds—looking for returns off the backs of farmers and those seeking to be fed, it seems unlikely that there is anyone in the world who won't feel the impact of this demand shock.

Kaufmann doesn't believe this market can be fixed. It's a classic bubble, and bubbles come about when everyone competes by doing the same thing. Like many people disgusted by the role that derivatives played in the eco-nomic crisis, Kaufmann joins the chorus clamoring for more transparency in what remains, to this day, a dark market. Although economists like Alan Greenspan argued that unregulated derivatives markets were safer because of their relative freedom from restraints, their extreme opacity and propen-sity for disaster proves such confidence ideological and obtuse.

In 2013, as part of the larger attempt to repair its reputation after scan-dals surrounding the manipulation of interest rates, Barclays Bank decided that it would no longer invest in food derivatives. Whether this was a tacit recognition that doing so was wrong or a decision based on a more tacti-cal sense that the market had peaked, no one would say. And while Fred Kaufmann was delighted by Barclays' exit, he still argued that the original law, restricting investment in agriculture to those primarily involved in pro-ducing food, should be reinstated and that the position limits, destroyed in the 1990s, need to be brought back. In other words, regulation—reverting to old rules—is the only way to curtail the human appetite for imitation.

The antidotes may be harder to find when it comes to pharmaceutical companies, for which imitation has proven so lucrative and yet so stun-ningly uncreative. Over the last fifty years, these businesses have gotten big-ger and are now spending in excess of $70 billion a year on R&D, but still they have not improved their ability to innovate. Many industry veterans argue that this is because they have become too big and sclerotic. That, at least, is the opinion of Jean-Pierre Garnier—and he should know, having run GlaxoSmithKline for eight years.

"The leaders of major corporations, including pharmaceuticals, have incorrectly assumed that R&D was scalable, could be industrialized, and could be driven by detailed metrics and automation. The grand result: a loss of personal accountability, transparency, and the passion of scientists in dis-covery and development."

In his own business, Garnier tried hard to restructure research to make it more productive, with questionable results. He hoped that smaller groups would make pharmaceutical research more akin to academic work and inspire the same qualities of dedication and commitment. But to this day the company's best-selling drugs remain glucocorticoids—the steroids beloved of athletes. What Garnier faced, and all pharmaceutical companies have to face, is the question implicit in their business: do they exist to maximize shareholder return (which is certainly what Garnier believed) or to discover and develop new medicines? Many in medical research dismiss as nothing more than a myth the idea that drug companies can be both investor-owned businesses and unbiased research and education institutions. Given that a genuinely new drug has such a high chance of failure, costs at least $1 billion, and takes, on average, twelve years to develop, the incompatibility between the two goals becomes obvious. To be prepared to be genuinely innovative requires a gamble on a scale that few CEOs would contemplate or survive— at least not while their eyes are firmly focused on the share price.

Some chemists are taking matters into their own hands, quite literally. Lee Cronin has pioneered the use of 3D printers to produce new molecules and treatments for disease. His dream—and it isn't yet a reality—is to do for drug discovery what Apple did for music: create an open network where anyone and everyone can publish their discoveries and share them.[17] Why shouldn't we be able, he asks, to download and print our own therapies? Whether this is a brilliant theoretical question or turns out to be a profound disrupter of me-too drug development remains to be seen.

What Cronin and others argue, however, is that technology ought to make the kind of innovation drug companies eschew easier and cheaper. After all, it's done that for almost every other industry—why not pharmaceuticals? It is in that context that industry thinkers have turned to open-source development as a possible alternative to corporate research. Software products like the Firefox web browser, the Thunderbird email client, and the Popcorn online video editor were all created by developers who collaborated online for free. Much of the Internet was built like this, and some of it continues to be. The reward for participants is the recognition and respect of their peers, combined with the excitement of cutting-edge software development and the knowledge of having contributed to something great. Many engineers contribute in their spare time or are encouraged by their employers to do so because building cool tools is how they develop their expertise.

Diagnosed with a brain tumor, the Italian artist Salvatore Iokanesi decided to crowdsource his treatment. He first hacked and then published all of his medical records online, asking for help and advice from strangers. Receiving over 500,000 responses was overwhelming, he said; he had to ask his respondents for help just organizing and tagging the contributions. Approaching the problem in this way was not, he insisted, anti-medicine or anti-doctor—surgeons removed his tumor—but it was the best way to surface a broad range of knowledge, to be confident in his decision-making—and to feel human.

The chief benefit of open-source development is that it combines an extremely divergent (often global) cross-section of people and thinking styles. That they are working for their own delight and generosity elicits more engagement and imagination. Unlike many research executives, open-source developers aren't clocking in, following orders, or playing politics. They're doing what they love to delight peers they respect. Often buried under the steep hierarchies that characterize large organizations, they express their expertise and their humanity by offering their contribution.

The quest for new drugs has also led to the pioneering of a particular kind of public-private partnership, modeled on open-source software development. One example is the Medicines for Malaria Venture, which posts its challenges, reviews submissions, and then selects a project to fund. Research is outsourced to a network of some three hundred scientists at forty institutions; some are universities, but drug companies and research institutions may also be included. At each stage, findings are reviewed and then continued or concluded. Critical to these partnerships is the determination to focus on neglected diseases; they have not been formed to create yet more me-too drugs but to confront some of the biggest medical challenges in the world. They have also been able to function on lean budgets and to attract a rich cross-section of participants and funding sources.

These partnerships seem more agile, more creative, and more willing to take on more risk than large pharmaceutical companies. They also move faster and attract a far wider array of people, from doctors with firsthand clinical knowledge of a disease to those with purely academic training. That diversity alone promises higher degrees of creative thinking. But it's too early to tell whether this new ecology of drug development will prove more than a fig leaf behind which the drug companies can hide. These partnerships are at least a creative attempt to escape the hypnotic attraction of imitation.

That software developers turned to software to develop more software doesn't seem much of a stretch. In 1998 Mozilla was launched as an open platform for software development and specifically aimed at giving users more choice and opportunities for greater innovation. The Mozilla browser Firefox, which merged the work of ten thousand contributors, has been downloaded over 3 billion times and is used on every continent on Earth—even Antarctica. The browser pioneered features aimed at giving users more control of their data (like "Do Not Track"). Fundamental to Mozilla's launch of its mobile phone operating system was to avoid offering just another me-too product: "We're not trying to get in the middle of an operating-system fight," CEO Gary Kovacs insists. "What we are trying to do is be the catalyst to drive more development around the open web." Existing phone systems didn't allow users to switch platforms: if you bought your apps on Apple, they wouldn't go with you when you moved to Android. But Mozilla's new FirefoxOS makes this possible. The goal, says Kovacs, isn't to steal market share—but to provoke other companies into giving users the freedom they want.

The idea that the way to influence a market is to give away your ideas isn't new. Andrea Palladio became the most influential architect in the world by publishing all of his ideas and designs in 1570 in his *I Quattro libri dell'architettura*. Had he not done so, his thinking might have remained obscure, as few of his buildings were in big public spaces; most of his villas were built in obscure parts of the Veneto in Italy, where even to this day they're rarely visited. It was the books, however, that changed Western architecture forever. Sharing his ideas and designs as widely as possible assured Palladio's immortality.

Mozilla's products are built by developers all over the world, from favelas to mansions. But human interaction still matters. Every year one thousand engineers come together at MozFest to join in science fairs, watch new product demonstrations, and debate new projects. New technology may have made it possible to work without ever meeting face to face, but it hasn't yet erased our desire to do so. Many of the world's most innovative businesses work the old-fashioned way: putting people in a building together and watching the sparks fly. For Adam Lowry and Eric Ryan, the heart of innovation is always human.

"You don't want to outsource your soul! Innovation is completely the heart and soul of everything we do, so we all do it, we all do it together—and we all need it for it to work."

Lowry is the most unlikely of detergent mavens. A tall, handsome advertising veteran, he set up Method Home Care with his school friend Eric because they'd always wanted to work together. Early in 2000, they couldn't help but notice that everyone was spending more time and money on their homes than ever before—yet they cleaned those homes with products that were toxic, that stank, and that were so ugly they had to be hidden in cupboards. This made no sense. Why not invent products that were beautiful enough to be left on display, made from ingredients that smelled great and respected both the planet and the home? Lowry and Ryan's determination to forge ahead didn't depend on an absence of competition—far from it. They had only to go into any supermarket to see the ferocious odds stacked against them. But their innovative new business was grounded in an awareness of the way people, values, and lifestyles were changing.

The desire of these two handsome young men to make domestic cleaning products had much going against it—and not just Procter & Gamble, Unilever, and a host of multinational behemoths. In a market besotted by virtual businesses like Pets.com and Google, they were proposing physical product sold in bricks-and-mortar stores. Moreover, they had just $45,000 each, no background in product manufacture, and few contacts. What they did have was a burning sense of mission and a belief that jobs should offer people more than just a salary. They weren't interested in motivating people with competition; they thought playing to human altruism—the opposite of competition—would prove more creative and long-lasting.

"We wanted to create work that had meaning," Ryan tells me, "that made people feel they were contributing to something important. Altruism is very motivating. Most of us want to know our work creates something positive in the world. If you're an educator, you want to know you're doing something bigger than just helping a few kids. If you are in business, you want to feel you're doing something more than just paying the rent. We wanted to build a company with new products, to create work that made people feel they were contributing to something important. Altruism is very motivating."

"It's not," Lowry tells me, "that I'm not a competitive person. I went to the Olympics as an alternate for the US sailing team in 2000! But I'm a big believer in not letting the competition—any competition—tell me what to do. I'm completely focused on sustainability. Eric's completely—obsessively—into beautiful design. The most sustainable product without beautiful representation won't fly here. And the most beautiful product that contains toxins, well, that's just shallow."

After founding the business, the two men hired a CEO whose primary job was to operate the business. They made that choice because they didn't want to jockey for position, and neither of them wanted to veer away from their core expertise. Wanting neither power nor the distance that comes with it, they don't believe they could get anyone else to collaborate if they don't do so as well. But just as fundamental as what goes on inside the business is their insistence that what goes on outside matters too.

"We don't steal from our competitors because we don't want what they make. Because they're always doing the old thing, and we don't want to end up being like them. I'd rather get my inspiration from the world of art or architecture," Ryan says, "or walking down the street or talking to people. It's far more rewarding, exciting, inspiring. It's the only way you redefine the game. You put things together in a new way."

This isn't just rhetoric. One of the first Method products signaled just how audacious and serious the two men were: a condensed laundry detergent.

"We knew that making things small was better for the environment— fewer trucks on the road making fewer journeys," Ryan recalls. "So we made small the big idea: we concentrated the detergent three times, which also made it easier to handle and less cumbersome to take home. It was a huge hit. So then Unilever did Small & Mighty. Then Walmart, P&G, everybody copied it. Warehouse and distribution costs came down. Today, anywhere you go, all the detergents are concentrated. We changed the norm. So our next goal is to change it again."

Because their competitors instantly copied Method's first innovation, the company had to provide another. Lowry was at pains to point out that this wasn't less risky for the small company but more so. Method had far more at stake: its very existence.

"If you look at P&G, Tide detergent is a $2 billion brand, and they make $100 billion. We are nowhere near those revenues! The point is, innovation is riskier for us than for P&G. And yet we take the risk and they don't. We do it from a philosophy that gets us out of bed every morning. It is something we believe very deeply: radical step-change innovation."

But isn't it intensely annoying, I ask them, to find their creativity so instantly and flagrantly copied?

"That's the way you change the world. It showed we were right! It showed we were on to something. We get copied all the time. It just means we have to be really good at coming up with new ideas."

Betting the whole business on innovation, Lowry and Ryan have had to think hard about how to provoke and sustain it. They put Method head-quarters in the center of San Francisco because they want the company not to be isolated but to be in and of the world. Subject to zoning laws, they are strictly controlled in the substances they can pour down their drains—but that's fine because they're committed to using nontoxic substances anyway. The offices are sparkling white—they're very serious about cleanliness—and the primacy of design is visible everywhere. We met in a conference room with walls emblazoned with a quote from the film *American Beauty:* I DON'T THINK THERE'S ANYTHING WORSE THAN BEING ORDINARY.

"We made a very deliberate decision not to outsource anything except hard manufacturing," Lowry says. "So we have vertically integrated all aspects of product development. We have chemical engineers here, packaging designers, ad designers—everyone is here. The traditional way to do this kind of business is to use lots of outside agencies. We don't do that. For us it is an imperative that everyone and everything we need is right here so that we can predictably create things that are innovative."

You only have to look around at the way Method employees are seated to see that there's very little hierarchy here. Ryan sits next to customer support because he wants to absorb the questions or complaints that customers call about. Information flows fast at Method because it sparks ideas. The walls are covered in continuous whiteboards: these "wiki walls" in hallways and around workplaces map a new product's development or its dead end. Anyone can add a comment, a thought, an inspiration. Key to the quality of the collaboration needed by the company are a few ground rules: Assume goodwill. Ask questions. Communicate directly ("You can't do anything new via email"). And just as in Uri Alon's lab, be supportive ("Yes, and …" replaces "Yes, but …").

Prototypes are everywhere: soap dispensers, dishwasher tablets, wood polish bottles, products that made it and more that did not. In the corner, a 3D printer whirs away, slowly accreting the layers of plastic that will model a body wash container. This is not just trendy: design is central to the strategic positioning of the business, whose beautiful containers were what earned its products shelf space in Target and Waitrose. Design thinking lies at the heart of the way the company works and succeeds.

"Design thinking," Ryan explains, "is about creating new choices that didn't exist before. It's holistic. It's not about line extensions or market research or copying the other guys. Most companies use agencies because they don't have (or want) the creativity they need. But that is what we are all about. So we mix everyone up here so we can hear each other, pay attention to each other. Everywhere you see what people are working on—and you think about it, add to it. It's fundamental that we're all in a design loop of failing and learning and getting better."

Research and development at Method isn't off on its own, in a different corner or floor of the building. It's at the center of the action where everyone can see what's being worked on. The purpose of all the displays is to provoke ideas and cross-fertilization. Just as at W. L. Gore, sharing ideas openly and uncompetitively is how Method gets better.

"It's important that everyone talks about the object, not about 'my idea.'" Lowry tells me. "We put stuff up on the walls so people talk about the design. We put whiteboards everywhere so all our work is visible, without politics or territory. In design you learn that ideas are currency, but you have to let go of them quickly so that they can grow. Design thinkers don't copy, they create."

The advantage of keeping everything in-house is that it allows the company to move fast. A good idea can be prototyped quickly, held, touched, passed around, sniffed or prodded, poured or pinched. As much energy goes into fragrance design as into figuring out the most efficient and greenest way to ship products halfway across the world. No discipline is pursued at Method without some element of design thinking, because everyone is highly committed to finding new and better ways to do business. Ryan and Lowry both came from families that had worked in the automotive industry. Growing up, they'd seen that industry dying on its feet because of its failure to innovate, and that left them both with a passion for creating a company that is, as Ryan says, "one giant continuous brainstorm."

"We've built a business that is fantastically innovative in organic green chemistry. We win prizes for our bottle design. People send love letters to our detergent! We have redefined the game. But there is *still* category management."

The bane of Method's existence is what's known as the "category captain." Most major supermarkets don't have or want to have buyers for every kind of product they sell. Instead, in every category—like detergent—they appoint representatives, and these are usually executives from the major suppliers, like Unilever or P&G. Those companies recommend to the supermarkets which products to stock; not surprisingly, they typically prefer their own.

"So the category—the trade—has a huge incentive *against* innovation," Lowry explains. "We often get in the back door because we're loss leaders: people come to the store just to get our products. So we have a direct relationship with the retailer. That means we have to develop and maintain really wonderful relationships with our retailers and serve them fantastically well. We have to think about our customers in a different way."

Nevertheless, a few years ago, having seen the growing appeal of Method products and having lost out to them in several categories, the major man-ufacturers started to fight back. Internally, some even developed teams with the mission: kill Method. Lowry and Ryan were not daunted.

"Everyone launched their green varieties—a million of them," Ryan tells me. "They all went in saying, 'You have this Method stuff, but here's our offering, and they aren't spending a million dollars on advertising and we will spend a hundred million—so we want that space.' It was dirty. But we just have to be very focused on the kinds of products we want to create, the companies we want to work with. And we can tell we're successful because people still keep trying to copy us!"

One school of thought argues that there is no absolute innovation, that every new thing is a combination of old things. The idea that weak artists borrow and great artists steal is variously attributed to T. S. Eliot, Pablo Picasso, or Steve Jobs. More recently, arguing that "everything is a remix," the filmmaker Kirby Ferguson has done a brilliant job identifying the many weird and wonderful sources of music, imagery, and language that have been borrowed to create work we all imagined was entirely original.[18] Led Zeppe-lin's "Stairway to Heaven" is a remarkably untransformed version of the song "Taurus" by the group Spirit, with which Led Zeppelin had earlier toured. The first Apple computer was famously a remix of technologies pioneered by Xerox Parc (and later reinterpreted by Microsoft). Henry Ford didn't invent the assembly line or the automobile, and Gutenberg didn't invent movable type. All of these inventions brought together elements that had previously been disconnected. That kind of innovation isn't driven by competition but by creativity and an engagement with the world that is able to see that the time is right.

Lowry and Ryan agree, arguing that many of their own innovations are sim-ply tremendous mash-ups. That the company has variously been described as the Herman Miller or the Aveda of home cleaning captures their debt to values and thinking in other industries. But in their determination—despite provocation—to keep coming up with new formulations and ideas, they show that deciding whether to clone or to genuinely innovate is a choice. Individuals and companies don't have to copy—they aren't forced to imitate or to join the herd. They could—and can—do better.

In his enthusiasm to demolish some of the more romantic and unhelpful myths around innovation, Kirby Ferguson almost—but not quite—argues that originality isn't all it's cracked up to be. His is a compelling postmod-ern argument, wittily and forensically assembled, and he's clearly right that much of what we enjoy borrows (often heavily) from other sources. But while imitation might be how we learn, it isn't all we can do. The patient whose tuberculosis is resistant to every known antibiotic or the Somalian farmer trying to feed her family is neither impressed by market share nor enraptured by the marketing millions spent to capture minute percentages of old business. From the discovery of the poliovirus to the reinvention of the humble laundry detergent, true innovators testify to the immense human gift for creativity and perseverance, sparked not by competition but by the sheer conviction that copying is a cop-out and solving problems and helping people is human.

CHAPTER 8

Supersize Everything

> People say to you: "I know a place where you can get more." It's
> very hard to say, "No, thank you, I'm happier with less." Hard to
> say that. People start thinking you must be stupid.
>
> —David Hare, *The Way to Yes*

On September 19, 1928, construction began on the Chrysler Building in New
York City. Walter Chrysler, founder of the eponymous car company, had
decided that, since his sons would probably settle in New York, they needed
something to be responsible for. (His two daughters, apparently, had no such
needs.) As the sons of one of the richest men in America, their requirements
were pretty special.

"They wanted to work, and so the idea of putting up a building was born,"
Chrysler later recalled. "Something that I had seen in Paris recurred to me.
I said to the architects: 'Make this building higher than the Eiffel Tower.'"[1]

A year after construction started, Wall Street crashed. But Chrysler persevered: his building had to be big. Not just big, but the biggest. With the
Bank of Manhattan under construction on Wall Street, the race was on to
build the world's tallest skyscraper. When his rival topped out at 927 feet, it
looked as though Chrysler had lost by just two feet. But his architect, William van Alen, had secretly assembled a spire in the fire shaft and just a few
weeks later, its twenty-seven tons were hoisted into place, giving the Art
Deco tower its full 1,048 feet—thus surpassing its New York rival and the
Eiffel Tower too.

Chrysler's triumph was short-lived. Three months after the Crash, in defi-
ance of economics and gravity, John Jacob Raskob and Pierre du Pont began
construction on the Empire State Building. The two men had made their
fortunes together at DuPont and General Motors, and they did nothing by
halves. Finished in just one year and forty-five days, the building was on
time and under budget; the Depression had brought down its labor costs.
At 1,250 feet, its record as the world's tallest building would endure for forty
years.

It's easy to dismiss the passion for size as simply the indulged idiosyncrasy of crazed tycoons. But the desire to build big is ancient: the Aztecs with their great stairs, the temples of southern India, the cathedrals of Europe—all make a statement about their builders and their culture by the confident mass of their presence. Skyscrapers are just the modern manifestation of an ancient feeling. "It's about power," the architect Philip Johnson wrote. "Power and domination. All those words we don't use anymore, but the feelings are still in the human breast, and they have got to find expression."[2]

Although he was perfectly content to design skyscrapers—most notably the AT&T Building in New York (now the Sony Tower), the Williams Tower in Houston, and the two leaning towers of Madrid's Puerta de Europa—Johnson recognized that they served no real economic purpose. "Our commercial skyscrapers are the result of the pushing and shoving of the competitive commercial world. There is no relationship between their size, their cost and their utility. In the commercial world, the skyscraper came into existence because we didn't have any religion to express. But it was an expression, not the result of economic needs. It was an expression that wanted to reach to heaven."[3] The size was the message.

But even if, as Johnson argues, power and dominance serve no meaningful purpose, they always incur costs. In biology, the cost can be painfully visible. During courtship, the argus cock pheasant spreads his large secondary wing feathers, which are decorated with beautiful eyespots; the bigger they are, the more they stimulate the female. And the longer the feathers, the more progeny the cock will produce. So the more beautiful cocks produce more descendants. That should be a competitive advantage. But the evolution of the argus pheasant has run itself into a blind alley because the most gorgeous cock has feathers so huge and unwieldy that he may be eaten by a predator because he can't fly away fast enough. Oskar Heinroth, the teacher of Konrad Lorenz, commented, "Next to the wings of the argus pheasant, the hectic life of western civilized man is the most stupid product of intraspecific selection!"[4]

In architecture between 1995 and 2005, the allure of size ran into an equally blind alley with the rise of "starchitects" and the huge blockbusting constructions that made their names. Big public commissions had long been decided by competition, but now these became big, showy, and controversial affairs that turned architects into brands. The contests were no longer about architectural firms but about celebrity designers. A plethora of new prize events sprang up, destabilizing careers and demanding bigger, flashier trophy buildings. America's Pritzker Prize (first won by Philip Johnson in 1979) had long been considered the Nobel Prize of architecture, its $100,000 award designating the winner as the "supreme genius" of the architectural world. But European institutions were keen to enter the game and update their image. The Royal Institute of British Architects' Stirling Prize, the Aga Khan Award, the Mies van der Rohe Award, France's Grand Prix National de l'Architecture, and the Deutscher Architekturpreis all fueled the new breathless rhetoric.

After building the Guggenheim Museum in Bilbao, starchitect Frank Gehry was assailed by requests from individuals and institutions who wanted to "have a Gehry"—a clone to show that they too had arrived. They didn't want anything very different—just more of the same big showy buildings with which to compete for tourists and renown. Renzo Piano, Daniel Libeskind, Norman Foster, Zaha Hadid—all the starchitects were begged to design not just buildings that fulfilled a human or social need but iconic structures that shouted out the names of those who had built and paid for them. It was, said architecture critic Miles Glendinning, the perfect marriage of big capital and big buildings. "The rhetoricians of architecture's capitalist revolution talk happily of architecture as an exercise in 'branding and advertising.' For them, the task of architects is not to make the world a better place, but 'to become tough, Machiavellian businessmen,' driven by 'hyper-rationality' in their incessant pursuit of market advantage."[5]

Architecture's most influential critic, Charles Jencks, wrote that the world of architecture was now one of "dog-eat-dog competition, requiring competitive capitalist training in how to get the job and keep it. At any one time, there are four isms, five trends, 100 architects who are competing on a world level." And their job, he said, was to "find out what makes a good iconic building and why." Sooner or later, everyone writing about architecture cited Howard Roark: the heroic protagonist and emblem of extreme individualism in Ayn Rand's novel *The Fountainhead*. Like Roark, every architect now had to tell a heroic career story and articulate a unique, radically individualistic style that proclaimed itself with volume. You just couldn't win with smaller, subtler buildings, and winning was what architecture was now all about.

One of the many architects caught up in the whirlwind was Richard Meier, who won the competition to design a new Getty museum in Los Angeles. Nothing about the project was small, which cost nearly $1 billion. The site required slicing the top off of a mountain to create the perfect position for a vast swath of white stone. Sixteen thousand tons of travertine marble were shipped from Italy to cover the 1.2 million-square-foot edifice. The model of the structure was so gigantic that it could not be loaded onto any of the museum's elevators.

As the building neared completion, even the board that had commissioned it started to balk at its daunting Aristotelian absolutism. It was, commented one member of the museum board, "all but overpowering," but that was its point. Meier proved that height wasn't needed to create a building of stunning dominance that left its spectators feeling small. The board had gotten what it asked for, but for many it was a shock. Late in the day, and over Meier's head, they brought in another artist—Robert Irwin—to design a garden around the building to soften its edges and humanize its tone. Meier saw the garden as his competitor, siphoning off attention and impact from his powerful, signature design, and he fought Irwin at every stage. When the site was finally opened, huge debate swirled around which was more remarkable—the building or the gardens. What nobody talked about was the art collection the museum was commissioned to showcase.

The fact that training to be an architect is one of the most expensive educations in the world, that the profession has very low starting salaries, and that there is an oversupply of trained graduates makes it more urgent for practitioners to enter competitions and win them with huge shiny buildings that bring attention, glamour, and notoriety. Miles Glendinning argues, however, that even starchitects have started to grow wary—and weary—of this passion for the big and the loud.

"There certainly was big pressure," he tells me, "to make big noisy buildings. But architects are quite subtle people, and around 2005 they started to feel pretty uncomfortable with some of this. There was a feeling that it was immoral, in bad taste, to do these extravagant buildings. That it was no longer so interesting. All that titanium and those big, computer-generated curves.

"You saw influential architects—Rem Koolhaas, for example, has excellent antennae—try frantically to distance themselves from it. Renzo Piano started to try to find a more ecological, more refined language. But of course, we're still stuck with Piano's Shard [in London]; in architecture, you always have the situation that the building starts to go out of fashion even while it's being built. Time moves on, leaving the building behind."

The problem with starchitects isn't just that their big showy buildings have had unfortunate side effects: the reflection from London's Walkie-

Talkie melted cars, the Los Angeles Walt Disney Concert Hall blinded drivers, and the Vdara Hotel's pool deck in Las Vegas singed hair and melted plastic. When these grandiose constructions were designed, what wasn't being addressed was how to house ordinary citizens in affordable houses whose energy consumption wouldn't bankrupt them or exhaust the earth's resources.

The age of austerity, Glendinning says, hasn't produced an aesthetic of austerity; in the West, architects are left feeling quite confused. They learned to compete, but the visual vocabulary of size they created to do so didn't lead anywhere. In the context of the economic crash, these huge, expensive buildings suddenly look irrelevant and crass, oblivious to the inequality they have come to symbolize. Renzo Piano's Shard may be the biggest building in western Europe, but it's hard to see what other role it plays in the London landscape. Once architects proved that they could build very big, very strange shapes, there has been nowhere left to go. The buildings famous for being big are, finally, only big, often overpowering their purpose, their environment, and the people who come to see them.

The pursuit of size for its own sake exerts a magical allure; bigger is better. The supersized Big Mac meal, 7-Eleven's Big Gulp drink, the armor-plated Hummer, and the hypercaffeinated energy drink are all expected to outperform their mundane rivals. The fantasy of more is that size makes you invincible and growth is its own reward. But the obsession with size always incurs costs, compromises, and sacrifices obscured by the sheer grandiosity.

In churches, bigger has long come to imply supremacy. Philip Johnson's Crystal Cathedral near Garden Grove, California, with its ten thousand panes of glass, stands isolated among big-box stores and gas stations. Acres of parking lots were designed to facilitate massive crowds; if the church itself overflowed, visitors could sit in their cars (just as in old-fashioned drive-in fast-food joints) and listen to services relayed through loudspeakers hanging from the trees. But the site proved so costly that in 2010 the church filed for bankruptcy and the buildings were sold to the Catholic Church. The lesson learned by all the independent churches was specific: size does matter, but it's safer to measure it in followers.

There's fierce competition to address the spiritual hunger that is one hallmark of modern American life. Scientology, Islam, Buddhism, and Pentecostal churches argue about which is the fastest-growing religion, but none question that they are all expanding rapidly. Sermoncentral.com ranks

American churches by attendance numbers. Topping the list is Joel Osteen's Lakewood Church in Houston, Texas, with over forty-three thousand worshipers every weekend. Those numbers count—and they're watched avidly.

"In late 1999, we had a core attendance of six thousand that came every Sunday," Steve Austin tells me. A former probate lawyer, Austin is now the senior director responsible for pastoral care and Christian education at Lakewood. As we sit talking in his windowless office, surrounded by standard-issue faux-wood furniture and filing cabinets, he could be reciting the metrics of any business.

"Our TV viewership is 10 million weekly and growing. But because we broadcast in over 150 nations, it is almost impossible to quantify how many people come to hear our message. We have 1 million people tapping our website every month. Joel has 1.2 million Facebook followers and about 800,000 Twitter followers."

Six months after I met with Austin, those numbers had doubled. Austin was pleased with the attendance numbers, but still worrying that the church's website content wasn't as successful as that offered by online rival Joyce Meyer.

"We still have a way to go to improve our online offering and infrastructure. But who knows exactly how many people Joel touches? People read his books, listen to his tapes, watch the TV. He is the number-one evangelist in the world today, bringing the lost into the kingdom of God."

Austin was the first of many people I spoke to who compared Lakewood's pastor, Joel Osteen, to Walmart founder Sam Walton. Like Walton, he says, Osteen is self-effacing but has a true sense of where he came from and where he's going. That sense of mission, according to Austin, drives spectacular growth.

"It was a rocket!" Austin says with enthusiasm as he reminisces. "Jim Collins's book, *Good to Great,* helped us a lot. The most stressful part was moving here, to this campus, and having to beef up the infrastructure of volunteers and personnel and putting systems in place to handle explosive growth. So when people came they would have a positive experience the minute they're in the door. That requires infrastructure."

Lakewood can afford infrastructure. While the big earners for the church are Osteen's best-selling books and recordings (his first book, *Your Best Life Now,* has sold over 4 million copies), worshipers are expected to tithe—to commit 10 percent of their income to the church. Attendance and revenue therefore grow together, generating a total estimated at between $77 million and $100 million a year. There's competition for that income, and Lakewood has proved astute at capturing and keeping it.

On the day I visit, the infrastructure works magnificently. Driving down Highway 59, I expected to spot the church easily, by its size or its crowds. Instead, I drive right past. The building—a former sports arena—is lost amid the mirrored towers and marble monoliths of corporate America. Nothing more than the logo of a flame indicates the country's largest church, which has no spire, no steeple, and no cross, only a long line of American flags. As for traffic, so many police officers are out directing drivers that there isn't a hint of gridlock. All the parking garages used to service the surrounding office blocks during the week are fully available on weekends to churchgoers, who turn up in the thousands.

Once inside, ferocious air conditioning assails the senses. This is familiar territory: the slowly curving outer corridor that rings the circular arena. An army of stewards point the way to available seats. It's quite a hike; along the way, signs point to rooms for children's services, crèches, bookstalls, restrooms, escalators, and seminar rooms.

At the Houston tourist bureau, I was told that Lakewood Church is the city's number-one visitor attraction. The sheer size of the church is what draws ever more people to it. No one is too young or too old for Lakewood; while the main services are addressed to adults, kids can go off in their age groups to play areas and Sunday school lessons in facilities decorated by former Disney designers. The main goal, I'm told, is to make the kids want to come back and bring their parents.

I am directed into the arena by a steward who opens a door, ushering me to the top of a steep staircase flanked by people standing up, arms aloft, palms up in prayer. On both sides of the stage are two huge rockeries and waterfalls; next to them, a pair of choir lofts with twelve rows of purple seats hold singers on either side of the stage. In the center of the stage, a vast, golden globe spins slowly. Absent are any religious symbols—no cross or crucifix, no image of God or Jesus, can be seen. Giant screens show musicians and celebrants while projecting lyrics so that everyone can sing along: "Nothing is impossible."

The audience, or congregation, is strikingly multicultural: black, white, Hispanic, Asian, Native American. Most are middle-aged and well dressed, and look affluent. No one acknowledges or speaks to me as I find my seat. Many congregants hold Bibles, and almost all are standing in a state that looks, but does not feel, like ecstasy. The auditorium is vast and strangely impersonal, too large for any real connection between pastors and congregation. Anyone arriving with some anxiety about being swept away by emotion and rhetoric would quickly relax.

> Nothing in this world can satisfy
> 'Cause Jesus You're the cup that won't run dry

Like the production values, the musicianship is technically perfect: Israel Houghton, winner of four Grammy Awards, has two gold albums to his name. Steve Crawford and Da'dra Crawford Greathouse are leading lights in the world of gospel music. Every one-hour service comprises roughly forty minutes of music, and when it's done, the stage sinks out of sight and is given over to twenty minutes of speech from Joel or Victoria Osteen.

Before each speech, the congregation is exhorted to hold up their Bibles and repeat together: "This is my Bible. I am what it says I am. I have what it says I have. I can do what it says I can do. Today I will be taught the word of God. I boldly confess my mind is alert, my heart is receptive. I will never be the same. In Jesus' name. God bless you." Then everyone sits and listens.

Physically, Joel Osteen is the most unlikely of preachers. A slight figure with huge white teeth, he seems startled to find himself onstage in front of seven thousand people attending the service, one of several he'll conduct throughout the day. Immaculately dressed in suit and shiny tie, brown curly hair perfectly in place, his tiny eyes try to make up with brightness what they lack in size. With his long, narrow, slightly lopsided face, Osteen works hard to connect with the audience in front of him and the one he knows is watching on television. Facing cameras on the ends of long cranes moving in for their close-ups, Osteen, like motivational speakers the world over, kicks off with a joke.

"I like to start with something funny. I heard about this eighty-five-year-old man. He was out fishing one day, and he heard a voice saying, 'Pick me up!' He looked around, didn't see anything, thought he was dreaming. He heard it again, and he looked down, and he saw a frog. He said in amazement, 'Are you talking to me?' The frog said, 'Yes. Pick me up and kiss me, and I will turn into a beautiful bride.' The man quickly picked him up and put him in his front pocket. The frog said, 'Hey, what are you doing? I said kiss me and I'll turn into a beautiful bride.' The man said, 'No thanks. At my age, I'd rather have a talking frog.'"

Osteen says that writing his weekly sermon is the single most important task of his week. He has perfected the art of communicating to a vast multicultural audience from the widest variety of backgrounds in language simple enough for everyone to understand. Pacing the vast empty stage, he speaks, beaming, without autocue or notes.

"You've been framed. God has put a boundary around your life. Nothing can penetrate your frame that God would not allow. Trouble, sickness, accidents … you don't have to worry about your future; there is a frame around your health, a frame around your children. It's a boundary set by the creator of the universe."

His audience loves him. As I watch the people to either side of me, they're rapt, Bibles open on their laps, grinning at the funny stories, intent upon the rising tide of repeated phrases.

"You will never run out of your frame. You will keep bumping up against it again and again. It will always push you back towards your divine destiny.… God has put a frame that you can't penetrate. The enemy can't penetrate. Drugs can't penetrate."

Replete with anecdotes about cars and kids, Osteen bounces between Bible stories and mundane lessons from daily life. He talks eagerly about his mother, who sits in the front row, and about his wife Victoria, who is almost as accomplished a speaker. The two of them look as though they stepped out of the cast of *Dallas:* polished, groomed, and brimming with health. Their story—the gawky boy who became the world-famous, wealthy preacher with the beautiful wife, gorgeous kids, massive house—smoothly implies that, if the American dream can come true for the Osteens, it can come true for everyone who listens to them. Everything about this service is technologically proficient and efficient. It has to be. To attract this many people and send them away satisfied demands the highest production values.

Osteen is deliberately, insistently ordinary: no fancy language, no difficult ideas, no complexity, no anxiety, no problems. His message is relentlessly upbeat: you are good, God will look after you, everything will be all right. Only believe.

The service features little in the way of prayer, and Osteen's theme is only faintly religious. He will cite scripture and recount stories from the Bible, but hard-core Christianity is neither his style nor his mission. He preaches family values, but accepts that families come in all shapes and sizes; everyone sins, but all are forgiven. Pressed hard by friends and critics alike to pronounce on the subject of homosexuality, he ducked and dodged until he came up with the formulation that homosexuality is a sin—the Bible says so, according to Osteen—but we are all sinners and can expect forgiveness.

At a time when one part of America has been campaigning for gay marriage while another wants gays locked up in concentration camps to prevent breeding, Osteen's is an astutely noncommittal position.

"I don't believe homosexuality is God's best for a person's life. I mean: sin means to miss the mark."[6]

Pressed by Piers Morgan on CNN to explain the problem of evil, Osteen did not, he said, know enough about Hitler's childhood background to comment. He has no view on capital punishment, even though his home state executes more inmates than any other in America. And following the December 2012 school shooting in Newtown, Connecticut, in which twenty children died, he felt that it was not his responsibility to take a stand for or against gun control.

"I really don't, because political issues divide us. I'm trying to reach as many people as possible. There are good people on both sides of the aisle, and I don't know what the best answer there is either, but I just try to guide them and give them hope in this time of need."[7]

To keep growing, Osteen must adroitly remain noncommittal, ambiguous, and bland. He can't be for or against gun control, for or against the shooter of Congresswoman Gabrielle Giffords, for or against homosexual rights. Saying nothing is the price Osteen pays for leading the biggest church in America. It would be wrong to call Osteen's language Orwellian—he does not use words in ways that are opposite to their meaning. Instead, he is supremely skilled at using words to evade meaning. Careful to avoid throwing fuel on the fire of American partisanship, he also does nothing to put it out.

Apart from tithing, Osteen can't tell his followers what to do; taking any position would alienate someone. If he wants to keep his numbers growing, all that is left for him is to flatter his followers—and this he does lavishly. If Osteen believes anything, it is that his millions of followers are all terrific. What he aims to do is just what his broadcast tagline says: "Discover the champion in you."

"You are someone to be celebrated. You are talented. You are smart. You are attractive. There's something great about you.… Listen, God breathed his life into you. He crowns you with his honor and favor.… Hold your head up high. Walk confidently. Talk confidently. Think confidently. Act confidently. People are going to treat you the way you present yourself."[8]

It's hard to imagine how the self-esteem that Osteen sells to his congregation could deliver on his promise that their dreams will be fulfilled. High self-esteem may be the outcome of hard work, discipline, and success—but it isn't the cause. Although the self-esteem movement has long argued the connection between high self-esteem and achievement, when the veteran social scientist Roy Baumeister reviewed the scientific literature, that wasn't what he found. Lab studies did not show that efforts to boost self-esteem lead to improved performance. Looking specifically at school performance, Baumeister clearly saw that, while those who do well feel better about themselves, the reverse is not true: merely encouraging students to feel confident doesn't make them do any better on tests.[9] The self-esteem movement, started by Ayn Rand's former lover Nathaniel Branden, promised much but has delivered nothing.

That finding is reinforced by the work of Carol Dweck, who has shown that blanket praise for children—telling them they're so smart, or so talented—far from motivating them to work hard encourages them to believe they're innately so brilliant that they need not work at all.[10] Although self-control, self-discipline, and perseverance are far more effective, the confidence instilled in children by self-esteem advocates may suggest to them that they don't need those traits at all, that they are already "someone to be celebrated."

What boosting self-esteem may also do is develop narcissists—people who look upon themselves as fundamentally special, entitled, unique. According to psychologist Jean Twenge, we are living through an epidemic of narcissism, represented by a generation of children who imagine that thinking positive thoughts *alone* will make good things happen. Citing numerous studies of college students, she shows that narcissistic traits rose as fast as obesity from the 1980s to the present day.

"Our country's focus on self-admiration has certainly been successful in raising Americans' opinions of themselves," Twenge writes. "Self-esteem is at an all-time high in most groups, with more than 80% of recent college students scoring higher in general self-esteem than the average 1960s college student. Middle school students, often the focus of self-esteem-boosting efforts, have skyrocketed in self-esteem, with 93% of late 2000s tweens scoring higher than the average eleven- to thirteen-year-old did in 1980."[11]

Many people insist that the world is now so competitive that you have to feel great about yourself—or at least act as if you do ("Walk confidently, talk confidently")—if you want to compete. But the problem with this behavior is that it separates feeling good from *doing* good, and the result, Twenge argues, is that we have become a nation of phonies.

We have phony rich people (with interest-only mortgages and piles of debt), phony beauty (with plastic surgery and cosmetic procedures), phony athletes (with performance-enhancing drugs), phony celebrities (via reality TV and YouTube), phony genius students (with grade inflation), a phony national economy (with $11 trillion of government debt), phony feelings of being special among children (with parenting and education focused on self-esteem) and phony friends (with the social networking explosion).[12]

Promoting self-esteem, as Joel Osteen so relentlessly does, may make his church grow, but it won't make his followers work better or smarter. Psychologist Don Forsyth and his team at Richmond University did an experiment with two groups of college students. They sent one group a weekly email containing a practice question, and they sent the other group a weekly practice question accompanied by messages reminding them of the importance of confidence and encouraging them to keep theirs up: "Bottom line: Hold your head—and your self-esteem—high."[13]

The students who had been encouraged to boost their self-esteem "showed a substantial drop in grades.... Feelings of unrealistic optimism," the researchers concluded, "can lead to complacency rather than active coping. Indeed, weak students may maintain self-esteem best by withdrawing effort and minimize the degree to which their self-esteem is contingent on good grades."[14]

The self-esteem that Osteen sells to his congregation won't deliver. The idea that feeling good alone will solve anything turns out to be neither true nor the Truth. But flattering his audience is a strategic way for Osteen to boost Lakewood's attendance and revenue; it is both cause and consequence of being big. Because the warm glow of self-esteem quickly fades, like addicts, churchgoers must go back for more.

Whether Lakewood is riding the rising tide of narcissism or contributing to it, the church's growth necessarily corrodes its message. After the service, as Joel and his wife Victoria stand in a reception line, shaking hands with visitors, I go behind the scenes to meet with Donald Iloff, Lakewood Church's chief strategist. We sit in what feels like the sitting room of a giant: huge chairs and sofas, empty tables, and fake book spines create the illusion of a home that is really a corporate reception area.

Iloff is a seasoned campaigner. He used to work in Washington as a lobbyist; at one point, he tells me, he had Enron as a client. A friend of Lee Atwater's, he was closely involved in Texas politics and the Bush-Quayle campaign in 1992, but there is nothing he takes more pride in than the achievements of Lakewood Church.

"Never in the history of the United States has there been a church this big! But you know," Iloff demurs, "we don't really go by numbers. We know our TV audience numbers. We're the number-one podcaster and always in the top ten worldwide. We're the third-biggest influencer on Twitter—we crushed Lady Gaga because we had more retweets and mentions."

To my ears, Iloff, just like Steve Austin, sounds like any corporate executive regaling me with his quarterly results. He is, after all, media-savvy and highly accustomed to monitoring his numbers.

"But we don't have size goals. We don't sit down and say, 'These are the numbers we want to hit this year.' We're really wanting something else. You know, if corporate executives were to look at what they do as spreading influence, they'd think about their models differently. Does Intel influence? It does. Does Apple influence the world? It does. That's how we think about growth. Are we influencing our community? How can we create the most influence? That's Joel's goal."

So how, I ask Iloff, does he see that influence growing?

"We see growth everywhere. It doesn't matter about the economy. We keep growing—and growing all over the world."

For an organization that purports to provide some kind of moral leadership, however, the example Iloff proffers to illustrate Lakewood's growing influence is, at best, puzzling.

"A few years ago I was speaking to the president of Liberia at a reception in Houston and he expressed his desire to have Pastor Osteen come to his country. He mentioned that Joel is very popular among his people and that he, himself, watched Joel's broadcast regularly."

As Iloff is proudly telling me this story, I am remembering that the current president of Liberia is female—Ellen Johnson Sirleaf—so that can't be who he means. The previous presidents were Charles Taylor and his close associate, Moses Blah. Taylor was indicted for war crimes, and Blah referred to Taylor as a brother. If Iloff was referring to either, such character references seem a strange way to illustrate the influence wielded by the biggest church in America.

You can't have a church as vast as Lakewood without coming in for a lot of criticism from your rivals. Osteen has been attacked for being too tolerant, too intolerant, too Christian, not Christian enough, too dogmatic, not dogmatic enough. But in order to maintain its top spot as America's biggest, Lakewood Church can purvey no real message; all it can do is sell itself. The atmosphere is glitzy and the moral compass of the organization distinctly weak, but its sheer size prevents it from being anything else.

I left Lakewood Church numbed by its scale, energy, noise, and banality. I had come looking for meaning—in what it did, in what it stood for. But I couldn't find any. As a religious experience, attending a Lakewood service was as moving as staying at a large, international chain hotel. For a religious institution, it was morally one of the most vacuous I'd ever encountered. All day I'd been given messages of self-confidence, of happiness, of destiny. I'd been entertained but not enlightened, talked at but not talked to. I was strangely troubled that I was repeatedly exhorted to feel good, but not to do good.

I don't believe that the church's growth was completely spontaneous, unplanned, or God-given. Nobody employs a chief strategist without believing in strategy, and while everyone at Lakewood denied the importance of numbers, they all recited them with pride. *Good to Great* was referenced more frequently than the Bible. This influential business book celebrates what it calls Big Hairy Audacious Goals (BHAGs™), but the problem with these is that they tend to overwhelm nuance, subtlety, and detail. That's what they're for—to keep eyes on the prize—but that is also the cost they incur.

The big promise of size is that it imparts invincibility. Organizations hope that being big will eliminate their competitors, allowing them to operate with impunity across a so-called free market. At the very least, they expect scale to command respect. That expectation underlies many, if not most, of the mergers and acquisitions that companies undertake in the face of the data showing that 50 to 80 percent of such deals fail.

"As a big company, we could drill more wells than a smaller company, and hence we could learn far more through greater experience," John Browne argued when becoming CEO of BP in 1995. "The bigger we were, the more we could leverage knowledge and experience and do the same things better. So scale and reach seemed like virtues worth having just on this basis.

"But there was more. We believed governments of oil-producing nations would increasingly prefer to work with very big and influential oil companies. They wanted to see a big balance sheet, global political clout and technological prowess and they wanted to be sure that you would be around for a long time."[15]

With the aim of transforming BP into a "super-major," Browne went shopping, trying and failing to buy Mobil in 1996, successfully buying Amoco in 1998, then Atlantic Richfield in 1999 and Castrol in 2000. These deals were big and expensive and garnered big headlines for Browne, large fees for lawyers, and huge amounts of debt for BP. Inevitably, these deals were followed by brutal cost-cutting across the board. Following the Amoco acquisition, the newly combined company ordered a 25 percent cut in fixed cash costs across all refineries, regardless of the condition of each site. And the cuts continued for the next three years. Everything was subject to being cut, it was said—down to the number of pencils.

In 2005 an accident at BP's Texas City refinery resulted in the deaths of 15 people, with 180 more injured. It was one of the most serious workplace disasters in the United States for twenty years. When the US Chemical Safety and Hazard Investigation Board came to study the accident, cost-cutting was deemed to have been a culprit.

"Cost-cutting and failure to invest in the 1990s by Amoco [which merged with BP in 1998] and then BP, left the Texas City refinery vulnerable to a catastrophe," the board wrote. "BP targeted budget cuts of 25 percent in 1999 and another 25 percent in 2005, even though much of the refinery's infrastructure and process equipment were in disrepair. Also, operator training and staffing were downsized."[16]

One year later, BP had another major industrial accident, this time in Alaska's Prudhoe Bay, where its pipelines leaked 212,252 gallons of oil into the delicate tundra environment—the worst spill ever recorded on the North Slope. The leak went undetected for as long as five days; upon analysis, the pipes were found to have been poorly maintained and inspected. And in 2010, cost-cutting was yet again implicated in the largest accidental marine oil spill in history—from BP's Deepwater Horizon rig in the Gulf of Mexico.

"Whether purposeful or not, many of the decisions that BP, Halliburton, and Transocean made that increased the risk of the Macondo blowout clearly saved those companies significant time (and money)."[17]

The first time I wrote about BP's cost-cutting and the Texas City refinery, I wondered whether, after the accident, the company had changed any of its views concerning the virtues of scale and reach. I began the delicate negotiations required to secure an interview with the chief executive, Tony Hayward. Yes, I was told, BP had been a mess under Browne, but now, after many years of reflection, discussion, and debate leading to root-and-branch restructuring, the company believed that it had finally put its house in order.

Perhaps talking to me might be a good way to start to spread that good news. Days later Deepwater Horizon exploded, and I never heard from the company again. BP's immense organizational complexity—which many inside the company had regarded as a competitive advantage and a strategic defense—had rendered the company incapable of fixing itself.

Because BP was bigger, John Browne had imagined it was stronger. Just before Deepwater Horizon exploded, he celebrated his creation of the super-major in his memoir *Beyond Business:* "BP Amoco was now a bigger, stronger business. It would become leaner and fitter as it safely pared its activities down to the essential, realizing more than the promised economies of scale."[18] Even after Texas City and after Prudhoe Bay, Browne couldn't see that his infatuation with size was inseparable from the cost-cutting that jeopardized human life and the environment. His appreciation of scale was simplistic and incomplete, overlooking its fundamental corollary: the risk implicit in being very big is that failures are very big too. Size acts on companies in just the way power acts on individuals: providing a sense of security that makes them reckless and more dangerous. The sense of invulnerability that comes with size is its hidden trap.

Yet the quest for size, through mergers and acquisitions, persists. The year 2013 kicked off with several: American Airlines merged with US Airways, Glencore merged with Xstrata, Berkshire Hathaway bought Kraft, Liberty Global bought Virgin Media, and Microsoft bought Nokia's phone unit. The financial press positively crowed—good times were back. Never mind the research that had linked such deals with narcissistic CEOs, and never mind the numbers showing that such transactions rarely create value. Once M&A came storming back, no CEO wanted to be left behind. "In the same way that success breeds success," one Heinz adviser swooned, "deals breed more deals."[19] He might more accurately have added, "… and failure breeds failure."

Much merger activity, dressed up as strategic activity, represents the pursuit of size for its own sake. After all, once you're a $30 billion company under pressure to maintain a 15 percent growth rate, it's easier to buy that than to build it from scratch.[20] The allure of size is necessarily tied up with status. Just as the biggest house, the biggest car, the biggest bank balance signify rank in a social pecking order, so companies are led by CEOs who care passionately about their standing in the industrial pecking order. That is what the Fortune 100, 500, and 1000 and FTSE equivalents are all about. The bigger the company, the more status its CEO acquires. To this day John Browne—now Lord Browne—is regarded in many circles with respect and admiration for having grown his little oil company into a super-major. That so much and so many died along the way is overshadowed by the sheer size of his creation.

Adam Smith saw the quest for size and dominance as inevitable; it is one of the reasons why he feared the growth of joint stock companies. If there were no limit to a company's size, might it not seek to overwhelm the market? Wouldn't every company aspire to be a monopoly? That, of course, is why antitrust legislation has tried to curb the egregious abuse of powerful market positions. But what Smith did not foresee was that those instincts might also overwhelm the ability of companies to manage themselves.

Internal sclerosis is one suspect when questions are asked about the failure of big pharmaceuticals to come up with important new drugs. It's been fashionable for these companies to buy competitors and start-ups and then, just as BP did, to go through several reorganizations and seasons of cost-cutting. But this doesn't improve new drug development. As these companies have grown bigger the share of experimental drugs that fail has actually risen. The bigger, sadder truth is that every one of these deals leaves behind a workforce traumatized and terrorized by the ever-present threat of layoffs and restructurings.

"Every time you re-org, you lose a couple of years' productivity," one insider confides in me. "You can see this in the product pipeline just like you can feel the air bubble in your heating system. A merger, acquisition, re-org is that air bubble; the heat goes out of the system, and it's a long time before you get the system up and functional again. In the meanwhile, everyone's running around wondering why—now that we're bigger—we aren't producing more! That is because everyone here is in pain.

"I've survived in business for nearly fifteen years. But even though I've stayed the course and done well, I know our organization is now so complicated that we get in our own way. Getting anything done is like playing 3-D chess. Everyone has become very cynical. They're incredibly defensive because they are so afraid of losing out in the next restructuring."

The insecurity introduced by mergers and acquisitions generates—or exacerbates—dog-eat-dog behaviors within the new big organizations. Everyone becomes very competitive—even more so when the CEO's personal competitiveness becomes legendary.

"Fred had to win, he always had to win," Malcolm Woods tells me when describing Fred Goodwin, CEO of the Royal Bank of Scotland from 2000 to 2008.[21] "He bullied his direct reports, and they bullied others the way they were treated. I learned a new verb: to 'Fred' people, because people Fredded each other all the time. He had to win every single encounter—it didn't matter how big or small. He had to dominate. RBS had a very strongly bullying culture. Everything in that bank was competitive."

After nearly two decades in financial services, Woods had never encountered a culture as ruthlessly competitive as RBS, where he now played a senior role in human resources. That culture, he tells me, flowed from the top, from a CEO keenly aware that his bank was a relatively small player in the banking world. Just as Goodwin wanted to bully everyone around him, so he sought to build a bank that could bully the market and, ultimately, national governments.

In 2000, as deputy CEO, he launched a hostile takeover bid to buy NatWest Bank—a business three times the size of his own. At £21 billion (about US$35 billion), the deal was the largest acquisition in UK banking history. The purchase of the very large and very old British institution by the smaller Scottish bank won Goodwin headlines, prizes (Best Bank CEO and Global Businessman of the Year), and the top job at RBS. Harvard Business School duly beatified him with a case study by Nitin Nohria (now dean of the school) that acclaimed RBS for being "masters of acquisition." Goodwin himself reveled in his nickname "Fred the Shred" as he exercised his much-lauded skills by eliminating eighteen thousand jobs.

Now that RBS was a force to be reckoned with, Goodwin went on a buying spree. Despite the fact that he was relatively new to banking and had no experience in investment banking, insurance, trains, or cars, he bought the Irish mortgage provider First Active, Churchill Insurance, Dixon Motors, Angel Trains, and a US investment operation with the world's largest trading floor. By 2004 he had also acquired a knighthood, and of course, he had to have a mammoth "world headquarters" replete with acres of stone and glass.

Like bullying leaders before and since, Goodwin injected a hefty dose of volatility into his big bank.

In his 2003 paper (revised in 2005), Nohria egged Goodwin on, writing: "Goodwin believed that RBS continued to have multiple options for growth.... He felt his entire organization was ready to meet this challenge."[22] Everyone working in RBS read the Harvard case study, and some believed it must be true. Eager to live up to that promise, Goodwin paid £8.3 billion to acquire the American bank Charter One. But shrill notes of criticism were starting to be heard over the chorus of approval.

"Some of our investors," challenged James Eden of Kleinwort Benson, "think Fred is a megalomaniac who cares more about size than about shareholder value."

"Oh yes," Malcolm Woods laughs, with hindsight. "Inside the bank every-thing was totally about being the biggest bank on the block. You couldn't explain some of the deals any other way. It was all about us, how big we were, how big we were going to be!" That the bank's strategy was driven by a lust for size and for no other reason was perceived at every level of the organization.

"What did we know about trains? About car companies?" John Berry wonders. Once deals were done, it often fell to him to lead integration projects—to make sure all the systems knitted together. That there was no strategic fit and very little due diligence made his job harder.

"We hadn't finished integrating NatWest—and here we were buying car companies. Angel Trains! Due diligence for Charter One was just about non-existent. We had no idea how to become an international bank. I'd worked in truly global banks before, and I can tell you: RBS was not ready to be a global bank. It was just size for its own sake."

When the RBS board forbade Goodwin from making further acquisitions, he visibly chafed—and then found another path to hypergrowth. The invest-ment arm of RBS went "hell for leather" into structured finance, becoming one of the leading players in the CDO (collateralized debt obligation) mar-ket. Here there were rankings too, and despite being relative novices in the business, RBS raced up them, becoming a top-five player, along with incum-bents Lehman Brothers and Bear Stearns. In 2006 alone, CDO volumes at RBS increased 134 percent.[23]

As revenue grew, the board could not deny Goodwin when he came to them with a startling new proposition: he wanted to create an international banking consortium to buy, and then divide, the Dutch bank ABN/AMRO.

For years ABN/AMRO had been struggling with its own internal demons and a wildly overambitious CEO, Rijkman Groenink. A big global bank with a complex and cumbersome management structure, it was already in talks with Barclays, which had proposed to buy ABN/AMRO outright and merge the two operations fully. Goodwin could not resist the challenge of another hostile takeover. But he could not afford all of the Dutch bank, so he created a consortium of Spain's Santander and Belgium's Fortis Bank. Together they hoped to buy ABN/AMRO and share the spoils: Santander would get Italy and Brazil, Fortis would get the Dutch bank, and RBS would get the rest. The deal would be the most complex as well as—at €71 billion (about US$97 billion)—the biggest banking deal the world had ever seen.

"Lots of people thought it was a bit of a leap," Bob Weston recalls, "but there were some good reasons to do the deal." Weston had only recently joined the bank and brought to it deep global experience. He thought RBS was too dependent on the British economy and that being bigger would enable the bank to spread some of that risk. But he never believed those business reasons lay at the heart of Goodwin's pursuit, which, he knew, was only ever about the status that came with size.

Within the Dutch bank, employees at ABN/AMRO were aghast and confused to find themselves at the center of a big public international fight between RBS and Barclays. Accustomed to a far more sedate style of doing business, they watched with wonder as their fate was determined.

"When the Barclays possibility was announced," Sunny Uberaii remembers, "jaws fell about two feet. And then when the RBS consortium came on the scene, jaws fell about four feet! No one had any experience of this kind of thing, and people were just in a state of total paralysis."

The Dutch bank had a workers' council that had to be consulted over any sale. Hans Westerhuis sat on the council, which worked hard not to let their shock overwhelm their thinking. When I met Westerhuis, he brought me a beautifully produced book commemorating the history of the Dutch bank. Today he remembers the merger as though recalling a family tragedy for which he is still in mourning.

"We talked to all parties involved in the merger. We wanted to understand the strategy in order to know how to implement it. On the RBS side, we had a session with the full board. They obviously expected us to be hard-core trades unionists and to want to discuss redundancies. We just wanted to ask about integration. But the RBS board knew nothing. It was a huge operational risk, and they didn't understand a single piece of it."

"We were asked our opinion by the ABN/AMRO board, and we prepared a long document comparing the two bids. It was a good analysis, which we also sent to investors—pension funds—and it focused on the relative risks of the two scenarios. Some pension funds did read it. But no one could stop Fred."

Weston, a veteran of takeovers, was less emotional about the unfolding disaster, but remained seriously skeptical about what was driving it.

"At the time regulators and politicians all believed that you would lower risk by being bigger and spread across multiple economies. But somewhere along the line, the arguments faded and the adrenaline of the chase took over. The sheer momentum—the players were so huge that the momentum was too great to be stopped."

"It was a race," John Berry recognizes. "The company was—is—stuffed with deeply competitive people, and they wanted to win the race. Due diligence? Anyone who raised any questions or doubts, they were just treated like wimps."

Not everyone hated the race. Many found the thrill of the chase, the size of the prize, galvanizing.

"I am an adrenaline junkie," Sunny Uberaii concedes. "And this was—it was—exciting. The largest financial services deal in the history of the world! Did that make it exciting? Absolutely. The fact that we would be one of the biggest, one of the top ten banks—which ABN/AMRO had once been in the past! We thought, 'Finally we'll be back on the world stage where we belong.'"

"It is very hard to stop these things," Bob Weston acknowledges. "There are huge face issues at stake. It's like you go to a dance and meet a girl, and she says she never wants to see you again. The risk you take as a man—there is just something in the male psyche that holds that issue. Near completion of a deal, if the market says no, you've failed, and you will always be known as a failure. There's just no way that you can walk away and feel a hero. Walking away in financial markets can never be positioned as winning."

Just as the credit crunch erupted in the autumn of 2007, Fred Goodwin closed on his prize. Neither the collapse of Northern Rock nor international jitters about the state of the world's economy had dampened his enthusiasm for making RBS the biggest bank in the world. Most wholesale banks did not want to lend him the money to fund his acquisition; the US Federal Reserve and the Bank of England ponied up £100 million (about US$160 million).

Goodwin's big deal was the largest cross-border banking takeover in history; with it, he achieved his dream of creating the world's largest bank. The fallout was predictably enormous too. The Belgian bank, Fortis, collapsed, and its part of ABN/AMRO had to be nationalized by the Dutch government. Santander fared better: it made a profit by keeping the South American businesses and selling the Italian part of ABN/AMRO to Monte dei Paschi di Siena, the world's oldest bank. (That bank too had to be bailed out later, in 2013.) In the United Kingdom, in February 2008, RBS announced a loss of £24 billion (about US$40 billion), the largest annual loss in British corporate history, and had to be rescued by the British government.

In October, Goodwin announced his resignation, and a month later Stephen Hester was brought in to run RBS. One of his first moves was to chastise and then eliminate much of the bank's management. They had not been leaders, he told them, but sheep.

The bank wasn't a master of acquisition after all. Left to knit the pieces together, John Berry was aghast at the mess he still struggles to make functional.

"Five years later, there are still huge parts of ABN/AMRO that are still not integrated to this day. They will remain unintegrated. Corporate clients who span both banks still have to call two different places for support! We have had to build a complete bank from scratch from IT resources. We've done that—up to a point—but all the legacy work was left. No one wants to touch it.

"They did have a program going round the world changing offices to blue and white from green and yellow. In some instances, that is all they've done! Had a staff party, changed the signage and the furniture. And when they're done, they have a party and bring over a Scottish piper to play bagpipes through the building to let them know they are now Scottish. It was that crass."

Stephen Hester worked hard to restore to the bank some sense of connectedness with its customers, using "customer charters" and implementing a policy called "Helpful Banking." But trying to inject the organization with some sense of social purpose after years in which it cared only about size proved tough. No one remembered anymore what they were there for; customers had never been on Goodwin's agenda. That the IT infrastructure kept failing was obvious to customers who were regularly denied their own money. But reprogramming 140,000 traumatized individuals, reminding them what business they were in and why, turned out to be a Sisyphean task for Hester, who left the bank after four and a half frustrating years.

There was a severe contradiction at the heart of his mission. On the one hand, he had to stabilize the bank's balance sheet by reducing the size of its bad debt. But one way to stabilize the balance sheet was to make more money, which the investment banking side of the business has continued to do. As a consequence, the bank still isn't small: in 2012 the balance sheet of RBS was the size of the entire British economy.[24] If scale was what Goodwin wanted, he got it.

Goodwin was not alone, of course, in his lust for scale: it takes at least two to make competition exciting. That Barclays was just as determined to be big and important on the world stage helped to fuel the race. Size alone seems to have been that bank's strategy too. "The closest the Barclays Group came to having a single vision was the strategy adopted by Group Chief Executive, John Varley, where he articulated the bank's goal to become a 'Top 5' bank," the Salz inquiry reported.

While this was a galvanising force, the stated aim was growth and improvement of competitive position.… Winning also extended to a keen interest in Barclays' position on industry league tables. However, we found that, particularly in the investment bank (but also in the retail bank sales force), the interpretation and implementation of "winning" went beyond the simply competitive. It was sometimes underpinned by what appeared to have been an "at all costs" attitude.[25]

The pursuit of size for its own sake devastated the bank's culture. Detail, nuance, and ethics, deemed trivial compared to grandiose schemes and global domination, went out the window.

One cost of size is insight—knowing what is going on. Leaders of institutions are surrounded by people who tell them what they want to hear. Organizational silence, inherent in all organizations and exacerbated by steep hierarchies, only gets worse in vast organizations where even those who dare to speak out are often lost in the crowd. The larger an institution grows the more extreme this insight problem becomes until, as many CEOs have told me, leaders are left relying on the numbers. But those numbers, while they contain a great deal of information, are also dangerous illusions—they appear to capture panoramic detail when in fact all they can convey are thumbnail sketches. In vast institutions, every top-line number summarizes hundreds, even thousands of data points, equations, and assumptions that themselves contain more. The sheer complexity of the cascade of information prevents leaders from ever fully knowing what they are seeing.

The allure of size and dominance, the promise that a business will progress more effectively if it can dominate the landscape, turns out to be a fatal chimera. Supersizing buildings or churches, oil companies or financial institutions, always comes at a cost: an artistic, moral, social, environmental, or financial dysfunction. Supersizing must incur that cost because competitive instincts don't stop until they fail. So they must fail in order to stop.

Public commitments to transparency don't get far in addressing this systemic issue. In a dazzling forensic analysis of Wells Fargo, one of America's smaller and more conservative banks, Frank Partnoy concluded that "banks today are bigger and more opaque than ever, and they continue to behave in many of the same ways they did before the crash."[26] The public accounts that banks file are governed in the United States by the Financial Accounting Standards Board. Don Young, an FASB board member from 2005 to 2008, now says that, "after serving on the board, I no longer trust bank accounting." Understanding accounts and risks—for this most qualified of assessors—is harder than ever. Other board members are adamant that they no longer trust these accounts either.

Partnoy more than knows his way through a balance sheet. After years of working on Wall Street, he left in disgust and wrote a shockingly honest (and often funny) book, *FIASCO,* about the madness he had witnessed and sometimes joined. After Enron collapsed, he helped the Senate understand derivatives, and from 2005 onward he tried to warn anyone who would listen about the ideological blind spots implicit in Federal Reserve chairman Alan Greenspan's love affair with deregulation. Now a professor of law and finance, Partnoy is relentless in separating financial rhetoric from reality.

Likening the levels of risk in Wells Fargo to the circles of Dante's inferno, Partnoy argues that each stage is replete with risk and obfuscation. In 2011 Wells Fargo had $81 billion in revenue and $16 billion in profit. But it also has $2.8 *trillion* invested in derivatives and $1.5 trillion exposed in entities that did *not* appear on its balance sheet. "These disclosures make even an ostensibly simple bank like Wells Fargo impossible to understand," Partnoy concludes. "Every major bank's financial statements have some or all of these problems; many banks are much worse."

The CEOs can't trust these statements either. JPMorgan Chase's Jamie Dimon, widely regarded as one of the smartest and most trusted of bank CEOs, was blindsided in 2012 by a $6 billion loss. In that context, it is hard to feel comfortable with the knowledge that in RBS (roughly the same size as JPMorgan Chase but run by a far less experienced CEO) the UK government finds itself trying to manage a bank as big as its own economy.

In the quest for growth and scale for their own sake, institutions around the world have expanded at such a pace and to such a size that their leaders can plausibly deny knowledge of widespread mis-selling, interest rate manipulation, and fraud. It may be tempting to imagine that each of these disasters was carefully planned and plotted by avaricious psychopaths, but the more prosaic and realistic explanation is that many vital institutions have become both unmanageable and unmanaged. Grandiosity for its own sake breeds complexity and an arrogance through which retail customers are regarded as "plankton" and investment bank customers as "muppets." To an institution whose revenue is larger than that of many nations and whose power in the marketplace exceeds that of governments, everyone looks small.

Altogether, America's nine biggest bank holding companies have almost

20,000 subsidiaries; JPMorgan Chase has 3,391 subsidiaries, Goldman Sachs 3,115, Morgan Stanley 2,884, and Bank of America 2,019. Does anyone seriously imagine that anyone can run such vast organizations or that any boards can exercise serious and trenchant oversight over them? Bearing in mind that all of these banks operate in at least forty countries, the result—if not the intention—of size is to make regulatory oversight as impossible as governance. As legislators around the world call for the banks to be broken up—former FDIC chair Sheila Bair in the United States, the Vickers Commission in the United Kingdom, Finnish politician Erkki Liikanen in the European Union—the ensuing political paralysis is a testament to the power these huge institutions have to intimidate reformers and stymie change. Banks bigger than governments wield more power than any legislature can regulate.

It's easy and comforting to imagine that this is a banking problem. It isn't. It's a size problem. The competitive drive to grow bigger and bigger—whether in buildings or pharmaceutical companies—always carries a concentration of risk that makes it ever harder for these organizations to do anything safely or well. Thinking otherwise is hubris. Economies of scale, if they can be achieved, eventually reach a point where they become counterproductive, creating so much complexity and internal and external friction that no one knows any longer how to make them work. The accrual of concentrated power means that no one can interfere—but neither can anyone, any longer, help.

What started as a banking crisis and turned into an economic crisis—and may yet develop into a democratic crisis—should have taught us not to expose our most crucial institutions to the risk carried by scale. We should have learned that no organization should be too big to fail and that the corollary of that insight is to keep all organizations small enough to fail with ease. And we should have learned to think more intelligently about growth itself and realized that increasing numbers on a balance sheet or a share price is not necessarily unmitigated good news.

"Being big doesn't protect anyone," Paul Purcell argues. "All bigness does is create scale—it doesn't mean you're good. You need to be good at what you do. It is all about, are you doing a good job for the client and adding value? Look at HSBC right now and Barclays. Did being big help them? You need to break up these institutions."

Purcell didn't join Occupy Wall Street, and he's as far from being a radical as it is possible to get. But as CEO of Robert W. Baird & Company, he does know what he is talking about. After a lifetime in financial services, he's reached conclusions somewhat different from those of his peers.

"The whole model is under attack—and so it should be. What's happened is, these big universal banks are too big to manage. The people are the risk. That's why they're losing value and why the government had to step in. They're always saying we have to be global, we have to be vast. But no, you don't. It doesn't work."

Based in Milwaukee, Wisconsin, Purcell's firm operates well away from the Wall Street whirlwind, and Purcell likes it that way. He keeps up with what other investment houses are doing but feels no compulsion to imitate or compete with them.

"You now have a situation where 10 percent of the largest institutions own 75 percent of the assets. By definition, that makes them too large to fail. And the very best of the bankers, Jamie Dimon, even he didn't know what was going on in his institution. You lose six *billion* dollars and you don't know why? That's good evidence that even he can't manage these things."

Apart from the outspokenness of its CEO, what makes Baird different is that, while it looks like other financial institutions, with investment banking, wealth management, capital markets, private equity, and asset management teams in the United States, Europe and Asia, the company is owned by its employees. And that, says Purcell, changes its priorities, its pace, its scale, and its culture.

"The strength of our model is that every decision we make is long-term. Our horizon is at least three to five years. And it is a basic principle here that we are fundamentally client-focused. We don't trade against our clients, and we never will."

In contrast to much larger companies like Goldman Sachs, which earned opprobrium for selling products to its clients while simultaneously betting against them, Baird and its employee shareholders appreciate that their clients are the only source of their revenue and that therefore their interests are aligned. The company is run, in effect, like a partnership—as many Wall Street firms used to be before they entered the public markets.

Purcell's passion for his business, and for its ownership structure, has been hugely influenced by his earlier career at Kidder Peabody. That firm too had been owned by its employees when Purcell joined. After it was sold to GE and became part of a publicly traded company, Kidder Peabody changed dramatically, and adventures in derivatives trading quickly destroyed it.

"I saw this terrific firm built, and I saw it wrecked—so my passion came from watching that. It galvanized my view that privately held employee ownership is the way to go. Your own money is on the line every day. This year we will achieve a return on equity of 11 to 12 percent, while most firms will struggle to get to 6. We are very metrics-driven because we care passionately about productivity and because we want to be able to pay our people well. But it isn't about bigness. Many banks got big just for the sake of getting big. We don't want to be big, we want to be good. Scale alone simply does not work."

More remarkable than Purcell's statement of principles is the coherence with which it is echoed throughout the organization. Sue Bellehumeu left her career as a dental hygienist to come to Baird as a receptionist. She was sufficiently intrigued by what she saw going on around her that she educated and trained herself—without much encouragement from her immediate, male supervisors—to become a financial adviser.

For Bellehumeu, organizational silence is not an issue; she has never had any fear of raising problems or challenging the merits of products. Because the bank doesn't sell its own products, there's no conflict of interest. And nobody at Baird would dream of emulating Lehman Brothers' example of posting daily earnings on the wall. What Baird wants, says Bellehumeu, is "to do what's right for the clients under every circumstance."

A petite blonde who sparkles with energy, she speaks with passion about her work and has never, she says with a laugh, been afraid to express herself; that's what she has always done.

"If you're an owner, you care about much more than just the money you take home each month. I know that if I have an issue, I can send Paul an email and hear back from him in twenty-four hours. I tell people this, and they don't believe me," she laughs. "But really—that's how it works here.

"There is a very strong sense that it is *our* business, so we have to keep trying to do the right thing. Intent always matters. You may make a mistake—people do—but what matters is intent. The company is everybody. Big and small producers have skin in the game. You need to be good at what you do—but being big doesn't help you do that."

The most stunning aspect of Baird's otherwise modest Milwaukee headquarters is the view over Lake Michigan. The frenzied hype I grew accustomed to in New York is absent; in its place is an unusual eagerness to show how careful the firm is.

"We are very risk-averse," Dustin Hutter, Baird's assistant controller, assures me. "What has helped me, learning the business here, is knowing that we are working with our own money. It's our firm, so that influences the strategic thinking. Being privately owned has allowed more of an entrepreneurial mind-set, but we approach new ventures very conservatively. We don't go in head first—we stick our toes in the water because it is our capital that we are putting at risk."

When I ask Hutter whether he ever feels competitive with his colleagues, he looks stunned and puzzled, unclear what I mean. I explain how some banks post daily earnings on the wall, how hedge fund managers won't talk to each other, and he looks at me as though I'm describing a different planet. Perhaps I am.

"If you don't share, you can't learn. What brought me here was wanting to learn, and that's what I've been able to do. What makes us successful is communication—Paul will share anything. Everything here is wide open, and that's what makes everyone very successful. Information is there not just to consume but to share. The more I share the more I learn."

But if openness and sharing are hallmarks of how Baird does business, doesn't that mean the company has to be careful about who it hires? If the major risk in banking, as Purcell says, is the people, then don't those people need to be well chosen?

"Gosh yes!" Hutter exclaims. "We have been hiring, but I reckon we only consider about two out of every eighty people who apply. We have Paul's famous 'no asshole' rule. If someone puts themselves before their client, they stand no chance. If someone misbehaves after they get here, it doesn't matter if they're a big producer—they're out.

"We did hire some people who came out of GE Healthcare. They were so full of distrust at first. I think they thought we were just saying these things but didn't really mean them. It's been hard for them to break down the walls that they've grown around themselves. But now those same people say there's no way they could ever go back."

Choosing people carefully, staying client-focused, not developing proprietary products, and giving employees in every function the chance to have skin in the game are strategies that have made Baird more resilient, more profitable, and more stable. Since 2007, Wall Street has lost 15 to 18 percent of its workforce; in the same period, Baird has increased its workforce by 12 percent. Purcell says that he does not want to manage his bank "like an accordion"; he wants to invest—in bonds, equities, companies, and people—for the long term.

Baird did not invest in CDOs, nor did it sell subprime mortgages. But it's the stories Baird tells about itself that most eloquently articulate the company's values under the stress of large transactions. One of those stories involves the investment banking group's sale of a large consumer services business. As negotiations closed in on a two-horse race, the Baird team grew concerned that one bidder was bound to lose. Should they encourage the losing bidder to keep throwing time and resources at the deal, knowing it would all be wasted? The fetid tradition of auctions is to always keep all the players in the game—never mind the cost, it keeps the competition going. But the Baird team felt uncomfortable wasting another party's time, effort, and good faith. So they let it be known that the deal was all but closed. Their reward was more business—both buying for and selling to the company with which they'd been so straightforward.

People at Baird love telling stories like this—and there are many more—because they're proud of them and because they recognize that telling them is one way to ensure that their lessons are repeated. If that means that Baird must stay a smaller player, that poses no problems for Paul Purcell. It is Baird's smaller scale that makes everything so personal. And because everything is so personal, what you do matters. And that attitude goes from Purcell down to the mail room.

"I just want to do my job well." A handsome, middle-aged African American in a crisp and spotless white shirt, Stacey Williams is keen to tell me about his sixteen years at Baird.

"I came here as a temp, and when the work was done I was sad to go, but Baird wasn't hiring at the time. Then, two years later, I come for an interview. I walk in and the supervisor, Marty, jumps up and says, 'Where you been? We've been looking for you! We remember you, you were a good worker. When can you start?'"

Stacey runs much of the back-office services; at his supervisor's insistence, he's been promoted often and now runs his own group. He's been an owner for the past nine years.

"Owning makes me feel part of something great. Other companies say everyone matters, but they don't really mean it. At other companies where I worked, I worked hard. But you never saw the bosses, they didn't know who you were. Paul knows me and is surprised when I call him Mr. Purcell—he looks around and wonders who I'm talking to! It's a blessing working for a company like this. That doesn't mean it's always perfect; there are bad days and people who get upset. But as long as I'm giving 110 percent, that's okay."

There are a few banks that work like Baird—William Blair in Chicago,

Donaldson in Montana, and Triodos Bank in Europe—but not enough of them. As I leave to go to lunch with some of the Baird team—a quick one, everyone has work to get back to—I reflect that what makes the company impressive is not just the people but the fact that the structure of the organization implicitly encourages them to do the right thing. They don't need a "customer charter" to remind them of the obligations of their relationship with the people they serve. Their obligations to each other, as owners, make their interdependency salient and real; the relationship is built into the structure of the organization, not mandated by a management pamphlet. The wild bets and flights of fancy that have characterized many of the giant banks are made more difficult and less abstract when the money is yours and your neighbor's. And it is just harder to make gigantic losses when you aren't gigantic yourself.

Many of the same dynamics can be seen within the peer-to-peer networks that have arisen as alternatives to banks. Zopa, Lending Club, and Funding Circle can't do everything that Baird can do, but they depend on the same characteristics: sharing, trust, and the desire to connect. Similarly, car-sharing (City Car Club, Greenwheels), house-sharing (Easyroommate, Airbnb), and even pet-sharing (Petstoshare) networks use technology to bring people together who don't want to work with domineering institutions but crave instead personal interaction and the daily experience of being human.

Size is not what matters. We need organizations that are robust and can survive the vicissitudes of political, social, and economic change. Expecting them to be infallible is madness or religion. What we want are organizations that are functional—but can fail safely. Making them functional may require that they stay small. The evolutionary biologist Robin Dunbar has devoted years to studying the evolution of the human brain as it affects the optimal size of social groupings, exploring what he calls the "social brain hypothesis." Analyzing the mathematical relationship between small- and large-scale societies, he has concluded that humans have a cognitive limit of approximately 150 people with whom they can maintain coherent personal relationships. That number has remained roughly the same, regardless of historical period, geography, or activity, and its constancy, Dunbar argues, is directly related to the physical size of the neocortex, the part of the brain responsible for higher functions, such as conscious thought, reasoning, and language. Brain size limits the number of relationships we can—literally—

keep in mind, and its size is a function of the groups in which our evolution has occurred. "Although the evolution of neocortical size is driven by the ecological factors that select for group size, we can use the relationship in reverse to predict group sizes for living species," he writes.[27]

This relationship between brain size and human groupings explains, Dunbar argues, the configuration of armies the world over and throughout history: most armies are largely constructed as platoons of ten to fifteen soldiers, companies of three to four platoons, and battalions of three to four companies. "Could it be," he asks rhetorically, "that the army's structures have evolved to mimic the natural hierarchical groups of everyday social structures, thereby optimizing the cognitive processing of within-group interactions?"[28]

Dunbar's work, while widely accepted, isn't without controversy, and as with much evolutionary biology, a great deal remains impossible to prove. The breadth, across geography and time, of Dunbar's evidence, however, is compelling, suggesting that more than culture is at work. However elaborate the systems and technologies we create to manage complex operations, sooner or later they always involve people; therefore, the size of organizations and how functional they are may have quite hard cognitive limits that we defy at our peril. This doesn't mean that units should never go beyond 150—armies quite clearly do. But they depend for their stability on a network of units, the smallest of which can't safely go beyond approximately 150.

These numbers have come to be known as "Dunbar numbers," and many organizations use them as a guide to the maximal efficiency of teams, groups, and departments. At the tomato processing company Morning Star, these numbers are used as a guide to how big the company should get, in the recognition that if it got any bigger, a different entity or structure would be required. At W. L. Gore, no business unit is allowed to go far beyond 150 people. That decision was reached before the publication of Dunbar's research, but nothing in the company's growth has challenged it. And one reason why the banking crisis hasn't proved as catastrophic in Germany as elsewhere is because 70 percent of its banking sector comprises small or community banks—in sharp contrast to the United Kingdom, where just five banks hold 80 percent of mortgages and 90 percent of company accounts.[29]

The point is not that companies can only ever be small, but that their ability to function may depend on how many relationships human beings can manage effectively. I might have hundreds or thousands of friends on Facebook or followers on Twitter, but everyone knows that these are not functional relationships and that my life would swiftly reduce to gibberish if I tried to live as if they were. When I look at the wildly complex matrix structures that many corporations design in a desperate attempt to be both efficient and creative, my respect for Dunbar numbers increases. To build organizations that demand greater cognitive capacity than our brains can provide is a perfect definition of hubris.

Geneticists exploring the concept of evolutionarily sustainable systems have come to similar conclusions: for a system to be capable of evolving, it must be robust—and that quality derives, in part, from multiple small parts that are only weakly linked; if one mutates, the whole being doesn't die. That is the premise of the emerging peer-to-peer lending networks like Lending Club, Prosper, Zopa, and Funding Circle, which enable individuals to lend to individuals. Taken as a whole the networks may be huge, but they are really just an aggregate of thousands, maybe one day even millions, of small, more personal transactions. Media rhetoric hypes the importance of these new lending organizations as deadly rivals of traditional banks, but their chief contribution lies in facilitating links between individuals—links that can be broken without endangering the whole system.

Another way to think about this is to look at the design of modern airplanes, whose automatic flight control systems are typically composed of three modules that have identical functions but are designed differently. The idea here is not only to introduce redundancy—if one module fails, another takes over—but also to ensure that the whole plane doesn't depend on a single technological approach. Whether you are talking about complex biology or engineering, the principle remains the same: multiple small parts, weakly linked, are safer because when one part fails the system as a whole is not fatally weakened. Such systems are robust because they are small. They are fail-safe.

Although technology can't be blamed for the passion for growth, it is a great enabler. We are only just beginning to realize the potential of big data: its capacity to deliver highly customized content and products and to predict human behavior. The vast accumulation of personal data by Google, Amazon, Apple, and national governments promises everything from automated, personalized health care to preventative law enforcement. But with these tantalizing powers come, necessarily, big risks. Just as Apple computers used to be safer from viruses because there were relatively fewer of them—which made them not worth attacking—so the vast accumulation of personal data makes it an irresistible target for hackers and malware. Governments and regulators worry about the personal information stored and exploited by Google, but it is precisely the scale of the accumulation of this information that makes Google's servers such tempting targets.

Google founder Larry Page may wax lyrical over the thought of all of his customers having Google implanted into their brains, but you don't have to be a civil rights activist to see that this vision poses huge risks of extravagant convergence: everyone knowing and thinking the same things would be conformity on a scale the world has never seen. Big data today promises to predict behaviors based on the actions and decisions of individuals who share characteristics, but just because the data is big doesn't guarantee that it will be right—only that mistakes will be more damaging.

In 2004 Solafa Batterjee's father, a philanthropist in Saudi Arabia, was placed by the United Nations Security Council on a terrorist watch list. His habit of traveling to dangerous places—Afghanistan, Chechnya—apparently fit the profile of an Al-Qaeda terrorist. For ten years, Solafa's father couldn't function—couldn't work, couldn't access funds—and the family had to sit and watch as their father was rendered impotent and immobile. Under continuous investigation, he could travel nowhere. In January 2013, he was delisted by the United Nations, which had failed to find any substantive information that he was other than what he said he was: an engineer trying to help people. As the data gets bigger, does it make people smaller?

The fact that the companies collecting our data compete with each other just increases our risk. As competitors, they've proved reluctant to share information about mistakes with their customers or about cyber-attacks between them and regulators or each other. Unlike doctors, who have started to learn the value of mistakes, these data gatherers don't want to reveal their weakness. But since no one can learn anything from unacknowledged mistakes, their refusal to share leaves everyone more vulnerable.[30] The bigger the data, the more alluring the prize; the greater the secrecy, the bigger the risk.

All of these companies hope that size will protect their commercial interests, while conveniently ignoring the degree to which their size increases their risks and ours. So it isn't just banks that consider themselves too big to fail. In hoping and assuming that governments will take responsibility for data security, most large corporations equally hope to outsource the cost of failure. Or as one computer security analyst put it, "No one is expected to provide for their own air defense. We have an army to repel a land invasion, so who is out there protecting the cyber lanes of control?"[31]

Why do we imagine that bigger is better, that size confers some implicit victory? We know that larger organizations struggle to be nimble, to adapt, and to innovate. We recognize that power, dangerous in itself, becomes more corrupt and even more destructive as it grows in scale and scope. We have had vivid, living proof from the shores of the Gulf of Mexico to the boardrooms of companies that vast enterprises can acquire the capacity to wreak havoc on a scale previously unimaginable. And we now know that few governments have the resources, insight, or political will to rein them in.

I'm not at all convinced that small is beautiful, but I am persuaded that big is dangerous. Size does not give organizations invincibility—indeed, their size is what makes them vulnerable—but does give them a kind of impunity: the confidence that when things go wrong, only governments can step in. As such, vast enterprises fundamentally outsource their risk to us all.

How Low Can We Go?

We are unsettled to the very roots of our being. We have changed
our environment more quickly than we know how to change
ourselves.

—Walter Lippmann, 1914[1]

On March 25, 1911, 146 garment workers, mostly women, died as they jumped
to their deaths or suffocated in a New York factory fire. The oldest, Provi-
denza Panno, was forty-three years old; the youngest were two fourteen-
year-old girls, Kate Leone and Rosaria Maltese. Nobody knows whether the
fire was started by overheated machines or an illicit cigarette, but it spread
fast because of the hundreds of pounds of fabric scraps that littered the floor.
The doors had been locked to stop the women from taking breaks and to
enable supervisors to check their purses before they went home. With no
access to fire escapes, many workers chose to jump from the building to certain death. In his poem "Shirt," the American poet Robert Pinsky describes
one of their male colleagues helping them out the window as though he were
"helping them up to enter a streetcar and not eternity."

Just over one hundred years later, on April 24, 2013, 1,127 garment workers, mostly women, died when their factory in Bangladesh collapsed on top
of them. A day earlier, cracks had appeared in the building and engineer
Abdur Razzak Khan had recommended that it be closed. But the company
had tough production deadlines to meet; it wouldn't get paid if the goods
weren't finished in time, and manufacturers would be sued if they attempted
to sell them to anyone else. After the accident, amid the rubble, photographer Shahidul Alam found a couple embracing each other, their torsos
immersed in concrete. Blood ran from the man's eyes, he said, like a tear.[2]

The Triangle Shirtwaist Factory fire in the twentieth century and the Rana
Plaza collapse in the twenty-first both derived from the remorseless logic of
competition: anything you can make cheap, I can make cheaper. Bangladesh
has the lowest labor costs in the world, with the minimum wage for garment
workers set at roughly $37 a month. For a consumer to get a bikini from

H&M or Walmart for $4.99, costs have to be very low. So wages go right down and safety considerations disappear. This is what economists call "the race to the bottom."

Companies like Li & Fung accelerate this race. Acting as a broker between low-wage factories and the companies that seek to use them, Li & Fung's brokers—"Little John Waynes"—search constantly for cheaper labor markets. These days sub-Saharan Africa is starting to appeal. Sourcing cheap labor is no small-time business—last year Li & Fung earned $20 billion[3]—and in theory, such brokers are supposed to monitor working conditions. In reality, this poses an impossible conflict of interest. In 2012, Li & Fung's suppliers had several disasters, including a factory fire that killed over a hundred workers. "We make our best effort to weed out bad factories," chief executive Bruce Rockowitz was quoted as saying at the time, "but we don't always succeed."[4]

The problem with the race to the bottom is that costs do not—cannot—simply vanish; they have to go somewhere. And so mostly they are shifted from those who have power and money to those who have nothing. The cost to the customer who buys the bikini may be just $4.99, but the cost to its maker is a working day of fourteen to sixteen hours, seven days a week, in cramped and hazardous conditions. Fires are frequent, made more dangerous by locked fire escapes. Safety is an easy, invisible thing to cut because it might never matter, and when it does it's too late. As far as possible, the risks of cheap manufacture have been passed down from the corporation to the local contractor, who passes them down to the individual workers. The garment can only be so cheap because its makers and the society they inhabit absorb the cost of its manufacture. Economists call this "externalization"—getting costs to move outside the business.

The competition to drive down costs predated the Great Recession, but economic decline since 2007 has made it more popular and, in some quarters, more palatable. With less money to spend, consumers seek out cheap bargains and companies compete eagerly with low prices. And the easiest cost to cut is always people.

In the summer of 2013, low-wage workers across the United States staged one-day strikes to protest against their working conditions. Employees from McDonald's, Subway, Taco Bell, Macy's, and Victoria's Secret walked out to protest earnings of $150 to $350 a week—too little to support themselves. They carried signs proclaiming FIGHT FOR 15, arguing for a doubling of their minimum-wage salaries to $15 an hour.

For many years, low pay was tolerated because people believed that cheap and temporary jobs provided an accessible route to greater opportunity. The National Restaurant Association claimed that the fast-food industry was "one of the best paths to achieving the American Dream."[5] That might once have been true—when most fast-food workers were teenagers living at home. But it is no longer true as workers have become older, more educated, and more likely to be supporting a family.[6] The suggestion that these jobs are the first step on "the path to achieving the American dream" is belied by the data, which show that an average fast-food worker in New York City gets an annual income of $11,000—less than one-quarter the median household income of $48,631. After seven years of working for Taco Bell, Joseph Barrera hasn't climbed any ladders or found a path; he cannot yet afford a meal every day, subway fares to work, or any new clothes. He doesn't think that getting married or starting a family is viable.

The other argument in support of low pay is that companies must stay competitive; to keep food or clothing cheap, they must keep wages low. "We seek to pay competitive wages and benefits" is how a Macy's vice president puts it. McDonald's insists that "employees are paid competitive wages and have access to flexible schedules." The reference to "access to flexible schedules" is telling—what sounds like a choice is in fact quite the opposite. Retailers use scheduling software to predict by fifteen-minute increments exactly how many staff members will be needed at what points of the day. Employees may be offered just twelve or fifteen hours a week, sometimes none. With these hours, they can't earn enough to live on, but companies like Abercrombie & Fitch, Jamba Juice, and Nine West use the software to keep their labor costs down. Jamba Juice claims it has saved them millions of dollars a year; the Bureau of Labor Statistics says the practice overall has eliminated over one million jobs. Temporary workers have no choice but to commit to being available, while their employer can choose whether to call them a little, a lot, or not at all. This makes household budgeting impossible and job-seeking risky: no one seeking a permanent job can afford to go to an interview in case they're called in for a few hours of paid employment.

In the United States, virtually all the job growth during the recovery has been an increase in the number of temporary jobs, with the result that the United States now has more temp workers—2.7 million—than ever before in its history. In some "temp towns"—places where there are, effectively, no permanent jobs—it isn't unusual to find warehouses staffed entirely with temporary workers. Anyone familiar with the film *On the Waterfront* would recognize the hiring practices that require that everyone turn up for work hoping to be one of the lucky few chosen for work that day. Temporary workers are less likely to have any savings, any pension, and, in the United States, any health care coverage. They're also twice as likely as permanent employees to suffer an injury at work.[7]

What all of these companies are doing is cutting prices by externalizing the costs of their operations onto individual employees, the weakest parts of the system. If employees can't earn enough to live on, they have to call on the state for help, with the result that, ultimately, the cheap prices are externalized to society at large. At the same time, the companies are aggressive in pursuing tax minimization strategies, so that they absorb as little of their own costs as they can get away with. That these companies can't find any other way (they say) to sustain their business than by keeping pay down merely testifies to the creativity they've lost. If these employers are looking to their frontline workforce for creativity, commitment, or innovation—well, they've created the precise conditions for their own disappointment. In the race to drive down wages, employers violate the trust and commitment of burned-out employees who could make their companies smarter and more dynamic.

Pay cuts have consequences well beyond the companies and industries that impose them—and nowhere has that been more apparent than in the newspaper industry. Until about five years ago, newspapers were profitable businesses. But as the Internet started to siphon off readers, pressure mounted to cut jobs. Fewer reporters led to poorer content, which only made newspapers less relevant—and less trustworthy. The once-respected *Chicago Tribune* and *Houston Chronicle* outsourced some of their journalism to the Philippines. Stories on local events and personalities were written for pennies, given fake, American-sounding bylines, and printed as though they had originated in their hometowns. When the agency responsible, Journatic, was identified, many of its exposed clients hastily withdrew from their contracts. But then James MacPherson, a Pasadena publisher, launched a competitor, Journtent, which pays pittances to freelancers in Mexico and the Philippines to watch and transcribe community meetings that are webcast online. MacPherson said, "This is how I solved the problem of time: I outsource virtually everything. I'm primarily looking for individuals who I can pay a lower rate to do a lot of work."[8]

The damage done to public trust in journalism is nowhere more evident than in the scandals that have dogged British newspapers in recent years. Under financial pressure to cut costs, newspaper proprietors turned news-rooms into competitive marketplaces, hoping that frightened journalists would be driven to uncover best-selling scandals and gossip. When legal means of finding stories didn't work, an epidemic of phone-hacking swept across the industry, incriminating journalists, police officers, Members of Parliament, and law firms. After Rupert Murdoch hastily shut down his best-selling Sunday paper, *The News of the World,* in July 2011 and was forced to testify before Parliament about what he did and didn't know about ille-gal dealings in his companies, the British government convened an inquiry into the media. Michelle Stanistreet, general secretary of the National Union of Journalists, compiled evidence for the Leveson Inquiry—but the cli-mate of fear remained so intense that much of the testimony had to remain anonymous.

What Stanistreet revealed was a stunning picture of a highly competitive culture in which journalists were all too aware of freelancers and interns competing for their jobs, a contest deliberately exploited by their bosses. Insecure in their careers, no one was ever going to argue or debate a ques-tionable editorial decision. Silence and compliance were the inevitable markers of a frightened workforce.

"The atmosphere was poisonous," one veteran reporter told Stanistreet. "It was unchecked bullying. When your boss said jump, it was a case of how high and where do you want me to jump from. It wasn't only me, there was talk of the 'revolving seat' in the office."[9]

Another veteran with twenty-five years' experience in print journalism described life within the *News of the World.*

"The way the paper was run was totally dysfunctional. The biggest rival of the news team—was our own features department! If news would bid on a story, features would outbid them. After the features department, the big-gest rival to news was *The Sun.* This was the regime that Murdoch created. It's dog eat dog. They enjoyed this fighting amongst colleagues. They'd set us off like wild dogs against each other. They thought it was all a great game to keep everyone on their toes. They'd light the touch paper, sit back and watch them kill each other. It was relentless, you could never rest."[10]

Working under these conditions, one journalist tells me, "Phone hacking was talked about openly in quite a jovial manner. It wasn't a dirty thing. 'Got it off the phone, didn't we?' No one thought bad of it. Maybe cheating a bit. The pressure is there and people cave. The temptation to dial a couple of numbers, maybe get a scoop—it was huge. Especially in a hire-and-fire kind of place where you're judged by the number of bylines and column inches you have. Along with a family, a mortgage, and bosses breathing down your neck saying you aren't bringing in enough."

To Stanistreet, it was clear that in this hypercompetitive environment no one would refuse to hack a phone or to practice what she called the "dark arts." "It is about delivering the goods. Being first. Not being shown up by a competitor. It is a cumulative pressure that makes people prepared to go to any lengths. The expectation is that you *will* go to any lengths. And if you won't, someone else will."

Editors, under intense pressure to deliver readers, passed their stress along to reporters, who competed with each other to do more work with fewer resources and less time, all the while knowing that budgets were shrinking and plenty of aspirants were eager to come and intern for free. Under these circumstances, phones got hacked and editorial standards plummeted.

"The ideal of the media holding power to account," said Richard Peppiatt, "when you're on the coal face [front line]—it just goes out the window. Some buckle up and get on with it, some leave, some embrace it and enjoy the competition. Some like winning at all costs. You get the front page and, if that involves manipulating the facts or lying, some don't mind doing it."

Working for Richard Desmond, owner of the *Daily Star* and the *Express* newspapers, Peppiatt watched as "chronic underinvestment in journalism allowed a corrosive culture to fester. I remember one shift there being just myself and two other reporters to write the whole of a national newspaper. It was so bad we had to use pseudonyms to make it appear there were more of us."[11]

"'If you won't write it, we'll get someone who will,' was the sneer *du jour*, my eyes directed toward a teetering pile of CVs.... You may have read some of my other earth-shattering exclusives. 'Michael Jackson to attend Jade Goody's funeral.' (He didn't.) 'Robbie pops pill at heroes concert.' (He didn't either.) 'Matt Lucas on suicide watch.' (He wasn't.) 'Jordan turns to Buddha.' (She might have, but I doubt it.)"[12]

Peppiatt is a smart, thoughtful guy who willingly admits that he enjoyed the celebrity parties and free champagne. He'd been willing to go along with many of the newspaper's stunts: dressing up in a burkha or proposing to Susan Boyle. But it was the newspaper's xenophobia that got to him.

"I nearly walked out the summer when the *Daily Star* got all flushed about taxpayer-funded Muslim-only toilets. Undeterred by the nuisance of truth, we omitted a few facts, plucked a couple of quotes, and suddenly anyone would think a Rochdale shopping centre had hired Osama Bin Laden to stand by the taps, handing out paper towels."[13]

"Decisions were made by the advertising and accounts departments, not by the editorial floor. Anti-immigrant and anti-Muslim stuff was always good for making money. Inflammatory headlines and then [toll pay] phone lines with questions like: Should we let immigrants take all our jobs? Five thousand readers calling up, each spending two pounds each—that was the real game."[14]

The race to the bottom that Peppiatt witnessed unnerved him. A newsroom might not look as grim or pose as great a physical danger as a sweatshop, but he came to see that it perpetrated something just as bad. He began to save his money so that he'd be able to leave. But then one day he just cracked.

"There was a story saying the English Defense League would become a political party. Big front-page story. I sat in the newsroom when it was concocted. It was just not true. But the readers were quite big fans—let's give them something they want. And I thought, 'There must have been a point in a newsroom in Germany in the 1930s when someone should have asked, "Why are we running pictures of Jews with hooked noses?"' I felt there was a big anti-Muslim sentiment building and we were building it up. And if one day it kicks off and there's violence and rioting and people getting killed—well, I can't escape feeling responsible. I played a part whipping that up. There can be no more insidious way to make profit than to whip up hatred and prejudice. That's not how I want to make a living. That's when I decided I didn't care about finances and just did it."

Peppiatt wrote a long, eloquent, and furious letter of resignation to Desmond and left the building.

"As much as I resigned from the *Daily Star* because I'd come to believe it was Islamophobic, my conscience was troubled by another, even more sinister, realisation," he told the Leveson Inquiry. "Their hate mongering wasn't genuine. It was a crude, morally deplorable play on the politics of fear in the pursuit of profit.... It makes victims of The Many by exploiting both public and journalist, to line the pockets of The Few."[15]

What Peppiatt recounted was more than just the damage to his hopes and career, more even than the story of a single newspaper that had lost its bearings. He described an industrywide acceleration: as one newspaper blew through one moral barrier, others raced past to blow through the next one, hitting new lows, until few knew any longer where they were or what they stood for. The racist and sensationalist journalism, some of it facilitated by phone-hacking, demonstrated how the race to the bottom not only had harmed the journalists who perpetrated it and the readers who bought it but had jeopardized an entire industry and abused the trust of a society that expected to be reliably informed. There may have been little sympathy for the stresses endured by tabloid journalists, but commercial pressures left the institutions of news reporting so frail and discredited that believers in a free and democratic society could only feel uncertain and afraid.

The corruption of the newspaper industry in Britain spread well beyond itself: to the police force, to broadcasters, and to Parliament. Those not immediately in the race to the bottom found themselves swept up in it, sucked in, or trampled as the runners sped past. Because industries don't operate in a vacuum but within a society, the impact of their race may spread far beyond their immediate operations. Nowhere is this more visible than in the meat business.

"I live in America!"

Don Webb, a big, lumbering man in his seventies, speaks with disgust and anguish, his fierce sentence and lingering stare challenging everything he used to believe in. What kind of America? Whose America? What happened to America? his single sentence seems to ask.

We are sitting inside an old wood-shingled house that once was used to dry tobacco. Outside, it's overcast and humid in the glowering August afternoon. The story that Webb has to tell is one he's told before; he will keep telling it until he's persuaded that something in America has changed—or until the day he dies. He's a charming, generous man, but he is also, palpably, full of rage. For all that he is a lifelong Republican, Webb is strangely reminiscent of Lyndon Johnson, speaking with the same good ol' boy drawl and the same raw language.

At six-foot-four and well over two hundred pounds, his powerful physique testifies to an earlier career teaching physical education and coaching the high school football team. But teaching paid poorly, and one day, when he was in Kinston, he heard some rich people saying that, if they were younger, they'd go into hog farming. The idea stuck, and Webb bought a dozen pigs. He did well from them, so he bought more and more until finally he was raising four thousand hogs.

"Then one day an elderly black gentleman, Mr. Lewis, waved me down.

He said, 'We can no longer sit on our porch if the wind is blowing in our direction. We can't use our window fans, and we don't have air conditioning. There's nights we can't sleep. And we've got a sick little girl at home; she can't sleep either. Can't you do something about the stench?'"

One hog produces three to four times the amount of waste that a human does. Like the farmers around him, Webb threw the feces and urine into open cesspits, known locally as "lagoons." Webb's pigs produced raw sewage roughly equivalent to the waste of a town. Lewis wasn't the only black neighbor to complain, and their words, Webb says, "bothered him bad."

"I talked to some of the government agents in Winton," he continues, "and they said I should put some yeast in my cesspool and stir it up with a ten-horsepower boat. So I did that; I opened up the engine and stirred those two cesspools up good. And then I cleaned my boat off and went home."

The next time Webb saw his African American neighbors, they were polite, but they were still unhappy.

"One more favor," they asked of him. "Whatever you did, please don't do it again. It's got worse."

Webb went home that night and thought hard about his pigs and about his neighbors.

"My home was out of the range of the odor, on nice streets, with curving gutters. Everything was fine in my house. And I remembered how, when I was growing up, we used to live with fans, and I remembered how it was if the fans weren't pulling in enough cool air. Suppose someone did to my mom as I'm doing to those people?

"On that day, well, I didn't feel very highly of myself. My greed—putting too many hogs in one place. Starting with twelve, ending with four thousand. Off the backs of hardworking people who couldn't move and couldn't sell. And I as a decent American could not live with myself. So I shut that operation down."

But if Don Webb cared about his neighbors, he was pretty isolated. Instead of abandoning the environmental mess that comes with intensive hog farming, big companies piled into it. Between 1992 and 1998, the hog population of North Carolina went from 2 million to 10 million, creating in just one state the waste equivalent of the entire human population of Canada.

Many of the big meat producers moved into North Carolina, where land was inexpensive, because it belonged to small farmers, mostly African American, who were in trouble. Tobacco had declined, soybeans weren't very profitable, and slaughterhouses, controlled by meat companies, wouldn't give access to smallholders. Many of them sold their farms cheaply to corporations, which then stipulated exactly what they could grow and at what price.

Bob Martin is a senior policy adviser at the Johns Hopkins Bloomberg School of Public Health; he headed up the Pew Commission inquiry into factory farming. He explained the meat producers' strategy to me.

"The whole idea was to get big, big enough to drive down costs. That meant buying up all the farms to ensure a steady supply to their slaughter facilities, which, to be efficient, got bigger and bigger. Individual slaughtering made dismembering the animal too costly, so they demanded absolute standardization. They invested in research in order to perfect certain narrow genetic lines of animals. The whole thing was about economies of scale: standardize everything to drive costs down as low as you can go."

Consolidation was extreme. In 1950 the United States had 3 million hog farms; by 2007 this was down to 65,640. Big companies producing a standardized product gave rise to CAFOs: confined animal feeding operations, also known more colloquially as factory farming. CAFOs handling hogs, chickens, turkeys, and cows are found all across America. In Europe, intensive farming has been introduced in Poland and Romania, and today 50 percent of the world's pork, 43 percent of its beef, 74 percent of its poultry, and 68 percent of its eggs come from CAFOs.[16] Don Webb may be distraught by his country's embrace of factory farming, but the American example turned it into a global phenomenon.

The economic premise behind CAFOs is simple: drive down costs. If you put enough animals into a confined space, you need very few people with few skills to look after them. Inject them with antibiotics and hormones and the animals will fatten fast so that, after five to six months, you can take them to the slaughterhouse and then start again.[17]

For large meat packers and producers, on the face of it, the race to the bottom has been fantastically successful. Americans are the world's largest consumers of meat, and they're eating more than ever, more cheaply than ever. In 1970 average Americans spent 4.2 percent of their income on 194 pounds of meat each year. By 2005 consumption had gone up to 221 pounds per person while the cost had halved.

For Smithfield Foods, the world's largest hog producer and pork processor, this has proved tremendously good business. Controlling roughly 75 percent of the market, the company manufactures more pork than the next five largest producers in the country combined—and it routinely outperforms the stock market.[18] Other large meat producers—Perdue Farms,

Tyson, Karmel, and Cargill—are privately traded, so it's hard to gauge just how profitable factory farming has been for them, but they are all large, flourishing enterprises that have made their fortunes by driving down costs to produce cheap meat.

But where did the costs go? Before meeting Don Webb, his friend and colleague, Rick Dove, took me up in a Cessna 172 Skylark to view one of the most intensive areas of pig farming in the Neuse River basin of North Carolina. Along with pilot Joe Corby, we weren't sightseeing but rather surveying a landscape that the Environmental Protection Agency (EPA) has neither the people, the money, nor the time to monitor. Dove, a retired Marine, used to be the water keeper of the Neuse River, and he knows the area like the back of his hand.

At first sight, the river and surrounding floodplain look like a Southern idyll: greenery as far as the eye can see, few towns, little traffic. Leaving New Bern, we fly over an elegant marina full of expensive yachts and lavish waterfront homes. A loose skein of canals meanders through lush vegetation. That this is hog country seems implausible.

But as we move inland, the houses give way to long steel barns sitting on breeze blocks, punctuated with ventilation fans. Inside of each barn are up to ten thousand hogs, chickens, or turkeys. They are kept permanently indoors, tightly packed together and confined to metal crates. Most animals lack the space to turn around or to lie down. Their feed incorporates antibiotics—penicillin, tetracyclines, microlides, streptogramins, and others—that both accelerate growth and protect against infections that can travel fast in such intense conditions. Arsenic fulfills a similar purpose for chickens, with the added effect of turning the meat an appealing pink.[19]

Next to the barns, and the length of two or three football fields, are what appear at first glance to be swimming pools. Except that what fills them isn't blue but a dull maroon brown. These are the lagoons that Don Webb described: clay-lined cesspits full of animal urine, feces, blood, and mucus, the waste that runs from the slatted floors of the barns, through pipes, and out into the open air. Alongside the lagoons, soybeans are showered by a rotary sprayer that sucks the excrement from the lagoon and atomizes it across the crops, fertilizing them. The US Department of Agriculture estimates that around 500 million tons of such manure are produced annually by factory farms; that is three times the amount of sanitary waste produced by humans living in America.[20] But this waste isn't treated; seventy-five times more concentrated than human sewage and five hundred times more concentrated than effluent from any municipal wastewater treatment facility, it is sprayed straight onto the crops.[21]

And this is a floodplain: the water table is high, the land laced with small streams and rivulets that feed into the river. Although it is early August and hurricane season hasn't yet begun, the water level is high enough for much of the dispersed spray to be visible sitting puddled on the soil or running off into the streams. The air we fly through may not be quite as pure as it looks either: up to 80 percent of the nitrogen in a hog lagoon can be emitted into the air in the form of ammonia, which eventually falls back to earth as rain onto crops, waterways, and river basins.[22]

The seeping of raw animal waste—together with the antibiotics, arsenic, and heavy metal from the lagoons—into the water supply poses serious environmental risks. The danger arises not just from the "dead zones," which kill off fish, but from what scientists describe as the "objectionable compounds" that can emanate from the livestock facilities: acetic acid, butyric acids, valeric acids, hydrogen sulfide, and ammonia. Decomposing manure produces at least 160 gases, of which ammonia, hydrogen sulfide, and methane are the most pervasive. One study of chronic exposure to hydrogen sulfide found that it can lead to such abnormalities as impaired balance, hearing, and seeing and also memory loss. Children living near these farms are more likely to be diagnosed with asthma and other respiratory conditions.

Moreover, meat companies have started to locate large poultry facilities within yards of the hog barns. For Bob Martin, the risk of cross-contamination is the most dangerous development he has seen in years.

"No one is concerned about 250,000 broiler chickens sharing the same ten acres with 25,000 hogs?" he exclaims. "These are perfect petri dishes for creating the new strains of avian and human flus!"

Yet the biggest environmental health risk comes from the widespread use of antibiotics to promote growth and prevent disease. According to David Kessler, former FDA commissioner, 80 percent of *all* antibiotics sold in 2011 went to the livestock industry.[23] Such profuse applications of antibiotics provoke resistance on a wide scale. The prolific appearance of methicillin-resistant *Staphylococcus aureus* (MRSA) is particularly alarming, as this bacterium is resistant to all common antibiotics. It is killed by cooking but can live on the skin, where it causes abscesses that are dangerous and difficult to treat. One study found that factory pig farmers were 760 times more likely to be colonized with the bacterium than the general population.

A 2012 report found that an increasing number of pathogens are resistant to antibiotics in supermarket meats: 38.2 percent of chicken breast and

51 percent of ground turkey hosted forms of *Salmonella* resistant to three or more antimicrobial classes.[24] Health authorities around the world now recognize the rise of antibiotic-resistant organisms as one of the toughest challenges we face today. The chance of disease increases as our ability to fight the disease decreases.

"It's easy to test for antibiotic-resistant bacteria on grocery store meat," Bob Martin tells me, "and the results are always shocking. But what happens when it is in the environment, no one can quantify. We know that it is very prolific and gets passed along to other bacteria that has never come into contact with antibiotics. It is amazingly resilient in groundwater and carried for miles by flies and in storms. It's really hard to test for that." In other words, the consequences of the way meat is produced touch everyone—even those who don't eat meat.

Of course, those most immediately at risk from CAFOs are the people who work inside them. The jobs these farms produce are few, unskilled, and poorly paid, attracting migrant and often undocumented workers who work long days and long weeks. Although privately they will talk about the smells that make them want to vomit, they have little protection, and few have health care. Slaughterhouse work is dangerous, and nerve damage, repetitive stress injuries, and accidents are common. Surrounded by animals treated without care and often with brutality, workers find themselves in the same position: treated like just another means of keeping meat cheap.

This is not the rural America of Aaron Copland or Andrew Wyeth. In North Carolina, 17 percent of the adult population and one-quarter of all children live in poverty.[25] Factory farming didn't create jobs; instead, it undermined the local economy because its centralization of the purchasing of feedstuffs and antibiotics, though it keeps costs down, brings no income into the region. Hog farms may produce cheap food, but the people who live near them are those most likely to need food stamps.[26]

When we finish flying over the farms, Rick Dove and I drive around them. Outside the long steel barns, we occasionally see a pickup truck, at most two: workers often live on-site, and the farms don't require much manpower. We drive through Brown Town, a cluster of houses on the edge of a farm. Refrigerators and rusting farm equipment sit for sale on the grass outside. A few African American men sit on the porches. Kids sit or stand, listless, on the grass; women don't look up as cars pass. The stillness is eerie. No urgency. No energy. What for? Nothing to do. Nowhere to go. The heat and the smell hang in the air, not moving.

Of course, they can't move. Elsie Herring, an elegant black woman, sat on her porch talking to me about her house. She'd inherited it from her mother, who had it from the plantation owner her father once belonged to. Sometimes the farmers spray at night, she says. You can't keep the mist or the smell out of the house.

Slavery feels near at hand on these roads. The past is very present, and the future seems hard to imagine. The region that once grew tobacco and now grows cheap meat finds it hard to attract new high-tech jobs because it isn't clean or skilled enough. The only new industries that want to come here are dirty jobs: recycling batteries and sludge, another form of industrial waste.

"People here are used to suffering in silence, and that is what these companies have exploited," Gary Grant later tells me. A former schoolteacher, Grant now runs the North Carolina Environmental Justice Network. Since the big hog farms started in 1991, he has campaigned vigorously against them, arguing that they specifically harm the poor.

"People are very afraid that if they speak up they will lose their jobs, they will lose their food stamps, they will just get whipped in the process. It's environmental racism, the last vestiges of Jim Crow."

Grant is a soft-spoken, mild-mannered man, with the patience and attention you'd expect of a teacher. He has fought the hog farms and their side effects for years, and in his county, Halifax, he's had a measure of success. That has only meant, however, that the big farms have gone to counties where the population is more passive or more afraid.

"In one county," he tells me, "I asked them why they didn't do anything. They just said to me, 'It's their land, what can we do?' And I said to them, 'But it's your *air!*'"

This was the source of Don Webb's anguish: what the farm had done to his neighbors, to their homes, to his community, and to his faith in America. He had tried to help them fight against the farms, breaking into barns to film what he saw, petitioning and protesting in every forum and legislature where he could gain admittance. He was threatened and offered money for his silence. He wouldn't shut up. He still won't.

"I wonder now how much of our world is for sale. When we turn our head away from one American, allow that person to be mistreated, then every man, woman, and child in this nation is at risk. I look at it with a sad heart to see that all I worked for all my life can be destroyed."

"Social capital" is the term sociologists use to define what Don Webb mourns. It's an academic term for mutual trust, reciprocity, and the shared norms that create quality of life and make a society resilient in times of stress.

"Communities with higher levels of social capital," wrote the Pew Commission on Industrial Farm Animal Production, "tend to have lower poverty rates, fewer incidents of violent crime, and stronger democratic institutions." Factory farming, the commission concluded, threatens social capital.

In the race to the bottom, social capital is what is destroyed when people are afraid to speak up and defend themselves. Social capital is what is destroyed when competitive pressures take precedence over community health. Social capital is destroyed when the occupants of Brown Town become invisible and impotent. When newsrooms hawk fakery and lies. When temporary workers contend with each other for a few hours' work.

"We got to have cheap pork, we have to have cheap chicken—but the people who benefit from it, they don't have to smell it, to eat the flies," is how Don Webb puts it. You don't need to tell him about power-distance relationships: he lives them, with his neighbors powerless to move and those making decisions a very great distance away. After decades of fighting, he is brokenhearted that his idea of America as a place where everyone matters and where everyone can be heard has turned out to be a fairy tale.

"They don't care about us. They don't care about me and some rural people who don't want to live with feces factories. My great nation under God with liberty and justice for all does not care for me and my family or for the poor black people who got it the hardest. And I live in America!"

In 2013 the Chinese firm Shuanghui Fuels agreed to buy Smithfield Foods for $4.7 billion—the largest-ever takeover of an American company by a Chinese firm. Among the issues that the deal raised for the US Senate was the question of the safety of the heparin supply. Heparin is an anticoagulant, used in dialysis and also to prevent and treat blood clots in the veins, arteries, and lungs. One of the oldest medicines still in use, heparin is administered in the United States to some 12 million patients annually and is made from pigs. In 2008 patients taking heparin began to have difficulty breathing, to suffer from nausea and sweating and, in some cases, such precipitate low blood pressure as to cause heart shocks. The heparin they had taken had been contaminated by a non-naturally occurring molecule, over-sulphated chondroitin, which costs a fraction of the drug. The contamination of the American heparin supply was linked to its manufacture in China.[27] The Senate similarly expressed concern over Shuanghui Fuels' link with the Clenbuterol scandal. Clenbuterol is a fat-burning drug that makes meat leaner but is poisonous to humans. In March 2011, Shuanghui issued an apology to investors and consumers who had become ill after eating Shuanghui meat products made from pigs that had Clenbuterol in their feed.[28]

It is always easier to push costs down to the poor, who can't move away, are afraid to speak up, and lack political influence. Threatened with increased regulatory oversight in the United States, meat companies have expanded their operations to Europe and South America, where they seek unfettered opportunities to keep up their race to the bottom. In Poland and Romania, they again find populations with a history of silence, peoples who are afraid to speak up and unaccustomed to the concept of rights. In 1999 Smithfield bought Animex, one of Poland's biggest pork producers, and by 2008, 600,000 Polish hog farmers had lost their livelihoods: consolidation, with its economies of scale keeping meat cheap, then moved on to Romania, where 90 percent of independent farms vanished. Then, in 2010, packets of frozen pork offal, subsidized by the EU, started to appear in African markets. They were so cheap that local farmers found it hard to sell their own products.[29]

Dennis Leary is frequently the spokesman provided by Smithfield Foods. A former environmental regulator, he is now an executive vice president who also acts as treasurer for the company's political action committee.[30] We met, not in North Carolina, but in Washington, DC, in the heart of the political lobbying district. Giving the world the "choice" of cheap meat is the company's strategic agenda.

"To feed the world," Leary argues, "modern intensive agriculture is the only way to go. Our task is to (I'm trying to avoid sounding noble here) make products that are sustainable so everyone enjoys the same thing. How are we going to feed people? Low prices are fundamental, so you have to start thinking about sustainable intensification. That is the current thought. That is where we all need to go."

Leary may be the chief sustainability officer and happy to talk about "sustainable intensification," but he can't and won't define "sustainability," and he discourages his staff from even trying.[31] Although the company proudly describes itself in its annual report as combining "leading brands and a commitment to sustainability to produce good food responsibly,"[32] the company is at pains to stress that sustainability must be pursued as part of "value creation"—in other words, it must never interfere with making money. The years 2011 and 2012 were the company's most profitable ever, but the sustainability initiatives they boasted of in their annual report seem trivial: reduced packaging at some plants, the replacement of cardboard bins with collapsible plastic ones, and donations to breast cancer research and the Red Cross.[33] New waste management technologies have been installed in some Missouri farms (where the company faces multiple lawsuits), and the company sponsored a livestock judging contest. It also boasts of having conformed to recent legislation that calls for phasing out gestation crates—the metal frames that hold pregnant sows before and during pregnancy—and replacing them with "group housing," which doubles the tiny space available for each sow. New lagoons can no longer be built in North Carolina, but the old ones remain. Antibiotic use is up, but food donations are down. Leary does not articulate a connection between the business and the society that supports it.

"It's hard enough," Leary writes, "to run a business even without considering the social concerns that have been injected in recent years."[34]

"Sustainable intensification" is the kind of oxymoron that George Orwell would have relished, since many—including the Pew Commission—argue that intensification is inherently unsustainable owing to the pollution, health problems, and cruelty it creates. But for Leary, a genial blowsy man who has clearly rehearsed these same arguments for years, any other approach is just romantic.

"I understand the romantic concept of the idealized farm; I live on a farm myself and buy from farmers' markets occasionally. That's our choice. But my wife can barely feed us from this small operation. And the people who believe in that stuff, they're always moneyed. Our job at Smithfield is to meet the expectations of a demanding population. That's where our planning comes from. And people want cheap meat."

Smithfield Foods is just one contestant among many in the race to the bottom; along with other private companies—Tyson, Karmel, Cargill, JBS—they all compete fiercely on price. Leary insists that, while the company isn't obsessed with its competition, there's no point resisting consumer demand: someone is going to fill that demand, and it might as well be Smithfield.

The true cost of cheap meat is poverty (which we all pay for), environmental degradation (which we all pay for), health care risks (to which we are all exposed), and the destruction of the social fabric on which we all depend. Even those who aren't meat-eaters inhabit a society stressed and divided by the costs of producing it. In externalizing their costs to society while retaining profits for themselves and their shareholders, these businesses hope to win the race. To do so, they fundamentally sever their connection to the world in which they operate. And if a corporation is big enough, there may be nothing that anyone is willing or able to do about it. This leaves such companies and their leaders feeling that they can do what they want to the environment.

"To me, ecology's just a source for raw materials and the place to (legally) flush our wastes."

That was Ray Anderson's view at one time, and having become one of the largest carpet manufacturers in the world, he thought he had every reason to feel self-satisfied.

"So what if each day just one of my plants sent six tons of carpet trimmings to the local landfill? It was someone else's problem, not mine. That's what landfills were for."[35]

Ray Anderson's soft Georgia accent and good ol' boy style could be deceptive; he described himself as a driven, cold-eyed businessman. After his college football career was cut short by injury, he studied industrial engineering and, in 1973, started his carpet tiles business, Interface. Carpet tiles turned out to be a perfect solution for the new economy, in which companies come, go, and change every week; Interface built alliances with architects and interior designers who loved the product. But then some of those architects and interior designers started asking: what is the company doing about the environment? Anderson's answer then was much the same as Smithfield's today: we comply with the law.

"We took it all for granted at that time," he recalled. "That's just the way it was. The energy was all coming from fossil fuels. The process is very energy-intensive and in some cases very abusive to the environment. That meant effluent going into the water system, maybe not treated. And with lots of chemicals in the process: dyes and surfactants."[36]

Customers and employees kept nagging Anderson for his environmental vision; he didn't have one. Recognizing that he had to come up with something more motivating than compliance, he happened to pick up *The Ecology of Commerce*. Because it was written by another successful businessman, Paul Hawken, he reckoned it would at least be pragmatic. Instead, it proved galvanic.

"I stood indicted as a plunderer, a destroyer of the earth, a thief, stealing my own grandchildren's future," Anderson later wrote. "And I thought, *My God, someday what I do here will be illegal. Someday they'll send people like me to jail.*"

Many of Anderson's employees thought he'd gone mad, but his epiphany set a new agenda for his company. Heretofore a huge consumer of fossil fuels and a generator of vast amounts of waste with tons of carpet going to landfill each year, Anderson decided that his company would no longer take anything from the earth that could not easily be renewed. Unlike Smithfield's Dennis Leary, Anderson could define sustainability.

"Sustainability," Anderson wrote, "is all about coming up with ways to meet our needs (not wants—needs) today without undermining the ability of other folks to meet their needs tomorrow." For his own business, he made it even simpler: "Take nothing. Do no harm."[37]

Most companies, he realized, were externalizing machines. In traditional businesses, when costs came down, they were imposed on people and places that were powerless to respond. That, Anderson determined, had to change. Businesses needed to identify all of their costs, and then they had to find or invent ways to eliminate them completely and permanently—not just pass them along.

In contrast to the race to the bottom, Anderson talked about "climbing Mount Sustainability" and challenged everyone to create "the first company that, by its deeds, shows the entire industrial world what sustainability is in all its dimensions: People, process, product, place and profits." Mission Zero meant that the company aimed to eliminate *all* negative environmental impact by 2020.

At the time, Anderson really had no idea how hard it would be to accomplish his vision, but he never wavered. His mission required completely different thinking about the full impact of the company on the environment and everyone who lived within it. In other words, Anderson vowed that he would no longer externalize anything. And he put his money where his mouth was.

"Make no mistake. Mission Zero is hard, hard work. It is not a 'program of the month.' And nobody is making us do it. We're under no pressure from our competitors to achieve sustainability."

Anderson wasn't driven by a passion to lower prices but by a determination that his company would accept all the responsibilities that its business incurred. Instead of seeing Interface as separate from society, he viewed it is integrally connected to the entire world. For a free market truly to exist, everyone would do this.

Interface is a billion-dollar, publicly traded business, operating in 110 countries. Changing a company this size would, Anderson knew, involve a lot more than creating a sustainability officer or a specialized team; every single person in the business had to get involved and contribute. His mission unleashed a whirlwind of innovation, leading the company to invent new processes and new technologies. Setting the bar high, not low, galvanized that creativity. It also forced everyone in the company to become a collaborator. In place of dog-eat-dog politics and departmental silos, the entire business could not be transformed without, as Anderson describes it, "a corporate 'ecosystem' to borrow a term from nature, with cooperation replacing confrontation." In everything the company learned along the way, Anderson found new lessons, ideas, and processes to share. Instead of keeping his discoveries to himself, he shared them broadly with anyone who would listen—Anheuser-Busch, PepsiCo, Google, Epson, Toyota, Bayer, Cisco—inciting them all to set new standards. After all, a free market would only ever be truly free if everyone stopped externalizing and instead absorbed the full cost of their activity.

Key to Interface's success was the determination not to outsource responsibility but to embrace it. Instead of trusting their suppliers to eliminate toxic substances, company chemists and engineers analyzed every material Interface used. Instead of trusting government lists detailing safety and side effects of substances, they developed their own chemical screening protocol. At every step of the way, instead of passing responsibility along to dependent suppliers, the company grabbed responsibility and set its own standards. "Trust but verify" was how Anderson summed it up.

Didn't this cost a fortune? It didn't. It made the business both more efficient and more creative. The idea that harm to people and the planet is the inevitable price paid for a successful business was one that Anderson repeatedly—and successfully—disproved.

"Any evaluation that concludes that it is cheaper and more cost-efficient to cause serious harm to the only world we have is not particularly logical," Anderson wrote. "You can be sure that externalities of some kind are disguising the true economics."

And he kept proving he wasn't a dreamer. Greenhouse gas emissions were reduced at Interface by 99 percent; water usage was down by 74 percent. In Europe, the use of all heavy metals was entirely eliminated. Since 2003, the company has sold 83 million square yards of one particular product—Cool Carpet—that has zero net global warming effect on the earth. It has been a runaway best-seller.

Not only did Anderson's radical approach to the environment make his business more successful and more influential, but it also made the company itself more resilient because of the commitment that everyone working for Interface brought to their work.

"It has had a profound effect on organizational cohesiveness," he said. "A shared higher purpose will do that."[38]

Interface's Mission Zero was full of creativity like this: breaking rules about what could and could not be economical, finding or inventing new technologies to solve problems everyone assumed just had to be accepted. And the more the company innovated the more lessons it had to teach—and wanted to teach—anyone who would listen.

Tragically, Anderson died from liver cancer on August 8, 2011, before he could see his company ascend to the summit of Mount Sustainability. But Interface continues to challenge itself to meet Anderson's 2020 goal and to prove to the world at large that externalizing can and must be a thing of the past. Anderson didn't try to win the race to the bottom; he just called it off.

"Will the new business model—investing in a truly sustainable future, a future characterized by new thinking, new products and new profits—see us through the economic downturn?" Anderson wrote. "I say, yes, and my money—my personal investment—is where my mouth is. And if we can do it, anybody can. And if anybody can, everybody can."

Although his leadership was uniquely inspiring, Anderson isn't the only business leader who has vigorously refuted the notion that the only way is down. At American Apparel, founder Dov Charney vigorously rejects the idea that making clothing requires sweatshops.

"Fast fashion is crass and cheap and sits on the backs of other people," Charney insists. "It looks sexy, but it is basically stolen goods, hot goods. Twenty cents an hour is slavery."[39]

American Apparel proudly labels itself "sweatshop-free." The company eschews outsourcing, and its factory in downtown Los Angeles, where he pays nearly twice the minimum wage, is the single largest garment factory in America.[40] Employees also receive subsidized public transport and meals, as well as low-cost health insurance, and can participate in a bike-lending scheme. All of this is aimed at keeping better, more committed workers and better quality control.

"I believe in bringing the worker *into* the company, knowing the face of the worker. Not relentlessly pursuing low wages. A $4.99 bikini doesn't exist unless you're screwing somebody. Focus on a better product!"

Charney has a talent for whipping up controversy about almost anything

—he calls himself "a complicated freak"—and he enjoys pushing boundaries. But he also means it when he urges consumers to reject sweatshop labor, comparing cheap clothes to the Outspan oranges his mother would never let him eat because they symbolized the injustice of apartheid. By refusing to outsource, Charney can bring everyone involved in the business under one roof where they can share ideas and "sculpt a sustainable business model that doesn't rely on exploitation."

But his argument against sweatshops goes beyond hating them because they represent a form of slavery. He also thinks that the race to the bottom is doomed. It isn't just that low wages are offensive—he doesn't think they're financially sustainable either. Today's low-wage countries, like Bangladesh, will become tomorrow's middle-class societies. Transportation costs will rise. Sooner or later prices will go up, and it's to the long-term advantage of any business not to get cheaper but to get smarter about what consumers really want and how to make good products well. Instead of cutting the wages of the least skilled, put pressure on the most skilled to be more creative.

Marketing American Apparel as "sweatshop-free" does not, Charney believes, make more than a 1 percent difference to his customers. But it proves that fashion doesn't have to be cheap and that sweatshops aren't a competitive necessity. He uses his company to show that businesses don't have to race to the bottom, they don't have to outsource, and they don't have to destroy the environment.

The wall of colorful bow ties displayed in the stores illustrates the company's "Creative Reuse" strategy: instead of wasting scraps or leaving them on the floor to cause fire hazards, American Apparel turns scraps into smaller items like tank tops, ties, and hairbands. His factory is solar-powered and makes a whole range of clothing from organic cotton. Charney believes in what he calls "win-win business" and is determined to prove that it works.

Emma Bridgewater has a gentler style than Charney, but their passion is the same. She started making mugs in 1985 when she couldn't find a gift for her mother's birthday. What began as a hobby soon became a business, but instead of doing what most entrepreneurs do—work from home until growth forces expansion into nearby industrial units—she sat down and thought about what kind of a business she wanted to build.

She knew her history. Aware that England's Stoke-on-Trent had once led the world in the production of both fine china and more homely pottery, it seemed the natural home for her new company. But contemporary Stoke was full of warnings about the desperate business that pottery-making had become. Brands that had once been world-famous were only just hanging on. Most had outsourced to China and, in doing so, lowered the value of their once-famous names: Minton, Royal Doulton, Wedgwood. Now the town featured abandoned warehouses, empty streets, and vacant houses—the Detroit of the pottery world.

"I was astonished by what I found: a post-industrial wasteland, really a desolate scene. There were only two manufacturers here who could supply the kind of clay we needed—it wasn't clear that they were going to be around all that long. We could only get the glazes we needed from one company, so that felt pretty risky too. And I knew we could get things done more cheaply abroad. But at the same time, I realized that this was where it had all started! And right from the start, I felt this business could grow from the grass roots. If it meant we were going to have high costs, so be it. That's what the brand would have to stand for. We would have to make things that had high value to people: because they were beautiful, well made, with great design, and worth the money."

Bridgewater wasn't blind; all around her, she could see the carcasses of dead businesses. But the lesson she took from them was that the race to the bottom was doomed. Those companies had cut costs and outsourced jobs—and it hadn't worked. Customers didn't want to buy British pottery made in Malaysia.

"Exporting a labor problem is just such crap; why aren't we ashamed to do that? Ashamed that we can't run our own businesses—the businesses we *invented*—well enough to make them work? As a new company, we couldn't cut costs—we didn't have any yet! So we had to be in tune with our customers. And what they wanted was really great design but something much more modern, less formal, than the old manufacturers had produced. We just had to think hard, and think creatively, about how to be relevant."

Walking through the Emma Bridgewater factory in Stoke today is an eye-opening experience. Crisply decorated bright mugs are still being hand-printed, and plates are being handled by people, not machines. There's an air of cheerful concentration about the place. When you stop and talk to the women painting polka dots and applying transfers or the men removing bowls from firing ovens, they're happy to chat about anything—but they don't stop working.

The factory is spotless, and visitors can take tours, stay for lunch, or just fill their baskets at the shop. Even midweek in a bleak winter, the atmosphere buzzes with visitors and the background hum of furnaces. Many visitors are shocked to see that their favorite mugs and plates are produced this way: by hand, by a person. But once she decided not to race to the bottom, to set up in Stoke and make it work, Bridgewater simply refused to compromise.

"Cutting your prices isn't a strategy. It isn't even thinking. Whenever you buy or sell something cheap—well, someone else must be paying, being exploited somehow. The environmental impact of buying crap is huge. When you buy a plate for two dollars, you have to think that someone somewhere is paying so you can do that. The race to the bottom—it's just total suicide."

Bridgewater runs the business with her husband, Matthew Rice, a talented furniture and print designer. They've doubled the firm's revenue in the last five years—straight through the recession—but the numbers didn't seem to excite them as much as the impact the company can make on its community. As we sit in the factory kitchen, Rice talks about the thrill he gets watching the company thrive.

"Companies are starting to come back to Stoke now—it's fantastic! It's as though we've given them courage. And of course, just being here, you keep suppliers in business. That means you don't lose the crafts, the talents, the skills you need for an industry like this. So if you can keep going—everyone can keep going."

Rice and Bridgewater have moved in some pretty swank circles; Rice's partner in his furniture business was the queen's nephew, Viscount Linley. But up in Stoke, glamour and the social whirl don't seem to be uppermost in his mind.

"You know what makes me happy?" Rice asks rhetorically. "What makes me happy is knowing that, the better we do, the more jobs we can create. We *like* employing people. That's what it is all about."

After I left Stoke-on-Trent, I reflected that I hadn't heard anyone in business say that they actually *liked* employing people for a long time. Had I ever heard it? After decades of working in the United States and the United Kingdom, almost all I'd ever heard was about cutting costs, cutting people. The race to the bottom has become so ubiquitous, its central tenets so pervasive and unquestioned, that most business leaders have entirely forgotten what companies are for.

Although wildly different in their businesses and personas, Ray Anderson, Dov Charney, and Emma Bridgewater have all followed firmly in the footsteps of Henry Ford, who maintained that all business exists to serve others and to do so must observe these principles: fearlessness, a disregard for competition, and putting service before profit. He also insisted that man-ufacturing is not about buying low, selling high, speculation, gambling, or "sharp dealing," and he had a pronounced disdain for financiers.

But Ford caused the greatest consternation when he doubled the wages of his factory workers. He did so in order to reduce staff turnover. To him, labor flexibility wasn't a strategy, and it wasn't even efficient—it was waste-ful. He considered every employee a partner—"the boss is the partner of his worker, the worker is the partner of his boss"—and insisted that any good business would aspire to keep good employees, train them, and pay them more.

"It ought to be the employer's ambition, as leader, to pay better wages than any similar line of business, and it ought to be the workman's ambition to make this possible.... What good is industry if it be so unskillfully managed as not to return a living to everyone concerned?"

Ford passionately maintained these principles because he believed abso-lutely in the value of human labor. But he also understood that, when he paid his workers more, he enabled them to earn enough money to buy his cars. You could say that Ford was the first evangelist for "trickle-up" economics: if you pay well at the bottom of the market, the whole economy will expand.

"If we can distribute high wages, then that money is going to be spent and it will serve to make storekeepers and distributors and manufacturers and workers in other lines more prosperous and their prosperity will be reflected in our sales. Country-wide high wages spell country-wide prosperity."[41]

Now that we know trickle-down doesn't work, it's an interesting thought that a "trickle-up" world might prove strikingly more successful. Instead of the entire economy sinking to the bottom, we would do better raising every-one's boat. What Anderson, Charney, Bridgewater, and Ford share is a vision of business in which nobody is left out. Everyone counts, and the secret of success lies not in being an expert at exploiting people and the planet, but in being smarter about getting them to work creatively together. Shortly before he died, Ray Anderson recorded a video message for his workforce, cele-brating the thirty-eighth birthday of his carpet company. He did not know whether he would live to see it achieve the audacious goal that had made it both successful and famous. But he knew what he wanted for the world he left behind.

"I can't say whether I'll see the view from the top of Mount Sustainability, but I want you to see it. And I want you to see the day when the Interface model has become the accepted business model of the most successful companies on earth. I want you to feel the joy of having led the transformation of the worldwide industrial system. I want you to appreciate the wisdom of doing well by doing good and the huge shift in thinking that has led to this journey."

CHAPTER 10

Top of the World

The more we sweat in peace, the less we bleed in war.
—Vijaya Lakshmi Pandit

China, India, Germany, and South Korea are 'not playing for second place.' And neither should we. The United States of America, we play for first place.
—Barack Obama

In 2009 Brett Pierce disconcerted his family by making regular trips to Iraq. He was neither a spy nor a member of the military. Having spent most of his professional life as a producer on *Sesame Street,* Pierce was on a mission to use television to educate Iraqi teenagers in communication, collaboration, and peace-building. His format of choice was a game show.

In *Salam Shabab* (*Youth Peace*), six regions fielded four teams of three kids each and competed to go through to a national final. A series of sports challenges, mental puzzles, and filmmaking and performance exercises were designed to teach collaboration through competition. Pierce ruled out anything too preachy. Years of making TV shows for kids had taught him that if they sense an iota of didacticism, he tells me, they tune out. The fact that girls and boys would be working together was radical enough.

"Keep in mind: the idea of putting a girl next to a boy where their knees might touch—it was mind-blowing! We didn't know how the kids would respond. They had never experienced this freedom before! It was a big thing for them to experience so much freedom, to think freely and to find a voice."

Building tricycles from spare bike parts, throwing water balloons, painting from memory—all of these challenges were designed to be met through collaborative interaction. Soloists would make teams fail. In the first regional rounds, the kids thrived. These were not the media-savvy, polished products of *The X Factor* but eager, shy, excited teenagers who felt lucky to be involved. Every participant in the show came across with a highly distinctive personality, energy, and sense of humor. Everyone was eager to do well;

there was palpable pleasure in the experience as a whole. The prize was kept deliberately low-key—a laptop and a video camera for the team—because the reward wasn't the focus of the experience.

"It mattered that it didn't matter," Pierce tells me. "There wasn't a lot at stake. That was deliberate. Being part of the show was enough. So the kids were very spirited but not mean. There was no nastiness, no rivalry—because they were all on such a unique trip."

Every challenge was part play, part work. The experience was supposed to be fun—and the show is certainly fun to watch. The filmmaking and performance sequences attract the largest number of points, and in these the results are voted on by the audience. It is a strange and moving sight to see the teenagers place their votes in a ballot box and then swipe their fingers with ink.

In the final round, Pierce introduced into the game what he called "the switch." At this point, the regional teams that had gone forward were broken up into new teams: black, white, red, and green—the colors of the Iraqi flag. Each team now had members from different parts of the country. In the very first season of the show, the "switch" had dramatic consequences. Many of the kids became sullen and resistant. What had been fun became seriously difficult and they were visibly angry at being made to collaborate with people from other parts of Iraq, some Shia, some Sunni, some Kurds.

The first season aired on Iraqi television in 2011. By the third season, shot in 2012, everyone knew that the switch was coming, so it wasn't such a shock. Most of the kids took it in stride; looking nervously at their new teammates, they were intrigued, and prepared to give them a chance. Some even looked quite excited, smiling shyly at their new friends.

"I'm convinced my team is strong—and the rest is for God and us to decide."

But not on the white team. There, one young woman from Tigris, named Baraa, decided that she simply could not get along with her teammate Fatma from Najaf. What was especially peculiar about this reaction was that, as part of her regional team, Baraa had been a great contributor. Alone among the teams, hers had scored in a water balloon challenge because she gave her teammate excellent support and advice. When they had struggled to make a boat from straws and hollowed-out eggs—and mostly failed—she conceded that "it was my mistake and next time I'll listen to them." Fatma too had done well on her regional team, particularly in the performance exercise, which attracted a large number of points.

But Baraa was adamant that she could not work with Fatma. The girl was too quiet, she was bound to let the team down. Baraa started to cry as she explained—in front of Fatma—that she was sure "this girl from Najaf" would make her lose.

Given odds and ends from bicycles, the three girls on the white team—Baraa, Fatma, and Buraq—were challenged to build a vehicle that could carry all three of them. The white team couldn't decide on their design, and Baraa pinned all her hopes on the weakness of the other teams. All the Rube Goldberg creations that emerged from the other teams were quirky and clumsy—but most still worked. The white team's vehicle, however, only loosely connected with string, could not hold together. A perfect image for the disjointed vulnerability of their teamwork, the machine lacked all coordination, and the three limped last across the finish line. All through the semifinal, whenever there was a break between challenges, Fatma and Baraa both retreated quickly to their regional friends.

In a subsequent challenge, the teams had to look at a grid of nine images, try to remember them all, and paint them. Once again, the dissentious white team struggled.

"I told her to draw a mountain—and she just drew a triangle," Baraa complained. The more she berated Fatma, the more withdrawn and sullen Fatma became. As Baraa took charge, the other girl relinquished responsibility for contributing. And as the contest progressed, the inability of the team to function—and the failure of the teenagers to relish their once-in-a-lifetime experience—became increasingly pronounced.

In the musical challenge, the three had to compose and play a piece of music using a rough assortment of pan lids, bottles, and sticks. The other teams quickly figured out that, in addition to the props they'd been given, they also had their own voices. What emerged was hilarious but charming cacophony. But the white team never saw their own voices as instruments. Lacking any melody, they hammered out a joyless series of rhythms that lacked structure, vigor, or finesse.

The best teams quickly resolved their individual difficulties. Some relished the chance to meet kids from other parts of the country, to learn a few words of Kurdish or hear about different foods and styles of dress. But the white team never figured this out. The more dominant Baraa became, the more Fatma withdrew, leaving their other teammate, Buraq, puzzled, isolated, and ineffective.

Salam Shabab won the UNESCO Prix Jeunesse in 2012 for its contribution to teaching the skills of collaboration and conflict resolution. It's easy to see why. On this small scale, with no high stakes and the lightest of oversight, the difficulty and potential of collaboration played out in miniature just as it plays out in life. It can feel quite easy and natural to work alongside people with whom you have much in common. The same work becomes far more difficult, contentious, and irrational when regional or national differences come into play. People are territorial animals, and that sense of defensiveness—irrational and counterproductive—can make the complex work of collaboration harder still. And the teams where one member tries to dominate lose.

Competitions always need a way to keep score. In *Salam Shabab,* it's done with points and votes. Schools, colleges, and hospitals have ranking and league tables, athletes use time, and companies compare stock price rises and market share. When it comes to international competition, nations use gross domestic product (GDP) to show how big their economies are and how energetic their growth rate is. Just like all competitive measures, GDP defines the game by what it measures—and what it doesn't. Like any single instrument trying to capture the value of a complex activity, it leaves a lot out. No one has summed this up better than Robert Kennedy in 1968, several weeks before he died.

> Gross national product, if we judge the United States of America by that ... counts air pollution and cigarette advertising, and ambulances to clear our highways of carnage. It counts special locks for our doors and the jails for the people who break them. It counts the destruction of the redwoods and the loss of our natural wonder, and chaotic sprawl. It counts napalm and it counts nuclear warheads and armored cars for the police to fight the riots in our cities. It counts Whitman's rifle and Speck's knife, and the television programs that glorify violence in order to sell toys to our children.[1]
>
> Yet the gross national product does not allow for the health of our children or the quality of their education, or the joy of their play. It does not include the beauty of our poetry or the strength of our marriages, the intelligence of our public debate or the integrity of our public officials. It measures neither our wit nor our courage, neither our wisdom nor our learning, neither our compassion nor our devotion to our country. It measures everything, in short, except that which makes

life worthwhile, and it can tell us everything about America except why we are proud that we are American.[2]

Had Kennedy been in America today, he might have added that current gross domestic product would include the war in Afghanistan, the cost of flooding, the medical care of injured athletes, the cost of steroids and antidepressants, the bills for legal services rendered in mergers and acquisitions as well as divorces and other litigation, and the food banks proliferating across the countryside. Because it represents total spending, GDP goes up in the wake of disasters but does not go down when fracking pollutes the water table, when gases evaporate from hog lagoons, or when athletes bow out because of their injuries. In GDP terms, it might be better for New Orleans to be flooded regularly than to install effective levees and other defenses. GDP doesn't reflect the lost capacity of kids who give up on education (or who are abandoned by it) or, among adults, the creative energy siphoned off by forced ranking and office infighting. Nor can it reflect parents' investments in their children, their efforts to look after their own parents and neighbors, or the time they devote to volunteering or community participation. Like all scores, GDP draws attention to one thing—spending—and erases the rest.

The inventor of GDP recognized this. Before the 1930s, governments had only a ragbag of data—stock price indices, freight train loadings—which made economic planning both impossible and highly susceptible to political manipulation or wishful thinking. With the onset of the Great Depression, what had been a chronic problem became acute, so the US Department of Commerce commissioned a Russian econometrician, Simon Kuznets, to design a method for measuring economic output. During World War II, the metric came into its own in the planning and financing of wartime production. When, in 1944, the Bretton Woods conference attempted to create a new monetary order throughout the world, GDP was adopted as the standard measure of a country's economy.

Kuznets himself, however, wasn't entirely gratified by this wholesale adoption of his work. A meticulous econometrician, he believed that a true measure of national output ought to include unpaid work—like housework. It made no sense that a parent cooking dinner for the family contributed only the ingredient costs to the economy, while a business executive dining alone apparently contributed more. The US Commerce Department didn't take the distinction seriously and refused to incorporate the value of unpaid labor, so Kuznets moved on to study inequality—but not before warning

Congress that "the welfare of a nation can scarcely be inferred from a measure of national income."

GDP is tweaked every five years; in 2013 the Commerce Department decided to give greater weight to intellectual property like movies, TV shows, and books like the one you are reading. But because they are free services, it can't reflect the value of Facebook or Twitter. So discontent with GDP has persisted: GDP doesn't capture externalities, it doesn't account for physical or mental health, and it doesn't reflect educational attainment, economic inequality, social stability, or environmental degradation. But in 1999 the Commerce Department threw a party to celebrate the invention of GDP as "its achievement of the century." Alan Greenspan, then the chairman of the Federal Reserve, crowed, "I personally would be inclined to say that the accuracy and conceptual rigor of our underlying data systems are more powerful and important than is commonly understood."[3]

Other countries occasionally toyed with alternative measures—as early as 1972, Bhutan proposed measuring gross national happiness; thirty years later, France and Great Britain did likewise. It turns out that happiness is a little complicated, in part because different cultures interpret questions about happiness in radically different ways, and also because surveys bring to light quite troubling anomalies. There is, for example, no relationship between increased gender equality and happiness, but there is a positive relationship between happiness and violent crime in the United States; nevertheless, it seems unlikely that any policymaker would use that data to campaign for more gender inequality accompanied by more murder.[4] The happiness indices, as a consequence, turned out not to provide much insight into the drivers of social welfare. In 2006 the Chinese introduced a "green GDP," which, applied to its own economy in 2004, would have knocked 3 percent off its growth rate. But still, GDP is the measure that has stuck. And because everyone uses it, countries can do what individuals and companies do: compare and compete.

What an insidious effect this has had. Every year, every quarter, even every week, just like companies on the stock market, countries compare their GDP numbers and growth figures to see who is winning. In recent years these numbers have incited something approaching panic, as Chinese GDP creeps closer and closer to that of the United States. As journalists wrote about the "last years of America's historic GDP reign," the 2012 presidential election echoed with candidates whipping up hysteria and promising bold action in the global competition.

"I want to beat China," Republican senator Rick Santorum said. "I want to go to war with China and make America the most attractive place in the world to do business."

"We can't just sit back and let China run all over us," Mitt Romney argued. "People say, 'You'll start a trade war!' There's one going on right now, folks! They're stealing our jobs, and we're going to stand up to China."

Even President Barack Obama has weighed in, using (as he often does) a sports analogy to insist that "the United States of America plays for first place."

While pundits placed bets about the exact year in which Chinese GDP would overtake America's, the public was already way ahead of them. Since 2011, Gallup polls have shown that China is widely regarded by most Americans as the world's top economic power.[5]

"Few would argue that China's rocketing economic growth looms as a formidable challenge to the United States' global economic leadership," Gallup commented. "However, the majority of Americans believe the US has already lost the challenge, and relatively few are confident that the situation will be reversed in 20 years."[6]

But what challenge is this? When the United States is not at war, lower defense spending brings down GDP, but that does not necessarily make American lives poorer or Chinese lives any richer. If there are no further oil spills in the Gulf of Mexico, it's hard to see this as a national calamity. Moreover, if American employment increases and those who have jobs now can afford iPhones and iPads, the fact that the FoxConn factory that makes them has more work does not make the US economy weaker. National economies are not zero-sum games in which one's gain is another's loss. In fact, as we've seen throughout the economic crisis, quite the reverse is true: one failure provokes multiple failures.

Yet world leaders endlessly talk about nations competing with one another. In the presidential debates, Obama argued about competing with China in education—as though well-educated Chinese children hurt American students. This rhetoric of competition plays to bias and prejudice, enflaming fear and distrust while illuminating nothing about why or how education needs to be improved for the children who receive it. The reason to upgrade schools or health care or road safety isn't to make the Chinese stupid or sick or dangerous; it is for their own sake, because these are the right things to do and because they make a society socially and environmentally sustainable. The "America Creating Opportunities to Meaningfully Promote Excellence in Technology, Education, and Science Act" makes perfect (if inelegant) sense; what seems spurious is its alternative title: "America Competes."

If, as Romney opined, the economic war has already started, what will "winning" look like? Will Americans truly thrill to see China languish in poverty, debt, and civil unrest? Would they feel safer if poverty in India grew and the youth of Algeria and Egypt were less well educated? Just what kind of victory do these evangelists for global competition have in mind? The drama of competitiveness attracts attention and engagement because it appears to simplify relationships that are, in fact, complex and delicate. It's far easier to demonize others than to improve ourselves. Crude political rhetoric studiously discourages awkward questions or rigorous insight. And the tropes of winning and losing are so pervasive and ancient that we assume they must mean something.

GDP is a poor indicator of national well-being, but it isn't the only culprit. All the global indices are sophisticated pecking orders that both represent and confer status. But they all contain agendas. Ever since 1979, the *Global Competitiveness Report* has been assembled and published by the World Economic Forum, the organization best known for its annual conference of government leaders and chief executives at Davos in Switzerland. The report is a rich mix of hard data (numbers like government debt and deficits) and a broad array of opinion that comes from "top management leaders."[7] Nobody at the World Economic Forum would tell me who these leaders were or what companies they came from—only that they all worked in the private sector. But whoever they were, it is their opinions that drive the data concerning the "12 pillars of competitiveness." These include, among other things, infrastructure, financial market development, education, health care, and labor efficiency. But drill down into these pillars a bit and what looks like hard data starts to feel a little squishy.

In addressing labor market efficiency, for example, the top management leaders are asked how easy or hard it is to hire and fire employees, what the costs of redundancy are, and to what extent pay is linked to productivity. The countries where hiring and firing are "flexibly determined by employers" top the list; countries where the cost of redundancy is nothing and countries that relate pay to productivity top the list. In other words, a labor market is deemed efficient where employers can hire and fire people at will and reward them according to performance. Yet there is no evidence that performance-related pay works or that it generates higher levels of productivity, creativity, engagement, or innovation—in fact, there is quite a lot of evidence that it has quite the opposite effect.

Moreover, we also know that being able to hire and fire people at will is negatively correlated to company performance. Swapping people in and out of jobs is expensive—new employees have to be found, hired, and trained—and it also harms corporate reputations and loses companies a great deal of knowledge, commitment, and efficiency.[8] While bringing new people into a business can be inspiring and galvanizing, turnover rates can get too high, not just because, as Henry Ford found, training is expensive, but because layoffs may damage corporate standing and erode the relationships that make work meaningful, creative, efficient, and engaging.[9] It's a rare company that spends a fortune recruiting talented employees because they want to be able to fire them quickly. And while zero-hours contracts create an illusion of efficiency, the fact that the workers on those contracts can't even afford to buy lunch restricts economic growth.

To get to the top of the competitiveness index, therefore, requires that a country and its larger corporations conform to a very particular business model of a kind that, at the very least, is highly debatable. Having investigated many aspects of the index, Australian academic Harald Bergsteiner concluded that the *Global Competitiveness Report* is ideology masquerading as data.

"I remember reading the report some years ago," Bergsteiner tells me, "and thinking this didn't make sense. There is more than one way to run an effective business, but the research really only looks for one model and puts that forward as though it's the only thing that works. So I sat down and looked at their metrics and discovered that many of them were ideologically biased. Then when you remove those questions from the questionnaire and add questions they should have had in there, distortions become huge. This stinks. It's poor science, and someone has to say that it's wrong."

Bergsteiner diagnoses a biased feedback loop that overemphasizes policies valued by dominant nations while not questioning the alternatives practiced by less influential countries. This, he says, produces the global equivalent of a Matthew effect: the dominant "efficient labor markets" are rewarded by a high ranking, while those who might dare to diverge from such thinking are condemned to languish further down the pecking order. The index therefore really measures how far a country conforms to a very specific agenda rather than to any objective definition of economic success. And because the World Economic Forum makes a big noise in the world, and leaders command respect at Davos according to the size and success of their economies, the *Global Competitiveness Report* has come to represent an authoritative report card on how well politicians and their economies are doing.

Much in the composition of the report provokes debate—or should. Not all citizens, not even all economists, would argue that foreign ownership of companies is infinitely beneficial; there must come a point at which the dominance of an economy by outsiders presents significant democratic and social challenges. But openness to foreign investment pulls countries up the league tables. Questions around such issues aren't posed, or explored, by the Global Competitiveness Index. Instead, for all the sophistication of the statistical analysis, what emerges is a doctrinaire picture of a thriving state in which anonymous management thinkers determine what constitutes a successful economy. Yet these scores form the basis of political rhetoric and policy.

That an economy is distinct from a society has only just begun to emerge within the rhetoric of the report. Growing discomfort with the implications of the World Economic Forum's formula for success led in 2013 to the first of its sustainability rankings. Even these effect little change in the overall rankings, however, and the degree to which countries are making little or no significant progress in social or environmental sustainability makes for demoralizing reading. Mostly what these supplementary league tables demonstrate is how poorly such rigid thinking maps onto the rich complexity of social communities.

Boston Consulting Group, a privately held advisory firm, has attempted to do better, creating a Sustainable Economic Development Assessment (SEDA) that distinguishes between different kinds of growth: the growth that improves well-being for everyone versus the growth that just benefits a few. "What is important," Boston Consulting Group maintains in its report, "is for rising national income to translate into greater well-being.... Countries with higher GDPs are not necessarily the best at converting their wealth into well-being for their citizens. A number of eastern European nations, such as Albania and Romania, and such Southeast Asian countries as Indonesia, the Philippines, and Vietnam, score particularly high in converting wealth into well-being."[10] What SEDA demonstrates that other metrics cannot is that a pro-poor approach to growth can make a positive impact without proportionate GDP growth.

"Brazil's record has been particularly impressive in this regard. While it averaged GDP growth of 5.1 percent over the past five years, Brazil generated gains in living standards that would be expected of an economy expanding by an average of more than 13 percent per year. New Zealand and Poland are among the other countries whose recent progress in improving well-being is greater than their GDP growth rates would suggest."[11]

One thing Boston Consulting Group did *not* do was to generate a league table with its data—in part because the way they've constructed their findings doesn't lend itself to so simplistic a display. More acid commentators have surmised that the company simply wished not to annoy prospective government clients. (After all, these reports all have to be paid for somehow.) But the main lesson of SEDA is that not all growth is equal and therefore growth alone isn't a useful measure.

Everyone knows—has known for over half a century—that GDP doesn't work and that the *Global Competitiveness Report* has its own agenda. So why is GDP all we continue to hear coming out of the mouths of politicians, economists, and policymakers? In part, it's a game of chicken: no one wants to turn away first. As long as the prevailing systems can somehow be gamed and dominant countries can stay on top, who wants to risk a different measure?

The rhetoric of competition and the alluring fantasies of victory impede our thinking about what meaningful progress might look like or require. It's simply impossible to frame effective policy when using a competitive metaphor. We know that the well-being of any nation depends on the stability and well-being of other nations, but competitive language omits dependencies, implying that winners live in a world untouched by the losers. Even those who might wish this to be true know that it is not.

Moreover, the competitive mind-set focused exclusively on GDP blinds us to other issues crying out for critical attention. We should be thinking about sustainable energy and food sources, but GDP doesn't draw attention to those issues. When the cost of solar energy starts to plunge, as has recently happened, this shouldn't register as a negative effect if it simultaneously reduces dependence on fossil fuels. The complex trade-offs between the longer-term benefit of sustainable technologies and the shorter-term benefits of extraction industries require a more sophisticated mind-set than win/lose can ever provide.

As new technologies continue to disrupt and eliminate entire industries, we need to think about how comfortable we are with the rising inequality that follows in their wake. As Jaron Lanier has described it so eloquently in *Who Owns the Future?,* advances in technology will make it easier and cheaper to automate a whole range of industries, from health care to transportation, leaving more and more people without work. At the same time, because the population will continue to grow by one billion people every twelve years, GDP will rise. A growing population with fewer and fewer job prospects should give anyone pause, but as long as we look only at GDP, with a competitive mind-set, these challenges don't even surface and cannot be addressed.

Once we recognize that even "winning" states have to coexist with everyone else, it becomes clear that the true challenge isn't competition at all. Some nation will always be the winner, as Britain was until it was overtaken by America around 1880, but one dominant nation doesn't make the others vanish—or even leave them powerless or poor. It does leave those societies that can't define their place in the world by being the biggest or the richest, the most aggressive or threatening, seeking alternative forms of identification. Like siblings, they must find their niche and, if they want to be productive, learn to play well with others. The challenge of cooperation and collaboration, it turns out, may be more demanding and subtle than dominance.

David Skilling argues that small countries tend to be better at addressing these questions because they have to be. Lacking the sheer economic dominance of the United States or China, they can't derive a sense of comfort or security from sheer size. Even if bigger were better, they have no choice. Finland, Switzerland, Singapore, and the Nordic countries are, he argues, more exposed—and that exposure makes them more alert.

"Small countries," Skilling tells me, "have less margin for error if you don't get things right. One small misstep and the ground falls away. If you're big, like the US, the size of your economy means that you can keep blundering along for quite a long time. Your size protects you. But small countries don't have that luxury, if you will. That makes policymaking much sharper. They're closer to the edge."

Skilling himself, a lanky New Zealander, knows what he's talking about. His own country is doubly disadvantaged: it's both small and remote. These days he spends much of his time in Singapore, where he advises policymakers keen to ensure that their tiny country makes as much as it can of its tiny landmass and population. He's been struck by the similarities between small nations around the world—countries that thrive because of their smaller size.

"They know," Skilling says, "that they can't be the biggest voice at the table. Therefore, they have to be allies, great partners, and collaborators. They're under no illusion as to their own importance, so they have had to develop relationships—with other countries and with regional and global organizations, like ASEAN [Association of South East Asian Nations] or WTO [World Trade Organization], that give them insight and influence. They invest a lot of time and effort in making these institutions work for them."

The greatest creativity in large countries like the United States, therefore, may be more likely to be found at the state level. It is there, after all, that the toughest gun laws have been passed quickly and there that the greatest steps have been taken to reduce carbon emissions and energy consumption.

"In the United States, you don't see this on a global scale, but you are starting to see it within the individual states and in some cities," says Skilling. "It is at that level—not the federal level—where you're starting to see the really creative initiatives and the ability to collaborate with one another. It's really at the level of smaller states and local economies that you're seeing innovation and reform."

Skilling sees the dynamic between small and large economies as analogous to Clayton Christensen's innovator's dilemma. In his classic business book, Christensen argues that large corporations—like Kodak—did not respond to disruptive technologies like digital photography because, when they first appeared in the market, these technologies represented a trivial challenge: they just didn't seem to warrant a strategic response and might, indeed, have gone away. By the time the challenge loomed large, change was too late and too expensive. Small companies, like Method Home Care products, can challenge big incumbents like Procter & Gamble because being adroit and creative is how they make their mark in the world.[12] Pursuing this analogy, small countries have to be clever and think ahead because they don't have the comfort or economic cushion afforded by scale. An example of such foresight is Norway, which, despite sitting on vast oil reserves, produces 99 percent of its energy from hydropower—not, obviously, because it has to, but because small countries learn to look ahead, knowing that sheer size or market heft will not protect them.[13]

"Small countries have developed a keen understanding of best practice and rapid learning. They're always looking, searching for new ideas, and bringing them in whenever they can. Singapore—it's a small country on steroids, constantly on the lookout for innovation in education, in health care, in technology. It's easier to introduce on a small scale, of course. But the benefit of being small is that you *have* to be more engaged with the world outside of your own."

You can see this, Skilling says, when you look at the number of people carrying passports or speaking other languages. And engagement with the world as a whole shows up nowhere more starkly than in exports.

"The US exports just over 15 percent," says Skilling. "But the average for a small country is 55 percent. The UK does reasonably well, but it's still in the 20 percent range, well short of Norway or Denmark. So these countries are—and know they are—highly dependent on how they relate to all the economies around them. The world cannot be binary for them. So it works two ways: they are more exposed to the pressures around them, and they know they have to develop the capacity internally to be excellent collabora-tors. That dominance isn't an option is what makes them nimble."

But for the United States, dominance has been an option and, for the last one hundred years, its recognized position in the world. No one wants to be the politician or statesman who stands up and points out the obvious: that falling down the economic league tables could be seen as a matter of historical or geographical inevitability that does not, in real terms, mean very much at all. Much of recent American geopolitics can be explained as nothing more than an existential crisis in which the United States slowly and painfully adjusts to a new role within a family of nations, developing and learning the skills and language needed for a new orientation to the world. What stands in the way of that is a cultural belief that acting inter-dependently, adjusting to the needs and beliefs of others, is fundamentally weak, that such behavior is lacking in America's signature independence.[14] Interdependence, being a great partner, developing the nuance, insight, and stamina required for creative global partnerships—this will be a hard role for America to adopt, not just because it represents a tectonic change, but because it is, simply, hard to do well. We've seen that some people view col-laboration as hard, only to discover in fact how difficult it is. If that's true within or across companies, it's nothing as compared to countries.

"The Human Genome Project had to be international for all kinds of rea-sons," John Sulston tells me. "Everyone wanted to contribute; that was a good reason. Everyone knew that a big public project was the best way to overcome intellectual property rights issues. That was a good reason. And some people wanted to make sure America didn't sweep the board with the whole thing. That was a less good reason. But whatever your reason, no one thought for one moment that this would be easy. But neither did anyone see just how tough it proved to be."

Sulston is invariably described as self-effacing and gentlemanly, as some-one who is keen not to step on toes. He's respected for his part in sequencing the genome of the worm, *C. elegans*, for which he was awarded the Nobel Prize. But what he's most famous for is the role he played in the Human Genome Project.

"He is the archetypal ethical, selfless scientist," according to Linda Par-tridge. "What he did with the project was quite altruistic insofar as it was extremely hard, terribly labor-intensive, and, for a scientist, somewhat unre-warding in the sense that the *science* wasn't the problem! The problem was getting everyone to work together."

A genial, shaggy man, accessible in his language and broad in his inter-ests and friendships, Sulston comes across as someone rather amazed and delighted to have been able to make a living doing what he loves. He had no great life plan, no conscious ambition, just endless curiosity about what could be discovered. In his autobiography, Sulston makes it clear that he'd never really imagined a life as an institutional manager or politician; the job fell on his shoulders, since the publicly funded project to sequence the human genome needed a home, a leader, and a fund-raiser. Sulston, it turned out, was gifted in all of these areas. He had a talent for making people want to produce excellent work; he was also quite (although not infinitely) patient, thoughtful, and difficult to provoke.

The Human Genome Project had begun in 1990 as a collaboration between American scientists funded by the National Institutes of Health and an international consortium led by Sulston and funded by the Medi-cal Research Council and Wellcome Foundation, the world's largest medical charity. The overarching goal was to map the whole of the human genome, but most scientists preferred to do this as a loose collaboration, with groups around the world contributing their data, rather than as a "big science" project masterminded by a single individual. Although personalities often clashed and conflicts over methodology were rife, the members of the inter-national group were united in their conviction that all of the data had to be published and shared as fast as it was produced. Their commitment to open data generated the trust required to collaborate. This sometimes made the project look chaotic or slow, but it also provided scale and diversity.

In 1994 Sulston received from his collaborator Bob Waterston an email with the subject heading "An Indecent Proposal": in effect, Waterston was proposing a concerted push to complete the entire genome by 2001. The plan was stunningly ambitious, not least because it included sequencing everything—including so-called "junk DNA," because Sulston believed (correctly) that it would turn out to be important. As audacious as the intel-lectual goal was the project's price tag: some $3 billion. Since no one orga-nization or even nation would foot the bill, the project could only survive if funded internationally. When Sulston succeeded at bringing massive UK funding to the table, the United States felt compelled to join in.

All of that was thrown into jeopardy in 1998 when a fellow scientist,

Craig Venter, announced that his commercially funded venture (eventually named Celera) could and would sequence the human genome better, faster, and with no cost to the public. Venter's methodology wasn't as thorough as that proposed by the Human Genome Project, but, he argued, it would be good enough. The stage was set for a competition the likes of which the media adored. The public project was portrayed as old, stodgy, academic, and impractical; Celera was positioned as the youthful, brash, ruthless, and practical upstart. National stereotypes sharpened the contrast: the public project featured British scientists (code for "old-fashioned"), while the American initiative was all about crass moneymaking. That all of this took place in the white heat of the Internet boom only fueled the drama. A historic moment in which breakthrough technologies were producing millionaires overnight focused all eyes on a wildly rising stock market that made heroes of the young men breaking conventions and making corpses of the institutional figures who stood in their way. In that context, Sulston played a fuddy-duddy Goliath to Venter's pugnacious David.

Although everyone followed the money with avid interest, what was at stake was more important and long-lasting. Venter attracted investors who hoped to be able to patent thousands of genes and create a business of renting out the data about them to researchers and drug developers. The idea was that Celera would become somewhat akin to Microsoft: an operating system for gene research, without which no research group could function. Sulston feared and fought this. He believed that genes are inherently not patentable, being a discovery and not an invention, and that charging for access to genetic information would both slow down subsequent research and make it all more costly. Moreover, if different companies "owned" different genes, research would become balkanized, making it more difficult to combine knowledge, insight, and research. The law offered little clarity because the field was simply too new. So the heated contest, between the public and the private projects, represented far more than the personalities or the culture clash relished by the media. At stake was not just whether a vast knowledge base would be privately owned or publicly shared—that was important enough—but whether a large, diffuse international collaboration could prove more effective than a single dominant (even domineering) player.

"There's only one human genome, one basic human reference genome," Sulston reflects. "Why compete over it? It's crazy! You want to pool resources, and it's not just a matter of getting the job done. It is very difficult to organize a consortium—we all know that. The point is scientifically and psychologically and in terms of ownership, it's much, much better to bring everybody into the same tent and to share the data. It was positioned as a race, but there's only one thing that matters—and that is the issue of data release."

Passions around sharing data ran explosively high. At one point, James Watson, the man most closely associated with DNA and the emerging field of genomics, compared the struggle to the Second World War. Venter's attempt to take over genome sequencing was analogous to Hitler's seizure of Poland, and the scientific community badly wanted a Churchill, not a Chamberlain.

"As I saw it," Watson said, "Craig [Venter] wanted to own the human genome the way Hitler wanted to own the world. And that was unacceptable for any person."[15]

In the contest between the global project and the American project, agreement was finally reached whereby Celera would agree to share its data, but only after a one-month delay; the public project, meanwhile, would continue to release its data daily and to everyone—including Celera. By combining the public data with its own, Celera would have everything—but the company refused to reciprocate. Anyone wanting access to its full data set would have to pay for it and would be forbidden from redistributing it. Either way, eventually all of the information would enter the public domain, but Celera could charge for access to its data because of its proprietary analysis and formatting. Moreover, that one-month delay gave the company crucial time to secure its intellectual property. Celera—whose tagline was "Speed matters. Discovery can't wait"—quickly perfected its ability to read a gene sequence in the morning and have the patent application in a lawyer's office by the afternoon.

Because his method was quicker and less granular than the consortium's, in effect Venter was externalizing much of the detail; that was how he was going to win. But rather than emulating his land grab, Sulston recognized that his best hope of reinforcing and protecting the public ownership of the information was to involve as many groups in generating and funding it as possible. The international consortium offered the advantage both of increased funding and broader ownership, and labs across the United States, the United Kingdom, France, Germany, and Japan did not want to be left out. But of course, that also made the Human Genome Project a bear to manage, with scientists, governments, lawyers, and politicians around the world piling onto what was rapidly becoming a gold rush. If the public research wasn't well managed, duplication and waste would be extreme—and Venter's claim that public projects were bloated, wasteful, and duplicative would be validated.

"Of course it was harder that the project was an international collaboration. Of course it was. But it had to be. It was too big to be owned by anyone, by a company or a country. And the spirit of the project had to be about sharing—the genome that we all share. It isn't yours or mine; it's ours."

Rhetoric around the two initiatives presented them as a race: which project would be first to complete its map of the human genome? Privately, Sulston felt that the contest was ridiculous—after all, the human genome wasn't going anywhere, and new technologies kept accelerating and simplifying the task. But he devoted the next six years of his life to shepherding the public project through to completion and—most important of all—publication. Through this period, what's remarkable is the amount of time that this eminent scientist—and many of his peers around the world—devoted not to the science but to media management. Press releases were as carefully drafted and reviewed as scientific papers. Public appearances had to be carefully stage-managed and rehearsed. That Venter turned out to have a great knack for publicity exacerbated the rivalry. Journalists loved the fact that Celera's headquarters were full of foosball tables, Nerf guns, and plastic Viking helmets. Wagner's "Ride of the Valkyries" blasting out of loudspeakers reinforced his image as the heroic soloist, single-handedly taking on both the scientific establishment and the human genome and wrestling both to the ground. When a *New Yorker* profile opened with the words "Craig Venter is an asshole," his fame was assured.[16]

Academic attempts at such color could not hope to capture the same kind of breathless attention. The Human Genome Project wasn't one superman but thousands of scientists, technicians, software engineers, and administrators performing precise, often dull, repetitive tasks, day after day. It didn't have a heroic leader but multiple advisers, evangelists, and silent partners. As Sulston shuttled between England and America, clearing up misunderstandings, keeping everyone aligned, committed, and focused, he found, much to his astonishment, that he had entered the world of politics.

"I was interviewed on the *Today* program on BBC Radio and pointed out that our problem was that Celera not only collected their own data but would hoover up all of ours—which of course was publicly available—call it their own, and charge others for using it. 'It's a sort of con-job, if that's not too rude a word,' I added. From its place deep inside the interview, *BBC Online* pulled out the word 'con-job' and flashed it around the world, to be seized on by journalists. And what did people say? Some approved. But many accused me of mud-slinging, jealousy, protecting my turf. I had been heard, but the world by and large divided along party lines."[17]

The party lines broke down, roughly, between an absolute belief in private, competitive commerce, as represented by Venter, and a belief in the public, international cooperation represented by Sulston, Watson, and the National Institutes of Health. Every prejudice against government involvement sprang to the surface; every fear of corporate dominance flowered there too.

Although Venter proved the superior showman, his life at Celera was not plain sailing. The company's aims competed with themselves. Investors and executives pursued a higher stock price and an expensive bioinformatics product, while the scientists concentrated on doing the same difficult work as their academic peers, but with less time, more pressure, and more showbiz. Caught in the cross fire between the scientific and the commercial missions, Venter's antagonistic relationship with the company's management left him abrasive, pugnacious, and often paranoid. His research team showed immense personal loyalty, but on some days, work ground to a halt when researchers watched in stunned silence as their net worth reached millions of dollars. And Venter felt his outsider status keenly; while he used this to whip up popular support, the personal animus he and the media drummed up made any meaningful collaboration impossible.

That it also put more pressure on the Human Genome Project was part of Venter's intent, but Sulston persevered. Together with his counterpart Francis Collins at the National Institutes of Health, he kept the project funded and shielded while scientists around the world just kept their nerve, working on academic salaries. (Sulston once said he saw no reason why scientists should be paid more than janitors.) But the politics of the contest were becoming disruptive.

"The negative side," Sulston tells me, "was that we started going for the wrong goal. We had to do a very stagey announcement, with [Prime Minister Tony] Blair and [President Bill] Clinton saying what a great thing it was—like going to the moon, terribly over-the-top, blah de blah—when it wasn't even finished at that point! But the reason for doing it was to make sure there was some kind of peaceful accord in the US. It was an election year for Clinton—and we wanted to ensure that we got some kind of publicity out to secure the intellectual property. But it was a slightly fake goal and quite a phenomenal waste of time."

Despite the ambient noise, Sulston and Collins fought the political fires together and work progressed at ever-increasing speed as the technology for gene sequencing kept improving. But had anyone ever asked who was running the public project, it might have been hard to provide an answer. Venter openly sniped at the Human Genome Project, calling it "the Liar's Club" and claiming that "it's just a bunch of disorganized academics and we [Celera] are the organized company." But the collaborators themselves thought differently. "Had any one party been able to dictate how the project was done," one commented, "I think it would have failed."[18]

In the end, Celera never made a business model out of charging subscriptions to its data, and Venter was eventually fired by management, who'd found him unworkably antagonistic. One year after the famous press conference, the public project published all of its data in *Nature* and Celera was compelled to publish its data in *Science.* The mapping of the human genome was complete. Venter had made millions and went on to run well-funded biotech businesses, and Celera (which is now part of Quest Diagnostics) still owns the patents on 6,500 genes. Sulston didn't make any money, but was at last able to retire from his role as super-collaborator. In 2004, along with Sydney Brenner and Bob Horvitz, when he was awarded the Nobel Prize, many of his colleagues muttered that he might equally have been a strong candidate for the Nobel Peace Prize.

Ten years on, I asked him whether competition had made the science any better. "I don't think so. Competition didn't make it any faster or any cheaper. And you can't make it better because, well, it is what it is. What is worrying is that we do now have a situation where several thousand genes have already been patented. Myriad, for example, is a company which has patented BRCA 1 and 2, which are small genes for breast cancer. They're very important in testing for family risks. If you want to be tested for this, you have to go to Myriad, which charges $3,000. That puts up the cost of health care. Many countries outside the US simply refuse to have anything to do with it. This is exactly why we wanted the project to be international and the data to be free. It does not seem in any way right that a country—any country—can own a patent on something which anyone, anywhere, might carry in their body."

In 2009 the American Civil Liberties Union took Myriad to court over the extreme level of patent protection it claimed. Four years and as many court cases later, the US Supreme Court ruled that the patents were invalid. But about 20 percent of human genes are now patented, and all that we know is that, as long as those patents are upheld, research will be more expensive and cumbersome and the promise of genetic medicine will be slowed. Had the Human Genome Project continued unchallenged, the problem would never have arisen.

"What we had originally wanted," Sulston explains, "was to hold all of the human genome inside a public database that could be added to and annotated all the time, enriched by knowledge that researchers everywhere were uncovering—just like Wikipedia. But once genes were patented, then—well, the whole area of whether you even can, or should, patent a gene still remains unclear. This makes multi-genic testing very difficult, a real roadblock. And it will make future collaborations a great deal more difficult. If you can't share the data, you can't build trust; the work suffers and the research suffers."

The Human Genome Project showed what could be achieved through international collaborations—but it also vividly demonstrated how hard it is, and how much talent it takes, to make them work. The ongoing legal wrangles continue to reflect what happens when coordination gives way to competition. Where there might have been an open, steadily improving, and refined knowledge base, there is now an infinite progression of contracts, negotiations, and lawsuits.

Everyone who has worked with Sulston—and thousands of scientists have, one way or another—talk about his fairness, patience, and ability to keep in mind a broad cross-section of interests: personal, political, national, scientific. More eager to tell me about the achievements of his grandchildren than about his Nobel Prize, he seems to epitomize many of the values that John Abele observed in great collaborators: humility, patience, curiosity. Perhaps that explains why he was asked and agreed to lead a more recent project commissioned by the Royal Society: People and the Planet.

"The idea was to look at how we are all going to live on this planet that gains a billion more people every twelve years. How do we work together, share resources? My perception is that in my lifetime, and especially over the last ten years, people have become more and more competitive. The recession has made that worse—but that was a result of competition too. All our governments do is tell us that we have to compete for growth, but this is becoming ridiculous; we can't all grow faster and faster. There are resource limits. So the idea of the Royal Society report was to think about this destructive competition and how we might find a way to adjust."

By now, you might have thought that Sulston has had his fill of destructive competition. But his experience with the Human Genome Project heightened his sense of how profoundly the world needs to find better ways to collaborate in order to tackle the problems and threats that grow by the day. Characteristically, he drew together a wide array of disciplines—scientists, economists, sociologists, demographers, theologians, and other thinkers—from all over the world: China, India, Egypt, Brazil, Ethiopia, Cameroon, Malawi, the United Kingdom, and the United States. The report they produced is detailed and thoughtful, the product of many minds, but Sulston's experience, living through fifteen years of full-throttle naked competition, hovers over the work.[19]

Consumption in the developed world, the report argues, has to be reduced. The extravagance and exhibitionism of pecking-order anxiety incurs too great a cost to be trivialized or ignored. Obesity, the by-product of overconsumption, now represents a significant mortality risk. Gross inequalities—in education and in health care—represent a waste of human potential and talent. Trickle-down doesn't deliver. Most of the health care issues discussed by the report are susceptible to low-tech solutions and medications—but these are the kinds of challenges that competitive businesses currently dodge. Environmental degradation of the kind perpetrated by externalizing pollution will only become increasingly expensive and difficult to repair. Whatever the carrying capacity of the planet turns out to be, we know that it is limited, and this challenges all of us, and our institutions, to devise constructive ways to share its wealth. Competition isn't solving these problems; if anything, it is making them worse faster.

One way or another, the critical issues raised in the Royal Society's report concern resource allocation: how to share what we have and how to handle the externalities that we generate. The report is fairly gloomy about our chances of resolving them, seeing each one as exemplifying "the tragedy of the commons." That parable, first described by ecologist Garrett Hardin, refers to what happens on common land: given the freedom to graze their sheep there, shepherds eventually let them graze the green to destruction. Confronted with a global tragedy of the commons, Sulston's report argues passionately for statesmen, legislators, and populations to think beyond competitive interests. "So long as an excess of competition between nations continues," the report concludes, "the future of humanity is in doubt."

When Hardin published his paper "The Tragedy of the Commons" in 1968, it was immediately controversial for his conclusion that there was no technical solution to the problem of resource allocation.[20] The only way forward was what Hardin called "a fundamental extension of morality," and this enraged people, in part because it seemed implausible and also because so philosophical a position seemed out of place in the pristinely objective pages of *Science*. For the most part, however, the tragedy of the commons came to be accepted as inevitable.

Two landmark concepts taken together, game theory and the tragedy of the commons, have illustrated in abstract the destructiveness of competitive self-interest. Whenever individuals compete by placing their individual interests above the common good, they prove collectively destructive. Believing that to be the case encourages people to imagine that their only choice—and chance—is to get there first, or with more force—or both. In a dog-eat-dog world, they can be bigger, better, faster, cheaper—or they can cheat. That, fundamentally, has been the sermon read out to all of us from free-market pulpits around the world for the last fifty years.

But an economist came along who insisted on arguing not from theory but from observation. Elinor Ostrom wondered whether Hardin's tragedies, where they existed in real life, really were inevitable or whether they could be averted. Could she find examples where the tragedy had been circumvented—and if so, how was that done? Even today it remains surprisingly uncommon for economists to adopt an empirical approach, but that is what she did.

At an early age, nobody would have selected Elinor Ostrom as a winner. Coming from a poor family in Los Angeles, she'd been steered away from studying mathematics because she was a girl and neither of her parents had attended university. Further dissuaded from studying political science because she stood no chance of getting a good university position, she found that, as a graduate, the only jobs she was offered were secretarial. And when she was finally offered a university post, it required teaching a class at 7:30 AM (the kind of assignment no one wanted). But she took on the challenge and never looked back.

Ostrom was the least owl-like of researchers. She and her husband Vincent worked, not in the grand palaces of Harvard or Oxford, but at Indiana University. An exceptional collaborator, she saw the competition between public and private, state and market, politics and economics, as an impoverished debate, unhelpfully polarized and contentious.[21] Ideologues liked to dismiss arguments about the commons as archaic; surely now all property was private. But Ostrom drew attention to intricate areas of cooperation in all our lives—whether in the management of condominiums, the Internet, school boards, or businesses.

One of her earliest studies boldly questioned the belief that big organizations, with their hierarchies and economies of scale, deliver services that are better because they are cheaper. She compared two different forms of policing in and around Indianapolis: one operated with a big, centralized organization, and the other was run with small, autonomous units. What she found both surprised her and laid the groundwork for her future work. The police forces of twenty-five to fifty officers proved more effective in every way than metropolitan teams of one hundred or more. Citizens were more likely to interact with the smaller teams, to report crimes, and to meet citizen demands for protection. Big wasn't better, and hierarchies didn't help.

A cheerful but rigorous iconoclast, Ostrom delighted in smashing silos, creating workshops and organizations where different disciplines could collaborate—to study collaboration. One of the many examples she analyzed was the provision of sanitation to poor communities in Brazil. A decade of large-scale public projects had failed, with the result that the absolute number of city-dwellers without adequate sanitation had risen by 70 million; putting large projects out to private contractors had created opportunities for bribery and corruption and left just 37 percent of Brazilian urban populations with access to sewerage services.

Rejecting the brutal simplification of market economics, Ostrom analyzed a Brazilian reform plan for sanitation that started with block meetings at which inhabitants had to be involved: if half of the households on the block didn't attend, the meeting was called off.[22] Residents decided on the layout they wanted, knowing their decisions would affect the cost of the system and the charges they would end up paying. Before construction started, residents had to sign a formal petition requesting the system that they themselves had chosen and committing themselves to the payment of fees. The process wasn't quick—it sometimes took four to six months to get the necessary agreement—but once a new sewerage system for a block was complete, other blocks learned from that block's experience and the process picked up momentum. Critically, the planners learned that they couldn't restrict the process to only the issues they thought belonged on the agenda. The residents knew their needs better than anyone, and the give-and-take in negotiations improved the design of the schemes.

Once designed, the water and sewerage systems weren't built by large multinational contractors with political connections to national leaders but no long-term commitment to the community. Instead, construction was undertaken by medium-sized local contractors who built better-performing systems because they cared about their reputation for high-quality work and were bound to encounter the users of their work in the future.

At every stage, Ostrom observed, the process encountered difficulties. Some neighborhood groups were more cooperative than others, and monitoring the performance of contractors wasn't always easy. But the process dramatically increased the availability of lower-cost services to the poorest neighborhoods in Brazilian cities—and was subsequently emulated in Kenya, Paraguay, and Indonesia. Critical to this success was the contribution of citizens who honored their promises and the good communication and collaboration between citizens and local government agencies. Knowledge-sharing, reciprocity, shared standards, and autonomy not only required but also developed large amounts of social capital.

Similarly, Ostrom's study of irrigation systems in Nepal found that those built and governed by farmers themselves were in better repair, delivered more water, and had higher agricultural productivity than the modern, commercial permanent systems funded by donors and constructed by professional engineering firms.[23] On many such projects, farmers face the perverse incentives to overconsume and undercontribute. But where they have been instrumental in designing both the systems and the sanctions, the rewards, incentives, motivations, and understanding have all been aligned.

Ostrom's work proved to her that what works best is collaborative pluralism: lots of different solutions, applied and devised locally by those with an immediate and personal investment. Left to their own devices, individuals can create solutions together that are superior to those imposed by external authorities or managing agents. Studying community projects as far apart as policing in Indianapolis, irrigation systems in Spain, mountain villages in Switzerland and Japan, fisheries in Maine and Indonesia, and condominiums in the United States, she found that individuals can and already do collaborate effectively in the management of shared, limited resources—and do so without tragic consequences. The commons, she argued, need not be a tragedy: the commons poses an opportunity.

Ostrom called this opportunity "polycentrism," by which she meant that the hard problem of managing limited resources creatively was best organized from the ground up in ways that fitted with, and articulated, social norms. As it turns out, communities are very good at organizing themselves, but design principles apply. Discussion must be face to face because it depends on and deepens trust. Smaller units work better than large ones. The solution to the vast ecological and environmental problems we face could be solved, not by a single, overarching agreement, but by thousands of individual initiatives at the city, regional, national, and international levels. Operating across multiple levels is both more sustainable and more robust. "Such an evolutionary approach to policy," Ostrom noted, "provides essential safety nets should one or more policies fail."[24] At all levels, collaboration is key, but even the finest collaborations fall apart if some individuals come to dominate the group or if participants start to form elites. The community must be self-monitoring, and it must design its own sanctions. Conflict is bound to occur—after all, Ostrom was describing real life, not theory—but low-cost conflict resolution mechanisms can resolve them.[25]

Ostrom's outline of the principles she discerned in effective collaborations around the world could describe many of the organizations discussed in this book. The emphasis on personal relationships and self-management, the absolute requirement of trust, the sharing of resources and denial of dominance—these principles lie at the heart of all successful collaboration. Collaborative efforts that run on these principles succeed not because they pursue a competitive agenda but because they define and develop fundamentally social goals. They refuse to choose between business serving society *or* society serving business; instead, they insist on keeping the two goals aligned. There can be no successful business that is antisocial; there is no successful society where work can't get done.

Most of all, Ostrom insisted that there are no simple answers. Following the example of the successful social projects she studied, she created workshops and institutes in which researchers from a range of different disciplines could share their knowledge in the search for common solutions. "No panaceas" was her mantra. Perhaps that's one reason why, after celebrating the fact that she was the first woman ever to win the Nobel Prize for Economics, so little public attention was paid to her work. She kept insisting that collaboration is hard—but that it solves problems better than any other kind of resolution. She was adamant that trust lies at the heart of all effective work—meaning that we all need to avoid competing with one another. She kept insisting that, working together, groups achieve optimal outcomes—with no winners or losers. She saw that we thrive when we acknowledge our mutual dependency—but that we all have to pull our weight and not try to buy our way out of social relationships.

In 2011, Elinor Ostrom was asked whether, given the vast problems the world faced, she was still optimistic.

"If we keep to our current theories, no," she replied. "If we can slowly but surely change the way we think about these problems, there are ways of doing much better multilevel thinking and understanding the diversity and the complexity and not rejecting it. So I think there's a good chance. But if we stay with our current narrow ways of thinking about the world, no, I'm very discouraged."[26]

On the day she died in 2012, Elinor Ostrom published her last article. In "Green from the Grassroots," she reiterated her faith in collaborative projects, but insisted that "everyone must have a stake in establishing them: countries, states, cities, organizations, companies, and people everywhere. Success will hinge on developing many overlapping policies to achieve the goals." And as a lifelong student of resource allocation, she left with one final observation.

"Time is the natural resource in shortest supply."

CHAPTER 11

A Bigger Prize

An era can be said to end when its basic illusions are exhausted.
—Arthur Miller

Following the events of September 11, 2001, Kenneth Feinberg was appointed special master of the Victim Compensation Fund. The statute establishing the fund was unlike anything enacted before, providing tax-free compensation to the families of those who had been killed and to those who had been injured on 9/11. Implicit in the fund were two aims. The nation as a whole, and the government as its voice, wished to help, console, and support the victims of the attack. More pragmatic, however, was the recognition that without federal compensation, the airlines would be bankrupted by the ensuing lawsuits. The prospect of courtrooms filled for years with bereaved families and maimed victims reliving their trauma was financially, politically, and culturally unacceptable. In these circumstances, the head-to-head contest of the courts was too grotesque for anyone to contemplate. Mediation was the only remedy that would both respect the individuals' lives and preserve a nation's transportation system. So urgent was the demand to address these issues with sensitivity and decorum that no cap was put on the amount of money Feinberg could give to the victims' families.[1]

It's telling that, under extreme pressure, no one believed that competition would work. The sorrow and pity of the events of that day remained so vivid that public contests over the value of life felt obscene. Knowing that the rich, with ample resources, were bound to fare better than those with none threatened to exacerbate the tragedy. That mediation was embraced as a better process was the culmination of several decades during which the gladiatorial showdowns of the legal system had come increasingly to look like slow, expensive, and inhumane mockeries of justice. For years, Feinberg had championed mediation as an effective, fast, and human alternative to epic courtroom pugilism. In his resolution of cases involving Vietnam War veterans and Agent Orange, asbestos, fraud, and a wide range of industrial accidents, he had demonstrated how much faster and more humane mediation could be. His appointment to lead the Victim Compensation Fund paid tribute to his achievement in positioning mediation as a true alternative to legal contests.

Mediators start by building relationships of trust. They have to be patient and leave their ego behind. Mediation isn't an absence of conflict; it's a creative approach to resolving it. So mediators have to come up with ideas that other people can take and own. Social connections and interdependence both enable and require this. Mediators deliberately do not frame conflict as a tournament in which there can be a winner and a loser, because then the quality of the exchange would get hollowed out. Communication would become positioning, and dialogue would turn into point-scoring. No one would listen—and it is only when people listen that they learn and change.

What happens when the talents of mediation are abandoned in favor of tournaments is all too easy to see in what is so appropriately labeled the political "arena." That we confront hard problems without skilled means of solving them is one of the higher prices we have paid for our long love affair with competition. That our political standoffs—sequesters, shutdowns, and filibusters—are embarrassing public rituals is bad enough; that they stymie creative thinking about critical problems is the bigger cost. Our politics is stalled because our problems are complex and our means of addressing them are crude and rigid. In the looming face-off between business, government, and society, a competitive mind-set can frame the contest, but doing so destroys all the mental maps that might lead us to a solution. The problem is a failure not of imagination but of courage: the willingness to relinquish fantasies of winning in exchange for the bigger prize of joint achievement and true progress.

Competition has proved so disappointing in part because it seems so promising: its simple, clean narrative beguiles us into imagining that life really can be so neat. And because, under some conditions, it is effective, it's tempting to imagine it works for everything. Speaking in 1912, Franklin Roosevelt argued that "competition has been shown to be useful up to a certain point and no further." It is a great way to focus on short-term problems and to enliven monotonous repetitive work. In small doses, competition adds spice to what might otherwise be mundane and dreary. And when the stakes are low, it can be an inspiring way to get things started, to galvanize participation, and to spark the imagination.

But when the stakes are high, and competition becomes the dominant driver, it backfires spectacularly, undermining exactly what it hopes to build. Competitive thinking, constrained by benchmarks, scorecards, and comparisons, cannot wander and explore new territory but stays fettered to old ideas and models. Cheating, corruption, subversion, silence, disenchantment, and the unwinding of the social fabric are not perverse but inevitable outcomes when societies are captive to the competitive mind-set and the ephemeral pleasures of winning.

But competition isn't the only source of our inspiration. Children given support and encouragement learn from, respect, and enjoy their siblings' differences. Teachers can inspire and develop a love of learning that doesn't die on graduation but adapts and grows as the world changes. Friends and couples find in each other an understanding of one another and of themselves that enriches, connects, and renews social bonds. Games and sports can teach fairness, integrity, stamina, self-discipline, and community when they're played for fun. These are bigger prizes, available to everyone for a lifetime, but only if, and when, we dare to relinquish our dependency on contests. "Cooperation," Roosevelt continued, "which is the thing we must strive for today, begins where competition leaves off."

Innovative institutions and organizations thrive not because they pick and breed superstars but because they cherish, nurture, and support the vast range of talents, personalities, and skills that sustained creativity requires. Collaboration is a habit of mind, solidified by routine and predicated on openness, generosity, rigor, and patience. It requires precise and fearless communication, without status, awe, or intimidation. It is hard because working together allows no passengers: everyone must bring of their best. And failure is part of the deal: mistakes, failed prototypes, dead ends, and clouds are necessary and inevitable stages in the process to be greeted with support, encouragement, and faith. The safest hospitals are those where it's easiest to acknowledge error. These are bigger prizes that grow as they're shared.

Conflict is inevitable because that's how new ideas emerge. So great collaborators do conflict well. "Scrapping," as the Wright brothers called it, is how we stretch, test, and develop new ideas and possibilities. The conflict-averse can't do this well, and those who love a fight can't either. But the mediators, listeners, and scrappers enjoy unfettered exploration, sure in the knowledge that intellectual risks and experiments are how new ideas emerge and that conflict is how organizations think. The impresarios of creativity make their breakthroughs because they support and unleash the genius and energy of the people around them. Like the pianist Fou Ts'ong, they recognize that the greatest originality comes from serving the needs and brilliance of others. These are prizes that unite the past with the future.

It's hard to create a climate of safety in times that feel so dangerous. But the failure to inculcate the habit of collaboration may be the biggest organizational, social, and political risk we face today. It's why companies hire armies of brilliant people, only to feel disappointed by what they produce; it's why citizens feel so disillusioned by politicians eager to attack but paralyzed when asked to work together. We don't lack for talent, but organizational silence and stalemates persist when the cost of honesty and sharing remains too high. Trust, not rivalry, is what makes relationships and institutions effective and efficient. Trust is both what we need and what we create when we learn to work together.

It would be wonderful to conclude this book with the perfect blueprint for collaboration, but the engineering concept of robust systems offers a cautionary tale here: single, dominant models are dangerous. Safety lies in plurality. For a collaborative mind-set to take hold, we need multiple systems—different sizes, shapes, ambitions, and goals. These systems have different forms of hierarchy, but they share salient characteristics. Extremes of power and distance are carefully, and structurally, avoided. Trust is valued more highly than secrets because giving ideas away is what makes them proliferate. Success is measured across two, three, four generations, by the impact and legacy left for children, grandchildren, and great-grandchildren. Success isn't pursued, like the Purdue chickens, by selecting superstars and seeing which is the last left standing; instead, true champions are fiercely protective of the principle that no one gets left out and that no one else pays the price of success. Just like the Finnish schools, these champions start and finish on the principle that success is only meaningful when everyone owns it. Instead of trophies for a few, collaborators seek the bigger prize.

The reason why employee ownership matters and proves so powerful is because it motivates and rewards mutual assistance and support, openness, and honesty. While every business leader says that people are a company's most precious asset, employee ownership makes this a structural reality, creating the conditions in which trust derives from mutual interest and success is shared. Cooperatives do this too, and their resilience through the economic downturn illustrates vividly that embracing our interdependence isn't weakness but strength. Brilliant innovations in technology demonstrate that we can radically reduce the costs of cooperation, making it easier to solve any problem and harming no one, if that's how we choose to define our goals.

We have science on our side. A team of scientists recently revisited game theory, challenging the original conclusion of mathematician John Nash that selfishness must always prevail. If Nash was right, why is it that cooperation prevails—in the animal kingdom, in the microbial world, and in human society? The answer turns out to be something that Nash left out of his equations: communication. Being able to talk to one another, to bring in a wide range of opinion and expertise to debate, argue, and negotiate, changes the game.

That's what super-collaborators excel at: they listen, make connections, and share. They're the interstitial people who keep family members in touch with each other, who make neighborhoods safe and functional, who make organizations smart and responsive. They have more tools with which to reach out than ever before. Some act on instinct, others because they enjoy social contact; unsung and often invisible, they make things work and drive change.

People giving each other time and respect is what makes organizations like Morning Star, Gore, Eileen Fisher, Ocean Spray, Interface, and Boston Scientific so creative. It's why Uri Alon's learning from improv, Mike North's lessons from comedy, Travis Tygart's crusade for real sport, and the classrooms of Martti Helstrom are so important. When the world has more teachers like Thiam Seng Ko or Beau Lotto, and more organizations like Gripple, Arup, TechShop, Lending Club, Mozilla, and Punchdrunk, our children will see for themselves that they can succeed without cheating, without gaming the system, and without making their friends lose.

As I was finishing this book, I was in Boston, Massachusetts, where I'd once lived and run technology companies. Just a few months before my visit, a bomb had killed three people and injured 264. Walking through familiar streets that had witnessed panic and mayhem, I thought about my friends and colleagues who had been present at the scene that day. All of their accounts had been saturated with a strange emotion. Yes, the day had been tragic and frightening, and yes, everyone had been angry and upset. But when they talked to me, that wasn't what I heard. What I heard was pride. Their stories told about what they'd done to help, who they'd put up for the night or the week, how generous everyone had been—about the kindness of strangers. It was as though, in the moment of disaster, they'd all been given permission to stop competing and to do instead what human beings are so great at: helping one another. What I heard was freedom.

Those feelings didn't last forever. But we don't need such tragedies to liberate the generosity latent in us all. The hopeful sign that I took from these stories—and they were everywhere—was the pent-up yearning all of us feel to connect, communicate, collaborate. We're just waiting for permission to live and work in ways that feel so much better than winning. That would be the biggest prize of all.

ACKNOWLEDGMENTS

Writing may appear to be the ultimate solo activity, but every author knows it is really a collaboration. I've been fortunate in the many men, women, and children who have helped me to understand how we manage our feelings of competitiveness and develop our ability to work together. Chief among these are my agent, Natasha Fairweather, and my editor, Clive Priddle, publisher and editorial director at PublicAffairs. They both had faith in this book early and throughout, offering excellent questions, challenges, and ideas that have made it richer. The additions, subtractions, and refinements offered so generously by Robert Kimzey and Cynthia Buck vividly demonstrated how we do better together.

I've been very fortunate to work again with Isobel Eaton, a gifted and imaginative researcher who seems to have a strong stomach for tough assignments, and I'm indebted to her for finding many of the remarkable people who have talked to me so honestly about their experiences of the competitive and collaborative life.

Everyone in these pages—many of them recognizable only to themselves—gave their time generously, offering insight, reflection, and openness of a kind that is a privilege to share. But many others form a deep, unseen foundation to my thinking: Philip Auger, Kate Bernhardt, Juliet Blake, Charlotte Calkin, John Carlisle, Judith Derbyshire, Jane Drabble, Paul Duggan, Tony Falbo, Clarissa Farr, Eileen Fisher, Mia Gray, Ava Griffith, Ginger Hardage, Erin Hoffman, Saj-Nicole Joni, the late Rush Kidder, Stef Kranendijk, Bernard Litaer, Donald Low, Ed Mayo, Christopher Meyer, Paul Moore, Patrick Moynihan, Bill Nemtin, Hilary Old, Daniel Oran, Frank Partnoy, Jessica Ronane, Rachel Rosenblum, and Michael Smith, all contributed to much that is in this book.

As I discovered, competitiveness or collaboration can be found everywhere, and I'm grateful to the many guides who showed me the impact of these two forces on their lives: Father Aidan Bellinger, Edmund Newell, and Dr. Anthony White on the church; Neil Tully on the world of wine; Mary King and Ferdi Alberg on competitive horse-riding; Gisela Stewart on party politics; Leonor Stjepic on competition among charities; Graham White on the law; and Jo Hawes and Jessica Ronane on child actors. Matthew Rock stopped me from speaking foolishly about cricket.

Kathy August, Clarissa Farr, Chuck Finkle, Beth Weiner, Elaine Goldberg, and Charles Fadel helped me find my way through the thickets of current education, while students from schools around the world were frank in sharing their thoughts and experiences with me. I'm also grateful to the Royal Academy of Dramatic Art and their audition candidates for letting me sit in on their very careful selection process. Nicolette Hahn Niman and Rick Dove were unstinting in showing me how the meat industry works. Simon Middlemass, Steve Phillips, Stephane Diagana, Ian Williamson, and Annie Skinner showed understanding and insight into sport that opened my eyes.

Alexandra and Caroline Paul, together with Prophecy Coles, Rosalind Edwards, Kate Gilbert, Albert Roux, Jan Seriff, and Tim and Jeff Lott, shed a great deal of light on sibling rivalry for me. My sister, Pamela Stewart, continues to show me how precious and wise a sibling can be.

As always, Albert Bandura was a great source of wisdom, support, and encouragement, and Robert Burton helped me distinguish the signal from the noise of neuroscience. Nick Bicat, Iona Bird, Dorothy Nancekievill, Lizzie Tocknell, Adam Tudhope, and John Williams were all terrific guides through the world of music. I am also indebted to Ben and Peter Stocks, who, together with David Erdal, taught me a great deal about the history and future of employee ownership. In Finland, Raila Pirinen, together with Glenn and Carita Orlando, were wonderful hosts as well as sources.

Many business organizations allowed me to explore and test some of my ideas at an early stage, in particular Footdown, the Caux Institute for Change, the Academy of Chief Executives, Tomorrow's Company, and Merryck & Co. Many companies and senior executives, working on the coalface of business, provided essential reality tests. At the University of Bath, I am fortunate in having such outstanding colleagues, especially Glynis Breakwell, Veronica Hope-Haley, Michael Mayer, Stephen Rangecroft, and Bruce Rayton. Their support of my work has proved a wonderful collaboration.

Like any researcher, I'm indebted to libraries and librarians, especially those at the University of Bath, Bristol University, and the wonderful London Library.

Crisscrossing the world was made more enjoyable thanks to warm welcomes, curiosity, and hospitality from Beth Edwards, Cindy Solomon, Cinta Burgos, Pam Esty, Witney Beals, and Rob and Fiona Wilson. Thank you for offering a warm and welcome respite from hotel rooms. I'm also indebted to Rebecca Lynn-Nicholson as well as David and Denise Nicholson for their patience and support.

For the study of competition and collaboration, there is no laboratory as intense (or uncontrolled) as my family. I would like to say that my children, Felix and Leonora Nicholson, were patient with my inquiries, but they were better than that: fierce, argumentative, at turns furious, hilarious, and chastening. I continue to learn a lot from them, and I hope that they feel they've learned something from me.

If at times during the darker moments of this book I began to lose faith in human generosity, I needed to look no further than my husband Lindsay for inspiration. His willingness to engage in exploration, debate, doubt, and challenge was inexhaustible, punctilious, and illuminating—proof, if it were needed, that altruism is not always self-interested.

Boston and Farrington Gurney
2013

NOTES

Chapter 1: Oh, Brother!

1 See Childhood Poverty Research and Policy Centre (CHIP), "Knowledge for Tackling Childhood Poverty," available at: www.childhoodpoverty.org/.

2 Sybil Hart and Heather Carrington, "Jealousy in Six-Month-Old Infants," *Infancy* 3, no. 3 (2012).

3 David Finkelhor, Heather Turner, and Richard Ormrod, "Kid's Stuff: The Nature and Impact of Peer and Sibling Violence on Younger and Older Children," *Journal of Child Abuse and Neglect* 30, no. 12 (2006): 1401–1421.

4 Vernon R. Wiehe, "Sibling Abuse," in *Domestic Violence and Child Abuse Source Book,* ed. Helene Henderson (Detroit: Omnigraphics, 2000), 409–492.

5 National Crime Prevention Council, *Helping Kids Handle Conflict: A Guide for Students Ages 5–12 on How to Handle Conflict* (Arlington, VA: National Crime Prevention Council, 1995).

6 Richard M. Ryckman, Cary R. Libby, Bart van den Borne, Joel A. Gold, and Marc A. Lindner, "Values of Hypercompetitive and Personal Development Competitive Individuals," *Journal of Personality Assessment* 69, no. 2 (1997): 271–283.

7 Mark N. Bing, "Hypercompetitiveness in Academia: Achieving Criterion-Related Validity from Item Context Specificity," *Journal of Personality Assessment* 73, no. 1 (1999): 80.

8 Allan Mazur and Alan Booth, "Testosterone and Dominance in Men," *Behavioral and Brain Sciences* 21 (1998): 353–397.

9 Paul van Honk, Dennis J. Schutter, Peter A. Bos, Anne-Wil Kruijt, Eef G. Lentjes, and Simon Baron-Cohen, "Testosterone Administration Impairs Cognitive Empathy in Women Depending on Second-to-Fourth Digit Ratio," *Proceedings of the National Acdemy of Sciences of the United States of America* 8, no. 8 (2011): 3448–3452.

10 Baris O. Yildirim and Jan J. L. Derksen, "A Review on the Relationship Between Testosterone and the Interpersonal/Affective Facet of Psychopathy," *Psychiatry Research* 197, no. 3 (2012): 181–198.

11 Nicholas D. Wright, Bahador Bahrami, Emily Johnson, Gina di Malta, Geraint

Rees, Christopher D. Frith, and Raymond J. Dolan, "Testosterone Disrupts Human Collaboration by Increasing Egocentric Choices," *Proceedings of the Royal Society B: Biological Sciences* 279, no. 1736 (2011): 2275–2280.

12 Baris O. Yildirim and Jan J. L. Derksen, "A Review on the Relationship Between Testosterone and Life-Course Persistent Antisocial Behavior," *Psychiatry Research* 200, no. 2 (2012): 984–1010.

13 Colin Blakemore and Richard C. Van Sluyters, "Innate and Environmental Factors in the Development of the Kitten's Visual Cortex," *Journal of Physiology* 248 (1974): 663–716.

14 Author interview, see: www.youtube.com/watch?v=aybKnSZ26Sw&-feature=related, and Allan N. Schore, "Effects of a Secure Attachment Relationship on Right Brain Development, Affect Regulation and Infant Mental Health," *Infant Mental Health Journal* 22 (1–2) (2001): 7–66.

15 Josef Perner, Ted Ruffman, and Susan R. Leekam, "Theory of Mind Is Contagious: You Catch It from Your Sibs," *Child Development* 65, no. 4 (1994): 1228–1238.

16 Judy Smith and Hildy Ross, "Training Parents to Mediate Sibling Disputes Affects Children's Negotiation and Conflict Understanding," *Child Development* 78, no. 3 (2007): 790–805.

17 Frances Fuchs Schachter, Ellen Shore, Susan Feldman-Rotman, Ruth E. Marquis, and Susan Campbell, "Sibling Deidentification," *Developmental Psychology* 12, no. 5 (1976): 418–427.

18 Frank J. Sulloway, *Born to Rebel: Birth Order, Family Dynamics, and Creative Lives* (New York: Little, Brown, 1996), 594. See also Darwin's *On the Origin of Species,* in which he explores one of the keystones of his theory, the principle of divergence, which causes "differences, at first barely appreciable, steadily to increase, and the breeds to diverge in character both from each other and from their common parent.... The truth of the principle, that the greatest amount of life can be supported by great diversification of structure, is seen under many natural circumstances." Charles Darwin, *On the Origin of Species* (London: John Murray, 1859), 104.

19 Sulloway, *Born to Rebel,* 21.

20 Benedict Carey, "Research Finds Firstborns Gain the Higher IQ," *New York Times,* June 22, 2007; see also Petter Kristensen and Tor Bjerkedal, "Explaining the Relation Between Birth Order and Intelligence," *Science* 316, no. 5832 (June 22, 2007): 1717.

21 It's important to acknowledge that, as in most scientific studies, general conclusions on vast topics like birth order may be meaningful about groups but meaningless when applied to individuals. Moreover, all studies of siblings suffer from small group size and (except in a few rare cases) periods of study that are short compared to the span of a human life.

22 Ralph Hertwig, Jennifer Nerissa Davis, and Frank J. Sulloway, "Parental Investment: How an Equity Motive Can Produce Inequality," *Psychological Bulletin* 128, no. 5 (2002): 728–745.

23 Ibid., 736

24 Frank J. Sulloway and Richard L. Zweigenhaft, "Birth Order and Risk Taking

in Athletics: A Meta-analysis and Study of Major League Baseball," *Personality and Social Psychology Review* 14, no. 4 (2010): 402–416.

25 Sulloway, *Born to Rebel*, 95-96, and Frank J. Sulloway, "Birth Order, Sibling Competition, and Human Behavior," from Harmon R. Holcomb, ed., *Conceptual Challenges in Evolutionary Psychology: Innovative Research Strategies* (Dordrecht and Boston: Kluwer Academic Publishers, 2001), 39–83. It's important to point out that many don't accept these birth-order hypotheses. It isn't at all clear whether the source of the difference lies primarily with parents or with siblings themselves, and of course, large patterns do not necessarily map to individual cases. But what all historical and psychological data do point to is the persistence and heat of this competition, which is a conflict not just between siblings but also between love and hate.

26 Frans de Waal, *Our Inner Ape: The Best and Worst of Human Nature* (London: Granta Books, 2005); see also Frans de Waal, *Chimpanzee Politics: Power and Sex Among Apes* (London: Jonathan Cape, 1982).

27 Darby Proctor, Rebecca A. Williamson, Frans B. M. de Waal, and Sarah F. Brosnan, "Chimpanzees Play the Ultimatum Game," *Proceedings of the National Academy of Sciences of the United States of America* 110, no. 5 (2013): 6, available at: www.pnas.org/content/110/6/2070.

Chapter 2: Making the Grade

1 David Leonhardt, "The Idled Young Americans," *New York Times,* May 3, 2013.

2 Michael Winerip, "Message from a Charter School: Thrive or Transfer," *New York Times,* July 10, 2011.

3 Scott Barry Kaufman, *Ungifted: Intelligence Redefined* (New York: Basic Books, 2013).

4 William J. Bushaw and Shane J. Lopez, "Which Way Do We Go? The 45th Annual PDK/Gallup Poll of the Public's Attitudes Toward the Public Schools," *Kappan* 95, no. 1 (September 2013), available at: http://pdkintl.org/noindex/2013_PDKGallup.pdf (accessed September 1, 2013).

5 Edward L. Deci, "Effects of Externally Mediated Rewards on Intrinsic Motivation," *Journal of Personality and Social Psychology* 18 (1971): 105–115; Edward L. Deci, "Effects of Contingent and Non-contingent Rewards and Controls on Intrinsic Motivation," *Organizational Behavior and Human Performance* 8 (1972): 217–229; Edward L. Deci, "Intrinsic Motivation, Extrinsic Reinforcement, and Inequity," *Journal of Personality and Social Psychology* 2 (1972): 113–120; Edward L. Deci and Richard M. Ryan, *Intrinsic Motivation and Self-determination in Human Behavior* (New York: Plenum, 1985); Edward L. Deci, Richard Koestner, and Richard M. Ryan, "Extrinsic Rewards and Internal Motivation in Education: Reconsidered Once Again," *Review of Educational Research* 71, no. 1 (2001): 1–27.

6 Sam Glucksberg, "Problem Solving: Response Competition Under the Influence of Drive," *Psychological Reports* 15 (1964); see also Sam Glucksberg, "The Influence of Strength of Drive on Functional Fixedness and Perceptual Recognition," *Journal of Experimental Psychology* 63 (1962): 36–41. A very accessible and detailed

exploration of this research can be found in Daniel H. Pink's wonderful book, *Drive: The Surprising Truth About What Motivates Us* (New York: Riverhead Books, 2009).

7 Daniel Fasko Jr., "Education and Creativity," *Creativity Research Journal* 13, nos. 3 and 4 (2000–2001): 317–327.

8 Beth A. Hennessey and Teresa M. Amabile, *Creativity and Learning* (Washington, DC: NEA Professional Library, 1987).

9 Adam Grant, *Give and Take: A Revolutionary Approach to Success* (New York: Viking, 2013); Michael Gove, "Passing Exams Make Children Happy and Satisfied," *London Evening Standard,* November 14, 2012.

10 Ke Xu, Monique Ernst, and David Goldman, "Imaging Genomics Applied to Anxiety, Stress Response, and Resiliency," *Neuroinformatics* 4 (2006): 51–64; see also Dan J. Stein, Timothy K. Newman, Jonathan Savitz, and Rajkumar Ramesar, "Warriors Versus Worriers: The Role of COMT Gene Variants," *CNS Spectrums* 11, no. 10 (October 2006): 745–748, available at: www.ncbi.nlm.nih.gov/pubmed/17008817.

11 Richard M. Ryan and Edward L. Deci, "Intrinsic and Extrinsic Motivations: Classic Definitions and New Directions," *Contemporary Educational Psychology* 25 (2000): 54–67.

12 See "Sneak Preview: An Interview with David Coleman, College Board President," *New York Times,* August 4, 2013.

13 Richard Vedder, Christopher Denhart, and Jonathan Robe, "Why Are Recent College Graduates Underemployed? University Enrollments and Labor Market Realities," Center for College Affordability and Productivity, January 2013, available at: centerforcollegeaffordability.org/research/studies/underemployment-of-college-graduates (accessed September 1, 2013).

14 Roger Cohen, "The Competition Drug," *New York Times,* March 4, 2013.

15 Vivian Yee, "Stuyvesant Students Describe the How and the Why of Cheating," *New York Times,* September 25, 2012.

16 Rushworth M. Kidder, "Ask Not for Whom the Students Cheat: They Cheat for Thee," Ethics Newsline, Institute for Global Ethics, February 28, 2011, available at: www.globalethics.org/newsline/2011/02/28/students-cheat/.

17 "Singapore: Rapid Improvement Followed by Strong Performance," in *Lessons from PISA for the United States* (Paris: OECD, 2010).

18 For the full details of this project, together with the published scientific paper, see Lottolab Studio, "Blackawton Bees," available at: www.lottolab.org/articles/blackawtonbees.asp. Further details of Beau Lotto's work are also available on this website.

19 Blackawton Primary School et al., "Blackawton Bees," *Biology Letters* 7, no. 2 (April 23, 2011): 168–172.

20 For sample PISA questions, see OECD, "Sample PISA Question," available at: http://pisa-sq.acer.edu.au/.

21 Charles Moore, *Margaret Thatcher: The Authorized Biography,* vol. 1 (New York: Alfred A. Knopf, 2013), 465.

22 Amanda Ripley, *The Smartest Kids in the World—And How They Got That Way* (New York: Simon & Schuster, 2013).

23 Richard Florida, "Cities: The World's Leading Nations for Innovation and Technology," *The Atlantic: Cities,* October 3, 2011, available at: www.theatlanticcities. com/technology/2011/10/worlds-leading-nations-innovation-and-technology/224/.

Chapter 3: The Morning After

1 In January 2005, Harvard president Lawrence Summers asked "whether innate differences between men and women might be one reason fewer women succeed in science and math careers" and subsequently left the university in the wake of a no-confidence vote.

2 Matthew Pearson and Burkhard C. Schipper, "Menstrual Cycle and Competitive Bidding," Working Paper 11, 10, University of California at Davis, Department of Economics, 2011, available at: www.econstor.eu/bitstream/10419/58389/1/717283119. pdf.

3 Niklas Zethraeus, Ljiljana Kocoska-Maras, Tore Ellingsen, Bo von Schoultz, Angelica Lindén Hirschberg, and Magnus Johannesson, "A Randomized Trial of the Effect of Estrogen and Testosterone on Economic Behavior," *Proceedings of the National Academy of Sciences* 106, no. 16 (April 21, 2009): 6535–6538.

4 Christopher Cotton, Frank McIntyre, and Joseph Price, "Gender Differences in Repeated Competition: Evidence from School Math Contests," *Journal of Economic Behavior and Organization* 86 (February 2013): 52–56.

5 Rachel Croson and Uri Gneezy, "Gender Differences in Preferences," *Journal of Economic Literature* 47, no. 2 (2009): 1–27; Muriel Niederle and Lise Vesterlund, "Do Women Shy Away from Competition? Do Men Compete Too Much?" *Quarterly Journal of Economics* 2, no. 3 (August 2007): 1067–1101; Anna E. Dreber, Emma von Essen, and Eva Ranehill, "Outrunning the Gender Gap—Boys and Girls Compete Equally," *Institute for Financial Research* (March 2010).

6 Hannah Riley Bowles, Linda Babcock, and Lei Lai, "Social Incentives for Gender Differences in the Propensity to Initiate Negotiations: Sometimes It Does Hurt to Ask," *Organizational Behavior and Human Decision Processes* 103, no. 1 (2007): 84–103.

7 Uri Gneezy, Kenneth L. Leonard, and John A. List, "Gender Differences in Competition: Evidence from a Matrilineal and a Patriarchal Society," *Econometrica* 77, no. 5 (2009): 1637–1664.

8 Ibid.

9 Stanley Siegel, "Penis Envy," February 13, 2012, available at: http://stanley-siegel.com/2012/02/13/penis-envy/.

10 Ibid.

11 Christopher Ryan and Cacilda Jetha, *Sex at Dawn: How We Mate, Why We Stray, and What It Means for Modern Relationships* (New York: Harper Perennial, 2010): 248.

12 "Married to the Mortgage," *The Economist,* July 13, 2013, 49.

13 Cindy M. Meston and David M. Buss, *Why Women Have Sex: Understanding Sexual Motivation—from Adventure to Revenge* (New York: Vintage Digital, 2010).

14 David M. Buss and David P. Schmitt, "Human Mate Poaching: Tactics and Temptations for Infiltrating Existing Mateships," *Journal of Personality and Social Psychology* 80, no. 6 (2001): 894–917.

15 Kate A. Ratliff and Shigehiro Oishi, "Gender Differences in Implicit Self-esteem Following a Romantic Partner's Success or Failure," *Journal of Personality and Social Psychology* 105, no. 4 (2013): 688–702.

16 Nathaniel Branden, interview with the author, Los Angeles, October 28, 2011. See also Nathaniel Branden, *My Years with Ayn Rand* (New York: Jossey-Bass, 1999), and Barbara Branden, *The Passion of Ayn Rand* (New York: Anchor Books, 1986).

17 "Women, the Main Breadwinners in Record 40 Percent of US Homes," *Financial Times*, www.ft.com/cms/s/0/7a185746-c869-11e2-acc6-00144feab7de.html.

18 Eric Klinenberg, *Going Solo: The Extraordinary Rise and Surprising Appeal of Living Alone* (New York: Penguin, 2012).

Chapter 4: Angry Birds

1 John Price, "A Remembrance of Thorleif Schjelderup-Ebbe," *Human Ethology Bulletin* 10, no. 1 (1995): 2.

2 Thorleif Schjelderup-Ebbe, "Contributions to the Social Psychology of the Domestic Chicken," trans. Monika Schleidt and Wolfgang M. Schleidt, in *Social Hierarchy and Dominance*, vol. 3, ed. Martin W. Schein (New York: Halsted Press/John Wiley & Sons, 1975), 35–49.

3 This quotation also appears in Thorleif Schjelderup-Ebbe, "Further Biological Observations of *Gallus Domesticus*" (translated by the author), *Psychological Research* 5, no. 1 (1924): 343–355.

4 Price, "A Remembrance of Thorleif Schjelderup-Ebbe," 3.

5 Ibid.

6 Ibid.

7 Caroline F. Zink, Yunxia Tong, Qiang Chen, Danielle S. Bassett, Jason L. Stein, and Andreas Meyer-Lindenberg, "Know Your Place: Neural Processing of Social Hierarchy in Humans," *Neuron* 58, no. 2 (2008): 273–283.

8 Robert Bales, "How People Interact in Conferences," *Scientific American* 192, no. 3 (1955): 31–35.

9 Akko Kalma, "Hierarchisation and Dominance Assessment at First Glance," *European Journal of Social Psychology* 21, no. 2 (1991): 165–181.

10 Amy Cuddy, "Your Body Language Shapes Who You Are," TED Talks, October 2012, available at: www.ted.com/talks/amy_cuddy_your_body_language_shapes_who_you_are.html.

11 Ibid.

12 Stanford W. Gregory Jr. and Stephen Webster, "A Nonverbal Signal in Voices of Interview Partners Effectively Predicts Communication Accommodation and Social Status Perceptions," *Journal of Personality and Social Psychology* 70, no. 6 (1996): 1231–1240.

13 Stanford W. Gregory and Timothy J. Gallagher, "Spectral Analysis of Candidates' Nonverbal Vocal Communication: Predicting US Presidential Election Outcomes," *Social Psychology Quarterly* 65, no. 3 (2002): 298–308.

14 Lynn Michell and Amanda Amos, "Girls, Pecking Order, and Smoking," *Social Science and Medicine* 44, no. 12 (1997): 1861–1869.

15 Marya Hornbacher, *Wasted: Going Back from an Addiction to Starvation* (London: Fourth Estate, 2010), 118.

16 Marya Hornbacher, interview with the author, February 16, 2012.

17 "Eating Disorders on the Rise in China," Cityweekend.com, April 11, 2011, available at: www.cityweekend.com.cn/beijing/articles/blogs-beijing/expat-life/eating-disorders-on-the-rise-in-china/.

18 Quoted in Tamara Lush, "At War with World of Warcraft," *The Guardian,* August 29, 2011.

19 "Money and Investing," *Wall Street Journal,* October 24, 2012, C1.

20 "About CultureGPS: A Global Positioning System to Navigate Through Intercultural Differences Based on the 5-D Model of Professor Hofstede," available at: www.culturegps.com/.

21 Geert Hofstede, *Culture's Consequences: Comparing Values, Behaviors, Institutions, and Organizations Across Nations* (Thousand Oaks, CA: Sage Publications, 2001), (emphasis added).

22 M. G. Marmot, S. Stansfeld, C. Patel, F. North, J. Head, I. White, E. Brunner, A. Feeney, and G. D. Smith, "Health Inequalities Among British Civil Servants: The Whitehall II Study," *The Lancet* 337, no. 8754 (1991): 1387–1393.

23 Zink et al., "Know Your Place."

24 Robert M. Sapolsky, "Social Status and Health in Humans and Other Animals," *Annual Review of Anthropology* 33 (2004): 393–418.

25 R. M. Yerkes and J. D. Dodson, "The Relation of Strength of Stimulus to Rapidity of Habit-Formation," *Journal of Comparative Neurology and Psychology* 18 (1908): 459–482.

26 Sendhil Mullainathan and Eldar Shafir, *Scarcity: Why Having Too Little Means So Much* (New York: Times Books, 2013).

27 Marianne M. Jennings, *The Seven Signs of Ethical Collapse: How to Spot Moral Meltdowns in Companies—Before It's Too Late* (New York: St. Martin's Press, 2006).

28 Peter E. Mudrack, James M. Bloodgood, and W. H. Turnley, "Some Ethical Implications of Individual Competitiveness," *Journal of Business Ethics* (2011), available at: doi:10.1007/s10551-011-1094-4.

29 Dacher Keltner, Deborah H. Gruenfeld, and Cameron Anderson, "Power, Approach, and Inhibition," *Psychological Review* 110, no. 2 (2003): 265–284.

30 Anthony Salz, with Russell Collins, *Salz Review: An Independent Review of Barclays' Business Practices,* April 2013, available at: http://online.wsj.com/public/resources/documents/SalzReview04032013.pdf.

31 Hofstede, *Culture's Consequences,* 135.

32 Geert Hofstede, Gert Jan Hofstede, and Michael Minkov, *Cultures and Organizations* (New York: McGraw-Hill, 2010), 87.

33 Adam Smith, *The Theory of Moral Sentiments* (Oxford: Oxford University Press, 1979), 308–313.

34 Thomas Piketty, Emmanuel Saez, and Stefanie Stantcheva, "Optimal Taxation of Top Labor Incomes: A Tale of Three Elasticities," Working Paper 17616 (Cambridge, MA: National Bureau of Economic Research, November 2011, revised March 2013).

35 Richard Wilkinson and Kate Pickett, *The Spirit Level: Why Equality Is Better for Everyone* (New York: Penguin Books, 2010).

36 "Pope Francis Denounces Income Inequality, Consumerism," November 24, 2013, available at: http://apps.washingtonpost.com/g/page/politics/pope-francis-denounces-economic-inequality-consumerism/619/.

Chapter 5: Keeping Score

1 Keith Hopkins and Mary Beard, *The Colosseum* (London: Profile Books, 2011), 80.

2 "Interview with Dai Greene, Olympic Captain of Great Britain's Athletics Team," Gulfnews.com, July 11, 2012.

3 Jack Wickens, "How Much Money Do Track and Field Athletes Make?" Track & Field Athletes Association, May 8, 2012, available at: http://trackandfieldathletesassociation.org/blog/how-much-money-do-track-and-field-athletes-make/.

4 "Estimated Probability of Competing in Athletics Beyond the High School Interscholastic Level," NCAA Research, available at: http://fs.ncaa.org/Docs/eligibility_center/Athletics_Information/Probability_of_Competing_Past_High_School.pdf.

5 Brad Wolverton, "Need Three Quick Credits to Play Ball? Call Western Oklahoma," *Chronicle of Higher Education,* November 9, 2012, available at: http://chronicle.com/article/Need-3-Quick-Credits-to-Play/135690/.

6 *Desert Island Discs,* BBC Radio 4, first broadcast February 10, 2012.

7 Andre Agassi, *Open: An Autobiography* (New York: HarperCollins, 2009), 214.

8 Frederick O. Mueller and Robert C. Cantu, "Catastrophic Sports Injury Research: Twenty-ninth Annual Report, Fall 1982–Spring 2011," University of North Carolina, National Center for Catastrophic Sport Injury Research, available at: www.unc.edu/depts/nccsi/2011Allsport.pdf.

9 Rose Eveleth, "Obesity Could Be the True Killer for Football Players," *Smithsonian,* February 4, 2013, available at: www.smithsonianmag.com/science-nature/mind-body/Obesity-Could-Be-the-True-Killer-for-Football-Players-189693981.html?c=y&page=2.

10 Frederick O. Mueller and Bob Colgate, "Annual Survey of Football Injury Research," American Football Coaches Association, 2012.

11 "Science News: Without Adult Intervention in Concussion Management, Youth Sports Can Become a Demolition Derby," *Science Daily,* November 3, 2012, available at: http://esciencenews.com/sources/newswise.scinews/2012/11/03/without.adult.intervention.concussion.management.youth.sports.can.become.demolition.derby.

12 "Most English Football Teams Don't Follow International Guidelines on Concussion, Study Finds," *Science Daily,* September 5, 2012, available at: www.sciencedaily.com/releases/2012/09/120905201255.htm.

13 Ken Belson, "Quitting the NFL: For John Moffitt the Money Wasn't Worth It," *New York Times,* November 18, 2013.

14 Ann C. McKee, Thor D. Stein, et al., "The Spectrum of Disease in Chronic Traumatic Encephalopathy," *Brain,* December 2, 2012, available at: brain.oxfordjournals.org/content/early/2012/12/02/brain.aws307.full.pdf+html?sid=010b634a-f023-430f-8488-2d220d3300f3.

15 Gary W. Small, Vladimir Kepe, et al., "PET Scanning of Brain Tau in Retired National Football League Players: Preliminary Findings," *American Journal of Geriatric Psychiatry* 21, no. 2 (2013).

16 Jonathan Mahler, "There Is No Concussion Crisis in Football," Bloomberg, December 5, 2012, available at: www.bloomberg.com/news/2012-12-05/there-is-no-concussion-crisis-in-football.html.

17 Sports Concussion Institute, "Concussion Facts," available at: www.concussiontreatment.com/concussionfacts.html.

18 André Le Gerche, Andrew T. Burns, et al., "Exercise-Induced Right Ventricular Dysfunction and Structural Remodelling in Endurance Athletes," *European Heart Journal* (October 5, 2011), available at: http://eurheartj.oxfordjournals.org/content/early/2011/12/05/eurheartj.ehr397.full.

19 Quoted in "New Research Links Endurance Exercise to Damage in the Right Ventricle of the Heart," European Society of Cardiology, December 7, 2011, available at: www.escardio.org/about/press/press-releases/pr-11/Pages/endurance-exercise-right-ventricle.aspx.

20 All quotes from "Thomas" and "Michelle" are from Natalie Barker-Ruchti, Dean Barker, Jessica Lee, and Steve Rynne, "Preparing Olympic Athletes for Life Outside of Elite Sport," final research report presented to the International Olympic Committee, December 30, 2011, available at: http://doc.rero.ch/record/28952/files/Barker-Ruchti_et_al_Final_Report_2011.pdf.

21 Scott Tinley, *Racing the Sunset: An Athlete's Quest for Life After Sport* (Guilford, CT: Lyons Press, 2003).

22 Bob Goldman, Patricia J. Bush, and Ronald Klatz, *Death in the Locker Room: Steroids and Sports* (Icarus Press, 1984).

23 "NFL Confidential: Why Should Roger Goodell Have the Last Word?" *ESPN The Magazine,* August 30, 2012, available at: http://espn.go.com/nfl/story/_/id/8316638/anonymous-nfl-players-share-secrets-player-safety-concussions-scandals-espn-magazine.

24 James M. Connor and Jason Mazanov, "Would You Dope? A General Population Test of the Goldman Dilemma," *British Journal of Sports Medicine* 43, no. 11 (2009): 871–872.

25 Owen Gibson, "Doping: Now Worse Than It's Ever Been," *The Guardian,* February 16, 2013.

26 Connor and Mazanov, "Would You Dope?"

27 Will Carling, "Cheating in Sport," Huffington Post: United Kingdom, January 10, 2013, available at: www.huffingtonpost.co.uk/will-carling/cheating-in-sport_b_2439325.html.

28 World Economic Forum, "Davos Underlines Economic Value of Sports," EurActiv.com, February 10, 2009, available at: www.euractiv.com/sports/davos-underlines-economic-value-news-221098.

29 Martin Breshear, "Balco Interview I," 20/20, March 10, 2008, available at: www.youtube.com/watch?v=lKqAUm1Tjek.

30 "What Sport Means in America: A Survey of Sport's Role in Society," U.S. Anti-Doping Agency, 2010.

31 Hannah Richardson, "Pressure to Win 'Turns Children into Sports Cheats,'" BBC News, April 14, 2013, available at: www.bbc.co.uk/news/education-22126301.

32 Sebastian Coe quoted this statistic on The World Tonight, BBC Radio 4, September 10, 2013.

33 Jill Haynes, "Socio-economic Impact of the Sydney 2000 Olympic Games," paper delivered at the 2001 Seminar of the International Chair in Olympism, available at: http://olympicstudies.uab.es/pdf/OD013_eng.pdf.

34 "True Sport: What We Stand to Lose in Our Obsession to Win," US Anti-Doping Agency, 2012.

35 Ibid.

36 Ibid.

37 Arijit Chatterjee and Donald Hambrick, "It's All About Me: Narcissistic CEOs and Their Effects on Company Strategy and Performance," University of Michigan, Ross School of Business, May 4, 2006, available at: www.bus.umich.edu/Academics/Departments/Strategy/pdf/F06Hambrick.pdf.

38 Steven Rattner, Overhaul: An Insider's Account of the Obama Administration's Emergency Rescue of the Auto Industry (New York: Mariner Books, 2011), 221.

39 Bob Lutz, "How Ed Whitacre Saved GM in Just 10 Months, and Other Fables," Forbes, February 28, 2013, available at: www.forbes.com/sites/boblutz/2013/02/28/how-ed-whitacre-saved-gm-in-just-10-months-and-other-fables/.

40 If you are interested in the science of fatigue, please see Chapter 3 of my book Willful Blindness: Why We Ignore the Obvious at Our Peril (New York: Walker & Co., 2011) for more details and references.

41 Marianna Virtanen, Stephen A. Stansfeld, Rebecca Fuhrer, Jane E. Ferrie, and Mika Kivimäki, "Overtime Work as a Predictor of Major Depressive Episode: A Five-Year Follow-up of the Whitehall II Study," PLoS ONE 7, no. 1 (2012): e30719; Marianna Virtanen, Archana Singh-Manoux, Jane E. Ferrie, David Gimeno, Michael G. Marmot, Marko Elovainio, Markus Jokela, Jussi Vahtera, and Mika Kivimäki, "Long Working Hours and Cognitive Function: The Whitehall II Study," American Journal of Epidemiology 169, no. 5 (March 1, 2009): 596–605.

42 Lynn Stout, The Shareholder Value Myth: How Putting Shareholders First Harms Investors, Corporations, and the Public (San Francisco: Berrett-Koehler Publishers, 2012).

43 "The Endangered Public Company," The Economist, May 19, 2012.

44 Stephen Denning, "Shift Index 2011: The Most Important Business

Study—Ever?" *Forbes,* January 25, 2012, available at: www.forbes.com/sites/steve
denning/2012/01/25/shift-index-2011-the-most-important-business-study-ever/;
see also Richard Foster, *Creative Destruction: Why Companies That Are Built to Last
Underperform the Market—and How to Successfully Transform Them* (New York:
Crown Business, 2001).

45 Stout, *The Shareholder Value Myth.*

46 Ibid., 65.

47 Marianne M. Jennings, *The Seven Signs of Ethical Collapse: How to Spot Moral
Meltdowns in Companies —Before It's Too Late* (New York: St. Martin's Press, 2006).

48 Roger L. Martin, *Fixing the Game: Bubbles, Crashes, and What Capitalism
Can Learn from the NFL* (Boston: Harvard Business Review Press, 2011).

49 Francesco Guerrera, "Welch Condemns Share Price Focus," *Financial Times,*
March 12, 2009.

50 Jim Collins, *Good to Great* (New York: HarperCollins, 2001).

Chapter 6: Only the Impresarios Thrive

1 Carl Djerassi, *The Pill, Pygmy Chimps, and Degas' Horse: The Remarkable Autobiography of the Award-Winning Scientist Who Synthesized the Birth Control Pill*
(New York: Basic Books, 1992), 33–34.

2 Ibid.

3 Ibid., 43.

4 Ibid., 44.

5 David Sloan Wilson, *Evolution for Everyone: How Darwin's Theory Can Change
the Way We Think About Our Lives* (New York: Random House, 2007), 33.

6 David Goodstein, "Scientific Misconduct," *Academe* 88 (2002): 28–31.

7 T. V. Rajan, "Biomedical Scientists Are Engaged in a Pyramid Scheme," *Chronicle of Higher Education* (June 3, 2005).

8 Melissa S. Anderson, Emily A. Ronning, Raymond De Vries, and Brian C.
Martinson, "The Perverse Effects of Competition on Scientists' Work and Relationships," *Science and Engineering Ethics* 13 (2007): 437–461.

9 John P. Walsh and Wei Hong, "Secrecy Is Increasing in Step with Competition,"
Nature 422, no. 24 (April 2003).

10 Raymond De Vries, Melissa S. Anderson, and Brian C. Martinson, "Normal
Misbehavior: Scientists Talk About the Ethics of Research," *Journal of Empirical Research on Human Research Ethics* 1, no. 1 (March 2006): 43–50.

11 Anderson et al., "The Perverse Effects of Competition on Scientists' Work and
Relationships."

12 The Official King James Bible Online, Cambridge Edition, available at: www.
kingjamesbibleonline.org/Matthew-25-29/.

13 Kary Mullis, "The Unusual Origin of the Polymerase Chain Reaction," *Scientific American* (April 1990).

14 Ferric C. Fang, "Reforming Science: Structural Reforms," *Infection and Immunity* 80, no. 3 (2011): 897–901.

15 Leonard Cassuto, "Big Trouble in the World of 'Big Physics,'" *Salon,* September 16, 2012, available at: www.salon.com/2002/09/16/physics/.

16 "Innovators Under 35: Jan Hendrik Schön, 31: Nanotechnologies," *MIT Technology Review,* 2002, available at: www2.technologyreview.com/tr35/profile.aspx-?TRID=395.

17 Eugenie Samuel Reich, *Plastic Fantastic: How the Biggest Fraud in Physics Shook the Scientific World* (London: Palgrave Macmillan, 2009), 150.

18 Ibid., 117.

19 Ibid., 131.

20 Ibid., 176.

21 Ibid., 181.

22 Deutsche Forschungsgemeinschaft, "DFG Imposes Sanctions Against Jan Hendrik Schön," October 14, 2004, meeting, available at: www.dfg.de/download/pdf/dfg_im_profil/reden_stellungnahmen/2004/ha_jhschoen_1004_en.pdf.

23 Yudhijit Bhattacharjee, "The Mind of a Con Man," *New York Times,* April 26, 2013.

24 Richard Van Noorden, "Science Publishing: The Trouble with Retractions," *Nature* 478 (October 5, 2011): 26–28, available at: doi:10.1038/478026a.

25 R. Grant Steen, Arturo Casadevall, and Ferric C. Fang, "Why Has the Number of Scientific Retractions Increased?" *PLOS/One,* July 8, 2013, available at: doi:10.1371/journal.pone.0068397.

26 Ibid.

27 K. M. Korpela, "How Long Does It Take for the Scientific Literature to Purge Itself of Fraudulent Material? The Breuning Case Revisited," *Current Medical Research and Opinion* 26, no. 4 (2010): 843–847.

28 Michael W. Kalichman and P. J. Friedman, "A Pilot Study of Biomedical Trainees' Perceptions Concerning Research Ethics," *Academic Medicine* 67 (1992): 769–775.

29 Ferric C. Fang, "Reforming Science: Structural Reforms," *Infection and Immunity* 80, no. 3 (2011): 897–901.

30 I wrote at greater length about Ruderman's ethical journey in *Willful Blindness.*

31 For more on cognitive limits and some of the experiments that explain them, see Chapter 4 of my book *Willful Blindness.*

32 Kurt Eichenwald, "Microsoft's Lost Decade," *Vanity Fair,* August 2012.

33 Ibid.

34 Duff McDonald, *The Firm: The Story of McKinsey and Its Secret Influence on American Business* (New York: Simon & Schuster, 2013); see also Duff McDonald, "McKinsey's Dirty War: Bogus 'War for Talent' Was Self-serving (and Failed)," *The New York Observer,* November 5, 2013, available at: http://observer.com/2013/11/mckinseys-dirty-war-bogus-war-for-talent-was-self-serving-and-failed/#ixzz2nLeSf74q.

35 See Andrew Munro, "What Happened to the War for Talent Exemplars," September 18, 2013, available at: www.slideshare.net/AndrewMunro/what-happenedtothewarfortalentexemplars.

36 David E. Terpstra, Mario G. C. Reyes, and Donald W. Bokor, "Predictors of Ethical Decisions Regarding Insider Trading," *Journal of Business Ethics* 10, no. 9 (September 1991): 699–710.

37 Uri Alon, "Together into the Unknown: What Science Can Learn from Improvisation Theatre," TedxTalks; see Alon singing "Scoop, Scoop" at: www.youtube.com/watch?v=RVoz_pEeV8I.

38 Uri Alon, "How to Build a Motivated Research Group," *Molecular Cell* 37 (January 29, 2010): 151–152.

39 John Abele, "Bringing Minds Together," *Harvard Business Review* (July–August 2011).

40 Po Bronson and Ashley Merryman, *Top Dog: The Science of Winning and Losing* (New York: Twelve, 2013), 207.

41 Anita Williams Woolley, Christopher F. Chabris, Alex Pentland, Nada Hashmi, and Thomas W. Malone, "Evidence for a Collective Intelligence Factor in the Performance of Human Groups," *Science*, September 30, 2010, available at: doi:10.1126/science.1193147.

42 Cranberries grow in a few other places in the world, notably Northern Ireland and some parts of China, but those bogs are small and have not been farmed.

43 Jerry Avorn, Mark Monane, Jerry H. Gurwitz, Robert J. Glynn, Igor Choodnovskiy, and Lewis A. Lipsitz, "Reduction of Bacteriuria and Pyuria After Ingestion of Cranberry Juice," *Journal of the American Medical Association* 271, no. 10 (1994): 751–754. For the Helicobacter reference, see Lian Zhang, Junling Ma, Kaifeng Pan, Vay Liang Go, Junshi Chen, and Wei-cheng You, "Efficacy of Cranberry Juice on *Helicobacter pylori* Infection: A Double-Blind, Randomized Placebo-Controlled Trial," *Helicobacter* 10, no. 2 (April 2005): 139–45, available at: www.ncbi.nlm.nih.gov/pubmed/15810945.

44 I am indebted to John Restakis and Ed Mayo for introducing me to the cooperatives of Emilia Romagna.

45 "Cooperatives in the U.S. Economy," University of Wisconsin Center for Cooperatives, available at: http://reic.uwcc.wisc.edu/issues/.

Chapter 7: Clone Wars

1 "Ne-Yo Slams Auto-Tune Singers: 'Take the Training Wheels Off,'" Thatgrapejuice.net, February 17, 2011, available at: http://thatgrapejuice.net/2011/02/neyo-slams-autotune-singers-training-wheels/.

2 Blake Snyder, *Save the Cat: The Last Book on Screenwriting You'll Ever Need* (Studio City, CA: Michael Wiese Productions, 2005).

3 Howard Suber, "Contradictions in the System," The Power of Film, February 21, 2012, available at: http://thepoweroffilm.com/pages/contradictions-in-the-system/.

4 For more on the neurological basis of the familiar, please see the first chapter of my book *Willful Blindness*.

5 Bernard Munos, "Lessons from 60 Years of Pharmaceutical Innovation," *Nature Reviews|Drug Discovery* 8 (December 2009): 959.

6 Ben Goldacre, *Bad Pharma: How Drug Companies Mislead Doctors and Harm Patients* (London: Fourth Estate, 2012), 146–148.

7 Iain M. Cockburn and Aslam H. Anis, "Hedonic Analysis of Arthritis Drugs," working paper 6574 (Cambridge, MA: National Bureau of Economic Research, 1998).

8 Pierre Azoulay, "Do Pharmaceutical Sales Respond to Scientific Evidence?" *Journal of Economics and Management Strategy* 11, no. 4 (2002): 551–594.

9 James Love, "Evidence Regarding Research and Development Investments in Innovative and Non-innovative Medicines," Consumer Project on Technology (aka Knowledge Ecology International), CPTech.org, September 22, 2003, available at: www.cptech.org/ip/health/rnd/evidenceregardingrnd.pdf.

10 Tom Clarke, "Drug Companies Snub Antibiotics as Pipeline Threatens to Run Dry," *Nature* 425, no. 18 (September 2003): 225.

11 Thomas Frieden, "CDC: Action Needed Now to Halt Spread of Deadly Bacteria" (press release), CDC Newsroom, March 5, 2013, available at: www.cdc.gov/media/releases/2013/p0305_deadly_bacteria.html.

12 Fergus Walsh, "Antibiotics Resistance 'as Big a Risk as Terrorism'—Medical Chief," BBC News Health, March 11, 2013, available at: www.bbc.co.uk/news/health-21737844.

13 Olivia Solon, "Bill Gates: Capitalism Means Male Baldness Research Gets More Funding than Malaria," *Wired,* March 14, 2013, available at: www.wired.co.uk/news/archive/2013-03/14/bill-gates-capitalism.

14 Frederick Kaufman, "How Goldman Sachs Created the Food Crisis," *Foreign Policy* (April 27, 2011), available at: www.foreignpolicy.com/articles/2011/04/27/how_goldman_sachs_created_the_food_crisis; see also Kaufman's book *Bet the Farm: How Food Stopped Being Food* (Hoboken, NJ: John Wiley & Sons, 2012).

15 Marco Lagi, Karla Z. Bertrand, and Yaneer Bar-Yam, "The Food Crises and Political Instability in North Africa and the Middle East," New England Complex Systems Institute, August 10, 2011, arXiv:1108.2455, available at: http://necsi.edu/research/social/foodcrises.html.

16 Michael W. Masters, Managing Member/Portfolio Manager, Masters Capital Management, LLC, testimony before the Senate Committee on Homeland Security and Governmental Affairs, HSGAC.senate.gov, May 20, 2008, available at: www.hsgac.senate.gov//imo/media/doc/052008Masters.pdf?attempt=2.

17 Lee Cronin, "Print Your Own Medicine," February 2013, available at: www.ted.com/talks/lee_cronin_print_your_own_medicine.html.

18 Ferguson's brilliant video series can be seen at Everything is a Remix, available at: www.allremix.ru.

Chapter 8: Supersize Everything

1 Judith Dupre, *Skyscrapers,* with an introductory interview with Philip Johnson (New York: Black Dog & Leventhal Publishers, 1996), 36.

2 Ibid., 8.

3 Ibid., 7.

4 Konrad Lorenz, *On Aggression* (London: Routledge, 2002).

5 Miles Glendinning, *Architecture's Evil Empire? The Triumph and Tragedy of Global Modernism* (London: Reaktion Books, 2010), 86.

6 Eryn Sun, "Joel Osteen Finally Gets to the Truth of Sin, with Piers Morgan," Christianpost.com, January 27, 2011, available at: www.christianpost.com/news/joel-osteen-finally-gets-to-the-truth-of-sin-with-piers-morgan-48685/#EetpxqSIaiiP91rj.99.

7 Katherine Weber, "Pastor Joel Osteen Addresses Gun Control After Conn. School Shooting," Christianpost.com, December 17, 2012, available at: www.christianpost.com/news/pastor-joel-osteen-addresses-gun-control-after-conn-school-shooting-86807/.

8 "Amazing Motivational Speech by Joel Osteen: Live with Confidence," available at: www.youtube.com/watch?v=rXktvy4Uv5Y.

9 Roy F. Baumeister, Jennifer D. Campbell, Joachim I. Krueger, and Kathleen D. Vohs, "Does High Self-esteem Cause Better Performance, Interpersonal Success, Happiness, or Healthier Lifestyles?" *Psychological Science in the Public Interest* 4, no. 1 (May 2003), available at: www.irc.csom.umn.edu/Assets/53495.pdf.

10 Carol Dweck, *Mindset: The New Psychology of Success* (New York: Ballantine Books, 2007).

11 Jean Twenge and W. Keith Campbell, *The Narcissism Epidemic: Living in the Age of Entitlement* (New York: Atria Books, 2009), 229 (ebook).

12 Ibid., 114.

13 Donelson R. Forsyth, Natalie K. Lawrence, Jeni L. Burnette, and Roy F. Baumeister, "Attempting to Improve the Academic Performance of Struggling College Students by Bolstering Their Self-esteem: An Intervention That Backfired," *Journal of Social and Clinical Psychology* 26, no. 4 (2007): 447–459.

14 Ibid.

15 John Browne, *Beyond Business: An Inspirational Memoir from a Visionary Leader* (London: Weidenfeld & Nicholson, 2010), 68–69.

16 US Chemical Safety and Hazard Investigation Board, "Refinery Explosion and Fire," Investigation Report 2005-04-I-TX, March 23, 2005, available at: www.csb.gov/assets/document/CSBFinalReportBP.pdf.

17 National Commission on the BP Deepwater Horizon Oil Spill and Offshore Drilling, *Deep Water: The Gulf Oil Disaster and the Future of Offshore Drilling* (Washington, DC: US Independent Agencies and Commissions, January 2011.)

18 Browne, *Beyond Business,* 74.

19 Peter Lattman, "Confidence on Upswing, Mergers Make Comeback," *New York Times,* February 14, 2013.

20 Christopher Meyer, with Julia Kirby, *Standing on the Sun: How the Explosion of Capitalism Abroad Will Change Business Everywhere* (Cambridge, MA: Harvard Business Review Press, 2012), 136.

21 Some of the interviewees quoted in this account of RBS have been given pseudonyms to protect their identity.

22 Nitin Nohria and James Weber, *The Royal Bank of Scotland: Masters of Integration,* Harvard Business School Case 404-026, August 2003 (revised June 2005).

23 Ian Fraser, "Loss of Trust," *Signet,* July 16, 2012.

24 "Royal Bank of Scotland's Balance Sheet Still as Big as UK Economy," *The Guardian,* Business Blog, January 12, 2012.

25 Anthony Salz, with Russell Collins, *Salz Review: An Independent Review of Barclays' Business Practices,* April 2013, available at: http://online.wsj.com/public/resources/documents/SalzReview04032013.pdf.

26 Frank Partnoy and Jesse Eisinger, "What's Inside America's Banks," *The Atlantic,* February 2013.

27 Robin I. M. Dunbar, "Coevolution of Neocortical Size, Group Size, and Language in Humans," *Behavioral and Brain Sciences* 16 (1993): 681–735.

28 Wei-Xing Zhou, Didier Sornette, Russell A. Hill, and Robin I. M. Dunbar, "Discrete Hierarchical Organization of Social Group Sizes," *Proceedings of the Royal Society B: Biological Sciences* 272 (2005): 439–444.

29 Andrew Simms, "Let's Play Fantasy Economics," *The Observer,* February 17, 2013.

30 Tim Adams, "I Still Haven't Found What I'm Looking For," *The Observer,* January 20, 2013.

31 "War on Terabytes," *The Economist,* February 2, 2013.

Chapter 9: How Low Can We Go?

1 Walter Lippmann, *Drift and Mastery: An Attempt to Diagnose the Current Unrest* (New York: Mitchell Kennerley, 1914), 92.

2 "A Final Embrace: The Most Haunting Photograph from Bangladesh," *Time,* May 8, 2013.

3 Ian Urbina and Keith Bradsher, "Linking Factories to the Malls, Middleman Pushes Low Costs," *New York Times,* August 7, 2013.

4 David Yin, "Li and Fung Fall Out of Favor," *Forbes Asia,* September 2, 2013, available at: www.forbes.com/sites/forbesasia/2013/08/28/li-fung-falls-out-of-favor/.

5 Sadhbh Walshe, "How America's Fast Food Industry Makes a Quick Buck," *The Guardian,* April 11, 2013.

6 John Schmitt and Janelle Jones, "Low-Wage Workers Are Older and Better Educated Than Ever" (issue brief), Center for Economic Policy Research, April 2012, available at: www.cepr.net/documents/publications/min-wage3-2012-04.pdf.

7 Michael Grabell, "The Expendables: How the Temps Who Power Corporate Giants Are Getting Crushed," *ProPublica,* June 27, 2013, available at: www.propublica.org/article/the-expendables-how-the-temps-who-power-corporate-giants-are-getting-crushe.

8 Hazel Sheffield, "Pasadena Publisher Launches a System for Outsourcing Local News," *Columbia Journalism Review,* August 27, 2012, available at: www.cjr.org/behind_the_news/pasadena_publisher_launches_a.php.

9 "In the Leveson Inquiry into the Press," available at: www.levesoninquiry.org. uk/wp-content/uploads/2012/02/MS-Exhibit-11.pdf.

10 "Second Witness Statement of Michelle Stanistreet on Behalf of the National Union of Journalists," January 23, 2012, available at: www.levesoninquiry.org.uk/wp-content/uploads/2012/02/Second-Witness-Statement-of-Michelle-Stanistreet.pdf.

11 Richard Peppiatt, testimony before the Leveson Inquiry, "Seminar 1: The Competitive Pressures on the Press and the Impact on Journalism," October 6, 2011, available at: www.levesoninquiry.org.uk/wp-content/uploads/2011/11/Witness-Statement-of-Richard-Peppiatt.pdf.

12 "Richard Peppiatt's Letter to *Daily Star* Proprietor Richard Desmond," *The Guardian,* March 4, 2011.

13 Ibid.

14 Richard Peppiatt, interview with the author, London/Farrington Gurney, January 19, 2013.

15 Peppiatt, testimony before the Leveson Inquiry, "Seminar 1—," October 6, 2011.

16 "Towards Happier Meals in a Globalized World," Worldwatch Institute, available at: www.worldwatch.org/towards-happier-meals-globalized-world.

17 In 2006 the European Union banned the administration of drugs for growth-promoting purposes. Since this action was taken, levels of antibiotic resistance, in both humans and animals, have decreased.

18 "Joseph W. Luter III (CEO of Smithfield Foods)," *Forbes,* available at: www.forbes.com/lists/2006/12/UQDU.html.

19 Nicholas D. Kristof, "Arsenic in Our Chicken?" *New York Times,* April 4, 2012. See also "Putting Meat on the Table," a report of the Pew Commission on Industrial Farm Animal Production (PCIFAP), a project of the Pew Charitable Trust and Johns Hopkins Bloomberg School of Public Health, 2008, available at: www.ncifap.org/about/. In October 2013, the US Food and Drug Administration (FDA) rescinded approval for three of the four arsenic-based drugs used in animal feeds after high levels of arsenic from poultry feces were found in rice.

20 Environmental Protection Agency, "Compliance and Enforcement: Clean Water Act," 2008, 1–3, quoted in PCIFAP, "Putting Meat on the Table," 23.

21 PCIFAP, "Putting Meat on the Table," 25.

22 David Kirby, *Animal Factory: The Looming Threat of Industrial Pig, Dairy, and Poultry Farms to Humans and the Environment* (New York: St. Martin's Press, 2010), 84.

23 David A. Kessler, "Antibiotics and the Meat We Eat," *New York Times,* March 28, 2013.

24 FDA, "Highlights of the NARMS Retail 2008 Report," available at: www.fda.gov/downloads/AnimalVeterinary/SafetyHealth/AntimicrobialResistance/NationalAntimicrobialResistanceMonitoringSystem/UCM237120.pdf.

25 US Department of Agriculture Economic Research Service, "County Level Data Sets," available at: www.ers.usda.gov/data-products/county-level-data-sets/poverty.aspx.

26 PCIFAP, "Putting Meat on the Table," 41.

27 US House of Representatives, Committee on Energy and Commerce, letter to C. Larry Pope, President and CEO of Smithfield Foods, Inc., July 24, 2013, 113th Congress, available at: http://energycommerce.house.gov/sites/republicans.energy-commerce.house.gov/files/letters/20130724Smithfield.pdf.

28 "Shuanghui Apologizes over Additive Scandal," *China Daily,* March 17, 2011, available at: www.chinadaily.com.cn/business/2011-03/17/content_12185197.htm.

29 Daniel Imhoff, ed., *The CAFO Reader: The Tragedy of Industrial Animal Factories* (Sausalito, CA: Foundation for Deep Ecology, 2010).

30 OpenSecrets.org, "Smithfield Foods," available at: www.opensecrets.org/pacs/lookup2.php?strID=Coo359075.

31 "Smithfield 2012 Integrated Report," 12, available at: http://files.shareholder.com/downloads/SFD/2790549716x0x590240/F33D665C-409C-4825-A50E-D7F90C10F399/smi_integrated_12.pdf.

32 Ibid., cover.

33 Ibid., 47.

34 Ibid.

35 Ray C. Anderson, *Confessions of a Radical Industrialist: Profits, People, Purpose—Doing Business by Respecting the Earth* (New York: St. Martin's Press, 2009), 8.

36 "Ray Anderson on *Confessions of a Radical Industrialist,*" available at: www.youtube.com/watch?v=HRkHJxQKM8A.

37 Anderson, *Confessions of a Radical Industrialist.*

38 "Birthday Message from Ray Anderson," available at: www.youtube.com/watch?v=oedz4E9vlDU.

39 "Dov Charney on Modern Day Sweat Shops," available at: www.youtube.com/watch?v=CG_T1fY3KTk.

40 Jaime Wolf, "And You Thought Abercrombie & Fitch Was Pushing It?" *New York Times,* April 23, 2006.

41 All Ford quotes come from his book *My Life and Work,* available in a Gutenberg Project edition at: www.gutenberg.org/cache/epub/7213/pg7213.html.

Chapter 10: Top of the World

1 In 1966 Charles Whitman killed sixteen people and wounded thirty-two in Austin, Texas, and Richard Speck raped and killed eight student nurses in Chicago.

2 Robert F. Kennedy, address at the University of Kansas, Lawrence, March 18, 1968, available at: www.youtube.com/watch?v=77IdKFqXbUY.

3 Bureau of Economic Analysis, "GDP: One of the Great Inventions of the Century," available at: www.bea.gov/scb/account_articles/general/0100od/maintext.htm.

4 Helen Johns and Paul Ormerod, *Happiness, Economics, and Public Policy* (London: Institute of Economic Affairs, 2008).

5 Jeffrey M. Jones, "In US, Majority Still Names China as Top Economic Power," GallupEconomy, February 26, 2013, available at: www.gallup.com/poll/160724/majority-names-china-top-economic-power.aspx.

6 "China the Top World Economy, Americans Say," CNN Politics, February 14, 2011, available at: http://politicalticker.blogs.cnn.com/2011/02/14/china-the-top-world-economy-americans-say/.

7 Klaus Schwab and Xavier Sala-i-Martín, *Global Competitiveness Report 2013–2014* (Geneva: World Economic Forum, 2013), available at: http://www3.weforum.org/docs/WEF_GlobalCompetitivenessReport_2013-14.pdf.

8 Jonathan Michie and Maura Sheehan-Quinn, "Labour Market Flexibility, Human Resource Management, and Corporate Performance," *British Journal of Management* 12, no. 4 (2001): 287–306.

9 Arie C. Glebbeek and Eric H. Bax, "Is High Employee Turnover Really Harmful? An Empirical Test Using Company Records," *Academy of Management Journal* 47, no. 2 (2004): 277–286; Steve Hillmer, Barbara Hillmer, and Gale McRoberts, "The Real Costs of Turnover: Lessons from a Call Center," *Human Resource Planning* 27, no. 3 (2004): 34–41.

10 Douglas Beal, Enrique Rueda-Sabater, and Teresa Espírito Santo, "From Wealth to Well-being: Introducing the BCG Sustainable Economic Development Assessment," Boston Consulting Group, November 12, 2012, available at: http://blair.3cdn.net/434880beeddae5e609_f7m6y5a4z.pdf.

11 Ibid.

12 Clayton Christensen, *The Innovator's Dilemma: When New Technologies Cause Great Firms to Fail* (Boston: Harvard Business Review Press, 2013).

13 Norwegian Ministry of Petroleum and Energy, "Energy in Norway," available at: www.regjeringen.no/en/dep/oed/Subject/energy-in-norway.html?id=86981.

14 MarYam G. Hamedani, Hazel Rose Markus, and Alyssa S. Fu, "My Nation, My Self: Divergent Framings of America Influence American Selves," *Personality and Social Psychology Bulletin* 37 (2011): 350–364.

15 John Sulston and Georgina Ferry, *The Common Thread: A Story of Science, Politics, Ethics, and the Human Genome* (New York: Bantam Press, 2002), 154.

16 Richard Preston, "The Genome Warrior," *The New Yorker*, June 12, 2000.

17 Sulston and Ferry, *The Common Thread*, 218–219.

18 Victor K. McElheny, *Drawing the Map of Life: Inside the Human Genome Project* (New York: Basic Books, 2010), 153.

19 The Royal Society, *People and the Planet*, April 26, 2012, available at: http://royalsociety.org/policy/projects/people-planet/report/.

20 Garrett Hardin, "The Tragedy of the Commons," *Science* 162, no. 3859 (December 13, 1968), available at: www.sciencemag.org/content/162/3859/1243.full.

21 "Rethinking Institutional Analysis: Interviews with Vincent and Elinor Ostrom," George Washington University, Mercatus Center, November 7, 2003, available at: www.mercatus.org/uploadedFiles/Mercatus/Publications/Rethinking%20Institutional%20Analysis%20-%20Interviews%20with%20Vincent%20and%20Elinor%20Ostrom.pdf.

22 Elinor Ostrom, "Crossing the Great Divide: Coproduction, Synergy, and Development," *World Development* 24, no. 6 (1996): 1073–1087.

23 Elinor Ostrom, "How Farmer-Managed Irrigation Systems Build Social Capital to Outperform Agency-Managed Systems That Rely Primarily on Physical Cap-

ital," keynote address to the Ford Foundation, 2002, available at: www.fordfoundation.org/pdfs/news/ostrom-2002-keynote.pdf; see also Elinor Ostrom and Roy Gardner, "Coping with Asymmetries in the Commons: Self-governing Irrigation Systems Can Work," *Journal of Economic Perspectives* 7, no. 4 (1993): 93–112.

24 Elinor Ostrom, *Governing the Commons: The Evolution of Institutions for Collective Action* (Cambridge: Cambridge University Press, 1990).

25 Ibid.

26 Patrick Love, "A Lesson in Resources Management from Elinor Ostrom," OECD Insights: Debate the Issues, July 1, 2011, available at: http://oecdinsights.org/2011/07/01/a-lesson-in-resources-management-from-elinor-ostrom/.

Chapter 11: A Bigger Prize

1 Feinberg wrote a tremendous account of running the fund in Kenneth R. Feinberg, *What Is Life Worth? The Unprecedented Effort to Compensate the Victims of 9/11* (New York: PublicAffairs, 2005).

Abele, John. "Bringing Minds Together." *Harvard Business Review* (July–August 2011).

Adams, Tim. "When Politics Is in the Blood." *The Observer*, September 6, 2010.

———. "I Still Haven't Found What I'm Looking For." *The Observer*, January 20, 2013.

Adewunmi, Bim, and Patrick Kingsley. "A Whole New Ball Game." *The Guardian*, June 21, 2011.

Adler, Nancy. "The Arts and Leadership: Now That We Can Do Anything, What Will We Do?" *Academy of Management Learning and Education* 5, no. 4 (2006): 486–499.

Adner, Ron. *The Wide Lens: A New Strategy for Innovation*. New York: Portfolio (2012).

Agassi, Andre. *Open: An Autobiography*. London: HarperCollins (2009).

Ahmadi, Sanaz Saeed, Mohammad Ali Besharat, Korosh Azizi, and Roja Larijani. "The Relationship Between Dimensions of Anger and Aggression in Contact and Noncontact Sports." *Procedia—Social and Behavioral Sciences* 30 (2011): 247–251.

Akerlof, George, and Rachel Kranton. "It Is Time to Treat Wall Street Like Main Street." *The Financial Times*, February 24, 2010.

Alling, Abigail, and Mark Nelson. *Life Under Glass: The Inside Story of Biosphere 2*. Santa Fe, NM: Synergetic Press (1993).

Almås, Ingvild, Alexander W. Cappelen, Kjell G. Salvanes, Erik Ø. Sørensen, and Bertil Tungodden. "Explaining Gender Differences in Competitiveness." January 1, 2012. Available at: tuvalu.santafe.edu/~bowles/GenderDifferencesCompetitiveness.pdf.

Alon, Uri. "How to Build a Motivated Research Group." *Molecular Cell* 37 (January 29, 2010): 151–152.

Anderson, Melissa S., Emily A. Ronning, Raymond De Vries, and Brian C. Martinson. "The Perverse Effects of Competition on Scientists' Work and Relationships." *Science and Engineering Ethics* 13 (2006): 437–461.

Anderson, Ray C. *Confessions of a Radical Industrialist: Profits, People, Purpose—*

Doing Business by Respecting the Earth. New York: St. Martin's Press (2009).

Andersen, Steffen, Erwin Bulte, Uri Gneezy, and John A. List. "Do Women Supply More Public Goods Than Men? Preliminary Experimental Evidence from Matrilineal and Patriarchal Societies." *American Economic Review: Papers and Proceedings* 98, no. 2 (2008): 376–381.

Andeweg, Rudy B., and Steef B. van den Berg. "Linking Birth Order to Political Leadership: The Impact of Parents or Sibling Interaction?" *Political Psychology* 24, no. 3 (2003): 605–623.

Armstrong, Lance. *It's Not About the Bike: My Journey Back to Life.* London: Yellow Jersey Press (2001).

Asthana, Anushka. "The Secret of a Happy Child: No Irritating Siblings to Get in the Way." *The Observer,* January 3, 2010.

Auger, Pat, and Timothy M. Devinney. "Do What Consumers Say Matter? The Misalignment of Preferences with Unconstrained Ethical Intentions." *Journal of Business Ethics* 76, no. 4 (2007): 361–383.

Austin, Elizabeth J., Daniel Farrelly, Carolyn Black, and Helen Moore. "Emotional Intelligence, Machiavellianism, and Emotional Manipulation: Does EI Have a Dark Side?" *Personality and Individual Differences* 43, no. 1 (2007): 179–189.

Baden-Fuller, Charles, and Mary S. Morgan. "Business Models as Models." *Long Range Planning* 43, nos. 2-3 (2010): 156–171.

Baird, Benjamin, Jonathan Smallwood, Michael D. Mrazek, Julia W. Y. Kam, Michael S. Franklin, and Jonathan W. Schooler. "Inspired by Distraction: Mind Wandering Facilitates Creative Incubation." *Psychological Science* 23, no. 10 (2012): 1117–1122.

Baker, Mike. "Should We Rank Pupils Instead of Grading Them?" *The Guardian,* March 20, 2012.

Bales, Robert F. "A Set of Categories for the Analysis of Small Group Interaction." *American Sociological Review* 15, no. 2 (1950): 257–263.

———. "How People Interact in Conferences." *Scientific American* 192, no. 3 (1955): 31–35.

Ball, Philip. "The H-Index, Also Known as the Stag's Antlers." *The Guardian,* January 6, 2012.

Barrett, David. "The Cheating Epidemic at Britain's Universities." *The Telegraph,* March 5, 2011.

Basu, Paroma. "Where Are They Now?" *Nature Medicine* 12 (2006): 492–493.

Baumeister, Roy F., Jennifer D. Campbell, Joachim I. Krueger, and Kathleen D. Vohs. "Does High Self-esteem Cause Better Performance, Interpersonal Success, Happiness, or Healthier Lifestyles?" *Psychological Science in the Public Interest* 4, no. 1 (May 2003). Available at: www.irc.csom.umn.edu/Assets/53495.pdf.

Bedford, Victoria Hilkevitch. "Sibling Relationship Troubles and Well-being in Middle and Old Age." *Family Relations* 47, no. 4 (1998): 369–376.

Beenstock, Michael. "Deconstructing the Sibling Correlation: How Families Increase Inequality." *Journal of Family and Economic Issues* 29, no. 3 (2008): 325–345.

Beggan, James K., David M. Messick, and Scott T. Allison. "Social Values and Egocentric Bias: Two Tests of the Might over Morality Hypothesis." *Journal of Personality and Social Psychology* 55, no. 4 (1988): 606–606.

Bell, Jarrett. "Vilma, Others Silent as NFL Makes Its Case." *USA Today,* June 19, 2012.

Bellafante, Ginia. "Forget the Downturn; Punish the Lazybones." *New York Times,* October 14, 2010.

Benenson, Joyce F., Timothy J. Antonellis, Benjamin J. Cotton, Kathleen E. Noddin, and Kristin A. Campbell. "Sex Differences in Children's Formation of Exclusionary Alliances Under Scarce Resource Conditions." *Animal Behaviour* 76, no. 2 (2008): 497–505.

Benjamin, Alison. "Sociologist Urges a Wider View of the Welfare State." *The Guardian,* March 20, 2012.

Bennet, Catherine. "Tiger Moms Are Pussycats Compared with Games Moms." *The Observer,* August 4, 2012.

Bensinger, Greg. "Sprint Abandons Blackberry Tablet." *Wall Street Journal,* October 27, 2011.

Berns, Gregory, and Scott Atran. "The Biology of Cultural Conflict." *Philosophical Transactions of the Royal Society B: Biological Sciences* 367, no. 1589 (2012): 633–639.

Bernstein, Richard. "The Chinese Are Coming!" *New York Review of Books,* February 23, 2012.

Bidgood, Jess. "Chicken Chain Says Stop, but T-Shirt Maker Balks." *New York Times,* December 4, 2011.

Bing, Mark N. "Hypercompetitiveness in Academia: Achieving Criterion-Related Validity from Item Context Specificity." *Journal of Personality Assessment* 73, no. 1 (August 1999): 80–99.

Birkinshaw, Julian. "Strategies for Managing Internal Competition." *California Management Review* 44, no. 1 (2001): 21–38.

Blitz, Roger. "Clubs with Contrasting Resources Fight to Stay Up." *The Financial Times,* May 11, 2012.

Blow, Charles M. "For Jobs, It's War." *New York Times,* September 16, 2011.

Blythe, Anne. "Hog Farm Fine to Clean River." *Raleigh News & Observer,* July 25, 2012.

Boksem, Maarten A. S., Evelien Kostermans, and David De Cremer. "Failing Where Others Have Succeeded: Medial Frontal Negativity Tracks Failure in a Social Context." *Psychophysiology* 48, no. 7 (2011): 973–979.

Boksem, Maarten A. S., Evelien Kostermans, Branka Milivojevic, and David De Cremer. "Social Status Determines How We Monitor and Evaluate Our Performance." *Social Cognitive and Affective Neuroscience* 7, no. 3 (2012): 304–313.

Booth, Alan, Douglas A. Granger, Allan Mazur, and Katie T. Kivlighan. "Testosterone and Social Behavior." *Social Forces* 85, no. 1 (2006): 167–191.

Boothman, Richard C., Amy C. Blackwell, Darrell A. Campbell Jr., Elaine Commiskey, and Susan Anderson. "A Better Approach to Medical Malpractice Claims? The University of Michigan Experience." *Journal of Health and Life Sciences Law* 2, no. 2 (January 2009).

Borgatta, Edgar F., and Robert F. Bales. "Sociometric Status Patterns and Characteristics of Interaction." *Journal of Social Psychology* 43, no. 2 (1956): 289–297.

Borger, Julian. "Who Creates Harmony the World Over? Women. Who Signs Peace Deals? Men." *The Guardian,* September 19, 2012.

Bos, Peter A., David Terburg, Jack van Honk, and Bruce S. McEwen. "Testosterone Decreases Trust in Socially Naive Humans." *Proceedings of the National Academy of Sciences of the United States of America* 107, no. 22 (2010): 9991–9995.

Boseley, Sarah. "Eye Doctor Resigns from US University After Research Fraud." *The Guardian,* April 19, 2012.

———. "NHS Director to Review Cosmetic Surgery Safety." *The Guardian,* August 14, 2012.

Boshoff, Alison. "The Other Winslet Girls." *Daily Mail,* February 20, 2009.

Bowers, Simon. "Glencore X-Strata Deal Threatened by Unimpressed Shareholders." *The Guardian,* February 7, 2012.

Bowles, Hannah Riley, Linda Babcock, and Lei Lai. "Social Incentives for Gender Differences in the Propensity to Initiate Negotiations: Sometimes It Does Hurt to Ask." *Organizational Behavior and Human Decision Processes* 103, no. 1 (2007): 84–103.

Bowles, Samuel. "Group Competition, Reproductive Leveling, and the Evolution of Human Altruism." *Science* 314 (2006): 1569–1572.

———. "Genetically Capitalist?" *Science* 318 (2007): 394–395.

———. "Policies Designed for Self-interested Citizens May Undermine 'the Moral Sentiments': Evidence from Economic Experiments." *Science* 320, no. 5883 (2008): 1605–1609.

———. "Did Warfare Among Ancestral Hunter-Gatherers Affect the Evolution of Human Social Behaviors?" *Science* 324 (2009): 1293–1298.

Bowles, Samuel, and Herbert Gintis. "Cooperation." In *The New Palgrave Dictionary of Economics.* London: Palgrave Macmillan (2007).

Bowles, Samuel, and Yongjin Park. "Emulation, Inequality, and Work Hours: Was Thorsten Veblen Right?" *Economic Journal* 115 (November 2003): 397–412.

Bradbury, Jane. "Social Opportunity Produces Brain Changes in Fish." *PLOS Biology* 3, no. 11 (November 2005): 1850.

Branden, Barbara. *The Passion of Ayn Rand.* New York: Anchor Books (1986).

Branden, Nathaniel. *My Years with Ayn Rand.* San Francisco: Jossey-Bass (1999).

Brickman, Barbara Jane. "Brothers, Sisters, and Chainsaws: The Slasher Film as Locus for Sibling Rivalry." *Quarterly Review of Film and Video* 28, no. 2 (2011): 135–154.

Broad, William J. "North Korea's Performance Anxiety." *New York Times,* May 5, 2012.

Brody, Gene H. "Sibling Relationship Quality: Its Causes and Consequences." *Annual Review of Psychology* 49 (1998): 1–24.

Bronson, Po, and Ashley Merryman. *Top Dog: The Science of Winning and Losing.* New York: Twelve (2013).

Brooks, David. "Testing the Teachers." *New York Times,* April 19, 2012.

Brosnan, Sarah F., and Redouan Bshary. "Cooperation and Deception: From Evolution to Mechanisms." *Philosophical Transactions of the Royal Society B* 365, no. 1553 (September 2010): 2593–2598.

Brown, Douglas J., D. Lance Ferris, Daniel Heller, and Lisa M. Keeping. "Antecedents and Consequences of the Frequency of Upward and Downward Social Comparisons at Work." *Organizational Behavior and Human Decision Processes* 102, no. 1 (2007): 59–75.

Brown, Helen Gurley. *Sex and the Single Girl.* New York: Open Road Media Iconic Ebooks (2012).

Browne, John. *Beyond Business: An Inspirational Memoir from a Visionary Leader.* London: Weidenfeld & Nicholson (2010).

Bruck, Connie. "The Art of the Billionaire." *The New Yorker,* December 6, 2010.

Buettner, Russ. "State Panel to Review Pay of Leaders of Nonprofits." *New York Times,* August 3, 2011.

Buhrmester, Duane, and Wyndol Furman. "Perceptions of Sibling Relationships During Middle Childhood and Adolescence." *Child Development* 61, no. 5 (1990): 1387–1398.

Bull, Andy. "Greene's Gold Silences the Critics." *The Guardian,* September 1, 2011.

———. "Bolt Knows He Can Be Beaten—but Only by Himself." *The Guardian,* August 26, 2011.

———. "Fast Learner." *The Observer,* 2011, September 4, 2011.

Burckle, Michelle A., Richard M. Ryckman, Joel A. Gold, Bill Thornton, and Roberta J. Audesse. "Forms of Competitive Attitude and Achievement Orientation in Relation to Disordered Eating." *Sex Roles* 40, nos. 11–12 (1999): 853–870.

Buser, Thomas, and Muriel Niederle. "Gender, Competitiveness, and Career Choices." Working paper 18576. Cambridge, MA: National Bureau of Economic Research (November 2012).

Buss, David M., and David P. Schmitt. "Human Mate Poaching: Tactics and Temptations for Infiltrating Existing Mateships." *Journal of Personality and Social Psychology* 80, no. 6 (2001): 894–917.

Bussey, John. "Subsidy Nation: Can Firms in US Compete with China?" *Wall Street Journal,* October 21, 2011.

Butler, Patrick. "Making an Impact." *The Guardian,* November 30, 2011.

Buunk, Abraham P., and Frederick X. Gibbons. "Social Comparison: The End of a Theory and the Emergence of a Field." *Organizational Behavior and Human Decision Processes* 102, no. 1 (2007): 3–21.

Byrne, John A. "B-Schools with the Most Competitive Students." PoetsandQuants. com, 2012. Available at: http://poetsandquants.com/2012/03/01/b-schools-with-the-most-competitive-students/.

Cadwalladr, Carole. "Have an Idea as Good as Jamie Oliver's and Win $1 Million to Make It Happen." *The Guardian,* August 9, 2012.

Callahan, David. *The Cheating Culture: Why More Americans Are Doing Wrong to Get Ahead.* New York: Harcourt (2004).

Cambers, Simon. "Why Does Women's Tennis Seem a Shadow of Its Former Self?" *The Guardian,* June 16, 2011.

———. "Pushy Parents Have Not Gone Away." *The Guardian,* June 24, 2011.

Cardenas, Juan-Camilo, Anna Dreber, Emma von Essen, and Eva Ranehill. "Gender Differences in Competitiveness and Risk Taking: Comparing Children in Colombia and Sweden." *Research Papers in Economics* 18 (2010).

Cashdan, Elizabeth. "Hormones and Competitive Aggression in Women." *Aggressive Behavior* 29, no. 2 (2003): 107–115.

Cassidy, John. "After the Blow-Up." *The New Yorker,* January 22, 2010.

———. "Mastering the Machine." *The New Yorker,* July 25, 2011.

Cassuto, Leonard. "Big Trouble in the World of 'Big Physics.'" *Salon,* September 16, 2012. Available at: www.salon.com/2002/09/16/physics/.

Centre for Effective Dispute Resolution. "Tough Times, Tough Talk." Human Resource Executive Online (2011).

Chang, Yang-Ming. "Transfers and Bequests: A Portfolio Analysis in a Nash Game." *Annals of Finance* 3, no. 2 (2007): 277–295.

———. "Strategic Altruistic Transfers and Rent Seeking Within the Family." *Journal of Population Economics* 22, no. 4 (2009): 1081–1098.

Cho, Adrian. "Particle Physicists' New Extreme Teams." *Science* (2011): 333.

Choi, Do Young, Kun Chang Lee, and Seong Wook Chae. "The Effect of Individual Psychological Characteristics on Creativity Revelation: Emphasis with Psychological Empowerment and Intrinsic Motivation." In *Brain Informatics,* ed. Fabio Massimo Zanzotto, Shusaku Tsumoto, Niels Taatgen, and Yiyu Yao. Berlin: Springer Berlin Heidelberg (2012).

Choi, Jung-Kyoo, and Samuel Bowles. "The Coevolution of Parochial Altruism and War." *Science* 318 (2007): 636–639.

Cicirelli, Victor G. "Feelings of Attachment to Siblings and Well-being in Later Life." *Psychology and Aging* 4, no. 2 (1989): 211.

Citigroup. "Revisiting Plutonomy: The Rich Get Richer." March 25, 2006.

Clark, Alex, and Peter Stanford. "Should Charities Use Shock Tactics?" *The Guardian*, February 18, 2012.

Clarke, Tom. "Drug Companies Snub Antibiotics as Pipeline Threatens to Run Dry." *Nature* 425, no. 18 (September 2003): 225.

Colapinto, John. "Looking Good." *The New Yorker,* March 26, 2012.

———. "Meet Trevor Neilson." *The Observer,* July 29, 2012.

Cole, Daniel. "Elinor Ostrom." *The Guardian,* June 15, 2012.

Coll, Steve. "Gusher." *The New Yorker,* April 9, 2012.

Collier, Paul. "Don't Look to China for Economic Salvation." *The Observer,* March 11, 2012.

Collins, Jim. *Good to Great.* New York: HarperCollins (2001).

Collins, Laura. "England, Their England." *The New Yorker,* July 4, 2011.

Colt, George Howe. *Brothers.* New York: Scribner (2012).

Coman, Julian. "The King and I." *The Observer,* March 25, 2012.

Conerly, Rachel. "The Collaborative Organization" (electronic presentation). March 21, 2011.

Conley, Dalton. *The Pecking Order: Which Siblings Survive and Why.* New York: Pantheon Books, 2004.

Conn, David. "Inspire a Generation?" *The Guardian,* August 25, 2012.

Connor, James M., and Jason Mazanov. "Would You Dope? A General Population Test of the Goldman Dilemma." *British Journal of Sports Medicine* 43, no. 11 (2009): 871–872.

Cook, Chris. "Oaksey House: The Service Station That Helps Bruised and Battered Jockeys Back in the Saddle." *The Guardian,* December 22, 2011.

Cookson, Clive. "Synthetic Life: The Revolution Begins." *The Financial Times Magazine,* July 28–29, 2012.

Cooper, Chris. "What if We Tested Athletes for Genes Instead of Drugs?" *The Observer,* May 6, 2012.

Corbett, Jo, Martin J. Barwood, Alex Ouzounoglou, Richard Thelwell, and Matthew Dicks. "Influence of Competition on Performance and Pacing During Cycling Exercise." University of Portsmouth, 2012.

Cotton, Christopher, Frank McIntyre, and Joseph Price. "Gender Differences in Repeated Competition: Evidence from School Math Contests." *Journal of Economic Behavior and Organization* 86 (February 2013): 52–56.

Coy, Peter. "You're So Bain." *Bloomberg Business Week,* January 11, 2012.

Crawford, Leslie. "Does Homework Really Work?" Available at: Greatschools.org.

Crocker, Jennifer, and Lora E. Park. "The Costly Pursuit of Self-Esteem." *Psychological Bulletin* 130, no. 3 (2004): 392–414.

Croson, Rachel, and Uri Gneezy. "Gender Differences in Preferences." *Journal of Economic Literature* 47, no. 2 (2009): 1–27.

Curtis, Guy J. "An Examination of Factors Related to Plagiarism and a Five-Year Follow-up of Plagiarism at an Australian University." *International Journal for Educational Integrity* 7, no. 1 (2001): 30–42.

Cyranoski, David. "Your Cheatin' Heart." *Nature Medicine* 12, no. 5 (May 2006): 490.

Dalisay, Francis, Jay D. Hmielowski, Matthew James Kushin, and Masahiro Yamamoto. "Social Capital and the Spiral of Silence." *International Journal of Public Opinion Research* 24, no. 3 (July 11, 2012): 325–345.

Daly, Martin, Margo Wilson, Catherine A. Salmon, Mariko Hiraiwa-Hasegawa, and Toshikazu Hasegawa. "Siblicide and Seniority." *Homicide Studies* 5 (February 2001): 30–45.

Darwin, Charles. *On The Origin of Species.* London: John Murray, 1859.

———. *The Descent of Man and Selection in Relation to Sex.* London: John Murray (1922).

Das, Andrew. "Less Is More: Less Practice Equals More Medals." *New York Times,* August 5, 2012.

David, M. Levy, and A. Ruckmick Christian. "Studies in Sibling Rivalry." *American Journal of Psychology* 49, no. 4 (1937): 691.

Davies, William. "All of Our Business: Why Britain Needs More Private Sector Employee Ownership." Employee Ownership Association (January 2012).

Davis, Anna, and Pippa Crerar. "'Gold Club' of Elite Schools to Put London Pupils on Top." *The Evening Standard,* October 18, 2012.

Davis, Jennifer. "Birth Order, Sibship Size, and Status in Modern Canada." *Human Nature* 8, no. 3 (September 1997): 205–230.

Dawkins, Richard. *The Selfish Gene.* 30th anniversary edition, with a new introduction by the author. London: Oxford University Press (2006).

De Botton, Alain. *Status Anxiety.* London: Hamish Hamilton (2004).

Decety, Jean, Philip L. Jackson, Jessica A. Sommerville, Thierry Chaminade, and Andrew N. Meltzoff. "The Neural Bases of Cooperation and Competition: An fMRI Investigation." *NeuroImage* 23, no. 2 (2004): 744–751.

De Dreu, Carsten K. W., Lindred L. Greer, Michel J. J. Handgraaf, Shaul Shalvi, Gerben van Kleef, Matthijs Baas, Femke S. Ten Velden, Eric van Dijk, and Sander W. W. Feith. "The Neuropeptide Oxytocin Regulates Parochial Altruism in Intergroup Conflict Among Humans." *Science* 328 (2010): 1408–1411.

Dehart, Tracy, Brett Pelham, Luke Fiedorowicz, Mauricio Carvallo, and Shira Gabriel. "Including Others in the Implicit Self: Implicit Evaluation of Significant Others." *Self and Identity* 10, no. 1 (2011): 127–135.

Delaney, Kevin. "In the Outgoing and the Introverted, Yin and Yang." *New York Times,* March 11, 2012.

———. "Change the World? Game On." *New York Times,* July 8, 2012.

Delios, Andrew. "How Can Organizations Be Competitive but Dare to Care?" *Academy of Management Perspectives* (2010): 24–35.

Denrell, Jerker, and Chengwei Liu. "Top Performers Are Not the Most Impressive When Extreme Performance Indicates Unreliability." *Proceedings of the National Academy of Sciences of the United States of America* 109, no. 24 (2012): 9331–9336.

Dent, Vivian. "Reply to Commentary by Juliet Mitchell: Siblings in Clinical Work." *Psychoanalytic Dialogues: The International Journal of Relational Perspectives* 19, no. 2 (2009): 171–174.

Depner, Charlene E., and Berit Ingersoll-Dayton. "Supportive Relationships in Later Life." *Psychology and Aging* 3, no. 4 (1988): 348–357.

Devine, Cathy. "We Should Not Fetishise Competitive School Sport." *The Guardian,* December 10, 2010.

De Vries, Raymond, Melissa S. Anderson, and Brian C. Martinson. "Normal Misbehavior: Scientists Talk About the Ethics of Research." *Journal of Empirical Research on Human Research Ethics* 1, no. 1 (March 2006): 43–50.

De Waal, Frans. *Chimpanzee Politics: Power and Sex Among Apes.* London: Jonathan Cape (1982).

———. *Our Inner Ape: The Best and Worst of Human Nature.* London: Granta Books (2005).

Djerassi, Carl. *Cantor's Dilemma: A Novel.* New York: Penguin Books (1989).

———. *Pill, Pygmy Chimps, and Degas' Horse: The Remarkable Autobiography of the Award-Winning Scientist Who Synthesized the Birth Control Pill.* New York: Basic Books (1992).

———. *This Man's Pill: Reflections on the 50th Birthday of the Pill.* New York: Oxford University Press (2001).

Doorn, G. Sander van, Geerten M. Hengeveld, and Franz J. Weissing. "The Evolution of Social Dominance I: Two-Player Models." *Behaviour* 140, no. 10 (2003): 1305–1332.

Dreber, Anna E., Emma von Essen, and Eva Ranehill. "Outrunning the Gender Gap—Boys and Girls Compete Equally." *Institute for Financial Research* (March 2010).

Duane, Buhrmester, and Furman Wyndol. "Perceptions of Sibling Relationships During Middle Childhood and Adolescence." *Child Development* 61, no. 5 (1990): 1387–1398.

Dunbar, Robin I. M. "Coevolution of Neocortical Size, Group Size, and Language in Humans." *Behavioral and Brain Sciences* 16 (1993): 681–735.

Dunn, Judy. *Siblings: Love, Envy, and Understanding.* London: Grant McIntyre (1982).

———. *Sisters and Brothers.* Isle of Man, UK: Fontana Paperbacks (1984).

———. *The Beginnings of Social Understanding.* Cambridge, MA: Harvard University Press (1988).

———. "Sibling Relationships: Theory and Issues for Practice." *Children and Society* 19, no. 4 (2005): 339–340.

Dupre, Judith. *Skyscrapers.* With an introductory interview with Philip Johnson. New York: Black Dog & Leventhal Publishers (1996).

Dweck, Carol. *Mindset: The New Psychology of Success.* New York: Ballantine Books (2007).

Dwyer, Jim. "A Billionaire Philanthropist Struggles to Go Broke." *New York Times,* August 8, 2012.

Dysvik, Anders, and Bård Kuvaas. "Intrinsic and Extrinsic Motivation as Predictors of Work Effort: The Moderating Role of Achievement Goals." *British Journal of Social Psychology* 52, no. 3 (September 2013).

Economist, The. "Move Over, Dalton." *The Economist,* September 1, 2012.

———. "Class Acts." *The Economist,* September 15, 2012.

———. "Working the System." *The Economist,* September 29, 2012.

———. "Body Politic." *The Economist,* October 6, 2012.

———. "Who's Shrugging Now?" *The Economist,* October 20, 2012.

Edmondson, Amy C. "Learning from Mistakes Is Easier Said Than Done: Group and Organizational Influences on the Detection and Correction of Human Error." *Journal of Applied Behavioral Science* 32, no. 1 (1996): 5–28.

Edsall, Thomas B. "Is This the End of Market Democracy?" *New York Times,* February 19, 2012.

———. "The Reinvention of Political Morality." *New York Times,* December 5, 2011.

Edward, Joyce. "Sibling Discord: A Force for Growth and Conflict." *Clinical Social Work Journal* 41, no. 1 (March 2013): 77.

Eichenwald, Kurt. "Microsoft's Lost Decade." *Vanity Fair* (August 2012).

eLearners. "Student Dropout Rates Linked to High Stress over Finances." Available at: eLearners.com.

Employee Ownership Association. "Case Study: Gripple." 2011. Available at: Gripple.com.

Enrich, David, and David Gauthier-Villiars. "Struggling French Banks Fought to Avoid Oversight." *Wall Street Journal,* October 21, 2011.

Erat, Sanjiv, and Uri Gneezy. "White Lies." *Management Science* 58, no. 4 (April 2012): 723–733.

Erdal, David. *Beyond the Corporation: Humanity Working.* London: The Bodley Head (2011).

Evans, Rhonda. "Is the Canadian Model Right for UK Schools?" *The Guardian,* January 4, 2011.

Falbo, Toni, and Dudley L. Poston Jr. "The Academic, Personality, and Physical Outcomes of Only Children in China." *Child Development* 64, no. 1 (1993): 18–35.

Fang, Ferric C. "Reforming Science: Structural Reforms." *Infection and Immunity* 80, no. 3 (2011): 897–901.

Farrer, Martin. "Olympics Effect on Economy May Be Short Lived, Says King." *The Guardian,* August 13, 2012.

Feinberg, Kenneth R. *What Is Life Worth? The Unprecedented Effort to Compensate the Victims of 9/11.* New York: PublicAffairs, 2005.

Feinberg, Mark E., Susan M. McHale, Ann C. Crouter, and Patricio Cumsille. "Sibling Differentiation: Sibling and Parent Relationship Trajectories in Adolescence." *Child Development* 74, no. 5 (2003): 1261–1274.

Feinberg, Mark, Anna Solmeyer, and Susan McHale. "The Third Rail of Family Systems: Sibling Relationships, Mental and Behavioral Health, and Preventive Intervention in Childhood and Adolescence." *Clinical Child and Family Psychology Review* (2011): 1–15.

Felson, Richard, B. "Aggression and Violence Between Siblings." *Social Psychology Quarterly* 46, no. 4 (1983): 271–285.

Fernandez-Araoz, Claudio. "The Coming Fight for Executive Talent." *Bloomberg Business Week,* December 7, 2009.

Festinger, Leon. "A Theory of Social Comparison Processes." *Human Relations* 7, no. 2 (1954): 117–140.

Finkelhor, David, Heather Turner, and Richard Ormrod. "Kid's Stuff: The Nature and Impact of Peer and Sibling Violence on Younger and Older Children." *Child Abuse and Neglect* 30, no. 12 (2006): 1401–1421.

Finnegan, William. "The Storm." *The New Yorker,* March 5, 2012.

Forsyth, Donelson R., Natalie K. Lawrence, Jeni L. Burnette, and Roy F. Baumeister. "Attempting to Improve the Academic Performance of Struggling College Students by Bolstering Their Self-esteem: An Intervention That Backfired." *Journal of Social and Clinical Psychology* 26, no. 4 (2007): 447–459.

Fowden, A. L., and T. Moore. "Maternal-Fetal Resource Allocation: Co-operation and Conflict." *Placenta* (2012). Available at: 10.1016/j.placenta.2012.05.002.

Frank, Robert H. *The Darwin Economy: Liberty, Competition, and the Common Good.* Princeton, NJ: Princeton University Press (2011).

———. "Will the Skillful Win?" *New York Times,* August 5, 2012.

Frank, Robert H., and Philip J. Cook. *The Winner-Take-All Society: How More and More Americans Compete for Ever Fewer and Bigger Prizes, Encouraging Economic Waste, Income Inequality, and an Impoverished Cultural Life.* New York: Free Press (1995).

Frank, Robert H., Thomas Gilovich, and Dennis T. Regan. "Does Studying Economics Inhibit Cooperation?" *Journal of Economic Perspectives* 7, no. 2 (1993): 159–171.

Franken, R. E., Ross Hill, and James Kierstead. "Sport Interest as Predicted by the Personality Measures of Competitiveness, Mastery, Instrumentality, Expressivity, and Sensation Seeking." *Personality and Individual Differences* 17, no. 4 (1994): 467–476.

Fraser, Giles. "Loose Canon." *The Guardian,* July 21, 2012.

Fraser, Ian. "Loss of Trust." *Signet* (July 16, 2012).

Frazier, Ian. "Out of the Bronx." *The New Yorker,* February 6, 2012.

Freedland, Jonathan. "The Markets Distrust Democracy." *The Guardian,* November 16, 2011.

Freeman, Richard, Eric Weinstein, Elizabeth Marincola, Janet Rosenbaum, and Frank Solomon. "Competition and Careers in Biosciences." *Science* 294, no. 5550 (2001): 2293–2294.

Frere-Jones, Sasha. "The Gerbil's Revenge." *The New Yorker,* June 9, 2008.

Frick, Bernd. "Gender Differences in Competitiveness: Empirical Evidence from Professional Distance Running." *Labour Economics* 18, no. 3 (2011): 389–398.

———. "Gender Differences in Competitive Orientations: Empirical Evidence from Ultramarathon Running." *Journal of Sports Economics* 12, no. 3 (2011): 317–340.

Friedman, George. "The Rise of Britain." *Geopolitical Weekly* (May 7, 2012).

Friedman, Stewart D. "Sibling Relationships and Intergenerational Succession in Family Firms." *Family Business Review* 4, no. 1 (1991): 3–20.

Friedman, Thomas L., and Michael Mandelbaum. *That Used to Be Us: What Went Wrong with America—and How It Can Come Back.* New York: Little, Brown (2011).

Fundenberg, Drew, David G. Rand, and Anna Dreber. "Slow to Anger and Fast to Forgive." *American Economic Review* 102, no. 2 (2012): 720–749.

Furnham, Adrian, D. Kirkcaldy Bruce, and Richard Lynn. "National Attitudes to Competitiveness, Money, and Work Among Young People: First, Second, and Third World Differences." *Human Relations* 47, no. 1 (1994): 119–132.

Gagne Joshua J., and Niteesh K. Choudhry. "How Many 'Me-Too' Drugs Is Too Many?" *Journal of the American Medical Association* 305, no. 7 (2011): 711–712.

Garcia, Stephen M., and Avishalom Tor. "Rankings, Standards, and Competition: Task vs. Scale Comparisons." *Organizational Behavior and Human Decision Processes* 102, no. 1 (2007): 95–108.

Garcia-Martinez, Jose Antonio. "Competitiveness, Cooperation, and Strategic Interaction: A Classroom Experiment on Oligopoly." *Revista Internacional de Sociologia* 70 (2012): 168–187.

Gay, Jason. "A Long, Amazing Ride to the Olympics." *Wall Street Journal,* August 12, 2012.

Gefter, Amanda. "Wilson vs. Watson: The Blessing of Great Enemies." *NewScientist* (September 10, 2009).

Gibbons, Frederick X. "Social Comparison and Depression: Company's Effect on Misery." *Journal of Personality and Social Psychology* 51, no. 1 (1986): 140–148.

Gibson, Owen. "Fewer Young People Playing Sport, Research Reveals." *The Guardian,* June 23, 2012.

————. "The Host Country Has Claimed Gold in Even More Sports Than the US Has." *The Guardian,* August 9, 2012.

————. "Doping: Now Worse Than It's Ever Been." *The Guardian,* February 16, 2013.

Gibson, Owen, and Patrick Wintour. "This Generation of Parents May Be Fitter Than Their Children, Says Coe." *The Guardian,* August 11, 2012.

Gilbert, Paul, John Price, and Steven Allan. "Social Comparison, Social Attractiveness, and Evolution: How Might They Be Related?" *New Ideas in Psychology* 13, no. 2 (1995): 149–165.

Glebbeek, Arie C., and Eric H. Bax. "Is High Employee Turnover Really Harmful? An Empirical Test Using Company Records." *Academy of Management Journal* 47, no. 2 (2004): 277–286.

Glendinning, Miles. *Architecture's Evil Empire? The Triumph and Tragedy of Global Modernism.* London: Reaktion Books (2010).

Glucksberg, Sam. "Problem Solving: Response Competition and the Influence of Drive." *Psychological Reports* 15, no. 3 (1964): 939–942.

Gneezy, Ayelet, and Daniel M. T. Fessler. "Combat and Cooperation: War Increases Prosocial Punishments and Rewards." *Proceedings of the Royal Society: Biological Sciences* (June 2011).

Gneezy, Ayelet, Alex Imas, Amber Brown, Leif D. Nelson, and Michael I. Norton. "Paying to Be Nice: Consistency and Costly Prosocial Behaviour." *Management Science* 58 (2012): 179–187.

Gneezy, Uri, Kenneth L. Leonard, and John A. List. "Gender Differences in Competition: Evidence from a Matrilineal and a Patriarchal Society." *Econometrica* 77, no. 5 (2009): 1637–1664.

Gneezy, Uri, Muriel Niederle, and Aldo Rustichini. "Performance in Competitive Environments: Gender Differences." *Quarterly Journal of Economics* 118, no. 3 (2003): 1049–1074.

Gneezy, Uri, and Aldo Rustichini. "Gender and Competition at a Young Age." *American Economic Review* 94, no. 2 (2004): 377–381.

Gogarty, Paul, and Ian Williamson. *Winning at All Costs: Sporting Gods and Their Demons.* London: JR Books (2009).

Goldacre, Ben. *Bad Pharma: How Drug Companies Mislead Doctors and Harm Patients.* London: Fourth Estate (2012).

Goldman, Bob, Patricia J. Bush, and Ronald Klatz. *Death in the Locker Room: Steroids and Sports.* Icarus Press (1984).

Gonzalez-Bono, Esperanza, Alicia Salvador, Jorge Javier Ricarte, M. A. Serrano, and M. Arnedo. "Testosterone and Attribution of Successful Competition." *Aggressive Behavior* 26, no. 3 (2000): 235–240.

Goodley, Simon. "Meltdown in the City." *The Guardian,* September 10, 2011.

Goodman, Paul S., and Emily Haisley. "Social Comparison Processes in an Organizational Context: New Directions." *Organizational Behavior and Human Decision Processes* 102, no. 1 (2007): 109–125.

Goodstein, David. "Scientific Misconduct." *Academe* 88 (2002): 28–31.

Gopnik, Alison, and Adam Gopnik. "Mom Always Liked You Best." *New York Times Book Review,* September 23, 2011.

Grabell, Michael. "The Expendables: How the Temps Who Power Corporate Giants Are Getting Crushed." *ProPublica*, June 27, 2013. Available at: www.propublica.org/article/the-expendables-how-the-temps-who-power-corporate-giants-are-getting-crushe.

Graf, Lorenz, Andreas König, Albrecht Enders, and Harald Hungenberg. "Debiasing Competitive Irrationality: How Managers Can Be Prevented from Trading Off Absolute for Relative Profit." *European Management Journal* 30, no. 4 (2012): 386–403.

Grafton, Anthony. "Our Universities: Why Are They Failing?" *New York Review of Books*, November 24, 2011.

Grandjean, Guy, Taylor Matthew, and Paul Lewis. "Deportation Contractor Faces Litany of Abuse Claims Against Staff." *The Guardian*, April 14, 2012.

Grant, Adam. *Give and Take: A Revolutionary Approach to Success*. New York: Viking (2013).

Grant, Adam M., and Sabine Sonnentag. "Doing Good Buffers Against Feeling Bad: Prosocial Impact Compensates for Negative Task and Self-evaluations." *Organizational Behavior and Human Decision Processes* 111 (2010): 13–22.

Gray, Peter. "As Children's Freedom Has Declined, So Has Their Creativity." *Psychological Today* (September 17, 2012).

Graziano, William G., Elizabeth C. Hair, and John F. Finch. "Competitiveness Mediates the Link Between Personality and Group Performance." *Journal of Personality and Social Psychology* 73, no. 6 (1997): 1394–1408.

Greenbaum, L. "Sibling Rivalry." *Lancet* 354, no. 9186 (1999): 1312.

Gregory, Stanford W., Jr., and Timothy J. Gallagher. "Spectral Analysis of Candidates' Nonverbal Vocal Communication: Predicting US Presidential Election Outcomes." *Social Psychology Quarterly* 65, no. 3 (2002): 298–308.

Gregory, Stanford W., Jr., and Stephen Webster. "A Nonverbal Signal in Voices of Interview Partners Effectively Predicts Communication Accommodation and Social Status Perceptions." *Journal of Personality and Social Psychology* 70, no. 6 (1996): 1231–1240.

Guala, Francesco. "Reciprocity: Weak or Strong? What Punishment Experiments Do (and Do Not) Demonstrate." *Behavioral and Brain Sciences* 35, no. 1 (2012): 1–15.

The Guardian. "The Secret Teacher Writes an Honest Letter Home." *The Guardian*, May 19, 2012.

Hacker, Andrew. "We're More Unequal Than You Think." *New York Review of Books*, April 23, 2012.

Hacker, Jacob S., and Paul Pierson. *Winner-Take-All Politics: How Washington Made the Rich Richer—and Turned Its Back on the Middle Class*. New York: Simon & Schuster (2010).

Hahn, Avital Lourisa. "Baird Revels in Its Independence." *Investment Dealers' Digest* (February 14, 2005).

Hamedani, MarYam G., Hazel Rose Markus, and Alyssa S. Fu. "My Nation, My Self: Divergent Framings of America Influence American Selves." *Personality and Social Psychology Bulletin* 37, no. 3 (2011): 350–364.

Hamel, Gary. "First, Let's Fire All the Managers." *Harvard Business Review* (December 2011).

Hamilton, W. D. "The Genetical Evolution of Social Behaviour." *Journal of Theoretical Biology* 7 (1964).

Hamlin, J. Kiley, Karen Wynn, and Paul Bloom. "Social Evaluation by Preverbal Infants." *Science* 450, no. 22 (2007): 557–558.

Hardin, Garrett. "The Tragedy of the Commons." *Science* 162, no. 3859 (December 13, 1968). Available at: www.sciencemag.org/content/162/3859/1243.full.

Harris, Judith Rich. *The Nurture Assumption: Why Children Turn Out the Way They Do.* London: Bloomsbury (1998).

Hasan, Mehdi. "The Schools Exam System Is No Longer Fit for Purpose." *The Guardian,* December 17, 2011.

Hatemi, Peter K., and Rose McDermott. "The Genetics of Politics: Discovery, Challenges, and Progress." *Trends in Genetics* 28, no. 10 (2012): 525–533.

Hayes, Christopher. *The Twilight of the Elites: America After Meritocracy.* New York: Crown (2012).

Heffernan, Margaret. *Willful Blindness: Why We Ignore the Obvious at Our Peril.* New York: Simon & Schuster (2011).

Heller, Nathan. "The Disconnect: Why Are So Many Americans Living by Themselves?" *The New Yorker,* April 16, 2012.

Hemming, Henry. *Together: How Small Groups Achieve Big Things.* London: John Murray (2011).

Hertwig, Ralph, Jennifer Nerissa Davis, and Frank J. Sulloway. "Parental Investment: How an Equity Motive Can Produce Inequality." *Psychological Bulletin* 128, no. 5 (2002): 728–745.

Hibbard, David R., and Duane Buhrmester. "Competitiveness, Gender, and Adjustment Among Adolescents." *Sex Roles* 63, no. 5 (2010): 412–424.

Hillmer, Steve, Barbara Hillmer, and Gale McRoberts. "The Real Costs of Turnover: Lessons from a Call Center." *Human Resource Planning* 27, no. 3 (2004): 34–41.

Ho, Violet T. "Interpersonal Counterproductive Work Behaviors: Distinguishing Between Person-Focused Versus Task-Focused Behaviors and Their Antecedents." *Journal of Business and Psychology* (2012): 1–16.

Hoare, Stephen. "In the Market for Mas." *The Guardian,* March 27, 2012.

Hochschild, Arlie Russell. "The Outsourced Life." *New York Times,* May 6, 2012.

Hofstede, Geert. *Culture's Consequences: Comparing Values, Behaviors, Institutions, and Organizations Across Nations.* 2nd ed. Thousand Oaks, CA: Sage Publications (2001).

Hofstede, Geert, Gert Jan Hofstede, and Michael Minkov. *Cultures and Organizations: Software of the Mind: Intercultural Cooperation and Its Importance for Survival.* New York: McGraw-Hill (2010).

Hopkins, Keith, and Mary Beard. *The Colosseum.* London: Profile Books (2011).

Hopkins, Nick. "G4s Using Untrained Staff to Screen Visitors." *The Guardian,* August 7, 2012.

Hornbacher, Marya. *Wasted: Going Back from an Addiction to Starvation.* London: Fourth Estate (2010).

Houston, John M., Sandra A. Mcintire, Judy Kinnie, and Christeine Terry. "A Factorial Analysis of Scales Measuring Competitiveness." *Educational and Psychological Measurement* 62, no. 2 (2002): 284–298.

Hughes, Claire, Alexandra L. Cutting, and Judy Dunn. "Acting Nasty in the Face of Failure? Longitudinal Observations of 'Hard-to-Manage' Children Playing a Rigged Competitive Game with a Friend." *Journal of Abnormal Child Psychology* 29, no. 5 (2001): 403–416.

Inman, Philip. "Brazil Passes UK to Become World's 6th Largest Economy." *The Guardian,* December 26, 2011.

———. "Skyscraper Craze Shows Chinese May Be Heading for a Fall." *The Guardian,* January 12, 2012.

Insley, Jill. "Farmers Fear Supermarket Offers Threaten British Food." *The Guardian,* August 12, 2012.

Irwin, Nancy, Carol Leonard, Ronald Clyman, and Roberta A. Ballard. "Sixty Follow-up of Siblings Present at Birth in an Alternative Birth Center." *Pediatric Research* 15 (1981): 449.

Jackson, Nate. "The NFL's Concussion Culture." *The Nation,* July 27, 2011.

Jacobs, Andrew. "Heavy Burden on Athletes Takes Joy Away from China's Olympic Success." *New York Times,* August 7, 2012.

Jacques, Martin "Why Do We Continue to Ignore China's Rise?" *The Observer,* March 24, 2012.

Jamshidi, Akbar, Talebi Hossien, Seed Saeed Sajadi, Khalil Safari, and Ghasem Zare. "The Relationship Between Sport Orientation and Competitive Anxiety in Elite Athletes." *Procedia—Social and Behavioral Sciences* 30 (2011): 1161–1165.

Janssen, Marco A. "Elinor Ostrom." *Nature* 172 (July 11, 2012): 487.

Jayson, Sharon. "From Brain to Mouth: The Psychology of Obesity." *USA Today,* August 1, 2012.

Jena, Anupam B., John E. Calfee, Edward C. Mansley, and Tomas J. Philipson. "'Me-Too' Innovation in Pharmaceutical Markets." *Forum for Health Economics and Policy* 12, no. 1 (2009): 1–19.

Jennings, Marianne M. *The Seven Signs of Ethical Collapse: How to Spot Moral Meltdowns in Companies—Before It's Too Late.* New York: St. Martin's Press (2006).

Jha, Alok. "Being Social 'Gave Humans Larger Brains.'" *The Guardian,* June 22, 2011.

———. "Research Fraud Forces Psychology to Take a Hard Look at Itself." *The Guardian,* September 13, 2012.

Johns, Helen, and Paul Ormerod. *Happiness, Economics, and Public Policy.* London: Institute of Economic Affairs (2008).

Johnson, Diane. "Finish That Homework!" *New York Review of Books,* August 18, 2011.

Judson, Horace Freeland. *The Great Betrayal: Fraud in Science.* New York: Harcourt (2004).

Kahn, Jennifer. "The Perfect Stride." *The New Yorker,* November 8, 2010.

Kalichman, Michael W., and P. J. Friedman. "A Pilot Study of Biomedical Trainees' Perceptions Concerning Research Ethics." *Academic Medicine* 67 (1992): 769–775.

Kalma, Akko. "Hierarchisation and Dominance Assessment at First Glance." *European Journal of Social Psychology* 21, no. 2 (1991): 165–181.

Kapner, Suzanne. "After Grueling Woes, CompUSA's Revival Efforts Fail to Spark Faith." TheStreet.com, December 30, 1999.

Karos, Leigh Karavasilis, Nina Howe, and Jasmin Aquan-Assee. "Reciprocal and Complementary Sibling Interactions, Relationship Quality, and Socio-emotional Problem Solving." *Infant and Child Development* 16, no. 6 (2007): 577–596.

Kaufman, Frederick. "How Goldman Sachs Created the Food Crisis." *Foreign Policy* (April 27, 2011). Available at: www.foreignpolicy.com/articles/2011/04/27/how_goldman_sachs_created_the_food_crisis.

———. *Bet the Farm: How Food Stopped Being Food.* Hoboken, NJ: John Wiley & Sons (2012).

Kaufman, Scott Barry. *Ungifted: Intelligence Redefined.* New York: Basic Books (2013).

Keltner, Dacher, Deborah H. Gruenfeld, and Cameron Anderson. "Power, Approach, and Inhibition." *Psychological Review* 110, no. 2 (2003): 265–284.

Kennedy, Maev. "Why Cross the South Pole in Winter? It's Just What I Do." *The Guardian*, September 18, 2012.

Kessel, Anna. "Athletics Is All I Ever Think About—It's Like Being Young and Falling in Love." *The Guardian*, May 1, 2012.

Kessler, David A., Janet L. Rose, Robert J. Temple, Renie Schapiro, and Joseph P. Griffin. "Therapeutic-Class Wars—Drug Promotion in a Competitive Marketplace." *New England Journal of Medicine* 331, no. 20 (1994): 1350–1353.

Khoja, Faiza. "Is Sibling Rivalry Good or Bad for High Technology Organizations?" *Journal of High Technology Management Research* 19, no. 1 (2008): 11–20.

Kidder, Rushworth M. "Ask Not for Whom the Students Cheat: They Cheat for Thee." *Ethics Newsline*, February 28, 2011.

King, Ronnel B., Dennis M. McInerney, and David A. Watkins. "Competitiveness Is Not That Bad—at Least in the East: Testing the Hierarchical Model of Achievement Motivation in the Asian Setting." *International Journal of Intercultural Relations* 36, no. 3 (2012): 446–457.

Kirby, David. *Animal Factory: The Looming Threat of Industrial Pig, Dairy, and Poultry Farms to Humans and the Environment.* New York: St. Martin's Press (2010).

Kirkpatrick, Doug. "Does Power Corrupt? Science Says Yes." Morning Star Self-Management Institute, May 20, 2012.

Klinenberg, Eric. *Going Solo: The Extraordinary Rise and Surprising Appeal of Living Alone.* New York: Penguin (2012).

Kluger, Jeffrey. *The Sibling Effect: What the Bonds Among Brothers and Sisters Reveal About Us.* New York: Riverhead Books (2011).

Korelitz, Jean Hanff. *Admission: A Novel.* New York: Grand Central Publishing (2009).

Koretz, Gene. "Are Women Less Competitive?" *Business Week*, December 9, 2002.

Korpela, Kalevi M. "How Long Does It Take for the Scientific Literature to Purge

Itself of Fraudulent Material? The Breuning Case Revisited." *Current Medical Research and Opinion* 26, no. 4 (2010): 843–847.

Koster, Raph. *A Theory of Fun for Game Design*. Phoenix, AZ: Paraglyph Press (2005).

KPMG Switzerland. "Profile of a Fraudster." June 15, 2011.

Kraus, Michael W., Paul K. Piff, and Dacher Keltner. "Social Class as Culture: The Convergence of Resources and Rank in the Social Realm." *Current Directions in Psychological Science* 20, no. 4 (2011): 246–250.

Kristensen, Petter, and Tor Bjerkedal. "Explaining the Relation Between Birth Order and Intelligence." *Science* 316, no. 5832 (June 22, 2007): 1717.

Kushner, David. "Machine Politics." *The New Yorker*, May 7, 2012.

Lafsky, Melissa. "Are Men Really More Competitive Than Women?" *New York Times*, February 6, 2008.

Lanier, Jaron. *Who Owns the Future?* New York: Simon & Schuster (2013).

Larrick, Richard P., Katherine A. Burson, and Jack B. Soll. "Social Comparison and Confidence: When Thinking You're Better Than Average Predicts Overconfidence (and When It Does Not)." *Organizational Behavior and Human Decision Processes* 102, no. 1 (2007): 76–94.

Lashewicz, Bonnie, and Norah Keating. "Tensions Among Siblings in Parent Care." *European Journal of Ageing* 6, no. 2 (2009): 127–135.

Lawrence, Peter A. "The Politics of Publication." *Nature* 422, no. 6929 (2003): 259–261.

Lehmann, Laurent, and François Rousset. "How Life History and Demography Promote or Inhibit the Evolution of Helping Behaviours." *Philosophical Transactions of the Royal Society B: Biological Sciences* 365, no. 1553 (2010): 2599–2617.

Lepper, Mark R., David Greene, and Richard E. Nisbett. "Undermining Children's Intrinsic Interest with Extrinsic Reward: A Test of the 'Overjustification' Hypothesis." *Journal of Personality and Social Psychology* 28, no. 1 (1973): 129–137.

Levine, George. *Darwin Loves You: Natural Selection and the Re-enchantment of the World*. Princeton, NJ: Princeton University Press (2008).

Levy, David M. "The Hostile Act." *Psychological Review* 48, no. 4 (1941): 356–361.

Lewis, Anthony. "The Shame of America." *New York Review of Books*, January 12, 2012.

Lewontin, Richard. "It's Even Less in Your Genes." *New York Review of Books*, May 26, 2011.

Lindquist, Gabriella Sjorgen, and Jenny Save-Soderbergh. "'Girls Will Be Girls'— Especially Among Boys: Competitive Behavior in the 'Daily Double' on *Jeopardy*." Linz, Austria: Johannes Kepler University, Swedish Institute for Social Research.

Lippmann, Walter. *Drift and Mastery: An Attempt to Diagnose the Current Unrest*. New York: Mitchell Kennerley (1914).

Littlemore, Sue. "Universities 'Need to Explain What Plagiarism Is.'" *The Guardian*, June 12, 2012.

Longman, Jere. "For Female Athletes, ACL Injuries Take a Toll." *New York Times*, March 27, 2011.

Lott, Tim. "As a Child, I Always Sought My Older Brother's Approval." *The Observer,* March 24, 2012.

———. "Did We Damage Each Other?" *The Guardian,* March 30, 2012.

———. "Get Over It, Guys." *The Observer,* August 18, 2012.

———. *Under the Same Stars.* New York: Simon & Schuster (2012).

Ludvig, Sandra, and Carmen Thoma. "Do Women Have More Shame Than Men? An Experiment on Self-assessment and the Shame of Overestimating Oneself." Discussion Paper 2012-15. University of Munich, Department of Economics (2012).

Lunn, Peter. *Basic Instincts: Human Nature and the New Economics.* Singapore: Marshall Cavendish (2008).

Machi, Ethel. "Improving US Competitiveness with K-12 Education and Training." Washington, DC: Heritage Foundation (2008).

Macilwain, Colin. "What Science Is Really Worth." *Nature* 464 (June 9, 2010): 682–684.

Magagna, Jeanne. "Transformation: From Twin to Individual." *Journal of Child Psychotherapy* 33, no. 1 (2007): 51–69.

Majendie, Matt. "The Brains Behind Our Mind Games." *The Evening Standard,* November 7, 2011.

Martens, Rainer, Robin S. Vealey, and Damon Burton. *Competitive Anxiety in Sport.* Champaign, IL: Human Kinetics (1990).

Martin, Roger L. *Fixing the Game: Bubbles, Crashes, and What Capitalism Can Learn from the NFL.* Boston: Harvard Business Review Press (2011).

Mathiason, Nick. "Square Mile in Spotlight as Tax Avoidance Trade 'Cheats' Europe." *The Observer,* December 17, 2011.

Matthews, Karen A., and Julio Angula. "Measurement of the Type A Behavior Pattern in Children: Assessment of Children's Competitiveness, Impatience-Anger, and Aggression." *Child Development* 51, no. 2 (1980).

Mayr, Ulrich, Dave Wozniak, Casey Davidson, David Kuhns, and William T. Harbaugh. "Competitiveness Across the Life Span: The Feisty Fifties." *Psychology and Aging* 27, no. 2 (2012): 278–285.

Mazur, Allan. "Sex Difference in Testosterone Response to a Video Game Contest." *Evolution and Human Behavior* 18, no. 5 (1997): 317–326.

Mazur, Allan, and Alan Booth. "Testosterone and Dominance in Men." *Behavioral and Brain Sciences* 21, no. 3 (1998): 353–363.

McCormich, Neil. "I Love My Brother—Just Can't Stand to Be with Him." *The Evening Standard,* October 13, 2011.

McElheny, Victor K. *Drawing the Map of Life: Inside the Human Genome Project.* New York: Basic Books (2010).

McGrath, Ben. "Queen of the D-League." *The New Yorker,* April 25, 2011.

McIntyre, Matthew H. "The Use of Digit Ratios as Markers for Perinatal Androgen Action." *Reproductive Biology and Endocrinology* 4, no. 10 (2006).

McKie, Robin. "Why We Are All in This Together." *The Observer,* August 24, 2012.

McWilliams, James E. "The Myth of Sustainable Meat." *New York Times,* April 12, 2012.

Meggyesy, David, and Dave Zirin. "How Players Won the NFL Lockout." *The Nation,* August 15–22, 2011.

Mehta, Pranjal H., Amanda C. Jones, and Robert A. Josephs. "The Social Endocrinology of Dominance: Basal Testosterone Predicts Cortisol Changes and Behavior Following Victory and Defeat." *Journal of Personality and Social Psychology* 94, no. 6 (2008): 1078–1093.

Meikle, James. "Cricketer Admits Being Bribed to Give Away Runs." *The Guardian,* January 13, 2012.

Melis, Alicia P., and Dirk Semmann. "How Is Human Cooperation Different?" *Philosophical Transactions of the Royal Society B: Biological Sciences* 365, no. 1553 (2010): 2663–2674.

Meston, Cindy, and David M. Buss. *Why Women Have Sex: Understanding Sexual Motivation from Adventure to Revenge.* New York: Vintage Digital (2010).

Meyer, Christopher, with Julia Kirby. "Runaway Capitalism." *Harvard Business Review* (January–February 2012).

———. *Standing on the Sun: How the Explosion of Capitalism Abroad Will Change Business Everywhere.* Cambridge, MA: Harvard Business Review Press (2012).

Michal, Perlman, and Hildy S. Ross. "The Benefits of Parent Intervention in Children's Disputes: An Examination of Concurrent Changes in Children's Fighting Styles." *Child Development* 68, no. 4 (1997): 690–700.

Michell, Lynn, and Amanda Amos. "Girls, Pecking Order, and Smoking." *Social Science and Medicine* 44, no. 12 (1997): 1861–1869.

Michie, Jonathan, and Maura Sheehan-Quinn. "Labour Market Flexibility, Human Resource Management, and Corporate Performance." *British Journal of Management* 12, no. 4 (2001): 287–306.

Midgley, Mary. *The Solitary Self: Darwin and the Selfish Gene.* Durham, UK: Acumen Publishing (2010).

———. "No Gain Without Pain." *London Business School Alumni News* 127 (2012): 34–35.

Millar, David. *Racing Through the Dark: The Fall and Rise of David Millar.* London: Orion Books (2011).

Miller, Geoffrey. *The Mating Game: How Sexual Choice Shaped the Evolution of Human Nature.* New York: Vintage (2001).

Miller, Greg. "The Prickly Side of Oxytocin." *Science* 328 (2010): 1343.

———. "Social Savvy Boosts the Collective Intelligence of Groups." *Science* 330 (2010): 22.

Mitchell, Heidi. "Competing for Scholarships on the Field and Online." *Wall Street Journal,* August 7, 2012.

Mock, Douglas W., and Geoffrey A. Parker. "Siblicide, Family Conflict, and the Evolutionary Limits of Selfishness." *Animal Behaviour* 56, no. 1 (1998): 1–10.

Moore, Don A. "Not So Above Average After All: When People Believe They Are Worse Than Average and Its Implications for Theories of Bias in Social Comparison." *Organizational Behavior and Human Decision Processes* 102, no. 1 (2007): 42–58.

Morgan, Mary S. "Economic Man as Model Man: Ideal Types, Idealization, and Car-icatures." *Journal of the History of Economic Thought* 28, no. 1 (2006): 1–27.

Morning Star Self-Management Institute. Newsletter (Fall 2011).

Mowen, John C. "Exploring the Trait of Competitiveness and Its Consumer Behav-ior Consequences." *Journal of Consumer Psychology* 14, nos. 1-2 (2004): 52–63.

Mudrack, Peter E., James M. Bloodgood, and William H. Turnley. "Some Ethical Implications of Individual Competitiveness." *Journal of Business Ethics* 108, no. 3 (2012): 347–359.

Mueller, Frederick O., and Bob Colgate. "Annual Survey of Football Injury Research, 1931–2011." American Football Coaches Association (2012).

Muir, William M. "Incorporation of Competitive Effects in Forest Tree or Animal Breeding Programs." *Genetics* 170, no. 3 (2005): 1247–1259.

Mullainathan, Sendhil, and Eldar Shafir. *Scarcity: Why Having Too Little Means So Much.* New York: Times Books (2013).

Mullis, Kary. "The Unusual Origin of the Polymerase Chain Reaction." *Scientific American* (April 1990).

Munos, Bernard. "Lessons from 60 Years of Pharmaceutical Innovation." *Nature Reviews|Drug Discovery* 8 (December 2009): 959.

Murayama, Kou, and Andrew J. Elliot. "The Competition-Performance Relation: A Meta-analytic Review and Test of the Opposing Processes Model of Competi-tion and Performance." *Psychological Bulletin* 138, no. 6 (2012): 1035.

Narain, Jaya. "Three Teachers at Award-Winning School Suspended 'for Helping Students Cheat in GCSEs.'" *Mail Online,* August 10, 2009.

National Crime Prevention Council. *Helping Kids Handle Conflict: A Guide for Stu-dents Ages 5–12 on How to Handle Conflict.* Arlington, VA: National Crime Pre-vention Council (1995).

Neville, Lukas. "Do Economic Equality and Generalized Trust Inhibit Academic Dishonesty? Evidence from State-Level Search-Engine Queries." *Psychological Science* 23, no. 4 (2012): 339–345.

Niederle, Muriel, and Lise Vesterland. "Do Women Shy Away from Competition: Do Men Compete Too Much?" *Quarterly Journal of Economics* 122, no. 3 (Au-gust 2007): 1067–1101.

Niman, Nicolette Hahn. *Righteous Porkchop: Finding a Life and Good Food Beyond Factory Farms.* London: HarperCollins (2009).

Nowak, Martin, with Roger Highfield. *Supercooperators: Evolution, Altruism, and Human Behaviour, or, Why We Need Each Other to Succeed.* London: Canon-gate Books (2011).

Okasha, Samir. "Altruism Researchers Must Cooperate." *Nature* (2010): 467.

Orr, H. Allen. "Is Goodness in Your Genes?" *New York Review of Books,* October 14, 2010.

———. "The Science of Right and Wrong." *New York Review of Books,* May 12, 2011.

Osnos, Evan. "Meet Dr. Freud." *The New Yorker,* January 10, 2011.

———. "The Han Dynasty." *The New Yorker,* July 4, 2011.

———. "Boss Rail." *The New Yorker,* October 22, 2012.

Ostrom, Elinor. *Governing the Commons: The Evolution of Institutions for Collective Action*. Cambridge: Cambridge University Press (1990).

Partnoy, Frank, and Jesse Eisinger. "What's Inside America's Banks?" *The Atlantic* (February 2013).

Paserman, M. Daniele. "Gender-Linked Performance Differences in Competitive Environments: Evidence from Pro Tennis." *VOX*, June 26, 2007.

Patil, Anita. "Status Anxiety Versus Status Updates." *New York Times*, December 4, 2011.

———. "Don't Fight It, Crowd-Source It." *New York Times*, March 4, 2012.

Paton, Graeme. "Schools 'Bribing Pupils' to Cheat Ofsted Inspections." *The Telegraph*, January 6, 2012.

Pearson, Matthew, and Burkhard C. Schipper. "Menstrual Cycle and Competitive Bidding." Working Paper 11, 10. Davis: University of California, Department of Economics (2011). Available at: www.econstor.eu/bitstream/10419/58389/1/717283119.pdf.

Peng, Wei, and Gary Hsieh. "The Influence of Competition, Cooperation, and Player Relationship in a Motor Performance Centered Computer Game." *Computers in Human Behavior* 28 (2012): 2100–2106.

Pepitone, Emmy A. *Children in Cooperation and Competition: Toward a Developmental Social Psychology*. Lexington, MA: Lexington Books (1980).

Perner, Josef, Ted Ruffman, and Susan R. Leekam. "Theory of Mind Is Contagious: You Catch It from Your Sibs." *Child Development* 65, no. 4 (1994): 1228–1238.

Petrecca, Laura. "Bullying by the Boss Is Common but Hard to Fix." *USA Today*, December 27, 2010.

Pettit, Nathan C. "The Eyes and Ears of Status: How Status Colors Perceptual Judgment." *Personality and Social Psychology Bulletin* 38, no. 5 (May 2012): 570–582.

Pfeiffer, Thomas, Lily Tran, Coco Krumme, and David Rand. "The Value of Reputation." *Interface: The Journal of the Royal Society* 9, no. 76 (November 2012): 2791–2797.

Piff, Paul K., Daniel M. Stancato, Stephane Cote, Rodolfo Mendoza-Denton, and Dacher Keltner. "Higher Social Class Predicts Increased Unethical Behavior." *Proceedings of the National Academy of Sciences of the United States of America* 109, no. 11 (2012).

Piketty, Thomas, Emmanuel Saez, and Stefanie Stantcheva. "Optimal Taxation of Top Labor Incomes: A Tale of Three Elasticities." Working Paper 17616. Cambridge, MA: National Bureau of Economic Research (November 2011, revised March 2013).

Pink, Daniel H. *Drive: The Surprising Truth About What Motivates Us*. New York: Riverhead Books (2009).

Pinto-Gouveia, José, Cláudia Ferreira, and Cristiana Duarte. "Thinness in the Pursuit for Social Safeness: An Integrative Model of Social Rank Mentality to Explain Eating Psychopathology." *Clinical Psychology and Psychotherapy* (October 1, 2012).

Porter, Michael E. *Competitive Strategy: Techniques for Analyzing Industries and Competitors*. New York: Free Press (1998).

———. "Clusters and the New Economics of Competition." *Harvard Business Review* (November 1998).

Porter, Michael E., and Mark R. Kramer. "Shared Value: How to Reinvent Capitalism—and Unleash a Wave of Innovation and Growth." *Harvard Business Review* (January 2011).

Preston, Richard. "The Genome Warrior." *The New Yorker*, June 12, 2000.

Price, John S. "A Remembrance of Thorleif Schjelderup-Ebbe." *Human Ethology Bulletin* 10, no. 1 (March 1995).

Price, John S., and Leon Sloman. "Depression as Yielding Behavior: An Animal Model Based on Schjelderup-Ebbe's Pecking Order." *Ethology and Sociobiology* 8, supp. 1 (1987): 85–98.

Price, John, Leon Sloman, Russell Gardner, Paul Gilbert, and Peter Rohde. "The Social Competition Hypothesis of Depression." *British Journal of Psychiatry* 164, no. 3 (1994): 309–315.

Puffer, Sheila M. "CompUSA's CEO James Halpin on Technology, Rewards, and Commitment." *Academy of Management Executive* 13, no. 2 (May 1, 1999): 29–36.

Quasem, Himaya. "Small Nations Can Also Be Tech Giants." *Straits Times*, November 12, 2011.

Rajan, T. V. "Biomedical Scientists Are Engaged in a Pyramid Scheme." *Chronicle of Higher Education* (June 3, 2005).

Ramesh, Randeep. "Britain Risks Catching the 'US Disease.'" *The Guardian*, December 7, 2011.

Rattner, Steven. *Overhaul: An Insider's Account of the Obama Administration's Emergency Rescue of the Auto Industry*. New York: Mariner Books (2011).

Recchia, Holly E., Hildy S. Ross, and Marcia Vickar. "Power and Conflict Resolution in Sibling, Parent-Child, and Spousal Negotiations." *Journal of Family Psychology* 24, no. 5 (2010): 605–615.

Reginato, James. "The World's Most Expensive House." *Vanity Fair* (June 2012).

Reich, Eugenie Samuel. *Plastic Fantastic: How the Biggest Fraud in Physics Shook the Scientific World*. London: Palgrave Macmillan (2009).

Reidy, Tess, and Conal Urquhart. "Sixth-Formers Pay Up to £350 to Cheat University Admissions System." *The Observer*, October 13, 2012.

Repak, Nick. "Emotional Fatigue: Coping with Economic Pressure." Available at: GradResources.com.

Reynolds, Gretchen. "Phys Ed: Will Olympic Athletes Dope if They Know It Might Kill Them?" *New York Times*, January 20, 2010.

Ricarte, Jorge Javier, Alicia Salvador, R. Costa, M. J. Torres, and M. Subirats. "Heart Rate and Blood Pressure Responses to a Competitive Role-Playing Game." *Aggressive Behavior* 27, no. 5 (2001): 351–359.

Richmond, Riva. "Web Site Ranks Hacks and Bestows Bragging Rights." *New York Times*, August 21, 2011.

Ridley, Matt. *The Red Queen: Sex and the Evolution of Human Nature*. New York: Harper Perennial (2003).

Rifkin, Jeremy. *The Empathic Civilization: The Race to Global Consciousness in a World in Crisis*. Cambridge: Polity Press (2009).

Ripley, Amanda. *The Smartest Kids in the World: And How They Got That Way*. New York: Simon & Schuster (2013).

Robbins, Alexandra. *The Over-Achievers: The Secret Lives of Driven Kids*. New York: Hyperion (2006).

Robertson, Ian. *The Winner Effect: How Power Affects Your Brain*. London: Bloomsbury (2012).

Ronay, Barney. "Wheldon's Death in Las Vegas Leaves an English Village Grieving over a Favourite Son." *The Guardian*, October 17, 2011.

Ronay, Richard, and Dana R. Carney. "Testosterone's Negative Relationship with Empathic Accuracy and Perceived Leadership Ability." *Social Psychological and Personality Science* 4, no. 1 (2013): 92–99.

Rosenthal, Elizabeth. "Troubled Marriage? Sibling Relations May Be at Fault." *New York Times*, August 19, 1992.

Rothstein, Jesse. "Does Competition Among Public Schools Benefit Students and Taxpayers? Comment." *American Economic Review* 97, no. 5 (2007): 2026–2037.

Rowe, Dorothy. *My Dearest Enemy, My Dangerous Friend: Making and Breaking Sibling Bonds*. Oxford: Routledge (2007).

Rustin, Margaret. "Taking Account of Siblings—A View from Child Psychotherapy." *Journal of Child Psychotherapy* 33, no. 1 (2007): 21–35.

Ryan, Christopher, and Cacilda Jethá. *Sex at Dawn: How We Mate, Why We Stray, and What It Means for Modern Relationships*. New York: Harper Perennial (2010).

Ryan, Richard M., and Edward L. Deci. "Intrinsic and Extrinsic Motivations: Classic Definitions and New Directions." *Contemporary Educational Psychology* 25 (2000): 56–67.

Ryckman, Richard M., Cary R. Libby, Bart van den Borne, Joel A. Gold, and Marc A. Lindner. "Values of Hypercompetitive and Personal Development Competitive Individuals." *Journal of Personality Assessment* 69, no. 2 (1997): 271.

Ryckman, Richard M., Bill Thornton, and J. Corey Butler. "Personality Correlates of the Hypercompetitive Attitude Scale: Validity Tests of Horney's Theory of Neurosis." *Journal of Personality Assessment* 62, no. 1 (1994): 84.

Saavedra, Serguei, Kathleen Hagerty, and Brian Uzzi. "Synchronicity, Instant Messaging, and Performance Among Financial Traders." *Proceedings of the National Academy of Sciences of the United States of America* 108, no. 13 (2011): 5296–5301.

Sahlberg, Pasi. "Education Reform for Raising Economic Competitiveness." *Journal of Educational Change* 7, no. 4 (2006): 259–287.

Sahlberg, Pasi, and Paul Michael Garcia. *Finnish Lessons: What Can the World Learn from Educational Change in Finland?* New York: Teachers College Press (2011).

Salmon, Catherine A. "Birth Order and Relationships." *Human Nature* 14, no. 1 (2003): 73–88.

Salmon, Catherine A., and Martin Daly. "Birth Order and Familial Sentiment—Birth Order, Family Dynamics, and Creative Lives." *Evolution and Human Behavior* 19, no. 5 (1998): 299–312.

Salz, Anthony, with Russell Collins. *Salz Review: An Independent Review of Barclays' Business Practices.* April 2013. Available at: http://online.wsj.com/public/resources/documents/SalzReview04032013.pdf.

Santora, Marc. "Amid Inquiry into Cheating, Stuyvesant Principal Will Retire." *New York Times,* August 3, 2012.

Sapolsky, Robert M. "Social Status and Health in Humans and Other Animals." *Annual Review of Anthropology* 33 (2004): 393–418.

Savikhin, Anya C. "Is There a Gender Gap in Preschoolers' Competitiveness? An Experiment in the US." *Journal of Economic Behavior and Organization* 92 (August 2013): 22–31.

Schachter, Frances F., Ellen Shore, Susan Feldman-Rotman, Ruth E. Marquis, and Susan Campbell. "Sibling Deidentification." *Developmental Psychology* 12, no. 5 (1976): 418–427.

Schjelderup-Ebbe, Thorleif. "Further Biological Observations of *Gallus Domesticus.*" Translated by the author. *Psychological Research* 5, no. 1 (1924): 343–355.

Schleien, Sara, Hildy S. Ross, and Michael Ross. "Young Children's Apologies to Their Siblings." *Social Development* 19, no. 1 (2010): 170–186.

Schmitt, John, and Janelle Jones. "Low-Wage Workers Are Older and Better Educated Than Ever." Issue brief. Center for Economic Policy Research (April 2012). Available at: www.cepr.net/documents/publications/min-wage3-2012-04.pdf.

Schneier, Bruce. *Liars and Outliers: Enabling the Trust That Society Needs to Thrive.* Hoboken, NJ: John Wiley & Sons (2012).

Schroth, Raymond A. "The Plagiarism Plague." *America: The National Catholic Weekly* 206, no. 16 (May 14, 2012).

Schwartzapfel, Beth. "The Brothers Moynihan." *Brown Alumni Magazine* (May–June 2010).

Schwarz, Alan. "From Big Leagues, Hints at Sibling Behavior." *New York Times,* May 24, 2010.

———. "Risky Rise of the Good-Grade Pill." *New York Times,* June 24, 2012.

Segal, David. "They Win Gold, but a Pot of It Rarely Follows." *New York Times,* August 4, 2012.

Segal, Nancy L., and Scott L. Hershberger. "Cooperation and Competition Between Twins: Findings from a Prisoner's Dilemma Game." *Evolution and Human Behavior* 20 (1999): 29–51.

Segal, Nancy L., Shirley A. McGuire, Steven A. Miller, and June Havlena. "Tacit Coordination in Monozygotic Twins, Dizygotic Twins, and Virtual Twins: Effects and Implications of Genetic Relatedness." *Personality and Individual Differences* 45, no. 7 (2008).

Sennett, Richard. *Together: The Rituals, Pleasures, and Politics of Cooperation.* London: Allen Lane (2012).

Sequino, Stephanie, Thomas Stevens, and Mark A. Lutz. "Gender and Cooperative

Behavior: Economic Man Rides Alone." *Feminist Economics* 2, no. 1 (1996): 1–21.

Sheffield, Hazel. "Pasadena Publisher Launches a System for Outsourcing Local News." *Columbia Journalism Review* (August 27, 2012). Available at: www.cjr.org/behind_the_news/pasadena_publisher_launches_a.php.

Shreeve, James. *The Genome War: How Craig Venter Tried to Capture the Code of Life and Save the World*. New York: Alfred A. Knopf (2004).

Sides-Moore, Lauren, and Karin Tochkov. "The Thinner the Better? Competitiveness, Depression, and Body Image Among College Student Women." *College Student Journal Publisher* 45, no. 2 (June 2011).

Silverman, Rachel Emma, and Leslie Kwoh. "Performance Review Facebook Style." *Wall Street Journal*, July 31, 2012.

Simms, Andrew. "Let's Play Fantasy Economics." *The Observer*, February 17, 2013.

Skilling, David. *The Observer* newsletter. Available at: Landfallstrategy.com.

Smit, Jeroen. *The Perfect Prey: The Fall of ABN/AMRO, or What Went Wrong in the Banking Industry*. London: Quercus (2010).

Smith, Adam. *The Theory of Moral Sentiments*. Oxford: Oxford University Press (1979).

Smith, Julie, and Hildy S. Ross. "Training Parents to Mediate Sibling Disputes Affects Children's Negotiation and Conflict Understanding." *Child Development* 78, no. 3 (2007): 790–805.

Smither, Robert D., and John M. Houston. "The Nature of Competitiveness: The Development and Validation of the Competitiveness Index." *Educational and Psychological Measurement* 52, no. 2 (1992): 407–418.

Snyder, Blake. *Save the Cat: The Last Book on Screenwriting You'll Ever Need*. Studio City, CA: Michael Wiese Productions (2005).

Solomon, Yvette, Jo Warin, and Charlie Lewis. "Helping with Homework? Homework as a Site of Tension for Parents and Teenagers." *British Educational Research Journal* 28, no. 4 (2002): 603–622.

Son Hing, Leanne S., D. Ramona Bobocel, Mark P. Zanna, and Maxine V. McBride. "Authoritarian Dynamics and Unethical Decision Making: High Social Dominance Orientation Leaders and High Right-Wing Authoritarianism Followers." *Journal of Personality and Social Psychology* 92, no. 1 (2007): 67–81.

Stadler, Christian. "The Four Principles of Enduring Success." *Harvard Business Review* 85 (July–August 2007).

Stapel, Diederik A., and Willem Koomen. "I, We, and the Effects of Others on Me: How Self-construal Level Moderates Social Comparison Effects." *Journal of Personality and Social Psychology* 80, no. 5 (May 2001): 766–781.

Steen, R. Grant. "Retractions in the Scientific Literature: Do Authors Deliberately Commit Research Fraud?" *Journal of Medical Ethics* (November 15, 2010).

———. "Retractions in the Scientific Literature: Is the Incidence of Research Fraud Increasing?" *Journal of Medical Ethics* 37, no. 4 (December 24, 2010): 249–253.

Steen, R. Grant, Arturo Casadevall, and Ferric C. Fang. "Why Has the Number of Scientific Retractions Increased?" *PLOS/One*, July 8, 2013. Available at: doi:10.1371/journal.pone.0068397.

Steinberg, Jacques. "Feeling Anxious, and Applying Now." *New York Times,* August 10, 2010.

Steinberg, Julie, Aaron Lucchetti, and Mike Spector. "At MF Global: Rush to Move Cash." *Wall Street Journal,* February 24, 2012.

Stevenson, Joan C. "The Evolution of Sibling Rivalry." *American Journal of Human Biology* 12, no. 5 (2000): 720–720.

Stewart, James B. *Tangled Webs: How False Statements Are Undermining America: From Martha Stewart to Bernie Madoff.* New York: Penguin Books (2011).

Stillwell, Robin, and Judy Dunn. "Continuities in Sibling Relationships: Patterns of Aggression and Friendliness." *Journal of Child Psychology and Psychiatry* 26, no. 4 (1985): 627–637.

Stocker, Clare M., and Lise Youngblade. "Marital Conflict and Parental Hostility: Links with Children's Sibling and Peer Relationships." *Journal of Family Psychology* 13, no. 4 (1999): 598.

Stout, Lynn. *The Shareholder Value Myth: How Putting Shareholders First Harms Investors, Corporations, and the Public.* San Francisco: Berrett-Koehler Publishers (2012).

Stross, Randall. "The Algorithm Didn't Like My Essay." *New York Times,* June 9, 2012.

Stuart, Keith. "Game Changers." *The Guardian,* December 9, 2011.

Sulloway, Frank J. *Born to Rebel: Birth Order, Family Dynamics, and Creative Lives.* New York: Little, Brown (1996).

———. "Birth Order and Intelligence." *Science* 316, no. 5832 (June 22, 2007): 1711–1712.

———. "Why Siblings Are Like Darwin's Finches: Birth Order, Sibling Competition, and Adaptive Divergence Within Family." In *The Evolution of Personality and Individual Differences,* ed. David M. Buss and Patricia H. Hawley. Oxford: Oxford University Press (2010).

Sulloway, Frank J., and Richard L. Zweigenhaft. "Birth Order and Risk Taking in Athletics: A Meta-analysis and Study of Major League Baseball." *Personality and Social Psychology Review* 14, no. 4 (2010): 402–416.

Sulston, John, and Georgina Ferry. *The Common Thread: A Story of Science, Politics, Ethics, and the Human Genome.* New York: Bantam Press (2002).

Sutton, Robert I. "Self-awareness, Competitiveness, and Cooperation." *Psychology Today* (June 15, 2010).

Tauer, John M., and Judith M. Harackiewicz. "Winning Isn't Everything: Competition, Achievement Orientation, and Intrinsic Motivation." *Journal of Experimental Social Psychology* 35, no. 3 (1999): 209–238.

Terpstra, David E., Mario G. C. Reyes, and Donald W. Bokor. "Predictors of Ethical Decisions Regarding Insider Trading." *Journal of Business Ethics* 10, no. 9 (1991): 699–710.

Thamotheram, Raj, and Maxime Le Floc'h. "The BP Crises as a 'Preventable Surprise': Lessons for Institutional Investors." *Rotman International Journal of Pension Management* 5, no. 1 (2012): 68.

Tharp, Twyla. *The Collaborative Habit: Life Lessons for Working Together.* New York: Simon & Schuster (2009).

Thornton, Bill, Richard M. Ryckman, and Joel A. Gold. "Competitive Orientations and the Type A Behavior Pattern." *Psychology* 2, no. 5 (August 2011): 411–415.

Tietz, Jeff. "Boss Hog: The Dark Side of America's Top Pork Producer." *Rolling Stone,* December 14, 2006.

Tignor, Stephen. *High Strung: Bjorn Borg, John McEnroe, and the Untold Story of Tennis's Fiercest Rivalry.* New York: HarperCollins (2011).

Tilton, Sarah, and Juliet Chung. "Mogulopoly." *Wall Street Journal,* October 21, 2011.

Tinley, Scott. *Racing the Sunset: An Athlete's Quest for Life After Sport.* Guilford, CT: Lyon's Press (2003).

Trilling, Bernie, and Charles Fadel. *21st Century Skills: Learning for Life in Our Times.* San Francisco: Jossey-Bass (2009).

Tsai, Terence, Michael Young, and Bor-shiuan Cheng. "Confucian Business Practices and Firm Competitiveness: The Case of Sinyi Real Estate." *Frontiers of Business Research in China* 5, no. 3 (2011): 317–343.

Tucker, Corinna, Genevieve Cox, Erin Sharp, Karen van Gundy, Cesar Rebellon, and Nena Stracuzzi. "Sibling Proactive and Reactive Aggression in Adolescence." *Journal of Family Violence* 28, no. 3 (August 2013).

Tugend, Alina. "Experts' Advice to the Goal-Oriented: Don't Overdo It." *New York Times,* October 5, 2012.

Twenge, Jean, and W. Keith Campbell. *The Narcissism Epidemic: Living in the Age of Entitlement.* New York: Atria Books (2009).

Ungrady, Dave. "From 10,000 Meters to 26.2 Miles in New York." *New York Times,* October 14, 2010.

Vaillancourt, Tracy, Denys deCatanzaro, Eric Duku, and Cameron Muir. "Androgen Dynamics in the Context of Children's Peer Relations: An Examination of the Links Between Testosterone and Peer Victimization." *Aggressive Behavior* 35, no. 1 (2009): 103–113.

Van Beest, Ilja, and Kipling D. Williams. "When Inclusion Costs and Ostracism Pays, Ostracism Still Hurts." *Journal of Personality and Social Psychology* 91, no. 5 (2006): 918–928.

Van Honk, Paul, Dennis J. Schutter, Peter A. Bos, Anne-Wil Kruijt, Eef G. Lentjes, and Simon Baron-Cohen. "Testosterone Administration Impairs Cognitive Empathy in Women Depending on Second-to-Fourth Digit Ratio." *Proceedings of the National Academy of Sciences of the United States of America* 8, no. 8 (2011): 3448–3452.

Venter, J. Craig. *A Life Decoded: My Genome: My Life.* London: Allen Lane (2007).

Vidal, Catherine. "The Sexed Brain: Between Science and Ideology." *Neuroethics* (June 8, 2011).

———. "Brain, Sex and Ideology." *Diogenes* 52, no. 4 (2005): 127–133.

Virtanen, Marianna, Archana Singh-Manoux, Jane E. Ferrie, David Gimeno, Michael G. Marmot, Marko Elovainio, Markus Jokela, Jussi Vahtera, and Mika Kivimäki. "Long Working Hours and Cognitive Function: The Whitehall II Study." *American Journal of Epidemiology* 169, no. 5 (2009): 596–605.

Virtanen, Marianna, Stephen A. Stansfeld, Rebecca Fuhrer, Jane E. Ferrie, and Mika Kivimäki. "Overtime Work as a Predictor of Major Depressive Episode: A Five-

Year Follow-up of the Whitehall II Study." *PLoS ONE* 7, no. 1 (2012): e30719.

Vivona, Jeanine M. "Sibling Differentiation, Identity Development, and the Lateral Dimension of Psychic Life." *Journal of the American Psychoanalytic Association* 55, no. 4 (2007): 1191–1215.

Walker, Stuart H. *Winning: The Psychology of Competition*. New York: Norton (1980).

Walsh, John P., and Wei Hong. "Secrecy Is Increasing in Step with Competition." *Nature* 422, no. 24 (April 2003).

Warneken, Felix, Frances Chen, and Michael Tomasello. "Cooperative Activities in Young Children and Chimpanzees." *Child Development* 77, no. 3 (2006): 640–663.

Warneken, Felix, and Michael Tomasello. "Varieties of Altruism in Children and Chimpanzees." *Trends in Cognitive Sciences* 13, no. 9 (2009): 397–402.

———. "The Roots of Human Altruism." *British Journal of Psychology* 100, no. 3 (2009): 455–471.

Watson, Michael. "The Secret World of Male Anorexia." *The Guardian*, September 9, 2012.

Wei, David. "The Long Game." *Insights* (alumni magazine of the London Business School) 123 (September 2010).

Weiner, Jonathan. *The Beak of the Finch: A Story of Evolution in Our Time*. London: Jonathan Cape (1994).

Whittemore, Irving C. "The Influence of Competition on Performance: An Experimental Study." *Journal of Abnormal and Social Psychology* 19, no. 3 (1924): 236–253.

———. "The Influence of Competition on Performance." *Journal of Abnormal and Social Psychology* 20 (1925): 17–33.

Wiehe, Vernon R. *Sibling Abuse: Hidden Physical, Emotional, and Sexual Trauma*. Thousand Oaks, CA: Sage Publications (1991).

———. "Sibling Abuse." In *Domestic Violence and Child Abuse Source Book*, ed. Helene Henderson. Detroit: Omnigraphics (2000).

Wilkinson, Richard, and Kate Pickett. *The Spirit Level: Why Equality Is Better for Everyone*. London: Penguin Books (2010).

Williams, Martin, and John Plunkett. "X Factor Takes 15 Places in Top 100 Ofcom Complaints." *The Guardian*, December 16, 2011.

Wills, Garry. "Verdi & Boito: The Great Collaboration." *New York Review of Books* (March 24, 2011).

Wilson, David Sloan. *Evolution for Everyone: How Darwin's Theory Can Change the Way We Think About Our Lives*. New York: Delacorte Press (2007).

Windschitl, Paul D., Justin Kruger, and Ericka Nus Simms. "The Influence of Egocentrism and Focalism on People's Optimism in Competitions: When What Affects Us Equally Affects Me More." *Journal of Personality and Social Psychology* 85, no. 3 (September 2003): 389–408.

Winerip, Michael. "When a Hazing Goes Very Wrong." *New York Times*, April 12, 2012.

Wingfield, Nick. "Why Microsoft Chose to Make a Tablet PC." *New York Times,* July 8, 2012.

Winnicott, D. W. *The Child, the Family, and the Outside World.* London: Penguin Books (1964).

Wood, Greg. "Gillespie Determined That Whip Rules Row Will Not Overshadow Cheltenham Festival." *The Guardian,* January 16, 2012.

Wozniak, David. "Gender Differences in a Market with Relative Performance Feedback: Professional Tennis Players." *Journal of Economic Behavior and Organization* 83, no. 1 (2012): 158–171.

Wright, Nicholas D., Bahador Bahrami, Emily Johnson, Gina di Malta, Geraint Rees, Christopher D. Frith, and Raymond J. Dolan. "Testosterone Disrupts Human Collaboration by Increasing Egocentric Choices." *Proceedings of the Royal Society B: Biological Sciences* 279, no. 1736 (2012): 2275–2280.

Wright, Robert. *The Moral Animal: Evolutionary Psychology and Everyday Life.* New York: Little, Brown (1995).

Wylie, Ian. "Schools Have the Final Word on Plagiarism." *The Financial Times,* April 9, 2012.

Yildirim, Bariş O., and Jan J. L. Derksen. "A Review on the Relationship Between Testosterone and Life-Course Persistent Antisocial Behavior." *Psychiatry Research* (July 28, 2012): 984–1010.

Young, Ed. "Girls Are as Competitive as Boys—Just More Subtle." *New Scientist* (June 25, 2008).

Yücel, Murat, Alex Fornito, George Youssef, Dominic Dwyer, Sarah Whittle, Stephen J. Wood, Dan I. Lubman, Julian Simmons, Christos Pantelis, and Nicholas B. Allen. "Inhibitory Control in Young Adolescents: The Role of Sex, Intelligence, and Temperament." *Neuropsychology* 26, no. 3 (2012): 347–356.

Zaimov, Stoyan. "Joel Osteen Asked by Interviewer: Was Jesus Poor?" *Christian Today,* September 18, 2012.

Zethraeus, Niklas, Ljiljana Kocoska-Maras, Tore Ellingsen, Bo von Schoultz, Angelica Lindén Hirschberg, and Magnus Johannesson. "A Randomized Trial of the Effect of Estrogen and Testosterone on Economic Behavior." *Proceedings of the National Academy of Sciences of the United States of America* 106, no. 16 (April 21, 2009): 6535–6538.

Zhou, Wei-Xing, Didier Sornette, Russell A. Hill, and Robin I. M. Dunbar. "Discrete Hierarchical Organization of Social Group Sizes." *Proceedings of the Royal Society B: Biological Sciences* 272 (2005): 439–444.

Zimmer, Carl. "A Sharp Rise in Retractions Prompts Calls for Reform." *New York Times,* April 16, 2012.

Zimmerman, Jenn, Tara Malone, and Jennifer Delgado. "More Top High Schools Eliminate Class Rank." *Chicago Tribune,* June 9, 2011.

Zink, Caroline F., Yunxia Tong, Qiang Chen, Danielle S. Bassett, Jason L. Stein, and Andreas Meyer-Lindenberg. "Know Your Place: Neural Processing of Social Hierarchy in Humans." *Neuron* 58, no. 2 (2008): 273–283.

Zitek, Emily M., and Benoît Monin. "'That's the One I Wanted': When Do Competitors Copy Their Opponents' Choices?" *Journal of Applied Social Psychology* 43, no. 2 (February 2013): 293–305.

Zoltners, Andris A., P. K. Sinha, and Sally E. Lorimer. "How to Manage Forced Sales Rankings." *Harvard Business Review* (July 27, 2011).

INDEX

FATIMAH NAMDAR

MARGARET HEFFERNAN is an entrepreneur, chief executive, and author of *Willful Blindness*, which was shortlisted for the *Financial Times*/Goldman Sachs Best Business Book award. Born in Texas, raised in Holland, and educated at Cambridge University, she was a prize-winning producer for the BBC before returning to the US to run multimedia companies. She now blogs for the *Huffington Post*, *CBSMoneywatch*, and Inc.com and teaches at business schools around the world. Her website is available at www.mheffernan.com.

PublicAffairs is a publishing house founded in 1997. It is a tribute to the standards, values, and flair of three persons who have served as mentors to countless reporters, writers, editors, and book people of all kinds, including me.

I. F. STONE, proprietor of *I. F. Stone's Weekly*, combined a commitment to the First Amendment with entrepreneurial zeal and reporting skill and became one of the great independent journalists in American history. At the age of eighty, Izzy published *The Trial of Socrates*, which was a national bestseller. He wrote the book after he taught himself ancient Greek.

BENJAMIN C. BRADLEE was for nearly thirty years the charismatic editorial leader of *The Washington Post*. It was Ben who gave the *Post* the range and courage to pursue such historic issues as Watergate. He supported his reporters with a tenacity that made them fearless and it is no accident that so many became authors of influential, best-selling books.

ROBERT L. BERNSTEIN, the chief executive of Random House for more than a quarter century, guided one of the nation's premier publishing houses. Bob was personally responsible for many books of political dissent and argument that challenged tyranny around the globe. He is also the founder and longtime chair of Human Rights Watch, one of the most respected human rights organizations in the world.

·   ·   ·

For fifty years, the banner of Public Affairs Press was carried by its owner Morris B. Schnapper, who published Gandhi, Nasser, Toynbee, Truman, and about 1,500 other authors. In 1983, Schnapper was described by *The Washington Post* as "a redoubtable gadfly." His legacy will endure in the books to come.

Peter Osnos, Founder and Editor-at-Large